DAUGHTERS OF THE COUNTRY

OTHER BOOKS BY WALTER O'MEARA

THE TREES WENT FORTH

THE GRAND PORTAGE

TALES OF THE TWO BORDERS

THE SPANISH BRIDE

MINNESOTA GOTHIC

THE DEVIL'S CROSS

THE FIRST NORTHWEST PASSAGE

THE SAVAGE COUNTRY

THE LAST PORTAGE

GUNS AT THE FORKS

THE DUKE OF WAR

WALTER O'MEARA

1897-

Daughters of the Country

THE WOMEN OF THE FUR TRADERS
AND MOUNTAIN MEN

HARCOURT, BRACE & WORLD, INC., NEW YORK

COPYRIGHT © 1968 BY WALTER O'MEARA

370.4

FIRST EDITION

LIBRARY OF CONGRESS CATALOG CARD NUMBER: 68-12590

PRINTED IN THE UNITED STATES OF AMERICA

To the memory of Evan A. Hart
un homme du Nord

FOREWORD

It is with a certain temerity that I offer this study of an aspect of the North American fur trade that has been oddly neglected by the many brilliant scholars in that field.

The relationships of Indian women and white men on the fur trade frontiers were so complicated by racial, cultural, sexual, religious, psychological, and other factors that it would be rash indeed to attempt a full-scale treatment of the subject in one volume. Single chapters, even paragraphs, of the present work could obviously be expanded to full-length books.

So I ask that this study be regarded as simply a general survey of a very broad and complex facet of American frontier history. And I hope that it may stimulate scholars more competent than myself in special fields to work the almost untouched materials in greater depth.

As anyone even casually familiar with the background of Indian-white relationships is aware, all source material on the subject is colored and distorted by prejudice, ignorance, romantic enthusiasms, and other personal and racial attitudes.

Except very incidentally, I have not attempted to comment on these widely varying and often contradictory attitudes, but have simply reported them as they are revealed in the writings and acts of white men in the Indian Country. For it was their mere existence in fact, not their soundness or acceptability by modern standards, that was the operative factor in determining the character of racial contact on the frontiers.

It will be seen that the study is based principally on journals, memoirs, chronicles, letters, and other writings left by men who lived among the Indians and generally married their women *à la façon du pays*. Page references to their works are given at the end of the book for the convenience of students who may wish to know from what specific sources the material was derived.

These source references will also serve as a means of acknowledging my debt to the many writers and scholars whose work has been helpful to me in my own research. I wish to express my sincere gratitude to them all. Their books, drawn on for this study, are listed in the bibliography, and specific acknowledgments are made in the page references.

I wish also to thank the staffs of the following libraries for courteous and efficient assistance: Yale University Library; Beineke Rare Book Library of Yale University; New York Public Library, American History Room; Public Archives of Canada, Ottawa; University of Arizona Library; and the Pequot Library, Stamford, Connecticut.

Finally, I am grateful to Mr. Anthony Wise, of Hayward, Wisconsin, through whose kindness I have been privileged to travel the ancient canoe roads with the Courtes Oreilles Chippewa; and to Mr. Hiram Haydn for his invaluable editorial help and encouragement.

W. O'M.

CONTENTS

PART THREE
LASTING AND NOT SO LASTING UNIONS

LIST OF ILLUSTRATIONS

Between pages 178 and 179

DAUGHTERS OF THE COUNTRY

INTRODUCTION

"White men, go home!" With this oddly familiar cry, the Nor'wester Charles MacKenzie tells us, the Crow women greeted the first traders among that remote tribe. "White men, go home—we are afraid."[1]

Fear was apparently the first reaction of the Indian woman to the hairy stranger who appeared suddenly from nowhere, offering her blue beads, vermilion, and silver crosses for beaver pelts, beat meat, or perhaps just a night in his blankets. Sometimes it was fear strong enough to kill.

When Jedediah Smith and his men galloped up to an Indian village in the Rockies, one of the fleeing inhabitants, a girl of nine or ten, fell down dead. "Could it be possible," the perturbed Smith asked himself, "that we who call ourselves Christians were such frightful objects as to scare poor savages to death?"

But the first fright wore off quickly. Soon the pale-skinned trader became simply an object of curiosity, then of feminine design and—if we may believe some of the more boastful traders—of extraordinary sexual interest.

Indian women soon got to know the white men very well indeed. Many became their wives, mistresses, casual bedfellows. The relationships that evolved were about as intimate as human contacts could well be. Yet there was a gulf that was never bridged: a chasm, not just of race but of archeological time,

1. The notes are on pages 309–340.

that perhaps no civilized man has ever succeeded in closing between himself and a primitive woman.

It shall be the purpose of this book to observe the ways of the white man with the native woman on the North American fur trade frontiers. But before we can begin, we need to learn something about this strange new phenomenon in the Indian world—this fur trader, trapper, *voyageur*, or mountain man, as he was called in his different roles.

Who was he? . . . Where did he come from? . . . What was he after in the Indian Country?

The answers to these questions cannot be simple, for we shall be dealing with a strange and oddly assorted lot of men. Among them will be found graduates of Oxford and Dartmouth College and trappers with a passion for Shakespeare; titled English gentlemen, like Sir David Douglas and Sir Alexander Mackenzie; rich and powerful merchants, like William McGillivray and Ramsay Crooks; and simply great men, like Dr. John McLoughlin, "the Father of Oregon," and David Thompson, who was perhaps the finest land geographer the world has ever known.

Among them, too, will be found greedy adventurers, scoundrels, no-goods, fugitives from justice, and what Sir George Simpson referred to as "the very scum of the country . . . the most unruly and troublesome gang to deal with in this or perhaps any other part of the world."

All these varieties of men, and many more, were to be found on the canoe roads and pack trails, at the trading posts and rendezvous, of the North American fur trade.

But whether they roamed the wilderness in high beaver hats, satin waistcoats, and ruffled shirts, or in greasy buckskins stinking of beaver dope, they all shared certain traits. Almost without exception they were hard, tough men of simple ways and soft speech, although sometimes given to boasts of personal prowess against Indians, grizzly bears, and women. Usually they were young men, for life was not ordinarily long in the Indian Country. Many of them were marked by a characteristic dignity, imparted perhaps by perilous living and grandeur of environment.

And they were all, without exception, obsessed with killing beaver. For beaver was the *raison d'être* of the fur trade.

The demand for beaver began in the elegant seventeenth and eighteenth centuries and lasted until the middle of the nineteenth. But it was not, as one might suppose, for skins to be worn as furs or linings of cloaks. It was for pelts to be made into hats—at first the big hats with wide rolling brims embellished with plumes, embroidery, braid, and jewels, later the high "beavers" that were the mark of a man of importance in the early days of the Republic.[2]

To manufacture a truly fine beaver hat, you had to have smooth, lustrous felt; and such felt, as it happened, could be made only from the soft, downy underhair of the beaver's pelt.[3] A genuine "beaver" became the status symbol of the European *beau monde*. Nothing less would satisfy a man, or woman, of fashion. To be without one, indeed, was to be quite hopelessly out of style.

As the demand for beaver hats spread, European prices for the pelts of *Castor canadensis* soared. In North America, where the finest skins were to be found, English fur hunters ransacked the mountains of Carolina and Tennessee, and were soon into the Ohio Valley, where they built a huge fur trading post at Pickawillany. The French drove to the eastern slopes of the Rockies. The search for beaver spread northward, almost to the Arctic Circle, and westward to the Pacific. By the time the American mountain man appeared on the scene, the wide-brimmed "beaver" had long gone out of style. But the finest felt for hats was still that made from the industrious little rodent's pelt; and American trappers carried the pursuit of beaver up the Missouri, across the Great Plains, into the mountains, and down to the ocean.

This feverish competition often erupted as violence, with traders deep in the bush killing one another as well as beaver. The French and Indians sacked Pickawillany. Nations became embroiled, and the fur trade figured as an important factor in world politics and the fate of empires.

Then John Jacob Astor uneasily reported a rumor that a way
had been found to make hats out of silk instead of beaver felt.
The rumor was true. Almost overnight the high silk hat put an
end to it all.

But before the end came, in the 1850's, the continent-wide hunt
for beaver had brought about one of the most far-reaching con-
frontations of a civilized race with an aboriginal people in the history of mankind. To grasp the nature and extent of this great racial
contact, it is necessary to review briefly the character and operations of the North American fur trade.

It was the French who set the pattern, defining in a general
way the lines the trade was to follow for two hundred years. At
first everything was a confusion of licensed and unlicensed traders,
explorers, and *coureurs de bois*, ranging the continent from Montreal to Louisiana, and adding to the roll of history's great such
names as Cartier, La Salle, Champlain, Bourgmont, and Du-
luth. But all this was changed by one of the greatest of them
all, Pierre Gaultier de Varennes, Sieur de la Vérendrye. In the
summer of 1731, La Vérendrye, striking west from Montreal,
began to build a chain of trading posts from Lake Superior to the
Saskatchewan. Soon the *commandants* had a line of forts reaching
for three thousand miles, to the foot of the Rockies. The fleur-
de-lis flew over the lands of the Huron, Ottawa, Sioux, Assiniboin,
and dozens of other remote tribes. The French were the first white
men from the East to meet the wild Indians of the West—and
their equally wild women.

But the English were not far behind. Around the middle of
the seventeenth century, two mysterious French adventurers,
Radisson and Groseilliers, prodded the British Crown into tapping
the great reservoir of furs surrounding Hudson Bay. Charles II
affixed his signature and a huge red seal to five pages of parchment
that created "The Governor and Company of Adventurers of
England trading into Hudson Bay." This historic document not
only set up in business a group of English gentlemen, but gave

them imperial control over 1,500,000 square miles of territory, with powers of making war, passing laws, and demolishing the trading post of anyone rash enough to trespass on their vast backyard. In time, their suzerainty became so absolute and awesome that the letters H.B.C. on their company flag were commonly accepted as standing for "Here Before Christ."

The Hudson's Bay Company proceeded at once to build posts at the mouths of the rivers emptying into the Bay. From these posts they sent out occasional explorers, like Samuel Hearne, who in 1770 was the first white man to reach the Arctic Ocean. But for the most part the Company of Adventurers were content to sit in their laced coats and wait for the Indians to bring furs to them from as far away as the Buffalo Plains.[4] And it was not until an upstart breed of Scottish traders began to threaten their monopoly from their headquarters in Montreal that the York boats and freight canoes of "the Great Company" appeared on the lakes and rivers of the West.

The Montreal traders—after a cutthroat competition among themselves, culminating in murder—finally buried the hatchet and formed the North West Company for the purpose of invading Hudson's Bay Company territory. The Nor'westers did not, like their great rivals, wait for the Indians to come to them; they made the long, incredibly difficult trip to the Indians. Each spring their big Montreal canoes, manned by a crew of ten and carrying a cargo of ten thousand pounds, left with trade goods and provisions for the Interior. Each summer they returned laden with the rich dark furs of the North Country. To gather these furs, the Nor'westers pushed forts and trading posts as far as Great Slave Lake and the Rockies. And finally, of course, they collided with the traders of the Hudson's Bay Company.

The easily predictable result was violence and bloodshed. Murders in the bush and attacks on lonely posts climaxed in a pitched battle at Seven Oaks, near present-day Winnipeg, in which a score of men were killed. The only answer to this destructive competition was union, and in 1821 this was effected. The warring companies formed a kind of shotgun marriage under the flag of the Hudson's Bay Company, and together they began to probe hopefully into Oregon and the upper drainage of the Missouri.

And here, on the high plains and in the cool canyons of the mountains, they met a wild apparition that boded no good for them or the peaceful pursuit of the fur trade in the Far West. They came up against the American mountain man.

❧

The American fur trade centered on St. Louis. It had a life span of only a few decades west of the Mississippi, but they were among the most colorful and exciting in American frontier history. And in some ways the most important. For it was the fur trader, not the people of the covered wagons or the bearded forty-niners, who led the westward march of the frontier. It was the fur trader with his packs and kegs of whiskey and the trapper with his Hawken rifle and "possible sack" who were the true spearheads of Manifest Destiny.

Until German-born John Jacob Astor arrived on the ground, the American fur trade was not dominated by one or two gigantic concerns, as it was in Canada. Instead, a number of daring and enterprising men led their own brigades up the Missouri, into the mountains, and eventually as far west as Oregon and California.

The Americans at first copied the trading techniques of their competitors to the north. Like the Hudson's Bay Company, they built big posts on the Missouri and its tributaries, and waited for the Indians to bring in furs. Then, like the Nor'westers, they built smaller posts nearer to the remote tribes and sent out trading parties to Indian villages. But neither of these plans worked out very well in dealing with the wild, independent, and often hostile tribes of the Great Plains and Rocky Mountains. So they invented the "rendezvous."

Under the rendezvous system, traders and trappers met each summer at a designated place deep in the Indian Country. To the rendezvous, trappers brought the furs they had taken during the fall and spring hunts; and there they met the pack trains from

St. Louis carrying trade goods and liquor. To the rendezvous, too, came hordes of Indians and their women; and it is doubtful if any mining town in the gold fields ever saw such wild revels as marked a rendezvous at Pierre's Hole or Cache Valley.

The Americans also freed themselves from dependence on unreliable Indian trappers. They formed parties of their own mountain men and half-breeds to work the beaver grounds, and so successfully that their Hudson's Bay rivals were soon forced to send out far-ranging brigades to trap the Rocky Mountain waters.

By the time it reached its peak in the mid-1800's, the fur trade had become an operation of vast scope and complexity. Its bounds were those of the continent, its logistical problems to scale. To meet these problems—which included not only the elemental factors of time, space, cold, and hunger but ruthless competition and murderous Indian hostility—the fur trade needed tough, courageous, resourceful men, with not too nice a regard for ethical principles. Such men were forthcoming—sometimes from the most improbable sources. Their day was short, but while it lasted they conducted one of the most remarkable operations, and wrote one of the most extraordinary chapters, in the history of North American commercial enterprise.[5]

The Shoshoni girl quietly beading moccasins in front of her tipi could hardly have cared less about all this. Yet to her and thousands of other Indian women, it was a historic fact of vast, and indeed fateful, importance.

The drive and organizing genius of the traders brought to the door of her lodge the marvelous products of white technology: woolen blankets instead of fur and hide robes, cloth for clothing instead of leather, steel knives and scraping tools, glass beads in rainbow hues, awls and needles, and hundreds of other items to delight her feminine heart. All this changed the life-style of thousands of native women in material and cultural ways. But far more profoundly it disturbed the depths of their Indian souls.

Now we shall observe what happened when civilized man met

primitive woman in one of the most dramatic of all racial con-
frontations. Against the backdrop of the fur trade and tribal life,
we shall trace what grew out of the Indian woman's first wide-eyed
glimpse of a pale hairy man offering her blue beads, vermilion,
and silver crosses for a few beaver pelts, a little bear meat, or
perhaps just a night in his blankets. And let us begin at the very
beginning.

PART ONE

Sex on the American Indian Frontiers

I

MEN WITHOUT WOMEN

The first woman to appear on the American scene was not an Indian but a blond Norse fury named Freydis.

In *The Saga of Eric the Red* we find Freydis plotting the destruction of two brothers who for some obscure reason have incurred her womanly hatred. She persuades her husband's henchmen to murder the sleeping brothers and their band. But, with the men disposed of, there still remain five women whom the assassins have no stomach for killing.

"Very well," says Freydis. "Hand me the ax."

From such diverting glimpses of life in Vinland around the year 1000, we learn that the Vikings brought their wives with them to America—a practice that later colonists thought better of. Unlike other newcomers, particularly the Spaniards, the Norsemen seem to have had nothing to do with the native women. Occasionally we catch a flash of some frightened female skraelling (possibly a Micmac girl) fleeing from a white man, but the sagas only once describe an Indian woman, and then in rather baffling detail.

Quite suddenly one night, *The Flat Island Book* relates, a mysterious figure appeared before Thorfinn Karlsefni's wife, Gubid, in the doorway of her house. "She was short of stature," the shaken Gubid afterwards reported, "and wore a fillet about her head; her hair was of a light chestnut color, and she was pale of hue and so big-eyed that never before had eyes so large been seen in a human skull." [1]

This ghostly female, who scarcely conformed to our common

13

notion of how an Indian should look, vanished abruptly with a loud crashing sound, and five hundred years pass before another woman appears in American history.

When she does, she is a lone small girl in a canoe among many canoes filled with men.

It is not reported what Columbus' sailors said when the *Santa Maria* dropped anchor off the island of San Salvador on October 12, 1492, but quite likely it was, "Where are the women?" For Columbus does tell us that among all the natives who swarmed out to welcome him to the New World with gifts of fruit and parrots, there was only one feminine figure, and that "a small girl, naked." [2] Apparently the Indians, unsure of what might happen to their wives and daughters, had taken the precaution of hiding them in the jungle.

It was not long, however, before the Spaniards had won the natives' confidence with baubles, blandishments, and edifying passages from the Gospels. By the time Amerigo Vespucci made his third voyage to America, he was able to write to his patron Piero Soderini, Gonfaloniere of the Republic of Florence, "When they [the Indians] returned, they led with them 16 of their girls, and entered with these into their canoes and came out to the boats, and in each boat they put four of the girls. How greatly we marvelled at this behavior, your Magnificence can imagine." [3]

It was behavior, however, that soon became routine. From such beginnings the Spaniards quickly progressed to an intimate, somewhat lurid, and in the end tremendously complex relationship with the women of the Indies. Before long, Pizarro's *caballeros* would rape three thousand nuns in the convent at Cuzco; De Soto would be passing out girl captives to his men in lots of three and four hundred; and all over the Indies, interbreeding would give rise to the patchwork of *mestizos*, *castizos*, and the innumerable other degrees of mixed blood that have become the racial pattern of half the Western Hemisphere.

The first contacts of the French with the Indian women of Canada were less spectacular but, in their somewhat bizarre way, equally interesting. When Jacques Cartier landed on the Gaspé

Peninsula in 1543, his Breton seamen gave an impressive demonstration of how to win the ladies with gifts of beads, mirrors, and hawk bells. "These women," the account of that first meeting runs, "were about twenty, who altogether in a knot fell upon our Captain, touching and rubbing him with their hands, according to their manner of cherishing and making much of one, who gave them each a little Tinne bell: then suddenly they began to dance and sing many songs." [4]

Having seduced the tawny belles of Canada with baubles and gewgaws, the French, with their practical attitude toward such matters, immediately began taking Indian girls as permanent mistresses. Early in the 1600's Samuel de Champlain sought to promote actual intermarriage, and offered a dowry of 150 francs to any French-Canadian who would wed an Indian woman. Few claimed the money, however, the *habitants* having found the other arrangement more to their taste.

The English were oddly reticent about their early relations with Indian women. Their explorers had little to say about the native girls, but there is definitely a wistful note in such recurrent references as "they seem to be somewhat jealous of their women, for we saw not past two of them" and "one of their canoes came not to us, wherein we imagined their women were, of whom they are (as all Savages) very jealous." [5]

Just what contacts the first English colonists had with the Indian women we do not know. But Sir Walter Raleigh's lost colony of Roanoke had only seventeen females for its ninety-one men, and a natural interest in the native girls may be surmised. Certainly, "the idle gentlemen, vagabonds, and libertines" who later founded Jamestown were not indifferent to them—although they virtuously refused to marry them "on account of their being pagans." But the gentle historian Robert V. Beverley says the Indian women were "generally beautiful, possessing an uncommon delicacy of shape and features." And results were predictable: the colony was soon compelled to import a shipload of nubile maidens as wives for its single gentlemen.

Even the Puritans admitted sexual relations with the native

women. From colonial court records and the writings of worried
Pilgrim Fathers, one learns that unhappily married native women
sometimes turned to the settlements for solace. One New England chronicler delicately observed that "these women often resort
to the English houses, where ex pares cum paribus congregate,
in sex, I mean, they do somewhat ease their misery by complaining, and seldom depart without relief." [6]

Wherever European men encountered Indian women, the
pattern was basically the same. There seems to have been no
instance—whether among the hot-blooded Castilians, the practical French, or the strait-laced Puritans—where the ancient law
of racial contact did not begin immediately to operate. This
law (with some sacrifice of euphony to propriety) has been expressed thus: When two strange races meet, first they fight, then
they interbreed. In the Americas, the fighting and interbreeding
went on for almost four hundred years, as the Indian frontiers
were pushed farther and farther back, and the natives were slowly
exterminated.

During this time the relationships of white men and Indian
women became a fearfully complex thing. But in the beginning
at least, the basic factor was simple sexual drive. Amerigo Vespucci
came close to summing it all up when in 1497 he wrote, "We
remained the night: where they offered us their women, so that
we were unable to withstand them."

Three hundred years later, David Thompson, a fur trader on
the Missouri, echoed Vespucci when he commented dourly: "The
curse of the Mandane [sic] is an almost total want of chastity.
This the men knew, and I found it almost their sole motive for
their journey thereto. The goods they bought were sold at 50 to
60 per cent above cost; and, reserving enough to pay their debts
and buy some corn, they spent the rest on women." [7]

It has been pointed out that sexual attraction was an important
force back of the westward advance of our frontier. When a callow
youth in the East decided to go west and "see the Elephant," he
was not thinking about the natural beauties of the Rockies. More

likely, he was recalling tales of amorous adventure retailed by
boastful frontiersmen back from the wild, free, uninhibited Indian
Country.

The Mandan girls were not without competition in drawing
lonely traders deeper and deeper into the vast reaches of the Far
West. Everywhere, *más allá*, there were always other, more remote
tribes—the Aricara, the Crow, the Arapaho—about whose women
even more interesting tales were told. And beyond them all lay
the Spanish settlements, with the charms of the dark-eyed *mestizas*
to lure a man along the Path of Empire.

In his counting house on the Bowerie, John Jacob Astor dreamed
of monopolies, political pull, ships to China, and a great fur
trading post on the Pacific. But the men who worked for him had
less grandiose dreams. Their thoughts reached no farther than
the next rendezvous, where the fruits of a trapping season's toil
would be spent on liquor and women.

"I'm a Salt River roarer, and I love the wimming!" Mike Fink
bellowed, and he was speaking for all his legendary breed. To the
Indians, indeed, the sex-hungry frontiersman was an object of
something like awe. "I was wondering," an Aricara chief mused,
"whether you white people have any women amongst you . . .
Why is it that your people are so fond of women? One might
suppose they had never seen any before." [8]

This, of course, is not to depreciate the nobler motivations of
the westward movement—the pioneer's love of land, independence,
hardihood, and all such traditional frontier virtues. But along
with them, oddly unreported yet powerfully operative, was the
factor of sexual compulsion. Together with greed, shiftlessness,
cruelty, lawlessness, and other less admirable traits of the west-
ward-trending population, our frontier history has chosen to
ignore it. But it was nonetheless true that, as much as they wanted
land, freedom, and adventure, the frontiersmen wanted women.

How badly they wanted women shows up over and over in the
journals and memoirs of the fur traders. Here is Alexander Henry
the Younger, a trader in what is now northern Minnesota, re-

cording the aching desire of one of his young *voyageurs* for an
Indian girl: "On the 12th, one of my men gave a mare that cost
him G.H.V.P. currency equal to £16 13*s*. 4*d*. for one single touch
at a Slave girl." [9]

And again the professionally cynical Henry: "One of my men,
who was much in debt, offered me his services as long as he could
perform any duty on condition that I clothe him and allow him to
take a woman he had fallen in love with." This proposal, Henry
adds, did not surprise him, several of his men having offered themselves in perpetual bondage for an Indian girl "who had struck
their fancy." [10]

It is not difficult to account for the sometimes extraordinary
preoccupation of the white frontiersman with Indian women. For
one thing, he was faced with an almost total lack of white females.
The first explorers left their wives—if they had any—behind them.
A single white woman accompanied De Soto's 1,500 troops. Cortés'
army numbered no more than three or four *castellanas*. The
early French on the Missouri, it was rumored in Santa Fe, had
beautiful white women "with their hair tied up on the crown of the
head," but this was just a rumor—like that other erotic Spanish
dream of the island of Matinino, inhabited only by women. Drake
and the other English explorers kept mostly to the sea, and their
ships carried no feminine passengers; nor did the first English
colonists bring their wives along.

In such circumstances, it is not surprising that the ineluctable
law of racial contact began to operate almost as soon as the white
men left their ships. Three centuries later it was still operating on
the Great Plains of North America, just as it had in the jungles of
Yucatán. And for precisely the same reason: at the beginning of the
nineteenth century, there was not yet a single white woman between the Mississippi Valley and the Rockies.

But this was not the whole reason. Aside from normal sexual
urges, the white man in the Indian Country was subjected to more
than ordinary temptations of the flesh. The Conquistadores—all
of them young men, probably averaging about nineteen years of
age—were at first astonished, then delighted with the sexual

customs of the New World. Particularly, they admired the easy
compliance of the native women. In his fine Italian phrasing,
Amerigo Vespucci expressed this with: "They showed themselves
very desirous of copulating with us Christians."

Polygamy flourished everywhere, Montezuma setting the pace
with three thousand wives, a hundred and fifty of them pregnant
at one time. Chastity, at least until after marriage, was a moral
concept unfamiliar to most of the natives. The gift-giving of girls
was a pleasant gesture of hospitality.

Nor was the fact that the Indians at first took them for gods—
or at least supermen—a disadvantage to the amorous *castellanos*.
The Aztec chiefs "offered their daughters as a token of friendship,
so that they might bear children by such valorous men and bring
into the world a new warrior caste." [11] Very flattering to the ego,
too.

And to all this must be added the physical and sexual attractiveness of many of the Indian women. The incidence of genuine
beauty seems to have been high. The Mayan girls were acclaimed
better-looking than most Spanish *señoritas*, "larger and better
made." The early chronicles leave no doubt that the ladies of
the Americas appealed powerfully to the Conquistadores.

Three centuries later, they still appealed strongly to the American mountain men. General Thomas James describes the women
of San Felipe marching into Santa Fe and "displaying the best-
formed persons I have yet seen in this country. . . . They are
extremely beautiful women, with fine figures and graceful, elegant
carriage." [12]

In the American West, everything that had so delighted the
youths from Castile and Aragon was still in evidence. Polygamy was
common. Girls were given freely as gifts to lonely traders, or lent
for a night. And Indian women were still beautiful and eager to
catch a blue-eyed white man and make him the father of her child.
The only difference now was the prevalence of organized prostitution wherever white men gathered in large numbers.

From the beginning to the end, the white men's relations with
Indian women were powerfully influenced by an environment

of primitive moral concepts and uninhibited sexual practices.
These concepts and practices—often misunderstood by the whites
—were without doubt a potent stimulus to the almost universal
interbreeding of the races. They profoundly affected the character
of frontier life. And, as has been suggested, they even contributed
to the impetus of our nation's westward advance.

Yet another aspect of the matter may well have been the
historic attraction of strange women for conquerors and explorers.
The sexual allure of what the Prophet Nehemiah called "outlandish
women" has always alarmed religious leaders and intrigued story-
tellers. In the most ancient of all living books, we find a running
preoccupation with alien girls: Leah of the tender eyes, beautiful
and well-favored Rachel, ill-starred Dinah. Even in the harsh
warnings of the Prophets, a fascination with the theme shows
through.

It is one of the traditional themes of literature, and one of misty
antiquity. Our own Western lore has it first in the tale of Odysseus
and his eight-year romance with the siren Calypso. But the Calypso
story, scholars say, is probably much older than the Odysseus
version; and its variants often incorporate the primitive concept
of women as symbols of evil—personified by such fascinating
females as Lilith and Circe. In our own time it has been the basis
of innumerable novels, plays, and song hits.

The women of primitive peoples have always possessed this
special attraction for men of civilized races. As, for example, in
the Pacific islands. The sailors off the windjammers found the
girls of the islands not only acquiescent beyond even a seaman's
dreams, but endowed with a sexual appeal so powerful that many
a tar jumped ship and remained behind for years or a lifetime.
And those who finally returned home—leaving behind them,
incidentally, a souvenir of venereal disease—added their yarns
to the ancient legend of "outlandish women" and their piquant
charm.

This same attraction, we cannot doubt, operated puissantly on the American Indian frontiers. From the Conquistador in his gilded morion to the beaver hunter in his fringed buckskins, all white men on the borders must have felt the spell of that mysterious allure. And reacted to it as adventurous men always have.

Yet the youth from New England or Ohio, suddenly aware of a Dakota girl's smoldering eyes, was responding to something even older, even more remote from the ordinary experience of nineteenth-century man. For the slim girl in her beaded doeskins was not just a creature of another race, or another culture, or even another world: *she was of another time.*

The American Indians were all Stone Age people. Technically, they belonged to the paleolithic or, at latest, neolithic period of human history. They made their weapons of flaked or polished stone, just as the Neanderthal and Magdalenian men had in Europe. Some grew maize, others kept alive by hunting and gathering, but except for the dog and the llama they had no domestic animals. Some made pottery, wove fabrics, even built magnificent temples of cut stone, while others lived like brutes on roots and insects. There was a vast disparity in their cultural levels, but from the Inca to the Digger they were all people of the Stone Age.

We should not equate them, however, with the squat, hairy, beetle-browed creatures we commonly associate with the idea of primitive man. Physically, they differed no more from contemporary white men and women than modern racial types do from one another. Culturally, they were simply people who had followed a different direction of evolution, and not necessarily an inferior one. "Primitive," it has been suggested, is a poorly chosen term for the American Indian; perhaps "preliterate" is better.

Between uncivilized people and ourselves, anthropologists remind us, there exists "not an irreducible difference but a fundamental identity." We are alike in more and deeper ways than we are different. And who can say that a Cheyenne girl, under her tawny skin, was so very unlike a Chicago secretary or a Vassar undergraduate?

Indian girls intrigued, baffled, frustrated, and delighted the white trader in exactly the same way their sisters of whatever skin tint have always intrigued, baffled, frustrated, and delighted men, and always will. The trader quickly discovered beneath the vermilion paint and barbaric trappings what we have rather fatuously come to call the "universal woman." In a short time, he hardly made any distinction between white girls and Indian girls. The term "squaw" was almost unknown on the early fur trade frontier. And in an 1805 census of the North West Company's posts, some four hundred Indian wives of *voyageurs* were actually listed as "white." [13]

Yet, despite the profound similarities, it must be said that they were, after all, different. They did live the lives of neolithic women. They did wear the skins of animals and work with flint tools, and delighted in torturing captives and dancing scalps. They were beset with innumerable taboos and terrors. They were, in fact, what the French quite realistically called *femmes sauvages*. And the Indian girl who took a fur trader as her mate was attempting to make a cultural leap of some thirty thousand years.

The wonder is how often she succeeded.

How these "women savages" fitted into the scheme of the North American fur trader's life—and he into their lives—is the substance of this study. To learn about this universal but little-reported relationship, we shall turn first of all to the fort journals and personal diaries of the traders themselves. But we shall also browse through the reminiscences of frontier "old-timers" and the first travelers to venture into the Indian Country. We shall even go back to the Spanish chronicles and the New England colonial records and writings, and to the documentaries of New France.

For only through a familiarity with their historical setting can we fully grasp the meaning of later attitudes and events. What happened under Pizarro in Peru was not unrelated to Spanish slave trading in New Mexico. The ruthless extermination of the Indians in New England was echoed at Wounded Knee. And by understanding the ancient attitudes, prejudices, and guilts we can see more clearly into the relations of white men and Indian women in more recent times.

So we shall review briefly the whole range of these relations. We shall observe the Indian woman as the victim of raw lust and brutal force. We shall view her as slave, concubine, prostitute, a "hospitality gift," or simply a loan for the night to a passing stranger. But we shall meet her, too, as the loved and respected wife of a distinguished, even great, white man. For she has appeared on the stage of her obscure and little-noted history in all these roles.

II

THE LADIES OF THE
AMERICAS

The hairy mammoth, the giant sloth, and the frightened little wild horse observed the first human intruders on the continent of North America.

The Indians had arrived.

Who were they? Where did they come from? What did they want in the dense forests and vast savannas of the two Americas?

For a while after the discovery of the New World, nobody bothered to ask these questions. Everyone was too busy killing Indians, enslaving them, and robbing them of their gold to wonder about their origin.

But after a couple of centuries, scholars began to speculate about America's aboriginal inhabitants. A favorite theory held them to be the lost Ten Tribes of Israel, a supposition based on the striking similarity of many Indian customs to those of the ancient Jews. Some were convinced that the Missouri Indians—because of their blue eyes, fair hair, and coracle-like skin boats—were descendants of a Welsh expedition under one Madoc. Others traced the red Americans back to Egyptian, Phoenician, or Irish wanderers—and so on.

But the racial memories of the Indians themselves came closest perhaps to the truth: tribal legends of a Land of Spirits *toward the west*—a land, moreover, of tall waving grass, suggesting irresistibly the steppes of Asia.

Although absolute proof is still lacking, no one any longer doubts that the Indians came to America across Bering Strait.

On a clear day you can see the coast of Asia from the American side. When the strait is frozen over, you can walk from one continent to the other on the ice. And all the evidence, archeological, linguistic, anthropological, and geological, suggests that this is exactly what the first Americans did.

After crossing from Siberia to Alaska, they worked their way slowly southward to Cape Horn. Other Asians may have reached South America by a more direct route from Polynesia, landing on the Peruvian coast from Easter Island and spreading north, south, and inland. Nobody knows for sure.

In any event, it took a long time for the trickle of hunters from Asia to swell, fan out, and eventually occupy the whole land mass of the Western Hemisphere. From bits of chipped stone, scratched bone, plant pollen, radiocarbon, and other evidence, we can tell that when the first immigrants arrived, the ice sheet that covered most of North America was still retreating northward. Herds of camels and elephants roamed the drying plains. But nothing human lived, *or ever had lived*, in the great empty spaces of the two continents.

These first Americans may have arrived as early as twenty millennia ago. Around 12000 B.C. they were quite certainly hunting mammoths near Clovis, New Mexico; one of their flint points was found embedded between the ribs of an Ice Age buffalo in that vicinity. Farther inland, the Paleo-Indians had settled down in the Great Lakes region.

The oldest human bones so far discovered in America—those of "Minnesota Man" and Texas' "Midland Man"—are really those of young females. And so, in the faint light of prehistory, our first glimpse of man in the New World is not one of hunters pursuing the wild horse, but of the women who kept their lodge fires and reared their children.

What were they like, these first "ladies of the Americas"?

To start with, we know quite surely that they were primarily of Mongolian stock. Some students find evidence that the Athabascan-speaking group of Indians—including the Apache and Navajo—still use a tongue closely related to primitive Chinese.

Complete skeletons of Indians found in a cave in Chile point clearly to Siberian origin. And all the historic Indians we know anything about closely resemble the Mongoloid peoples. So there is good reason for concluding that American dawn-women looked very much like their near relatives in eastern Asia today.

That is to say, they had skins varying in color from yellowish to chocolate brown; their hair was straight and glossy black; their eyes were slightly oblique, but without the so-called "Mongolian fold" characteristic of some Asian stocks; their bodies were probably shapely and graceful, since the demands of their active and often dangerous lives weeded out the deformed and poorly co-ordinated; and they were occasionally born with a purplish mark at the base of the spine—the "Mongolian spot" that is sometimes found on the backs of Japanese, Mongolian, and American Indian people to this day.

We know almost nothing about how they dressed, but it is reasonable to suppose that, in summer at least, they wore very little. Perhaps a brief skirt of some animal's skin, basketwork sandals, a head covering of sorts, a few strings of beads on special occasions, maybe a little vermilion paint, and possibly a bit of tattooing. They were not without the normal feminine wiles and vanities.

How did the women of the Americas look to the first white men who appeared among them—before several centuries of racial mixture, disease, alcohol, vice, and despair had left their mark? Here our sources of information are the writings of explorers and chroniclers, the drawings and engravings of early artists, and a study of modern types. But none are wholly reliable.

The first writer to describe Indian women was, of course, the man who discovered them: Christopher Columbus. It can be said that his comments were polite and generally favorable, but not enthusiastic. Quite possibly he was mindful of the *señoras* at home. At any rate, he placed himself in no jeopardy by observing, "I saw two young women as white as any that could be found in Spain." [1] That was about as far as Columbus committed himself on the ladies of the Indies.

The Spaniards who followed him were less restrained. Amerigo Vespucci in particular was much impressed by the physical charms—as well as the complaisance—of the women who welcomed him and his gentlemen to the New World. "They are women of pleasing person," he reported, "very well proportioned; so that one does not see on their bodies any ill-formed feature or limb. . . . Only exceptionally will you see a woman with drooping breasts, or with belly shrunken through frequent parturition, or with other wrinkles; for all look as if they had never given birth." A charming American lady, Frances Calderón de la Barca, wrote three centuries later of the beauty of the Mexican Indian girls "who enchanted Cortés"; and, indeed, not only the Great Captain but all his men found many of them fascinating—prettier than the Spanish women they had left behind, "larger and better made." [2]

The gaily bedecked, freshly bathed, and perfumed daughters of the Inca and Aztec appear time and again in the warlike chronicles of the Conquistadores as brief flashes of feminine allure in the grim accounts of Spanish violence and cruelty. Of the Chachapogas women, Pedro de Cieza says: "We found them the most fair and good-looking of any I have seen in the Indies . . . exceedingly beautiful, fair and well-formed." Many of them, he adds, were worthy of being wives of the Inca and inmates of the Temple of the Sun.[3] Francisco López de Gómara sees the Cholnan women as "elegant in appearance, and handsome in features, and very clever." They were also, he doesn't forget to mention, good silversmiths. Of the women of the Spice Islands, he says simply: "The women are beautiful . . . all wear their hair long." [4]

The doughty Bernal Díaz del Castillo, a soldier with Cortés, expressed his appreciation of the Mexican women's charms in his own original and practical terms. After describing the rich presents brought by the Indians to the Spanish conquerors—diadems, masks, earrings, little dogs, five ducks, "and other trinkets," all of pure gold—he adds: "But all this was nothing compared with the twenty women, among whom was an excellent one who was named Doña Marina when she became a Christian." [5]

Hernandez de Soto described the Pacaha ladies of Arkansas as "symmetrical, tall, and full." Other Spaniards frequently referred to the statuesque figures of the women of the Indies. Yet the native drawings show them to have been small and dainty, with delicate features, and probably averaging well under five feet in height.[6]

Not all the Indian women were good-looking, of course; even Gómara, who generally admired them, says some who were brought to Cortés' camp were "about as dirty as gypsies." And when the same Gómara says, "The Xuarez girls were pretty, for which reason and because there were few Spanish women about, they were much sought after," [7] one might question whether the Xuarez girls were considered pretty precisely *because* there were so few Spanish women about. We can never know how objective the judgment of the Conquistadores was in the matter of female Indian beauty.

As we progress northward and nearer to our own time, we find fewer descriptions of Indian women in the writings of explorers and colonists. But one of the most glowing and intimate pen pictures of all has come down to us from John Lawson in his *History of North Carolina*. Writing in 1714, Lawson says:

As for the Indian women which now happen in my way, when young and at maturity, they are as fine-shaped Creatures (take them generally) as any in the Universe. They are of a tawny Complexion, their Eyes very brisk and amorous, their Smiles afford the finest Composure a Face can possess, their hands are of the finest make, with small, long fingers, and as soft as their cheeks, and their whole Bodies of a smooth Nature.[8]

At about the same time, the Frenchman Baron de Lahontan was describing the native women of Canada as "generally handsome," and "with wonderfully pretty complexions." He was less complimentary, however, about their figures.

The early New England colonists, while not immune to the

charms of their tawny female neighbors, had little to say about their physical appearance. And it was not until the missionaries, traders, explorers, and travelers began to move west that we again get sharp and realistic pen sketches of the North American Indian women.

Our second source of information about how the Indian women looked to white men is to be found in the pictures left us by early white artists and by the Indians themselves. In the very early Spanish drawings—if not in the violent pre-Spanish Mayan paintings—we are introduced to small, tastefully dressed women with serene and comely but somewhat melancholy faces. They lack the sex appeal of their verbally described sisters, but watching them at their looms or shaping tortillas between their graceful, long-fingered hands, it is not difficult to see why a soldier of Cortés'— or even a *hidalgo*—might want to marry one of them.

Then European artists began to depict a race of Indians never beheld by the Conquistadores or, for that matter, by anyone else. The first illustrations of the early popular chronicles were produced by painters who had never seen an Indian; nor, it would seem, had they paid much attention to the descriptions of those who had. One of the first of these fanciful pictures, an engraving entitled "A Renaissance Gentleman in America," depicts the Indians offering their nude girls to a blushing Amerigo Vespucci. They are beautiful girls, with classical forms, wavy waist-length hair—which is surely blond!—and demurely seductive features. But they certainly are not Indians.

Yet for two centuries these oddly imagined Indian women were offered to the world, and generally accepted, as true to life. For the most part, they were voluptuous creatures, something between Greek goddesses and court ladies of the Renaissance: long-limbed, global-breasted, with Rubensesque bodies carefully disposed in the classical attitudes of the current fashion. When they wore any clothing at all, it was likely to be a scanty fringed dress which left the breast, arms, and legs bare, with maybe a rope of massive beads around the neck. Yet so firmly were these unlikely damsels established as true Indian types that even Lahontan, who surely knew what an Indian girl looked like, allowed them to appear in his own book of travels.

Not unnaturally perhaps, attempts by some artists to get away from this romantic stereotype were resisted by a public who preferred the pretty to the true. Thus John White received little encouragement when he tried to come a little closer to reality. His watercolors of the Roanoke Colony Indian women show them with broad noses, thick lips, and huge eyes in round faces—caricatures neither white nor Indian, but still an attempt to escape from the obviously false types so popular in Europe. Yet when Theodore de Brey turned these watercolors into his famous engravings, White's ugly Indian girls reverted to the classical cliché —voluptuous bodies, serene faces, blond hair, languorous poses and all.

Large-scale portraits of Indian women are practically unknown before the late 1700's, and when they first appear they tell us little. There are several portraits extant of that celebrated lady Pocahontas, for example; but all are different, and none of them look much like an Indian woman. The one in the National Portrait Gallery titled "Pocahontas in England, 1616" is admittedly an appealing likeness, but as John C. Ewers points out, it is hard to find in it any trace of Indian facial structure. We must wait until the nineteenth century before we encounter anything like realistic portraiture—flesh-and-blood figures that are not only women but Indian women.

French artists had no firsthand contact with North America prior to 1800, and purely imaginative pictures of Canadian Indian women continued to be published in Europe well into the nineteenth century. In the English colonies, however, portraits began to be more truthful. There was still the old fascination with the picturesque and romantic, but along with it an increasing realism. Nonetheless, while dress and other details became more authentic, faces long continued to be European, and for this reason it is difficult to know how the women of the eastern tribes really looked.

The matter is further complicated by interbreeding—Indian with white, Negro, and other Indian tribes—which had already begun to take place. But it is probable, anthropologists say, that the eastern Indians, particularly their women, had less prominent cheekbones, faces more oval, and looked more European than did the Plains Indians.[9]

It is the Plains women who first stand before us as real people— thanks to the energy and courage of a New Yorker named George Catlin. In 1832 Catlin went west with the intention, as he expressed it, of "mingling with the red men, and identifying myself with them as much as possible." He remained eight years, visiting forty tribes, then returned with 310 portraits in oil and 200 other paintings of village and tribal life. Catlin was an incurable romantic, a showman, an atrocious draftsman, and not always too reliable as a reporter. His Indian women are stiffly posed, and he outrageously idealized his fair subjects. But he was first to paint Indians at home, and in his pictures the women of the tribes at last come to life.

Close on the heels of Catlin was Karl Bodmer, a young Swiss artist who accompanied Prince Maximilian of Wied up the Missouri in 1833. He was warned that he might not come back alive from the Sioux country, but he did—and with a portfolio of some of the finest paintings ever made of the Plains Indians. Bodmer was followed by Alfred Jacob Miller, who, in addition to vivid factual reporting on Indian life, left us such romantic confections as his famous picture of a Shoshoni maiden swinging from the branch of a tree. Other artists who set up easels in the Indian Country included the Canadian Paul Kane, George Winter, Peter Rindisbacher, Samuel Seymour, Rudolph Friedrich Kurz, Gustavus Sohon, the popular Eastman Johnson, and Father Nicolas Point, whose Chagall-like miniatures are one of the delights of frontier painting. They all added something to our knowledge of how the women of the tribes looked before the pure Indian line was diluted by the white man's blood and Indian character corrupted by "civilization." And we can be thankful that such generally able and dedicated painters set down their impressions on canvas before the camera began its grim recording of a later day.

In addition to the painters who ventured among the wild Indians, others "took the likeness" of chiefs and tribal delegates who visited Washington. James Otto Lewis and James Bird King, in particular, turned out a large number of highly professional portraits for the government (at $33 apiece). Most were of male Indians, but a few of women found their way into the Indian gallery and added much to its interest.[10]

All in all, thousands of paintings and sketches were left by the Catlins, Bodmers, and Millers who labored with such a keen sense of history to show us the girls of the tribes as they saw them. It is remarkable that their sitters were almost without exception good-looking women. Occasionally they are beautiful. And invariably they exhibit a dignity that somehow seems inseparable from their primitiveness.

Kurz, who delighted in sketching the Missouri maidens in the nude, gave as his expert opinion: "Forms more beautiful than those I have found among the Iowa Indians I cannot imagine, though I have been accustomed during my studies from life for many years to all that is finest in the human form. . . . No individual of the white race can compare with them [in grace of carriage]."[11]

It would be too much, of course, to suggest that there were no uncomely women in the lodges, or that a painter would not turn naturally to young and attractive subjects. But as specimens of the best, the Indian women whose portraits have come down to us compared well, it would seem, with the best of any race.

Turning from the artist with his pencil and brushes to the scientist with his calipers and microscope, we get still another view of the Indian woman. We would expect the specialists in racial anthropology to discourse on blood types, dentition, genetic variations, nasal bone growth, cranial measurements, and so forth; and we are not disappointed. But occasionally we find a reference to some determining factor that is closer to a layman's understanding—the "shovel-shaped" incisors, for example, that are frequently found in Indian types. We can comprehend, too, the theory of Asian origin, and wonder, as anthropologists themselves sometimes do, about non-Mongoloid strains—Caucasoid and Negroid—that seem to be present in some American Indian groups.

One anthropologist, Aleš Hrdlička, we can comprehend very well indeed when, in writing of "Beauty Among the American Indians," he gives us a very explicit blueprint of what he considers to be the characteristics of a beautiful Indian girl. Here, in slightly abridged form, are his specifications for a Miss Amerind, as she might well have appeared to some trader's delight in an Aricara or Pawnee village in the mid-nineteenth century:

SKIN: medium to light brown.
HEAD: black, lustrous hair, a little coarser than that of the whites.
FOREHEAD: medium height, nicely arched.
EYES: slightly oblique—no "Mongolian fold." Pupil black, iris fine dark
    hazel brown.
NOSE: straight or a little concavo-convex, or a little convex.
LIPS: a trace fuller than the whites', well formed, red with a dusky tinge.
MOUTH: medium size.
TEETH: clear, white, medium size, very regular.
CHIN: moderately prominent, nicely rounded.
EARS: well molded.
NECK: medium height and thickness.
BREASTS: never very small or large, inclining to conical in form, areola
    dark, nipple larger than whites'.
SHOULDERS: slightly sloping.
WAIST: rather small.
ABDOMEN: never pendant.
HIPS AND LEGS: less adipose and more shapely than whites', calves shapely.
ARMS: feminine.
HANDS AND FEET: small.[12]

But one can no more generalize on the physical characteristics of American Indian girls, of course, than on those of their modern French, Swedish, or American counterparts. They came in all shapes, sizes, and degrees of pulchritude—just as women do today. There was much variance from tribe to tribe. The faces of the eastern Indians, we have already noted, may actually have been more "European" than those of the western tribes. And the strongly aquiline profiles of the Sioux could hardly have been more different from the flat Asiatic features of the West Coast peoples. Skin tones also ranged from almost Caucasian to a deep brown. "The women were so white," wrote the missionary padre Francisco Garcés of some Havasupais girls, "I saw one who looked like an Española."

It was the Mandan women whose fair skin, long platinum-blond hair, and gray eyes most fascinated the traders. La Vérendrye, the first white man to appear among them, reported: "The women are rather handsome, particularly the light-colored ones; they have an abundance of fair hair." From La Vérendrye's time on, the women of the blond Indians of the Missouri were a magnet that—as David Thompson has already told us—drew traders from all quarters of the West. Many of these traders made their own anthropological observations on the Mandan girls' special style of beauty. Thompson recalled them "as fair as our french canadians; their eyes of a dark hazel, the hair of dark brown or black, but not coarse." Catlin, however, better expressed the wonder that most white men seem to have felt on first seeing the Mandan beauties:

A stranger in the Mandan village is first struck with the different shades of complexion, and various colors of hair which he sees in a crowd about him; and is at once almost disposed to exclaim that "these are not Indians!"

There are a great many of these people whose complexions appear as light as half-breeds; and amongst the women particularly, there are many whose skins are almost white, with the most pleasing symmetry and proportions of features; with hazel, with grey, and with blue eyes,— with a mildness and sweetness of expression . . . which render them exceedingly pleasing and beautiful.[13]

Nobody knows from what source the Mandan derived their fair complexions; speculation has ranged all the way from ancient Welsh and Scandinavian explorers to natural mutation. But they and some closely related peoples, such as the Crow, afford dramatic evidence of how widely physical norms—and hence feminine beauty—varied from tribe to tribe.

It has been suggested, however, that one rather surprising peculiarity of Indian physiognomy was to be noted. "Strange as it may appear," General Robert B. Mitchell wrote in 1864, "all the Indians had extremely feminine faces, except the Big Mandan. Spotted Tail looked exactly like a woman . . . the Indian men seem to have a rather feminine look and the women to have a rather masculine look, which increases as they grow older." [14]

The fort journals and old-age reminiscences of trappers, traders, guides, and scouts have much to say about the Indian girls, and one might expect them to be the most reliable of all sources of information. But one cannot accept uncritically the judgments of even such distinguished traders as Alexander Mackenzie or Edwin Thompson Denig. A great many emotional and psychological factors no doubt influenced the white man's viewpoint on Indian femininity.

The truth probably was that, as time passed in the *pays sauvage*, the daughters of the country looked less and less like Indian women and more and more simply like women. Veteran traders, as we have noted, seldom referred to them as "squaws." In the journals they were called "women"; or if the traders happened to be married to one of them, "my woman" or "my girl," or perhaps "the mother of my children." The passing years faded the "polished copper" tones of the Indian girl's skin to a lighter and lighter shade, until at last the trader was hardly conscious of any difference between her and the half-forgotten girls back home.

And, in fact, the difference may not have been nearly so great as is generally supposed. François-Antoine Larocque, an early trader on the Missouri, mentions the Crow women's skin as being white, *except where exposed to the sun*. And many another trader, speaking from direct observation, agrees. Naked, or almost naked, as both sexes often were in the family lodge, the Indian woman may have scarcely looked darker than, say, a Mediterranean brunette to unprejudiced eyes.

It is quite probable, incidentally, that while the Indian girl's frequent state of undress may have heightened the white man's appreciation of her charms, the opposite was also true. A Sioux or Aricara maiden in her snowy elkskins, ornamented with colored quill embroidery, must have been a splendid sight. Nor was the costume of a fully dressed Indian belle necessarily without a seductive quality. Thus David Thompson, describing some Mandan dancers:

The dancing women were twenty-four young women of the age of sixteen to twenty-five years. They all came in their common dress, and went to a place set apart for them to dress; and changed to a fine white dress of thin Deer Skins, with ornamented belts, which showed their shapes almost as clearly as a silk dress.[15]

"They were all courtesans," he adds, "a sett of handsome, tempting women."

Many traders, surprisingly enough, adopted a rough scientific approach in describing the tribes. At remote Fort Chipewyan, Roderic McKenzie, *bourgeois* of the North West Company's vast Athabasca Department, distributed printed questionnaires to his still more remote flying posts, requesting ethnological data on the local Indian bands. Most of the more literate traders took pains to note in their journals the tribal peculiarities of the nations they visited, usually appending a vocabulary. And it is from such writings that we get our clearest idea of how the Indian women measured up, tribe by tribe, to the white man's standards of feminine beauty. Often, of course, there is disagreement, sometimes so violent that one might suspect the amateur ethnologists of writing about entirely different tribes. But the women of some nations did have a widespread reputation for beauty, while others are treated rudely by every trader articulate enough to express his views.

Among those most admired were the daughters of the Cree, that vast nation stretching across half of Canada. "The women of this tribe are often comely and sometimes pretty," Catlin says. And as early as 1790, Alexander Mackenzie declared, "Of all the nations which I have seen on this continent, the Knisteneaux [Cree] women are the most comely. Their figure is generally well proportioned, and the regularity of their features would be acknowledged by the more civilized people of Europe." [16]

Cree girls painted their faces with red ochre, and some of them had faint tattoo lines on the chin. They parted their hair in the middle, defining the part with a line of vermilion—as was the custom of all tribes east of the Rockies—and fastened it behind each ear in a large bun from which hung bunches of blue beads. But their springtime freshness was fleeting. "The mild countenances of the women," Thompson wrote, "make many, while young, appear lovely; but . . . the softness of youth soon passes away." [17]

The Ojibway (or Chippewa) girls seem to have fascinated the traders not only by their good looks, but with a vivacity and sexy charm that comes through the routine journal entries of many a white man in the *pays d'en haut.* Duncan Cameron, at his post in the Nipigon country, wrote:

They are in general very well featured, especially their women, some of whom would be real beauties if their complexion was fair, although it is generally more so than those inhabiting warmer climates. They all have excellent teeth and pretty black eyes, which they know very well how to humor in a languishing and engaging manner whenever they wish to please.[18]

Alexander Henry, an early American trader at Chequamegon Bay on Lake Superior, noted that the Ojibway women "have agreeable features and take great pains in dressing their hair, which consists in neatly dividing it on the forehead and top of the head and in plaiting and turning it up behind." [19]

A peculiarity of the Ojibway women mentioned by Peter Grant, a North West Company trader, was their toeing in while walking. This, Grant suggests, detracted somewhat from their otherwise graceful and erect carriage. But he hastens to add apologetically: "They have a softness and delicacy in their countenance which rival the charms of some of our more civilized and accomplished *belles.*" He also mentions their "soft, shrill voices," contrasting pleasantly with the sound of drums.[20]

At the Grand Portage Rendezvous in 1800, young Daniel Harmon, fresh up from Montreal for the North West Company, was not only impressed with the beauty of the Ojibway girls in their party finery, but mildly astonished at their social charm. He wrote in his journal:

In the daytime the Natives were permitted to dance in the fort. . . . In the evening the gentlemen of the place dressed, and we had a famous ball in the dining room. . . . At the ball there was a number of the ladies of this country; and I was surprised to find that they could conduct with so much propriety and dance so well.[21]

Finally, to the almost universal admiration of rough traders for the Ojibway maidens must be added that of the cultivated Englishman Nicholas Garry. While on a border survey in 1821, Garry noticed that "the Ladies were not quite decently clad," but he found them to be very pretty, and some who would have been thought beautiful in London or Paris. Of one in particular he says, "She had the most beautiful intelligent Countenance and the finest black eyes, and a Complexion which would have been considered as a Brunette and not darker in any Country." [22]

Of the other northern Indians, the Chipewyan tribe, inhabiting the desolate maze of bogs and water south and west of Hudson Bay, was the most numerous. The beauty of its girls does not seem to have impressed the traders. Mackenzie describes the tribe as swarthy of complexion, with coarse features, lank hair, and dull eyes. And the best he can say for the distaff side is: "The women have a more agreeable aspect than the men, but their gait is awkward, which proceeds from their being accustomed, nine months of the year, to travel on snow-shoes and drag sledges of a weight from two hundred to four hundred pounds." [23]

The Hudson's Bay Company factor Samuel Hearne, however, writes that "their skins are soft, smooth, and polished; and when they are dressed in clean clothing they are as free from an offensive smell as any of the human race." But, having gone that far, he generalizes: "Take them as a body, the women are as destitute of real beauty as any nation I ever saw, though there are some few of them when young who are tolerable." [24] Yet it was from the women of this unattractive tribe that some of the greatest *bourgeois* of the North West Company chose companions to share their lives in the lonely *pays sauvage*.

As the fur hunters moved westward and southward, they met the mounted Indians of the Great Plains, a wild, free, fierce, and virile people who have become the archetype of the noble red man.

The Sioux women were described as shorter than the men, but still of remarkable stature, often willowy, with long legs that made them look short-waisted, and long delicate fingers. Most of them, according to Royal B. Hassrick, "had softer faces than those of the men, more finely chiseled and carefully polished heads . . . and some appeared Mongoloid." [25] At Fort Leavenworth, the American trader Nathaniel Wyeth called them "really beautiful women." But William H. Keating describes the women of an earlier tribe of Woods Sioux as having clumsy figures, with "a great breadth of hips." [26] And still earlier, a French missionary, Father Guignas, reported to the Governor of Canada on the same Sioux: "The men are almost all large and well made; but the women are ugly and disgusting." [27]

Catlin, who called the Mandan girls "exceedingly pleasing and beautiful," was no less complimentary to the Gros Ventre's "many beautiful and voluptuous-looking women . . . shedding bewitching smiles." [28] But even Catlin had trouble finding something nice to say about the charms of the Crow girls. He remarked simply that they were not handsome. And Edwin Thompson Denig, commander of Fort Union, who knew them perhaps better than any other white man in the West, gives us this devastating appraisal:

It would seem that nature on this occasion has done so much in favor of
the Crow men that she has entirely neglected the women. Of all the
horrid looking objects in the shape of human beings these women are the
most so. Bad features and worse shapes, filthy habits, dresses, and persons
smeared with dirt and grease, hair cut short and full of vermin . . .[29]

And so on. However, the Nor'wester Charles MacKenzie, that
most charitable and humane of all traders, did say that "the
[Crow] women are handsome, but their beauty fades early, even
children have gray hairs." [30]

Of the other Plains and Missouri River women, we have for the
most part favorable reports. Denig—who seems to have been a
hard man to please—makes his usual sour comments on the
Aricara girls, but the naturalist Henry Marie Brackenridge says
that "some might be considered handsome anywhere"; [31] and the
journals of the Lewis and Clark expedition describe them as "handsome and lively" and "disposed to be amorous." [32]

But it is the wandering painter Kurz who gives us the liveliest
and most attractive picture of the Aricara maidens:

Had an interesting view of about 50 girls and women bathing. As they
thought themselves well concealed, they were sportive and animated in a
natural way. There were several dainty figures among them—so slender
yet round, so supple yet firm.[33]

Kurz watched them for a while as some romped and splashed,
while others "dreamily dried themselves in postures and move-
ments so natural and unrestrained, yet such grace."

Catlin describes many of the Comanche, Pawnee, and Kiowa
girls as "exceedingly pretty in feature and form, and also in expression, although their skins are very dark." To Ross Cox, a
young Irishman with John Jacob Astor's Pacific Fur Company, the
Flathead girls (whose heads, incidentally, were *not* flattened) were
"remarkably well made, rather slender," and "comparatively very
fair," with complexions "a shade lighter than the palest new
copper after being freshly rubbed." [34] David Thompson voices
cautious approval of the Piegan: "The women have in general

good features." And Alexander Henry is equally restrained about the Assiniboin: "Some of the women are tolerably handsome, considering how they live." [35]

All in all, one gathers from the widely scattered and often contradictory field reports of the traders and mountain men that the proud, fierce warriors of the Plains and mountain tribes were more favored by nature than their women, although instances of feminine comeliness and even spectacular beauty were by no means unknown.

When the traders crossed the mountains and descended the rivers of the West, they came to an altogether different kind of Indian—people who lived in large plank houses with carved doorways and took to the sea in huge, fantastically adorned war canoes. But the women of this intelligent and relatively advanced race, they found, had been rendered singularly unattractive by excessive drudgery, and by head-flattening and other bodily deformations.

With a few exceptions—notably the Kootenai—what seems most to have impressed white men on the Columbia was the filthiness of these Indians. "Disgusting creatures," the Nor'wester Alexander Henry the Younger called them. And Father Pierre Jean De Smet, a missionary whose pride in his Flathead flock absolves him of any suspicion of racial bias, says of them: "The women are very filthy. Their hands, faces, and feet are black and stiff with dirt. They rub them every morning with a composition of red and brown earth mixed up with fish oil. Their hair, always long and dishevelled, serves them for a towel to wipe their hands on." [36] "They had no beauty to spare," David Thompson remarked mildly, "and wanted the agile step of those who dwell in tents." [37]

To this symposium of ugliness, the journals of the Lewis and Clark expedition add: "The women [of the Columbia] are small and homely in appearance, their legs and thighs much swelled, and their knees remarkably large; deformities, which are no doubt owing to the manner in which they sit on their hams." [38] And it must have been with relief that traders on the Columbia left these

unfortunate females sitting on their hams and turned southward
to the beguiling beauties of the Spanish Borderlands.

Without exception, it would seem, explorers, traders, and travelers agreed on the good looks and sexual attractiveness of the
southwestern Indian girls. The American trader James O. Pattie
was particularly enthusiastic about the Navajo maidens. "They are
much handsomer and have lighter complexions than the men,"
he wrote. "They are altogether the handsomest women I have seen
among the red people, and not inferior in appearance to many
Spanish women." [39] Nor was he less complimentary to the Mohave,
Yuma, Coco, and Maricopa girls, whose charms owed nothing to
clothing or adornment; and all early visitors to these tribes agreed
with him. Of the Maricopa women, "Uncle Dick" Wootton, a
famous mountain man who was never distinguished as an admirer
of Indians of either sex, felt impelled to write: "The Maricopa
women struck me as the handsomest lot of Indian women I had
ever seen. They were fine-featured, well-developed, and much
fairer-skinned than any of the other southern or western
Indians." [40]

Father Francisco Garcés, writing in his journal in 1775 and 1776,
paused to drop this compliment to the girls of the San Fernando
Valley: "The women are very comely and clean, bathing themselves every little while; they take great care of their hair and do
it up in a topknot; they wear petticoats of antelope skin and
mantas of fur, although they are not very coy [*aunque son peco
recatadas*]." [41] And General James, in a somewhat later review of
feminine charm among the northern Mexican Indians, tops him
with: "Their women are fascinating and far superior in virtue and
beauty to the greater number of Spanish females." [42] To find a
negative, or at least noncommittal, comment on the women of
the Hispanic Southwest, one must go back to Colonel Juan Bau-
tista de Anza, who reported to the Governor of New Mexico on
the Yuma: "The women were of good size like the men and their
faces were about like those of other Indian women; none especially
ugly, and none noticeably beautiful." [43]

Thus we see that, tribe by tribe, the Indian women varied in physical appearance quite as markedly as those of such ethnic groups as the Mediterranean, Scandinavian, and Central European females in modern society. Some the traders and mountain men thought ugly; some they considered beautiful and worth a staggering bride-price; and the majority they found to be, in De Anza's jaded words, "none especially ugly, and none noticeably beautiful." Which, of course, might be said of any cross section of femininity anywhere, at any time.

The women the traders and mountain men encountered in the forests, plains and mountains were physically very much like the girls they had left behind them. Racial taste in primitives sometimes finds expression in deformation of the body—flattened heads, pierced noses, enlarged lips, elongated ears, and so on—in attempts to embellish the person. But with a few exceptions, such as the head-flattening people of the Pacific Northwest, the North American Indians did not indulge in these practices.[44] Unclothed, their women were not even very dissimilar in color from the women of the white cities and settlements. Dressed in their finery, they were a little on the extravagant side perhaps, but who could blame a mountain man for finding the beaded antelope-skin slip of a Pawnee belle a more beautiful, not to say seductive, mode of dress than the hoop skirts and pantalettes of civilized fashion?

To the average fur trader's somewhat elementary taste in women, there was nothing about an Indian girl's physical appearance and dress to inhibit his natural yearning for feminine company. And there was much in her temperament and training that made it highly desirable for the white man to form an alliance with a sultry daughter of the country.

III

THEIR LIVES . . .

When a fur trader or mountain man bought himself a tawny teen-ager for a wife, he was braving not only the universal unpredictables of feminine nature, but also a cultural and racial complication far beyond his simple experience and understanding.

The Indian maiden, for all her fundamental resemblance to the rest of womankind, was conditioned culturally, morally, and emotionally to a life-style completely different from that of her white sisters. She had been reared to accept a marital status that made her the chattel of a husband who could lend her for a night to any stranger, swap her for a friend's wife temporarily, sell her to a well-heeled *bourgeois* for a string of horses, or kill her if she proved unfaithful.

Even when she was taken in hand at a very young age, missionaries found it almost impossible to effect an exchange of an Indian girl's thoughts and customs for white ways. In 1668, after a disastrous attempt to encourage little Indian girls to adopt the white mode of life, the Jesuits in Quebec reported in despair:

It is however a very difficult thing, if not an impossible one, to adapt the Indians to French customs or to civilize them. We have had more experience with it than anyone else, and we have observed that of a hundred girls who have passed through our hands [in the seminary of Quebec and the Ursuline convent], we have scarcely civilized one.[1]

For matrimony, or even simple cohabitation with a civilized white man, one might conclude that an Indian girl's preparation could hardly have been more inadequate. Yet these "women

savages" often did make good and even lasting unions with white
men. Something in their primitive background and training, instead of inhibiting the success of such unions, seems actually to
have furthered it.

To understand the alliances of white traders and native girls,
it is necessary to examine the background of the Indian woman's
tribal life. We must observe her in her environment, as a member
of tribal society, lodge mother, nubile maiden, and sexual partner.
It is even necessary to probe the springs of her emotional life—the
primitive sources of her loves, hates, jealousies, loyalties, cruelties,
and despairs—if we are to discern in what ways she was, after all,
simply the eternal female, the universal woman, and in what ways
a creature alien to any of her sex the white man had ever before
encountered.

In the eyes of most traders, the Indian woman was treated
by her husband as a drudge, a pack animal, a slave.

Early in the nineteenth century a particular model of tomahawk
began to be called a "squaw ax." One might suppose such a term
would apply to a light ax, suited to a woman's strength. On the
contrary, it designated heavy two- and three-pound hatchets, used
by Indian women for cutting wood.[2] Equally revealing was the
Ojibway custom of burying a woman with her ax, portage collar,
blanket, and kettle, while her husband took along to the Land
of Spirits only his gun, blanket, firesteel, flint, and moccasins.

Traders and early travelers almost always stressed the dreary
lot of the Indian wife. La Vérendrye, speaking of a Cree chief,
wrote: "I clothed his wives, or rather his slaves." The Hudson's
Bay Company factor Matthew Cocking had to travel as far as the
Blackfoot country before he found Indian women who were not,
in his view, "beasts of burden." Jonathan Carver, the early American trader and travel-book writer, noted that Indian women
were allowed only a few hours' rest after childbirth before returning
to their laborious tasks. And the naturalist John Bradbury wrote
that Sioux women frequently hanged themselves (on the smallest

possible tree, since they would have to drag it with them through
the spirit world) to escape a life of pure misery; to save their babies
from the same fate, they often practiced infanticide.[3]

Yet, it was not altogether true that an Indian woman's work
was nothing but heavy drudgery. Much of it consisted of the usual
tasks performed by all women in every age: cooking the meals,
keeping the house, rearing the children, fashioning clothes. The
Indian woman's skill as cook, tailor, and nursemaid was, as
Frances Densmore has pointed out, the product of careful training
from earliest childhood:

The companionship of a Chippewa girl and her mother was very close
and the child learned many household tasks by watching and helping her
mother. Thus a little girl was early taught to chop wood and carry it on
her back, and as she grew older she carried larger and larger bundles of
wood until she could carry enough into the wigwam for a night's use. A
girl was taught to make little birch-bark rolls like those which covered the
wigwam, her mother saying, "You must not grow up to live outdoors
and be made fun of because you do not know how to make a good wigwam." She was also taught to make maple sugar, gather wild rice, and do
all a woman's tasks.

A little girl was trained in what might be termed the accomplishments of
a feminine life, as well as in household tasks. Her first lessons in applied
beadwork were the decoration of her doll's clothing. . . . A simple
pattern [in woven beadwork] for a child consisted in a stripe of contrasting
colors down the middle of the chain, after which she might attempt a
diagonal or zigzag pattern in two colors. In such easy, yet intelligent
lessons a Chippewa girl was trained by her mother.[4]

A rather attractive picture can be drawn of Indian women at
their household duties: sitting in the sun at the doors of their
wigwams and netting snowshoes; smoking, gossiping, and enjoying
themselves as they work together on a new lodge cover; chattering
and laughing as they gather berries into birchbark *makuks* slung
from gay beaded belts; having a fine time in the sugar bush;
fashioning their beautiful quillwork. They were drudges when the
hard life of their primitive world demanded it, but they were also
industrious and carefully trained keepers of the lodge, skilled in

the arts of making a man comfortable and happy at home, taking pleasure in their wifely tasks. And it is not difficult to see how this proficiency—testified to by many a trader, and even by missionaries' white wives—fitted them well for marriage to a white man. A trader's needs, after all, did not differ much from a male Indian's.

A Sioux girl's domestic accomplishments, for example, were highly appreciated. If she was especially expert in beading or moccasin-making, she kept a record of her work, just as a warrior counted his coups. On her elkhorn scraping tool's handle she placed a dot for each robe she had tanned; when she had accumulated a hundred dots, she could make a raised circle at the base of the tool. The women often held contests at which they displayed their moccasins, dresses, cradleboards, and beaded belts.[5]

It was in articles of dress, her own and her husband's, that the Indian woman expressed her domestic talents most freely and often beautifully. A Sioux woman decorated her snowy leather shift with colored quills, later with beads; and one trader describes "the new Madame out in her finery, a scarlet dress with six hundred elk teeth." Contradicting Denig's wholesale dismissal of the Crow women, Catlin, while admitting that they "are not handsome," added that many of them were dressed with great beauty and taste; "their dresses are all of deer or goat [*sic*] skins, extending from their chins down to their feet . . . in many instances trimmed with ermine, and ornamented with porcupine quills and beads with great ingenuity." [6]

Fashions varied from tribe to tribe, of course, and changed with the times, tanned leather giving way to cloth, quills to glass beads, and elk teeth to disks of silver or tin. But the Indian woman's love of colorful decoration was universal and timeless. It found expression in what the elder Henry called "the fantastic harmony" of the Assiniboin women's dresses, the lower edges trimmed "with small bells, deer hoofs, pieces of metal, or anything capable of making a noise. When they move the sounds keep time." Traders remarked it in the beautifully ornamented leggings of the Cree, and a tribal cap of blue cloth profusely decorated with beads of many colors. Navajo women wove their beautiful blankets, so

prized by the Cheyenne, in which they danced around their enemies' scalps.[7]

From the time of the Aztec women, whose exquisitely woven
huipils Bernal Díaz found so "rich and beautifully ornamented,"
down to the era of complete corruption of native taste by cheap
traders' goods, the women of the tribes spent endless hours with
awl and deer sinew, vying with one another in the production of
elegant clothing and accessories for formal occasions. And one
wonders where they found the time.

There was, of course, the cooking—always left to the lodge
mother. Meals were simple, but not so simple as to consist only
of strips of meat half broiled over the fire or fish boiled in a pot.
The Indian woman was often a skilled, even sophisticated, cook,
and one of her meals was likely to include a rather surprising
variety of dishes. Ojibway women, for example, mixed pounded
hazelnuts into their maize cakes to give them a buttery taste.
They thickened their soups with "swan potatoes," dried pumpkin
blossoms, and "trout herb." They seasoned their food with wild
ginger, bearberry, mountain mint, and—above all—with maple
sugar, a large *makuk* of which was always handy at mealtime.
They strove, in short, to make their families' fare attractive and
varied as well as filling.[8] And all this took time.

Keeping the lodge clean and neat took still more time. Crowded
quarters did not simplify housekeeping, and an Indian dwelling
was likely to be filled with adults, children, dogs, and perhaps a
few horses. It was also, traders sometimes ungraciously observed,
rather noisome. The pious Reverend E. D. Neill, in describing
the Sioux of a later day, generalized: "The heathen, in their manner
of life, are essentially the same the world over. They are all given
up to uncleanliness. . . . In an Indian village all is filth and
litter." [9]

But, while this may have been true of the particular band of
Sioux Neill knew, it could hardly be said of all Indians. Many a
trader, grateful for the hospitality of an Indian lodge, did not
neglect to compliment his hostess on her housekeeping. The Rocky
Mountain trader Osborne Russell wrote of a Flathead woman,

with whose family he had spent a pleasant night: "The neat manner in which her lodge and furniture was kept would have done honor to a large portion of the 'pale faced' fair sex in the civilized world." [10] Paul Kane, the artist, said of a Cree woman in whose tipi he had found shelter: "She was so civil and kind, and the lodge was so comfortable, that we were induced to stop." [11] Even the critical eyes of Juliette Kinzie, wife of the famous Chicago trader, noted the order and cleanliness of an Indian wigwam she visited: "The fire in the center; the neat new mats on the floor; the leather bags containing food and other household treasures"; the kettles and ladles, all "very neatly arranged." And she tells of an Indian woman who, wanting to learn the housekeeping ways of the white woman, asked permission to come on washing day and observe her servants at work.[12]

Yet it would appear that all this—the cooking, sewing, child rearing, and housekeeping—was only a small part of an Indian woman's tasks. She also gathered wild berries and fruits, root vegetables, and herbs. She helped to harvest the wild rice and boil down the sap of the sugar maple. She dried the surplus meat her husband brought in from the buffalo hunt—or, more likely, left on the spot for her to bring in. She tanned the hides and from them fashioned lodge covers. She made the tipi, set it up, and took it down when the encampment moved on. She cut wood and brought it to the lodge fire. On the move, she packed the horses, and when a new camp site was reached, "she unpacks the animals, pitches the lodge, makes the beds, brings food and water, and does everything that is to be done, and when her husband returns from the hunt, is ready to take and unsaddle his horse." [13]

Her assigned tasks conformed to her tribe's economic environment. Among the agricultural Indians such as the Huron, the women were, as Pierre François Xavier de Charlevoix noted, "charged with the culture of the fields"—that is, they planted and hoed the maize, pumpkins, and beans, harvested them, and processed them for winter storage. The women of the canoe Indians plied their own paddles and carried their share on the back-breaking portages. Captain William Clark was astonished to find a Chinook woman shouldering a load that was "almost as much as a man could lift, and above one hundred pounds in weight." [14]

Samuel Hearne's guide Matonabbee gives us a fair idea of a woman's role on a canoe journey. "Women," he said, "were made for labor; one of them can carry, or haul, as much as two men can do. They pitch our tents, make and mend our clothing, keep us warm at night; and, in fact, there is no such thing as travelling any considerable distance, or for any length of time, in this country, without their assistance." [15]

Women as a rule accompanied war parties only as drudges and prostitutes, but there were individual cases of females taking the war road on their own and becoming famous as warriors. At La Pointe, a young Ojibway girl joined the fighting men of her tribe, raised the scalp of a wounded Sioux, and won great acclaim when she returned from battle.[16] And Denig tells of a Crow girl captive, "tolerably good-looking," who not only became a full-fledged brave but rose to the rank of a chief. She led raids against the Blackfoot, killed and scalped with her own hands—and, in keeping with her character of a warrior, married three women according to the rites of her tribe.[17]

And, of course, there was Pine Leaf, the spectacular Crow maiden, sweetheart of the no less spectacular mountain man James P. Beckwourth; she was "endowed with extraordinary muscular strength, with the activity of a cat, and the speed of an antelope." Besides this, she possessed great intellectual powers, "her features were pleasing, her form symmetrical," she was the bravest woman (in Beckwourth's opinion) that ever lived, and she counted coups by the score. She steadfastly refused, however, to marry Beckwourth until he should find her "a red-headed Indian." [18]

Although it was only in desperate circumstances that Indian women joined their men in battle—as the Aricara women did, "fighting like demons" against Colonel Leavenworth's troops— they were expected to perform special duties in time of war. The Apache women formed a reserve corps which rounded up horses while the men attacked, and by their numbers thus made the war party look larger and more formidable than it actually was.[19] Women, as in all warrior societies, were skilled in treating the wounded after battle. And the Pueblo Indians sent their girls "to excite the Spaniards to lewdness," in preparation for a surprise night attack.[20]

All in all, it can be seen that the Indian woman led a rather active life. Even when she grew too old to cut and fetch firewood, hoe corn, or carry heavy loads, she was set to weaving mats, taking care of the children, disciplining the dogs, and performing other "light" tasks about the lodge.[21]

It might be observed, of course, that contemporary white women had it no better. As, for example, the one pictured in a seventeenth-century manual for farm wives:

First in the mornying, when thou art wak'd and purpose to rise, lift up thy head and blis and make a sign of the holy cross . . . then first swepe thy house; dress up thy dys chebords, and set al thynges in good order within thy house, milk ye kine, take up thy children and aray them, and provide for thy husband's breakfast, diner, souper, and for thy children and servauntes, and take thy parte wyth them. And to ordeyne carne and malt to the myll, to take and brue withal the nede is. And mete it to the myll and fro the myll, and see that thou have the measure agayne besides the toll or else the myllner dealeth not truly wyth thee, or else thy corne is not dryed as it should be; thou must make butter and chese when thou may, serve thy swine both mornying and eveninge, and give thy polen meate in the mornying, and when the tyme of the year cometh thou must take hede how thy henne, ducks, and geese do lay, and to gather up their eggs . . .[22]

Also, the goodwife must make a garden, sow flax and weed it, after which it must be "pulled, watered, washen, dried, beten, braked, tawed, hucked, spon, wound, wrapped, and woven." Then, having attended to such routine chores as baking bread, making soap, and so on, she went to market with her butter, cheese, eggs, pigs, and geese. In her spare time she kept the accounts.

At about the same period, white women in Europe were laboring on the land, sometimes yoked to a plow. Children were put to

work in the flax fields. Little girls toiled at spinning wheels when
they were so small they had to stand on footstools. And a little
later, women and children were the principal victims of the horrors
perpetrated in the lofts and mills of the industrial revolution.
Perhaps the Indian woman, hard as her lot often was, carried no
heavier a load than many of her white contemporaries.

Life was simply a hard, unrelenting struggle in the forest and
on the prairies, and a woman shared with her man the unending
battle against cold and starvation. For his role in the stark drama—despite the stereotype of the fat, lazy Indian buck taking
his ease while his squaw did all the work—was not a soft one. As
in all primitive societies, the male accepted those tasks calling for
relatively short bursts of energy, muscular exertion, and exposure
to danger, while the woman performed routine work demanding
patience, endurance, and manual skills. Chief among a man's
duties was the procurement of meat. Meat was the staff of life,
and the hunter was the real breadwinner. So hunting was anything but a sport. It was hard, serious, dangerous work, with lives
often depending on the hunter's success. Here is a description of
a meat hunt in the deadly cold and deep snow of a Canadian
winter, as recalled by John Tanner, a white captive who grew up
as an Indian:

As the most incessant and the most laborious exertions alone could save
us from perishing, I immediately went out to hunt again, and having
started a bear, I pursued him for three days without being able to come
up with him. At the end of this time, I found myself so exhausted that I
knew I could never overtake the bear and I should not have reached
home had not some Indians less miserable and hungry than myself
happened to meet me. . . . It not infrequently happens that the strongest
men and the best hunters perish from absolute hunger.[23]

In most tribes a fair division of labor seems to have obtained,
and perhaps the Indian woman spent no more time complaining
of her lot than the modern suburban housewife does of hers. She
was sure, at least, of her place in the domestic economy, and
plagued by no sense of unfulfillment, nor any confusion about her

role in society. Even in the pages of the most cynical traders, we frequently catch glimpses of her gay and happy at her work. Walter McClintock, who lived with the Indians and knew them well, says: "Women considered it a disgrace for men to do any of their work—put up lodges, tan skins, cook food at home or look after provisions; all this was a woman's work in which they were trained from childhood, and they resented any interference from the men." [24]

The Cheyenne, a frontier army officer observed, ranked the good things of life in the order of whiskey, tobacco, guns, horses, and women.[25]

But it was not always the good fortune of Indian women to be listed among life's blessings, even after guns and horses. In some tribes, it would seem, she was not even accorded the dignity of a soul; she was not, in other words, quite human.[26]

Anthropologists speculate that the abysmal status of Indian women in some tribes may have been an expression of innate hostility between the sexes. Women were regarded as dangerous adversaries, foes to be conquered and humiliated. For this reason they were hedged about with innumerable taboos. They must spend their menstrual periods alone in tiny segregation huts. They must prepare the meals but eat apart from the men. They must dance by themselves and never touch a warrior's hunting or fighting gear. In some tribes they were thrown on their husband's funeral pyre, then hauled off by friends, then thrown on again, and so on, until dreadfully burned and insensible. (Wootton says the Ute sometimes burned wives with their dead husbands.)[27] In other tribes, a widow was condemned to carry her husband's ashes about with her for two or three years and remain a slave to his nearest kin. And in almost all Indian societies a certain amount of mutilation and disfigurement was expected of women as part of their mourning for lost mates.

Apart from the taboos, there were other tribal expressions of sexual hostility and contempt: the Sioux custom, for example, of the young men counting coup for coitus, and the enforced use of chastity belts.[28]

All this, it has been suggested, was rooted in the male's "unresolved masculine fear" that his physical powers would be lowered by sustained sexual intercourse—a view which was advanced by Lahontan at a very early date—and certainly a worrisome possibility to people whose existence depended on the physical fitness of the men.[29]

As in most other aspects of Indian life, a woman's status varied from one tribe to another. Much depended on her importance in the economy. Where the men were the breadwinners, Ross Cox points out, the women were condemned to a life of drudgery; where the women were important as root-gatherers, "they assume an air of liberty and independence." [30] Captain Meriwether Lewis agrees with Cox:

> The importance of the female in savage life, has no necessary relation to the virtues of the men, but is regulated wholly by their capacity to be useful . . . Where the woman can aid in procuring subsistence for the tribe, they are treated with more equality, and their importance is proportioned to the share which they take in that labor; while in countries where subsistence is chiefly procured by the exertions of the men, the women are considered and treated as burdens.[31]

Sometimes the standing of women within the tribe changed with a shift in the economic or cultural situation of the tribe itself. Thus, when the Comanche took to the plains, where game was abundant and easy to kill, the old taboos in connection with menstruation were relaxed. As competition for game disappeared, hunting medicine became less important, and the activities of the men became channelized largely in competition for women.[32]

To observe womanhood at its most abject, we must visit the northern tribes, such as the Chipewyan of the Lake Athabasca region. It would be hard to imagine a degree of degradation lower than the one reflected in a report from Fort Wedderburn by Sir George Simpson, governor of the Hudson's Bay Company: "The Bustard's wife died this morning, or more properly speaking a termination was put to her sufferings as she was actually buried before the vital spark was extinguished." [33] So little were the women of the Chipewyan valued, and so harshly were they treated, that David Thompson tells us:

This hard usage makes women scarce among them, and by the time a girl is twelve years of age she is given as a Wife to a man twice her age. . . . The hardships the Women suffer, induce them, too often to let the female infants die, as soon as born; and they look upon it as an act of kindness to them. And when any of us spoke to a women who had thus acted, the common answer was: "She wished her mother had done the same to herself." [34]

The men of the Cree, the Arctic explorer Sir John Franklin wrote, kept up a curious pretense of despising their womenfolk while treating them well; they surrounded them with many taboo reminders of their inferiority and grew furious with a white man who so far forgot himself as to treat an Indian wife tenderly.[35]

But it was not only among the bleak northern tribes that women were considered inferior, if indeed human at all, and were saddled to boot with a vague primitive onus of harboring something innately evil. Even the advanced Plains nations were something less than chivalrous. The Sioux, as we have seen, despite the romanticizing indulged in by the admirers of that great people, had little basic respect for their women. The Mandan women, although "beautiful and modest," were gladly sold for a couple of horses and a gun; and Catlin relates that the men of the tribe were outraged when he painted their women's portraits— thus giving squaws an importance equal to that of warriors.[36]

The Blackfoot showed their contempt for women by encouraging their young men to practice seduction, and then to scorn the women who yielded to their advances; or, if the woman was married, to mutilate or even kill her. As for the Aricara, "the sex is much more debased and unfortunate here than among other savages," the Missouri trader Pierre-Antoine Tabeau observed. But it may be noted that the Aricara women were not unconscious of their deplorable state, and made efforts to escape it—preferably by running off with a white man. "If enough white men came here," they told Tabeau, "the Ricaras would have no women." [37]

Like many another trader, Daniel Harmon drew some general conclusions about the Indian's treatment of his women, and they are not very favorable. "All the Indians," he said, "consider women as far inferior in every respect, to men; and among many tribes, they treat their wives much as they do their dogs. The men chastise their wives frequently, with an axe, or with a large club; and in the presence of their husbands, the women dare not look a person in the face." Having thus generalized, however, Harmon proceeds to make some important exceptions:

Among the Sauteaux [an Ojibway band], Crees, Muscagoes, and Assiniboins, however, the women are treated with more gentleness and respect. The husband shares the labor with his wife; and the women govern everything in their tents, so that the husband presumes not to dispose of the most trifling article, without the consent of his wife. Among them the husband kills animals and generally brings the meat to his tent, where his wife prepares it for drying, and melts down the fat. She also generally does the cooking; not, however, without the occasional assistance of her husband.[38]

He also assisted her, Harmon tells us, in taking care of the children, and if his wife was too heavily laden on the march, he even went so far as to take one of the children on his back.

It seems to have been true that in some tribes wives enjoyed a respect and influence comparable to that of modern American women. The most frequently quoted example, of course, is that of the Iroquois. This great federation of powerful tribes possessed the most highly organized social and political life of any Indian nation, and its core was the "fireside," consisting of the mother and all her children. The nation was composed of clans, the clans of *ohwachira*, and the *ohwachira* of all the descendants of a particular woman. From generation to generation, the eldest daughters succeeded to leadership of the *ohwachira*, and all basic authority stemmed from the *ohwachira* and the women who headed them.

Thus, in theory at least, Iroquois women were the dominant sex.[39]

In reality, however, not even the Iroquois society was a true matriarchy. Descent, to be sure, was traced through the mother, and nominal leadership was in the hands of the *ohwachira,* but most of the Iroquois woman's authority was symbolic. As Charlevoix pointed out, there was much pretense, much form, but little substance.[40]

Still, the women of the Five Nations did take part to a remarkable extent in a male-oriented culture. Girls were as fondly and permissively treated as boys. Women accepted a fair share of labor, but were not burdened. And, although not ruling in a true "matriarchal" sense, they could and did exert a strong influence on the decisions of the sachems in council. Even today, it has been pointed out, Iroquois women are remarkably resolute and self-reliant, and seem to be more secure in their feminine role than their masculine counterparts.[41]

The western Pueblo Indians and the Navajo also inherited through the mother; and the women, Cabeza de Vaca noted at a very early date, were "treated with more decorum than in any part of the Indies we had visited." Among the Natchez, the chief's nearest female relative (through whom succession to the "throne" was traced) was accorded great honor but had no real authority in council. She did, however, possess considerable power; and, according to Charlevoix, when she pointed at one of her people and said, "Go, rid me of this dog," she was taken quite literally. Those she passed on the road were, indeed, required to howl like dogs.[42]

In various other tribes women were accorded at least a symbolic authority in such matters as arranging marriages. An Ojibway woman could gain full membership in the Midewiwin, her people's Grand Medicine society.[43] In many tribes women were given power of life or death over prisoners of war. Sometimes, as we have seen, a woman even became a chief; but although a girl might dream of fighting with the war bands and taking scalps, she rarely succeeded in escaping from the reality of male domination in a warrior society.

White women who were captured and married into a tribe often preferred life with their Indian husbands to a return to "civilization." Mary Jemison, taken by the Shawnee in 1755 and married to a Delaware at the age of seventeen, described her husband as "good, tender, generous," and said that "strange as it may seem, I loved him." Cynthia Ann Parker, captured by the Comanche in 1836, returned to her husband's tribe after her "rescue," and her son Quanah Parker became a famous Comanche war chief. The early chroniclers often tell of white women refusing to leave their Indian husbands; Mary Harris may have spoken for many of them when she wondered aloud to the famous frontiersman Christopher Gist "how the white men could be so wicked as I have seen them in these woods." Despite the cruelties and outrage they suffered, many white women agreed with the Comanche's numerous *mestiza* captives that the Indians treated them better than the whites.

The Indian woman's status was clearly revealed by her rights— or lack of them—as a wife. And perhaps no other aspect of her life influenced so strongly her attitude toward the white man—and what he offered her as a mate.

The Indians considered marriage strictly a private affair, an agreement between a man and a woman to live with each other; and the event was usually marked by nothing more ritualistic than the young couple's going to bed together. Some tribes, such as the Iroquois, the Huron, and the ceremony-loving peoples of the Pacific Coast, asked friends and neighbors in for a little dancing and drinking, but for the most part Indians reserved their more elaborate rites for burying and name-giving. A wedding had no overtones of sanctification or religious import.

The events leading up to marriage, however, might have their interesting aspects. The Athabascan Indians, for example, often wrestled for wives; and a strong man might collect half a dozen young and good-looking girls, while a weakling had to content himself with a tribal reject or no wife at all.[44] The Shoshoni, following an ancient primitive ritual of chase and capture, ran a foot race for a mate, giving the girl a head start and pursuing her with a lasso; if he caught her, she was "tied to him for life." [45] The Ute Indians had a still simpler system: the man seated himself on a log outside the village and waited for the girl to come and sit down beside him; the courtship was then considered ended, and married life began without more ado. An Assiniboin warrior tied two horses outside the girl's lodge, then another, then another, until she gave in or sent him packing.[46]

Sometimes, it would seem, the girl boldly took the initiative. When she came of age, she might spread her blanket in front of the family tipi and invite suitors to share it with her. Young men lined up—with members of the family, and even other villagers, passing by—to pay her court.[47]

This matter of sharing a blanket was, in one form or another, a basic aspect of Indian courtship. It was an outgrowth, perhaps, of the custom of the man's lying down at night outside the tipi and reaching in to where the object of his desire was sleeping. What ensued, anthropologists inform us, went a good way beyond a mere tugging at the blankets, with the outcome more than likely to lead to matrimony.[48]

Blanket-sharing was observed and reported on by Lahontan, Peter Pond, Jonathan Carver, Alexander Henry, and other early commentators on Indian customs. It involved a stealthy nocturnal visit to the girl's lodge after a careful daytime reconnaissance of her sleeping place. The procedure, described by the American trader Peter Pond in his original orthography, was as follows:

When all the famaley are quiet and perhaps a sleep he slids soffely into that [place] and seat himself down by her side. Preasantlay he will begin to lift her blanket in a soft maner. Perhaps she may twich it out of his hand with a sort of sie and snore to gather but this is no killing matter. He seats awhile and makes a second atempt. She may perhaps hold the blankeat down slitely. At lengh she turns over with a sith and quits hold of the blanket.[49]

Henry describes a variant of this mode of courtship. The young man comes into the tipi with a splinter of wood, which he lights in the embers of the lodge fire. When he has found the young woman by its light, he whispers to her—after perhaps having had to awaken her—and if successful takes part of her mat. "I consider this practice," Henry adds, "as precisely similar to the bundling of New England and other countries; and to say the least, is not more licentious." [50] The young man, Henry makes clear, brought his own blanket.

Lahontan gave a Gallic embellishment to the procedure. The girl, he informs us, signified her acquiescence by blowing out the young man's light. This symbolic act seems to have fascinated the French imagination; one of their engravers produced a popular sequence of pictures depicting such a courtship—and ending with the young woman extinguishing her suitor's match with unmistakable enthusiasm. [51]

It might be noted, however, that William Keating and others deny the prevalence of this custom (among the Ojibway, at least) as a prelude to marriage. "It is not true," Keating wrote, ". . . that men visit the cabins of those whom they wish to marry, and commence their intercourse by nocturnal assignations; the young man will frequently resort to this, but never when they wish to take a woman as a wife." [52]

On the whole, marriage among the Indians was a casual matter and courtship little hampered by subtle conventions. A youth might begin by gently pelting his sweetheart with bits of earth, snowballs, small sticks, or anything else at hand; if she returned the compliment, he would be emboldened to engage her in some rather ribald repartee, and marriage followed not long after. Or perhaps he would throw a deer's carcass down in front of the girl's lodge, and keep this up until her father demanded to know what his intentions were. An Apache warrior simply staked his horse in front of the girl's lodge at night; if she took the horse within four days, fed and watered it, and returned it to the hopeful owner, everything was settled. [53] It does not seem that the historic phenomenon we call romantic love was an especially complicating factor in most cases.

We have the word of Lahontan that the Indians were "altogether strangers to that blind fury which we call love." Another early commentator, John Lawson of North Carolina, was of the opinion that an Indian woman's passion was "never of that force and continuance that any of them ever runs mad, or makes away with themselves, on that score." [54] And most whites appear to have rated the Indian woman's capacity for real love—at least for a white man—as rather limited.

Strong sexual attraction, and even one woman's desire for one man—something to be found in the lowest of societies—was certainly much in evidence. There were, John Lawson to the contrary, suicides over unrequited love, and a good deal of jealous killing. But true romance? Early traders and travelers were definitely skeptical. What John Dewey calls "phenomena which are peculiarly symptoms of the civilization of the West at the present time," and not at all fixed native impulses of human nature, were seldom apparent to the eye of the Indian traders.

Yet Indian lore and myth are rich in love stories. Callow youths mooned about the encampments playing melancholy music to their mistresses on courting flutes. Indian girls not infrequently resorted to love potions and charms, such as figurines carved from wood representing a man and a woman, and tied together face to face with a hair from the head of the desired one. The seeds of the false gromwell (*Onosmodium hispidissimum*) were supposed to have "great attractive power." [55]

Jealousy among Indian girls was rampant, Frances Densmore found in her study of Chippewa life, and often resulted in spirited fighting. "The hair," she says, "seems to have been the special point of attack, being ferociously pulled and frequently the braid being cut with a knife." And she tells of one young girl who, having "flirted with several young men," was waylaid by her group, severely beaten, and thrown into a mudhole.[56]

Indian torch songs, if somewhat repetitious and monotonous, were often lyrically tender. And sometimes a boy's appeal for a girl's hand was true poetry; as, for example, this one, taken down at Nipigon by the trader John Long:

Father, I love your daughter. Will you give her to me, that the small roots of her heart may entangle with mine, so that the strongest wind that blows shall never separate them? [57]

Thus, while an Indian marriage did involve such practical details as trading between parents, preliminary gift-giving, and payment of a bride-price, the element of romance was not always lacking. Young people could usually contrive to make their own choice of mates; and not infrequently elopements frustrated the best-laid plans of scheming parents. In some tribes, however, brides were bestowed at ages as early as six or seven—to make sure of their virginity, the trader Duncan Cameron cynically surmised.[58]

The Huron, Samuel de Champlain noted in his *Voyages*, carried the Indians' casual attitude toward marriage to its logical conclusion: trial marriage. The customary presents were exchanged, the young couple lived together for a week or two, and if it did not work out, each felt free to try again with another mate. The whole experiment was simplified by the fact that, among the Huron, a girl was under no chastity requirements before marriage; although, Champlain says, "after marriage the women were chaste and their husbands generally jealous." [59]

The simplicity of Indian marriage arrangements was, of course, much to the taste of fur traders and mountain men, who readily adapted to the customs of the tribes—even, in some cases, to the extent of taking brides of nine or ten years old. Very convenient, too, was the Indian attitude toward divorce, when the time came for a man to cast his wife *à la façon du pays* adrift.

Indian marriages could fall apart as easily as they were put together. Either husband or wife commonly felt free to get rid of a spouse for the lightest of reasons. "The Sioux," Kurz observed, "especially regard it as a very great honor to cast off as many wives as possible." [60] Of his beloved Flathead people, Father De Smet had to write: "We have not found even one of the best disposed who, after marriage had been contracted in their own fashion, did not believe himself justified in sending away his first wife whenever he thought fit to take another." [61]

Usually, the way to divorce was extremely simple. Of the Chipewyan, for example, Hearne wrote: "The Ceremony [of divorce] . . . consists of neither more nor less than a good drubbing and turning the woman out of doors, telling her to go to her paramour or relations, according to the nature of her crime." [62] All a Sioux husband had to do was beat the drum and announce that he had thrown out his woman; not infrequently, Kurz remarks, without distressing "the little wife" too much, since she was tired of her mate anyhow.[63]

So divorce was a two-way street in Indian society, with the woman as free as the man to pack up and leave. In most tribes she had only to pile her husband's personal gear in front of their lodge—public notice that she intended to go her way without him. (We shall see, however, that the life of a lone woman in an Indian encampment or trading post could be so dreadful that release from an unendurable marriage was sometimes sought in suicide, rather than through divorce.)

In the eighteenth century, the women of the Shawnee amazed colonial army officers with a mass divorce of their husbands and the selection of new mates more to their liking. On this memorable occasion, they opened festivities with a proclamation that all marriages were dissolved. Then followed a three-day feast, during which the women sang, "I am not afraid of my husband, I will choose what man I please." On the third day, a hundred men danced past the women, each of whom chose the one she wanted and danced with him. "After which," Colonel Mercer, an eye-witness, wrote to Christopher Gist, "the dance ended, and they all retired to consummate." [64]

Many of the whites—including such cultivated and intelligent ones as Edwin Thompson Denig—did not find even the Indian practice of polygamy incompatible with their own inclinations. Some of them, like the Missouri trader Larpenteur, were quite open in their admiration for the Indian who could support a string of wives in the hard, competitive world of the Plains. "It is a fine sight," Larpenteur said, "to see one of those big men among the Blackfoot, who has two or three lodges, five or six wives, twenty or thirty children, and fifty to a hundred head of horses . . . I can assure you, such a man has a great deal of dignity about him." [65] Larpenteur, however, has nothing to say about the dignity of the chief's wives, or how they felt about sharing their man with so many others.

It is possible that the frustrations and jealousies arising from such an arrangement had something to do with the Indian woman's eagerness to attach herself to the white man—but unlikely. Polygamy, among the Indians, was imposed by economic necessity and by an excess of women in a warring society. It was part of the pattern of survival, and as advantageous to wives as to husbands. "Polygamy among the Indians is no indication of sensuality," Kurz explained, "but simply shows their system of labor." An extra wife, in other words, was an extra "hand."

The more successful an Indian was as a hunter, the more wives he needed to prepare skins, dry meat, and so on. And, with the coming of the white trader, the stepped-up demand for pelts increased the need. This was especially true among the Plains Indians, where the bison economy made the support of large polygamous families possible.[66] It was less true of the forest Indians, where a man often found it difficult to support even one wife and her offspring. Hence polygamy, while not unknown, was less prevalent among such tribes as the Ojibway and Woods Cree.

The economic basis for plural marriage was a fortunate circumstance for older and less attractive women. A man did not refuse a woman because she was no longer young or beautiful; if she was willing and able to work, she had a place in the lodge. "Of course,"

Kurz says, "a man aims to have always apart a dainty one for his own private pleasure, but the others are for the most part working women—old maids or widows—who are glad to belong to a family."

Aside from economic reasons, an Indian often took on additional wives from a sense of social responsibility, or for political motives.[67] It was quite common for a man to marry his dead brother's wife or wives. Sisters were often married collectively; and some tribes recognized a man's right to all the younger sisters of his bride, or even his obligation to support them. Where wife-lending and wife-swapping were practiced extensively, it was necessary for important men to have a supply of wives— preferably young and good-looking—in order to extend the hospitality their position in society required. As a demand for more wives arose, the age of brides tended to decrease, and it was customary for all wives lower in the scale than No. 3 or No. 4 to be known as "slave wives," kept chiefly for lending purposes.

One might suppose it difficult to maintain harmonious relations between half a dozen women, or even fewer, in the same lodge. But Indian wives, as a matter of fact, seem seldom to have quarreled or engaged in jealous feuds. There were not many Leah-Rachel situations in the lodges; the first wife was in charge, and her authority was accepted by the others, who were often her sisters. A husband with a roving eye was even likely to find his wives united on keeping him in line.[68]

Polygamy tended to lighten the burden of the Indian woman, and to provide a certain security for her in old age. She was not abandoned by her husband, since he felt free to take a younger wife or two while keeping the old ones. And most Indian wives seem to have enjoyed the sociability of the polygamous lodge, especially if the other wives were her sisters.

Even under such conditions of drudgery, tyrannical domination, summary divorce, and the husband-sharing of a polygamous marriage, the Indian wife was not invariably discontented with

her role. If the journals of the traders are sprinkled with recitals
of domestic misery, they are also lightened occasionally with
little stories of wifely devotion and the love of Indian husbands
for their lodge mates.

One of the forces that acted to hold Indian marriages together
was the parents' love for their children. "All travelers concur
in representing them as very proud of the number of their children," Keating says. "Where the mild and humane provisions
of the Christian faith do not prevail, children form almost the
only link that binds man to woman for life." And much earlier,
Cabeza de Vaca noted that "it was the custom of men without
children to leave their wives at pleasure and unite with another
woman, but, having children, they never abandoned their wives." [69]

Children aside, a deep and enduring attachment seems often
to have existed between Indian couples. Indian women resented
belittlement of their husbands. "It is offensive to an Indian
woman," Walter McClintock says, "to have a report spread
about that anything is the matter with her man. She feels ashamed
and humiliated, as though she had neglected him." [70] Indian
women, Thompson says, forgave their men everything but a
lack of courage.

John Tanner tells of a Sioux prisoner who, having taken an
Ojibway wife, refused at imminent peril of his life—while "crying
like a child"—to leave her when an exchange of captives was
negotiated. [71] Sir John Franklin gives us another glimpse of hus-
bandly devotion on the bleak shores of Great Slave Lake: "Kes-
karrah, the guide, remained behind with his wife and daughter.
The old man has become too feeble to hunt, and his time is almost
entirely occupied in attendance upon his wife, who has long been
affected with an ulcer on her face, which has nearly destroyed
her nose." [72] And Denig tells of a Sioux chief who, after losing
his favorite wife by sickness, sacrificed his life "through reckless
grief" in a buffalo hunt.

The four female virtues, the Sioux held, were bravery, generosity, truthfulness, and childbearing. The feminine goal was "to
be loving, industrious, generous, and kind to all men and ani-

mals." [73] That many Indian wives and mothers sought and possessed these virtues is well attested by the loyalty and devotion of their men. "The Spokane women," Ross Cox says, "are good wives and most affectionate mothers. . . . The women of the Flatheads are excellent wives and mothers . . . and we have never heard of one of them proving unfaithful to her husband." [74] Over and over, the fort journals and wilderness diaries pause to pay similar tribute to the loyalty, courage, and devotion of the Indian woman. And, as the frontier advanced westward, the white man did not fail to find the same qualities in the native wife he chose to share his own rugged and often dangerous life.

♣ IV

AND LOVES . . .

Indian patterns of sexual behavior had their inevitable effect on the relationships of white men and native women. The sex life of the Indian female was a factor both in conditioning her for cohabitation with a white trader, and in his acceptance of her as a natural mate. While Indian practices did not exactly parallel those of civilized white society, in general they were not—like those of many other primitive people—so shockingly different as to cause revulsion on the part of the white partner or confusion in the mind of the Indian woman. On both sides, the relationship was a natural, even familiar one.

Indian women probably did not differ much in their sexual impulses and needs from their white counterparts. It is difficult, of course, to obtain reliable data from early reports—just as, up to Kinsey at least, it has been in our own day. The very first impressions recorded by white men were not very flattering. Thus Vespucci: "They . . . are libidinous beyond measure, and the women far more than the men; for I refrain out of decency from telling you the trick which they play to satisfy their immoderate lust." Lahontan remarked that "the men are as cold and indifferent as the girls are passionate and warm." From later observers we hear that "the Ricara women are disposed to be amorous," the Carrier girls "very free with their persons," and Indian women generally "of an amorous temperament." [1]

Traders, travelers, and missionaries—especially missionaries—tended to take a moralistic view of the Indians' sexual attitudes

68

and practices. Often their reports were distorted by prejudice, sometimes based on misconception. But if we disregard all this, we are still left with a considerable body of observed fact that explains why the uninhibited sex life of the Indian girl made it easy for her to adapt to the role of a trader's sexual partner—for a night or for a lifetime.

While the pattern of behavior varied across the land and through the years, certain practices were widespread enough to qualify as almost universal norms. First, the conditions of living. Children were brought up in crowded lodges, where they were exposed nightly to the mysteries of physical love. Adults—including even the most reserved and modest women—were notoriously ribald and obscene in their conversation, with no attention paid to little jugs with big ears.[2] Clothes were worn for warmth or decoration, not for decency; men and women bathed together in the nude; boys and girls ran naked through the village streets. There was absolutely no religious stricture on sexual freedom. There was very little of anything to retard most Indian girls' sexual inclinations from the time they first began to notice boys.

Even so, chastity was considered a virtue by many of the Indian nations. Among the Ojibway—a people of generally high moral standards—a girl's honor was peculiarly the concern of her brother (as it was in some other tribes), and chastity, Keating tells us, was a thing of high repute. Lacking it, he says, "no woman could expect to be taken as a wife by a warrior." [3] The Chipewyan confined their girls after the age of eight or nine to the wigwam, keeping them under strict watch to preserve their virginity until marriage—which often took place at the age of ten or twelve. The Iroquois maidens, Charlevoix avers, had a reputation for chastity before they were corrupted by the Illinois and other southern Indians.[4]

Here and there we find other defenders of Indian girlhood, or at least apologists. Among the latter is Lahontan, who explains disarmingly:

The [Huron] girls are indeed a little foolish, and the young men play the fool with them not infrequently: but then you must consider that a young woman is allowed to do what she pleases; let her conduct be what it will, neither father nor mother, brother nor sister, can pretend to control her. A young woman, say they, is master of her own body, and by her natural right to liberty is free to do what she pleases.[5]

This completely permissive attitude seems to be reflected in the sexual mores of the other eastern tribes. Alexander Mackenzie flatly denies that among the Cree chastity was of any importance. Before marriage, Carver observes of Indians in general, there was no restraint on a girl's conduct: "Indian women, before they are married, are not the less esteemed for the indulgence of their passions."[6]

After crossing the Mississippi, white traders encountered a variety of sexual practices that seem to have intrigued, amazed, bewildered, and occasionally disgusted them. It is difficult to draw any general conclusions from the often contradictory reports of the whites; but what they came upon appears to have been the familiar behavior pattern of primitive peoples, modified by contact with traders bringing rum, gewgaws, and a preoccupation with sex that astonished the natives.

Although Catlin called them beautiful and modest, the Mandan girls enjoyed—if that is the word—a reputation for wantonness along the fur trade frontier. But all the Plains Indians, in the judgment of most whites, were notoriously careless about the moral standing of their daughters. The Blackfoot and Sioux were said to have encouraged seduction. The Crow, it was alleged, found encouragement unnecessary. Of this picturesque tribe, Denig says:

The women, whether married or not, appear to be perfectly unaware that virtue or chastity has any existence even in the imagination. Their conduct in these matters is carried on in broad daylight, without any regard to bystanders or lookers on. Indeed, it would appear that they are as destitute of the ideas of decency or modesty as any part of the brute creation, and they prefer to be seen rather than to conceal any and all transactions between the sexes. . . . The married women are not a whit better than the others as they usually have had more or less connection before they were taken as wives by one man. Before marriage a woman is not thought impudent if she has but one lover; more, however, stamps her character as a courtesan.[7]

Maximilian noted also that the women of the Crow "are the most dissolute of all the tribes of the Missouri." Indeed, there seem to have been few defenders of the Crow girls' honor.

The Aricara maidens fared no better. Jean-Baptiste Trudeau echoes the opinion of most of the Missouri River traders when he says that the girls and young women "seem to be common property among them, living in full liberty, are so dissolute and debauched that, according to the reports of those who have studied them, there is not one whose modesty is proof against a bit of vermilion or a few strands of blue glass beads." [8] Trudeau, Denig, and others noted that incest was also common among the Aricara; and this at least, according to Osborne Russell, could not be said of the Crow.[9]

The Sioux made much of their young girls' virtue, but their use of chastity belts and the custom of tying a girl's legs together at night might raise a few eyebrows. Pierre-Antoine Tabeau, noting how Sioux maidens mingled with the men and laughed at their obscene jokes, had his own doubts about their reported virginity, even up to the ages of eighteen or twenty. "Truth," he remarked dryly, "exceeds probability here." The most that Tabeau will concede is that the Sioux women, "although not very strict, are more reserved than the Ricara women." [10]

On the whole, traders' views on premarital sexual practices of the western tribes add up to a picture of rather permissive conduct—even by the Indians' own standards of morality. Denig said of the Assiniboin women: "There are few handsome women among them, and virtue is a still rarer commodity, except in the very young females." He concedes, however, that "in these matters they are very shy and modest," and not at all like the brazen Crow hussies. The Prairie Cree, Franklin wrote, did not consider chastity a virtue in a female before marriage. Farther west, the Carrier Indians allowed their young girls "every liberty . . . for the purpose of keeping the young men from intercourse with married women." It was Ross Cox's opinion that Chinook women led depraved lives before marriage, but "made excellent wives afterwards." The Navajo, an early Franciscan father noted, did not prize virginity in their young women. The Zuñi regarded sex casually, as simply "an incident in a happy life." And so on—with, however, the usual number of traders giving us completely opposite views of sexual behavior, sometimes even in the same tribe.

Daniel Harmon, contradicting Mackenzie and others, says that "chastity in young women is considered as a virtue by the Indians generally, on the east side of the Rocky Mountains; and many mothers among some tribes are so particular that they never allow their daughters who have arrived at a certain age, to go from home alone, but always send some person with them as a protector." Indian women, Harmon adds for good measure, "sit down in a decent attitude, with their knees close to each other." [11]

But Harmon is by no means alone in his defense of feminine virtue among the Cree, Assiniboin, Sioux, and other tribes east of the Rockies. The Cheyenne girls, Colonel Richard Irving Dodge tells us, were modest and chaste—at least until they came under the influence of the "squaw man." Osborne Russell speaks warmly of the decorous conduct of the Shoshoni maidens. Alexander Henry found the Assiniboin women "perfectly modest, both in dress and demeanor." Thompson wrote of the Salish: "The Saleesh Indians were a fine race of moral Indians, the finest I have seen, and set a high value on the chastity of their women." Even among the much maligned Aricara, want of virtue was not universal. Brackenridge tells of a chastity ordeal in which a beautiful young girl of seventeen successfully flung at the male population of her village the challenge: "Where is the Arikara who can bring any accusation against me?" He ends with, "I feel pleasure in adding for the honor of the ladies of Arikara, that others followed [successfully], though I did not take the trouble of counting the numbers." [12]

A white man who lived much of his life among the Indians, as an Indian, attributed the seeming looseness of the native girls'

morals to the seductive skill of the whites, and to liquor. Mountain
man John D. Hunter, speaking of the Osage, Kickapoo, Kansas,
and other western tribes, says, "We find chastity as common a
virtue among those Indians who have never been corrupted by
intercourse with the whites, as it is, or ever has been, among any
people on earth . . . their girls' innocence and artlessness render
them the more liable to become the dupes of accomplished white
villains." [13]

Who was right—Harmon or Mackenzie, Denig or Brackenridge,
Trudeau or Hunter? We can never be sure, for it is impossible
to check at the source the reliability and representativeness of the
often conflicting reports. Yet, from the fragmentary and frequently disparate evidence, perhaps a few reasonably safe conclusions may be drawn.

First, the Indian woman's sexual behavior differed somewhat
from tribe to tribe. While some nations placed a high value on chastity, most North American Indians appear to have taken an extremely permissive view of a young woman's premarital conduct.
Despite innumerable taboos and prohibitions, her sex life was
generally governed by very lenient, if any, social controls. Restraints were often nonexistent. Intercourse before marriage was
sometimes actually encouraged, as we have noted, to safeguard
the virtue of married women.

Perhaps the voice that comes to us most clearly from the past
is that of Lahontan's Huron girl, declaring that "a young woman
is master of her own body, and by her natural right to liberty is
free to do what she pleases."

After marriage the picture changed abruptly. The girl who had
been as free as the prairie wind suddenly found herself to be the
property of one man—possibly a stranger—who could lend her,
swap her, sell her, beat her, or kill her if she played him false.
Although marriage and divorce were casual affairs, adultery was
no laughing matter. It could cost a woman her nose and ears, if
not her life.

Under conditions of tribal existence, with polygamy and easy separation prevalent, fidelity on the part of an Indian wife was no mean accomplishment; and there is little evidence that extramarital relationships were rare. Lahontan, to be sure, tells us of the Huron: "I do not believe that in the space of fifty years there has been one instance among them of the invasion of another man's bed." [14] The Chipewyan, Thompson says, exacted chastity from their wives and seemed to practice it themselves.[15] But among most tribes, particularly those on the western plains, adultery appears to have been a serious problem.

This is attested to by the fantastic "fidelity rites" observed by married women, and by the stringent punishments meted out to wives who took lovers. Sioux women, for example, proved their fidelity at feasts to which no men were admitted. After protesting the purity of her conduct, a woman proved the truth of her claims by "biting the knife." If her lips bled, she was counted a liar and a cheat. If, on the other hand, any woman contested her and, after biting the knife, displayed a lacerated mouth, her honor was saved.[16] So much trouble, one might think, to prove what should have been taken for granted!

The penalty for adultery was often severe. With the Blackfoot it was death for a guilty woman and forfeiture of the man's property. But actual illicit intercourse, it would seem, was not necessary to justify revenge. When an Indian "saw his wife make too free with young men," Larpenteur says, "the penalty is a piece of her nose. I have seen several who have undergone this punishment, and awful they did look." The Assiniboin, he adds, had no particular law against adultery, but left the matter in the hands of individual husbands. Their name for an unfaithful wife was *wittico-weeon*, literally "fool woman," but signifying a sort of second-degree prostitute.[17]

The Salish and Fall (Gros Ventre) Indians, according to Thompson, decreed death for both parties; but it was rare that punishment of any sort was actually carried out against either the man or woman, and even rarer for the death penalty to be exacted.

Although some tribes, such as the Creek and Crow, handled adultery cases severely, others let offenders off lightly; and some tribes did not punish them at all.

But whatever the penalties—or lack of them—not a few extra-marital affairs appear to have been carried on in most encampments and villages. Even among the remote Beaver Indians, Mackenzie says, conjugal fidelity was rare:

The women are of a contrary disposition, and the slaves of the men . . . They are very subject to jealousy, and fatal consequences frequently result from the indulgence of that passion. But notwithstanding the vigilance and severity which is exercised by the husband, it seldom happens that a woman is without her favorite, who, in the absence of the husband, exercises the same submission, and practices the same tyranny.[18]

Not infrequently, tensions between husbands and wives erupted in violent rebellion on the part of the woman. Colonel Dodge tells of a young Cheyenne woman who,

having become for some reason greatly exasperated with her husband, murdered him with an axe while asleep. About a month afterwards she gave birth to a child, which, as soon as it was born, she threw as far as possible into a thicket, saying she would "have nothing to do with anything belonging to that dead man." No notice whatever was taken of either of these crimes . . . her only punishment has been her inability to get another husband, the bucks wisely steering clear of a woman of such vigorous action.[19]

Sometimes it was sexual frustration under polygamy that led to open revolt on the part of the woman. One of Matonabbee's young wives, for example, turned on her husband and accused him of having more wives than he could properly attend. Then, deserting him for a younger man, she declared that she "chose rather to be the sole wife of a sprightly young fellow of no note, than to have the seventh or eighth share of the affections of the greatest man in the country." The outcome of that affair was the brutal murder of "the sprightly young man" by the outraged Matonabbee and the hardly less brutal beating of his wayward young wife.[20]

Quite often Indian women unhappy in their married lives sought escape in self-destruction. Peter Skene Ogden relates a familiar instance on his 1825 Snake-country expedition:

This day one of our guide's wives, as he has three and can afford to lose one, in a fit of jealousy committed suicide by hanging herself. This is the second instance of this kind since we started. This woman left four young children who no doubt will experience the inconvenience of being without their mother.[21]

Celebrated in Ojibway legend was the pathetic case of Dark Day. When Dark Day's husband decided to improve his social prospects by taking another wife, she placed her children in a light canoe, sang her death song, and plunged over the falls of St. Anthony—thus adding to the rather numerous and lugubrious Indian stories of a similar nature.

Often the discontented mate fled, with or without a lover, to another tribe. Kurz tells of one, a young Aricara girl, "hardly fifteen years of age, rather small, to be sure, but beautiful, and to all appearances modest and unassuming in manner," who eloped with a Mandan warrior. Such an elopement of a wife with a lover, Kurz explains, was a dangerous matter, but the husband was obliged to feign indifference, lest he be ridiculed. His revenge when the opportunity offered, however, was sure to be barbarous.[22]

Occasionally an Indian woman who could no longer endure either her husband or the drudgery of her tribal life fled to the whites. As early as 1540, such an instance was recorded by Hernando de Alacrón, commanding the sea arm of Coronado's expedition. While sailing up the Colorado, he took aboard an Indian woman, who then refused to leave. Her husband, she explained, had taken another wife, by whom he had children, and she could no longer live with him.[23] Three hundred years later, Indian women were still seeking refuge in white forts from hated men or intolerable conditions. Captain Bonneville told of a young Blackfoot woman who one night galloped into his camp and silently joined his band of trappers. "I love the whites," she said, "I will go with them." [24]

When an Indian wife was released from her hard lot by the

death of her spouse, she sometimes openly rejoiced. It is not unlikely that many an Indian woman displayed the same cold indifference to the loss of a husband that the Nor'wester Duncan
M'Gillivray describes in his journal of Fort George:

This woman . . . beheld her husband last Fall cruelly stabbed to the
heart without any extraordinary emotion or regret: and so unconcerned
was she at the event, that the night on which it happened she resigned
herself in marriage to a Canadian . . . Indeed from the barbarous
treatment of the women of the savages in this country, it can scarcely be
expected that they would have any degree of affection toward their
tyrants, or that they should be much affected at their death.[25]

Some of the sexual practices of the Indians, it must be acknowledged, were of a spectacular nature, and enough to boggle the
senses of a youthful fur trader who, quite likely, had never experienced anything more bizarre than the furtive rakehelling of
a New England village or frontier settlement. Prominent among
these were the communal orgies—or what most whites took to be
orgies—that were a feature of Indian life from the Atlantic to the
Pacific.

General Edward Braddock's soldiers described how the ceremonies were conducted at Fort Cumberland, where the British
were gathering for the ill-fated campaign against Fort Duquesne.
One of them wrote:

It is the custom with them, once or twice a year, for the women to dance
and all the men to sit by. . . . Each woman takes out her man that she
likes, dances with him, and lies with him for a week, and then [they]
return to their former husbands and live as they did before.[26]

The demoralizing effect of these rites on Braddock's troops, it
might be added, contributed to the bad blood between them and
the Indians, and finally to the desertions of desperately needed
Indian scouts. Braddock's disaster on the Monongahela could
thus be attributed in no small part to the involvement of his
troops with Indian women.

In a Mandan village on the Missouri, David Thompson observed a somewhat similar but even more curious ritual:

These people annually, at least once in every summer, have the following detestable ceremony, which lasts three days. The first day both sexes go about within and without the village, but mostly on the outside, as if in great distress, seeking for persons they cannot find, for a few hours, then sit down and cry as if for sorrow, then retire to their houses. The next day the same is repeated, with apparent greater distress, accompanied by low singing. The third day begins with both sexes crying (no tears) and eagerly searching for those they wish to find, but cannot; at length, tired with this folly, the sexes separate, and the men sit down on the ground in one line, with their elbows resting on their knees, and their heads resting on their hands as in sorrow. The women, standing and crying heartily, with dry eyes, form a line opposite the men; in a few minutes, several women advance to the men, each of them takes the man she chooses by the hand, he rises and goes with her to where she pleases, and they lie down together. And thus until none remain, which finishes this abominable ceremony.[27]

As was true of all such rites, no woman was allowed to choose her own husband. But Thompson was charitable enough to add: "Women who love their husbands lead away aged men."

In another Mandan village, that picturesque Nor'wester Alexander Henry the Younger was the bewildered witness of a lurid nocturnal ceremony:

About midnight we were awakened by some extraordinary noise in the village. On going to the outer porch door I saw about 25 persons of both sexes, entirely naked, going about the village singing and dancing. At times they withdrew in couples, but soon rejoined their companions in the dance and song. During this short separation from the rest they appeared to be very closely engaged, and not withstanding the night was dark I could perceive them occupied in enjoying each other with as little ceremony as if it had been only the common calls of nature. This affair continued about two hours, during which they made the tour of the village several times. What was the meaning of this ceremony I could not learn; but certainly there could be no performance more lascivious than the one I witnessed.[28]

Occasionally white men were involved in these rites. Maximilian describes his own rather passive participation in what he calls the Buffalo Medicine Feast in an Aricara village. First came dances and ritualistic performances by the men. Then:

When the ceremony had continued a couple of hours, the women began to act their part. A woman approached her husband, gave him her girdle and undergarments, so that she had nothing on under her robe. She then went up to one of the most distinguished men, passed her hand over his arm, from the shoulder downwards, and then withdrew from the lodge. The person so summoned follows her to a solitary place in the forest; he may then buy himself off with presents, which, however, few Indians do. This honor was offered to us, but we returned to the lodge, after having made a present.[29]

The Lewis and Clark journals also describe this ceremony, with the additional information that "the young men who have wives back of the circle go each to one of the old men with a whining tone and request the old man to take his wife (who presents herself naked except a robe)." The journals add: "We sent a man to the Medicine Dance last night: they gave him four girls." [30]

Whatever their significance may have been, many of the Indian tribes conducted festivals, dances, rituals, and celebrations that were often attended by a general communal orgy. During these festivals—among which may be mentioned the Shasta and Maidu girls' adolescent ceremonies, the Karok salmon dance, and the Maidu spring dance—general license was not only tolerated but almost obligatory.

Like Henry and Thompson, fur traders were generally ignorant of the religious or shamanistic significance of these strange rites. But Catlin, describing the orgiastic aftermath of the gruesome Mandan *o-kee-pa* ceremony, hazards a guess at their meaning: "Let us inquire whether it is not, more or less, an inherent propensity in human nature (and even practiced in some enlightened and Christian communities) to end extreme sorrow, extreme penitence, and even mourning for kindred the most loved in *debauch?*" [31]

In most instances, it would appear that a feature of these pan-tribal ceremonies was wife-swapping. A temporary exchange of wives, however, was also practiced as a non-ritualistic custom. La Vérendrye described the Indians around Lake Winnipeg as having two wives each and lending them now and then from one lodge to another. Alexander Henry noted:

The Cristenaux [Cree] have usually two wives each, and often three; and make no difficulty in lending them, for a length of time, to a friend. Some of my men entered into agreement with the respective husbands in virtue of which they embarked the women in their canoes, promising to return them the next year.[32]

Among the Beaver Indians, brothers apparently swapped wives as a matter of course: "Brothers cohabit with one another's women openly," George Keith reported of them.[33] Hearne protested that the Chipewyan, on the other hand, held such practices "in abhorrence." [34]

To some degree, at least, wife-swapping appears to have been practiced in most of the tribes; and despite its social acceptance, it was not without occasionally disastrous results. Mackenzie tells of an "unfortunate event" in the Athabasca country involving two comrades, one of whom became enamoured of one of the other man's wives:

The husband consented to yield her to him, with the reserved power of claiming her as his property, when it should be his pleasure. This connection was uninterrupted for near three years, when, whimsical as it may appear, the husband became jealous, and the public amour was suspended. The parties, however, made their private assignations . . .[35]

And the end of the story, as might have been foreseen, was murder.

If a more profound reason than a sexual one is to be sought for the custom of wife-swapping, either on a ceremonial or a private level, it may be found in the possible influence on the fecundity of the tribes. Among the Eskimo, Edward Weyer points out, the trading of wives for a night or for a longer period may have a purely practical purpose: "In strict pair marriage, if either party is sterile the union remains unproductive; whereas if the exchanging of wives is practiced there is greater probability that every fertile person will have intercourse with a fertile mate." [36]

The Eskimo, however, seem to have turned a practical necessity into something of a diversion by blowing out the igloo light, after which each man found a mate in the dark.

☙

Other peculiar sexual practices claimed the attention of white traders and trappers in the Indian Country. Among these were various forms of perversion. The very earliest chroniclers note the burning alive of Incan sodomists in Cuzco, and Garcilaso recorded the destruction of a whole city of them by an outraged angel from heaven.[37] In North America, such early reporters as Joliet and Marquette describe "those wretches who from their youth dress as girls and pander to the most shameful of all vices." Homosexuality, as a matter of fact, seems to have been widespread, and the "berdache," as he was called by the whites, a fixture in many Indian communities. [38]

A famous berdache was Yellow Head, the son of a celebrated Ojibway chief. "This person," Alexander Henry the Younger wrote, "is a curious compound between a man and a woman. He is a man, both as to members and courage, but pretends to be womanish, and dresses as such. His walk and mode of sitting, his manners, occupations, and language are those of a woman. His father, who is a great chief among the Saulteurs, cannot persuade him to act like a man." [39]

There was a tribal variance of attitude toward such deviates. Some Indians considered their condition an unfortunate slip-up on the part of the Manitou, with no special opprobrium attaching to the victim of the Great Spirit's bungling. Others regarded the *agokwa*, as the Ojibway called them, with contempt and pity; and parents were anguished to see signs of perversion developing in their sons. According to Catlin, some of the Plains Indians made a public thing of it, with an obscene and "humorous" dance cere-mony.[40] Some tribes attributed magical powers to the *agokwa*, some feared them. The Illinois trained youths to be concubines of the men.

While sexual abnormalities, incidentally, are sometimes glossed over as "of so filthy and disgusting a nature as not to admit of being published," fur traders are often remarkably explicit and matter of fact in reporting the Indians' most bizarre practices. Thus Alexander Henry the Younger on the Crow: "I am informed they are much addicted to unnatural lusts, and have no scruple in satisfying their desires with their mares and wild animals fresh killed." [41]

Except for occasional mention of a warlike female like Beck-wourth's Pine Leaf, or the "Absaroka Amazon" described by Denig, there is little evidence that Indian women engaged in homosexual relations. One of the rare instances of female trans-vestitism reported by a white trader was the "prophetess" who complicated David Thompson's life. When a young Indian and his wife appealed to Thompson for protection, he took a good look at them:

In the man I recognized the woman who three years ago was the wife of Boisverd, a Canadian and my servant; her conduct was then so loose that I requested him to send her away to her friends. . . . She found her way from tribe to tribe to the sea, she became a prophetess, declared her sex changed, that she was a man now, dressed and armed herself as such, and also took a young woman to wife, of whom she pretended to be very jealous.[42]

The Nor'wester Gabriel Franchère, however, surmised that "the prophetess" dressed herself as a man so as to travel with more security.

In the matter of private love-making, traders in the Indian Country found nothing very different from what they had been accustomed to in civilized life, judging from their lack of comment on the subject. And they seem to have experienced little difficulty in adapting to whatever small peculiarities distinguished the Indian mode of private sexual behavior.[43]

Overt expressions of affection were considered uncouth, or at least in bad taste, by most Indians. Sweethearts were never seen holding hands, and not even married couples showed their feeling for each other in public. A woman seldom looked directly at a man; to do so stamped her as a bold hussy.[44]

But this did not mean that the Indians were indifferent to the subtleties of love-making, or failed to employ them in private. Kissing, including the so-called "deep kiss," was a usual preliminary to sexual intercourse among many tribes. Apparently kissing was an indigenous custom, since the earliest white men among the North American Indians were greeted with kisses, sometimes so enthusiastically as to become embarrassing. Later traders mention, often with no relish, the same propensity on the part of tipsy females at post dances. Fondling of the breasts was another common prelude to more intimate relations. In the observance of such sex play, the Indians seem not to have differed from civilized whites of their time—or, if we may believe Kinsey, from the majority of educated Americans today.

Grooming and delousing, as a preliminary to sexual relations— practiced, for instance, by the Plains Cree—was a new note, no doubt, to early explorers and traders. But the giving of gifts was familiar enough, and some of the mountain men seem not only to have fallen in line with this Indian courtship custom, but to have carried it to extremes. There were few features of Indian lovemaking preliminaries, indeed, that tended to inhibit the white man's solicitation of a native belle's favors, or to put him at a disadvantage in awakening her amorous inclinations.

Nor was he likely to be nonplussed by the Indians' techniques of sexual intercourse. Unlike some other primitive societies, such as certain African and Pacific peoples, the Indians did not go in for bizarre or highly athletic sexual exercises. The sex act was commonly practiced in the face-to-face relationship, and the variants were not so unusual as to perplex the white partner.

It was the Indians, in fact, who seem to have been puzzled at times by the whites' sexual practices. Lahontan's friend, the Indian chief Adario, censured the immoderateness of the French and "the inconvenience" of their sexual techniques: "For when you have just done eating, or are newly come off a fatiguing bout, you lie with your Women as often as ever you can, and that either upon Chairs, or in a Standing Posture, without considering the Damage that accrues from such indiscretions." [45]

Custom varied, of course, among the tribes, as did the tribal notion of what was expected of the woman—or what she could expect for herself. Among some tribes (according to recent anthropological studies) we find the Victorian stereotype—that of the passive female—prevailing, with the Chiricahua women forbidden even to display any emotion. The Hopi, on the other hand, expected the female partner to be aggressive and vigorous. Crow women desired and achieved as much satisfaction as their partners. All the tribal variants were doubtless well known to the traders and mountain men, and the topic of much campfire discussion.

In such areas as frequency of intercourse, we again find a good deal of variation, ranging all the way from the Hopi, who indulged themselves several times a week, to the Crow, who thought it weakening to have intercourse every night but found it "difficult to do so less frequently." Among all the tribes, however, there seems to have been generally widespread agreement that seclusion was desirable for love-making, and that night was the proper time for it, although many scenes of open abandon, described by Denig and other traders, appear to contradict this conclusion.

Certain sexual taboos, such as those proscribing intercourse after the onset of menstruation, before taking the warpath, and so on, were everywhere observed. Abortion—whether to escape the burden of childbearing or to spite a husband—was widely employed.[46] In fact, most of the familiar sexual behavior of women the world over—including various dodges to discourage or deceive an overamorous husband—was to be found among the daughters of the country.

On the whole, there seems to have been little about private

sex for the lad from New England or Ohio to learn from the Indians; and if there was, plenty of Indian girls were willing and eager to teach him.

Almost everything we know about the sexual behavior of the Indians we have learned from men. What, it might be asked, could an ignorant fur trader, or even an educated traveler, possibly tell us about the emotional reactions of a Sioux or Blackfoot girl to her tribal environment; and, particularly, what could they tell us about her sex life?

Most of these men—even such fair and objective observers as Mackenzie, Thompson, Charlevoix, and Brackenridge—took a moralistic view of what they saw. Theirs was the puritanical Western outlook on sex, which related "morality" to sex alone and connected sexual behavior in some vague way to religious concepts. The fact that the Indians recognized no such relationship between sex and religion was ignored. And so, time after time, otherwise well-disposed men committed what one of their number, Ross Cox, called "the cardinal sin of history": they judged the morals of one age, one society, by the standards of another.

They not only condemned the Indians for not observing the Christian Western sex taboos, but they misunderstood much of what they saw. The communal orgies described by Thompson, Henry the Younger, and others, for example, doubtless had a religious significance; and this, quite surely, was also true of the "mass divorce" reported by Colonel Mercer.

In addition, white men frequently came into contact with the worst types of Indian womanhood, the tarts, trollops, and prostitutes—and not even the best of them. White visitors to the Indian villages, Hearne complained, were "always served with the worst commodities, though perhaps they pay the best price for what they have." [47] It was, Franchère says, as if English womanhood in general were judged by the morals of London costermongers.

Among the most complete—and damaging—reports on the

sexual conduct of Indian women were those of traders who visited
the Mandan villages on the Missouri. But Edward M. Bruner
observes: "The sexual behavior of Mandan women toward white
men was rooted in basic premises of Indian culture; the inter-
pretation of the white traders was a gross cultural misunderstanding." [48]

As a blanket statement, this may possibly be open to question.
But it is doubtless true that white men often misread the sexual
behavior not only of the Mandan women, but of Indian women
generally. Even so astute an observer as Edwin Thompson Denig,
it may be suspected, did not deal fairly with the women of the
Crow, that virile, warlike, ribald nation so much admired by all
white traders.

The sex life of the Indian woman was observed by untrained
investigators, without benefit of controlled experiments, measured
pulse rates of couples in coitus, or computerized data. The traders
were mostly rough, often illiterate men, who simply reported
what they saw and experienced—or heard from other traders.
Sometimes they wondered, as Henry the Younger did, "what was
the meaning of this," but none ever came close to finding out. [49]

Yet in their very misunderstandings and false conclusions there
is a certain value, for they help to explain many of the characteristics of racial contacts on the fur trade frontiers. It was what
the white man believed to be true, rather than the truth itself,
that shaped his attitudes and determined his relationships with
the Indian women.

AND INFINITE VARIETY

Not many Americans of this generation could give you the names of more than one or two Indian women. Most would start with Pocahontas. Some would follow with Sacajawea—although few would know how to spell or pronounce it. After that we might get some fumbling allusions to heroines of legends and sheet music— Minnehaha, Nokomis, Red Wing, Winona.

Today, actually, the list has dwindled to almost nothing. Who sings songs about Indian girls any more, or writes poetry about them, or paints romantic chromos of them mourning for lost warriors? The Indian woman as an individual with a name and personal identity has vanished with the plaster bust of the dusky maiden (in full war bonnet) on top of the upright piano. She has been reduced to the vaguest of stereotypes, and the Indian heroines of television have not done much to bring her alive again.

Despite their highly personal contacts with native women, even traders and mountain men tended to oversimplify. The Sioux women had "unhappy faces and a tendency to suicide," the Chipewyan were "the mildest and most virtuous of females," the Beaver women were "of a contrary disposition," the Cree "quiet and sweet tempered." One must dismiss most of this testimony, often discrepant; but at the same time one may take note of certain traits, imposed by a neolithic culture and a savage environment, that did seem to be widely observable among Indian women.

The most arresting of these was cruelty. The torture of pris-

oners, for example, was regularly turned over to the women, and
there is no evidence that they showed much distaste for it. After
a battle between the Crow and the Piegan under Fort McKenzie's
walls, Bodmer was aghast at the mutilation of the body of a fallen
Crow warrior by the Piegan women, "whose fury was particularly
directed toward the privy parts." [1]

The torment of captives varied in degree and character, from
the fiendish inventions of the Iroquois—who forced their victims
to eat their own flesh—to the total absence of torture among the
Pueblo Indians. But wherever it was practiced, the females played
a prominent part. The women greeted the bedraggled captive with
blows, insults, and lamentations for their own dead. The women
were in line with their clubs when the unhappy prisoner was forced
to run the gantlet. And usually it was the women who, after
setting fire to the wood around his stake, strove to prolong his
agony by every subtle means their ingenuity could devise.

When Colonel William Crawford, a friend of George Washington's, was captured by the Shawnee in 1782, he had nothing in
store for him so quick and merciful as simple burning at the stake.
After a nightmare trek to the Indian village of Sandusky, he was
stripped naked and made to sit down. He was then turned over to
the women, who beat him and otherwise amused themselves while
the warriors fixed a heavy post in the ground and laid a circle of
hickory firewood around it.

But Colonel Crawford was not bound to this post. A man
enveloped in flames might die in a few hours, even in minutes.
So Crawford, his hands tied behind his back, was attached to the
post by a long rope. The fire was kindled. Suddenly the warriors
swooped at him, yelling like demons. They cut off his ears and
fired gunpowder into his naked body. Then they retired to watch
the female professionals work.

The women pelted him expertly with live coals, jabbed at him
with burning poles. They shrieked with laughter when Crawford
began to run around the post, leaping and frisking in a macabre
dance through the flames. After two hours of this, Crawford
became all but insensible to pain. He walked slowly, around and

around, heedless of his tormentors, asking God in a low voice to be merciful and let him die. Finally, he stumbled and fell on his face in the burning embers. Sensing the end was near, a warrior pounced on him and tore off his scalp with his teeth. A woman rushed forward and emptied a shovel full of live coals on his exposed skull. But Crawford got up and resumed his slow walk around the stake. It was long after dark, when the women were almost too weary to lift a burning pole, that Crawford died.[2]

Many attempts have been made to explain the strange joy that Indian women took in torture. Perhaps, it has been conjectured, this was their way of dulling their grief for sons and husbands killed by the enemy. But the women of the tribes often exhibited an equal ferocity when no such motive operated. Here, for example, is the Nor'wester Charles MacKenzie telling of a beautiful young slave girl's escape from a Mandan village, and its mournful aftermath:

A young man, brother of the Great Chief, sent for me to his lodge or tent. After exchanging the usual civilities, he observed that during my absence, in the summer, he had been at war.

"I killed," said he, "a Serpent [Snake] chief, two young men, with several women and children. I saved a young slave and brought her here; I used her kindly, for I intended her for you, but at the end of three days she deserted in the night, and carried off a fine horse from my tent." "Where did she go?" I said. "She went to her relations where she is arrived before now. . . . She is very pretty; none of our own women equal her; she is the greatest beauty of all the Indian tribes, and we know the White Man would love her and would give a generous price for her. I saved her life on account of the White Man."

"I wish you had not been so merciful, my Son," exclaimed an old woman. "I wish you had killed the bastard [*sic*], for she has stolen my knife; it was a good knife, only the handle was broken." "Yes," said a young woman from the opposite corner of the tent, "the bad slave has stolen my knife also; I wish she was dead!"

These wishes, MacKenzie adds, were not in vain. Shortly afterwards, four young men who had been sent in pursuit of the beautiful fugitive returned with her head on a pole. They planted

the pole in front of the tent from which she had escaped, and made
no more of the incident. Nor did the other men of the village,
regarding the head or scalp of a woman beneath their notice. But—

Not so the women. Overjoyed by the spectacle, they collected around in
great numbers, dancing and turning it into ridicule. They pulled it by
the hair from the pole, tossed it with their feet from tent to tent throughout the village, exclaiming, "There is the enemy: take care! be kind to
her!" At length the head was consigned to the boys as a mark for their
arrows.[3]

Anthony Henday says that when a captive Blackfoot girl
aroused the resentment of an Assiniboin warrior's jealous wives,
she was summarily hacked to pieces.[4] The journals of the traders
frequently recount similar acts of almost unbelievable ferocity.
It was in actual fact a "woman savage" that a fur trader took to
wife.

Yet beneath her streak of savagery the Indian woman frequently revealed a tenderness and compassion that touched even
the casehardened trader. Often it was she who saved the victim
from the slow fire, and perhaps adopted him to replace a lost son.
Generally it was she who took pity on the abused captive, as the
Otter Woman did when John Tanner was tomahawked in his
sleep by his captors: "The old woman and her daughter having
found me, discovered some signs of life, and had stood over me for a
long time, crying, and pouring water on my head." [5] Or as when
Mary Rowlandson, hungry and cold, wandered through the town
of her Indian captors, and the women took her in: "Going among
the wigwams, I went into one and there found a squaw who showed
herself very kind to me, and gave me a piece of bear. . . . She
bade me come again, and told me they would buy me if they were
able, and yet these were strangers to me that I never saw before." [6]

These same women who delighted in torturing prisoners and
mutilating the dead reproved their dogs "very tenderly," Franklin tells us. When they saw them fighting, " 'Are you not ashamed,'
say they, 'are you not ashamed to quarrel with your little brother?'
The dogs appear to understand the reproof and sneak off." [7]

And they were the most loving of mothers. "I believe it will not be disputed," John Long wrote, "that the Indian women love their children with as much affection as parents in the most civilized states can boast." And Keating: "Their fondness for their children is extreme, especially that of mothers for their daughters." Catlin leaves us a charming word picture of young mothers at Fort Snelling "anxious to show off their children."

"Their whole life," Charles MacKenzie exclaimed, "is a life of extremes!" They were at once cruel and tender, courageous and timid, stolid and emotional, sad and merry, silent and loquacious, loyal and faithless, cold and amorous. And, indeed, the testimony of scores of whites in the Indian Country seems to bear out MacKenzie's baffled judgment. The woman of the tribes, the primitive daughter of a harsh and elemental environment, was far from an uncomplicated being. She was so complex, in fact, that the astounding contradictions of her character are almost impossible for us to grasp in our "sophisticated" time.

Among all of them, pitifully few have survived—even as fleeting shadows in some forgotten trader's journal—to show themselves to us as women of flesh and blood. But in the long procession of history, one occasionally does pass who left the impress of her personality on a royal chronicler or frontier yarn-spinner. A few have been remembered, to remind us that every Indian woman was, after all, a unique person—a woman, with all the fascinating qualities of her own individual feminine nature. And the first of these to appear in history was

DOÑA MARINA

She was lovely as a goddess, *hermosa como diosa*, the Spaniards said, and very clever. When the chiefs of Tabasco brought gifts to Hernando Cortés, they also presented him with twenty beautiful girls, and Marina was among them. She was from near Jalisco, the daughter of a chief, stolen in wartime and carried off to Xicalduco, and afterwards sold in the market place to the cacique of Potonchan.

Marina spoke the tongues of both Cortés' enemies the Mexicans and his allies the Tlaxcalans—which made her, through the interpreter Aguilar, the Spaniards' only means of communicating with the Aztec chieftains. Quick to sense her immense value to him, Cortés took her aside and promised her "liberty and more than liberty" if she would become his interpreter and secretary. She accepted the offer, became a Christian (at which time she was given the name of Doña Marina), and thereafter Cortés' talks with the Mexicans were always reported "through Doña Marina." Cortés gave Doña Marina as a gift to his favorite captain, Alonzo Hernandes Puertocarrero, who was later to receive still another Indian beauty, Doña Francisca. But when Puertocarrero returned to Spain, Cortés made Doña Marina his own mistress, and she bore him a son.

Doña Marina's importance to Cortés far transcended that of interpreter. Through her diplomatic skills, her native understanding of the Mexican mind, her courage—and, it must be said, her treachery—she played a vital role in the Spanish conquest of Mexico. Doña Marina rode at Cortés' side wherever the fighting was heaviest and the outlook blackest. She cajoled, pleaded with, and threatened her countrymen on behalf of her white lord and lover. Once, she undoubtedly saved the whole expedition from disaster by uncovering an elaborate Cholulan plot to exterminate the Spaniards in the night. Cortés, "on horseback, with Doña Marina at his side," was rather embittered about this. "So, for coming like brothers and telling you what our Lord God and our king ordered," he rebuked his enemies, "you would pay us by killing and eating us, and your pots already prepared with peppers and tomatoes." He then turned his soldiers loose on them in an enclosed courtyard, with Doña Marina at his side looking on.[8]

So, "with affectionate words" and "in the way she knew so well," Doña Marina continued to serve the Great Captain in his bloody conquest of her countrymen. She was in his company so constantly that the Mexicans gave Cortés the name *Malinche*, which was Marina's Indian name. She quickly became fluent in Castilian, and added the weight of her promises or, if necessary, her threats to

Cortés' negotiations with the Mexicans. And it was Marina who, in her gentle manner, persuaded Montezuma at last to give himself up to imprisonment and death.

What does all this make Doña Marina? She was beautiful and gifted. She was a woman of quick intelligence, strong character, and apparently generous nature. The Spaniards loved her, at any rate, for we find hard-bitten Bernal Díaz adding to his account of some particularly rough treatment at the hands of the Mexicans: "I have forgotten to write how glad we were to see that our Doña Marina was still alive . . ." And, oddly enough, even the conquered people of Mexico seem to have thought of her kindly—as they do to this day.[9]

Yet, in purely objective terms, Doña Marina was a traitor who betrayed her own people and, perhaps more than any other single person in Cortés' expedition, brought them to their knees. And here we happen on a phenomenon that, in William Christie MacLeod's words, is both surprising and abundant: "the constant betrayal of their own people by Indian women," usually to white lovers.[10] Catherine, the Chippewa mistress of Major Henry Gladwin, foiled Pontiac's surprise attack on Detroit. A native woman's treachery upset the Natchez' plan for wiping out the French Fort Rosalie. Garcilaso reports the betrayal of their own people by Indian women as far back as De Soto's time. Weetamo, "the Queen of Pocasset," went over to the English side when things became too hot for her in King Philip's camp. And, apart from overt treachery, we have numerous instances of young Indian girls conniving in the escape of white captives. Such conduct, it has been noted, is not marked among any other people, and it is especially surprising to find it in women whose sense of loyalty was otherwise so strong. It has been suggested that matters sexual may be at the bottom of it.

After Marina, other women of the Americas appear frequently in the chronicles of the Conquistadores. We see the cacique of Pacaha giving his two sisters, Macanoche and Mochila ("they

were symmetrical, tall and full"), to De Soto as wives, and Balboa
receiving a similar present from the chief of a Panama tribe. We
find two Indian women making history by leading Cabeza de Vaca
to the Rio Grande pueblos. Women aplenty move across the stage
of early America, play out their obscure roles, and disappear. But
they are all—except for Doña Marina—impalpable, spectral figures. We do not meet another woman of solid substance until we
come to

POCAHONTAS

She was "a little girl wrapped in a robe of deerskin, lined and
edged with pigeon down," with "a white heron's feather in her
black hair"; and her name (in polite terminology) meant "Little
Wanton." As everyone knows, she was the daughter of the powerful chief Powhatan, and she is supposed to have saved the life of
Captain John Smith from her father's executioner—although the
captain himself failed to mention the incident in the narrative
of his life in Virginia.

That she grew up to be a comely young lady, with a good deal
of sparkle and spirit, is proved by her portrait, painted in England
when she was twenty-one. It is possible, indeed, that John Rolfe,
a pious English gentleman, fell in love with her for herself—and
not, as the circumstances strongly suggest, as a step toward
promoting trade and peace between the Virginia colonist and his
bride's people. Pocahontas had already been married to an Indian
of no exalted rank (who was dead or whom she had divorced), and
Rolfe was a widower with one child. But, on her part at least, it
seems to have been truly an affair of the heart. What it was on
Rolfe's remains a question.

If he was in love with her, he chose strange ways of showing it.
There was no race prejudice in Virginia at the time, but Rolfe
seems to have thought it necessary to explain in torturous detail
why he wished to marry a savage. In the process, he became so
entangled in his own rhetoric that he came close to comparing his
bride with the loose women of the colony.

In a letter to Sir Thomas Dale, Deputy Governor of Virginia, Rolfe reviews "the grounds and principall agitation" that "should provoke me to be in love with one whose education hath been rude, her manners barbarous, her generation accursed." He explains it all with:

Now, if the vulgar sort, who square all men's actions by the base rule of their own filthiness, shall taxe or taunt me in this godly labor: let them know, it is not the hungry appetite, to gorge myself with incontency; sure (if I would, and were so sensually inclined) I might satisfy such desire, though not without a seared conscience, yet with Christians more pleasing to the eye, and less fearful in the offense unlawfully committed.

But he protests that he is really in love with her, and however doltish his manner of expressing it, his sentiment seems to ring true. "An unbelieving creature," he described her to Dale, "namely Pokahuntas, to whom my harte and best thots are, and have been a long time, so intangled and inthralled in so intricate a labrynth that I was ever wearied to unwind myself thereout." Then he mentions "her great appearance of love to me, her desire to be taught and instructed in the knowledge of God," and so on and on. Poor mixed-up young man! Poor Pocahontas!

They were married, at any rate, "for the good of the Plantation and the glory of God," although Powhatan was not on hand to give away the bride. Pocahontas gave birth to a son, Thomas, who became the ancestor of an astonishing number of Eminent Virginians. In 1614 she went with her husband and child to England, where she was shown off and made much of. And there she died.[11]

❧

Pocahontas' pathetic story bears little resemblance, of course, to the nursery-school tale of the Indian princess and doughty Captain John Smith, which is the only one that most Americans are familiar with. But we shall continue to tell and believe the legend, just as we continue to cling to our vague stereotypes of the Indian woman. It is difficult to rid the mind of old beliefs, smoothed and polished by endless repetition. Who, for example, would ever expect to meet an Indian girl like

TSHUSICK

We skip two hundred years. On a blustery night in the winter of 1826, a "wretched, ill-clad, way-worn female," wrapped in a ragged blanket and wearing an old pair of men's boots, knocked at the door of Colonel Thomas L. K. McKenney, Commissioner of Indian Affairs, in Washington, D.C.

This forlorn creature turned out to be a young Chippewa woman from distant Michilimackinac. Her name, she said, was Tshusick, and for reasons somewhat obscure, she had come all the way from Detroit on foot to see the President's Lady.

Moved by her story—and possibly by her pretty face—the Commissioner took her in and installed her in a comfortable apartment in a nearby hotel. Next morning, he brought her some scarlet and blue cloth, beads, and other finery, from which Tshusick ran up a fetching costume. A few days later, she was introduced to Washington society by Mrs. McKenney, and instantly became the darling of the capital.

Not since the 1821 visit of "the Eagle of Delight," the beautiful wife of an Oto chief, had an Indian woman created such a sensation on the Potomac. "So agreeable a savage," it was declared, "has seldom, if ever, adorned the fashionable circles of civilized life." For not only did Tshusick converse brightly in English, but her French was so good that a visiting Parisian suspected some sort of hoax. "No Indian," he maintained, "could speak the French language with such purity and elegance."

Captivated by her beauty and vivacity, the elite of the capital continued to "invite and caress" Tshusick; and it was not until she had left, loaded with presents, that the deplorable truth about her became known. Tshusick was not at all the helpless widow she had claimed to be, but the wife of "a short, squat Frenchman who officiated as a scullion" in the household of the Indian agent at Mackinac. Her Washington adventure, indeed, was only one of a long series of amiable deceptions that had taken her across Canada from Quebec to Montreal, and down the Mississippi to St. Louis.

So exit Tshusick, laughing no doubt. It would be nice to record that she left behind her the pieces of a shattered cliché—the then-prevalent two-faced cliché of the American Indian woman, bearing on one side the romantic image of "the noble savage," on the other "the dirty squaw" of the hostile frontier. Clichés, however, do not fracture that easily, and this one is still with us, more or less intact. But this much can be said for Tshusick. In her brief appearance she demonstrated, to Washington society at least, how infinitely varied, complex, and unpredictable a female Indian could be—just like a diplomat's wife.

After Tshusick's visit to Washington, even the capital dimly suspected what was well known to every white man in the Indian Country. James Hall thought it appropriate to express this feeling in words: "We are forcibly struck with the boldness, subtlety, and singleness of purpose, with which the individuals of that race plan and execute any design in which they are deeply interested." But what Mr. Hall was really talking about, of course, was not Indians, but women.[12]

Of America's few national heroines, one was an Indian—a woman whose courage and greatness of soul left their impress not only on history, but on the hearts of the brave and distinguished men with whom she shared one of our people's great adventures. She was "a good creature of a mild and gentle disposition and greatly attached to the whites," and her name was

SACAJAWEA

When Lewis and Clark started on their great exploration in 1804, one of their assignments was to inform the Indians in the vast Louisiana Purchase that they were now living on land owned by the United States. This was a delicate business, since the warlike tribes west of the Missouri had always thought of this land as belonging to nobody but themselves. Most of them, in fact, had never heard of the United States. How to break the good news to them was a bit of a problem.

First of all, it was necessary to find someone who could speak their languages. The Americans had interpreters who knew the tongues of the Missouri Indians, but no one who could talk with the Plains tribes. At a Mandan Village, near the site of Bismarck, North Dakota, they found what they wanted—the eighteen-year-old wife of a no-good French-Canadian trapper named Toussaint Charbonneau.

Lewis and Clark needed Charbonneau about as much as they needed a mule skinner on the Missouri, but the girl—whose name, Sacajawea, meant Bird Woman—satisfied their requirements exactly. She belonged to the tribe of Shoshoni Indians, whose territory stretched from Montana to Idaho, but had been captured as a child by the Hidatsa and raised among them by a captive Shoshoni woman. Sacajawea thus grew up speaking both the language of her own people, the Shoshoni, and that of her captors, the Hidatsa. It was really for this reason that Charbonneau was hired, although he was allowed to believe that Sacajawea, the only woman in the party, was permitted along as a special favor to him.[13]

Sacajawea first appears in the journal of the expedition in February, 1805, when the Americans were still in winter quarters on the Missouri. On the eleventh, Lewis noted, along with some details about sleds, horses, and the weather, that "about five o'clock one of the wives of Charbonneau was delivered of a boy." She didn't have an easy time of it with her first child, and Lewis sought to hasten the delivery by giving her, on the advice of a French-Canadian guide, "a small dose of the rattle of the rattle-snake."

Sacajawea's baby was six weeks old when she tucked him into his cradleboard, strapped him to her back, and started with the expedition up the Missouri. It was not until late in July that she could prove her special usefulness, but she is mentioned frequently in the journals, and in terms that reveal how quickly she won the hearts of the Virginia aristocrats who led the party, as well as the thirty-one rough men who followed them. There is a note of sincere relief, for example, in the entry for June 16: "Since leaving Maria's river the wife of Charbonneau, our interpreter, has been dangerously ill, but she now found great relief from the mineral water of the sulphur spring." Sacajawea, in fact, had been near death. She was not a strong woman; she was small and frail, and all her strength was in the stoutness of her heart.

Sacajawea, it seems necessary to add, was not a guide. Contrary to popular belief, she did not show the Americans the way through the mountains. Even when the party had reached her own country, she was not always sure of the trails and passes. The mountain men were pretty well able to find their own route to the Pacific; what Sacajawea offered was something even more important. In the midst of warlike, perhaps hostile, tribes—although not a single Indian had yet appeared—she alone would be able to communicate with the chiefs and win their friendship for the intruding whites. Her very presence was proof enough of the party's peaceful intentions; for Indian women with infants on their backs did not, as John C. Ewers has said, accompany war parties.

At the foot of the Rockies, with the Americans in critical need of horses to get them over the mountains before snowfall, Sacajawea dramatically proved her great value to the expedition. Some historians consider that she saved it. What happened on the early morning of August 17 was written down by Clark: "On setting out at seven o'clock, captain Clark with Charboneau [*sic*] and his wife walked on shore, but they had not gone more than a mile before captain Clark saw Sacajawea . . . begin to dance and show every mark of the most extravagant joy." Sacajawea had sighted an encampment of Shoshoni. "We soon drew near to the camp," Clark continues, "and just as we approached it a woman made her way through the crowd toward Sacajawea and recognizing each other, they embraced with the most tender affection."

The woman, it turned out, had been captured as a little girl with Sacajawea, but had also escaped from the Hidatsa. From her Sacajawea learned that all her family was dead except two brothers and a son of her sister's. So it was a sorrowful as well as a joyful homecoming; all through the ensuing council, Clark tells us, Sacajawea "attempted to interpret for us, but her new situation seemed to overpower her, and she was frequently interrupted by tears."

Thanks to Sacajawea, the expedition was now well supplied with pack-horses, and the journey to the Columbia and down to the Pacific was resumed. Sacajawea begged Clark to take her and her husband along. She wanted to see the ocean—and one of those monstrous fish she had heard so much about. How could she be refused? "So reasonable a request," Clark agreed, "could not be denied; they were therefore suffered to accompany captain Clark, who after an early breakfast set out with twelve men in two canoes."

So Sacajawea saw the ocean and her whale. She was the first woman of any race to cross the continent from the Missouri to the Pacific, and she became one of America's most famous heroines. Certainly, she deserves the innumerable statues that have been erected to her throughout the country, for she served well the exploding young nation of whose existence she could have been only dimly aware. But it is for her dauntless spirit really, her tender but courageous womanhood, that she is remembered and honored.

Sacajawea did not end her days in happiness. After the return of the expedition, Charbonneau, with Clark's assistance, bought a tract of land on the Missouri and tried to farm. But in 1811, Henry Brackenridge, on a trip up the Missouri with Manuel Lisa, wrote:

We have on board a Frenchman named Charbonet, with his wife, an Indian woman of the Snake nation, both of whom accompanied Lewis and Clark to the Pacific, and were of great service. The woman, a good creature, of a mild and gentle disposition, is greatly attached to the whites, whose manners and dress she tries to imitate, but she has been sickly, and longed to revisit her native country . . .

The following year, John Luttig, at Manuel Lisa's fort on the Missouri, made this entry in his journal: "This evening the wife of Charbonneau, a Snake squaw, died of a putrid fever. She was good and the best woman in the fort, aged about 25 years; she left a fine infant girl."

Captain Clark, whose admiration and affection for Sacajawea shines through so many of his journal entries, made good a promise to Charbonneau and adopted both of Sacajawea's children. Baptiste, the baby she had carried on her back to the Pacific, was educated at Clark's expense. In 1823 Prince Paul of Württemberg met him at a trading post at the mouth of the Kansas River and took him to Europe. Baptiste toured Europe for six years and learned to converse fluently in English, French, Italian, and Spanish. He was, we are told, equally at home in discussions of French philosophy, Spanish dances, or beaver-trapping. After returning to America, he spent some time as a trader, guide, justice of the peace, and miner in the California gold fields. But in the early fifties he returned to his mother's people in Wyoming, and died a Shoshoni.[14]

When we turn to the fort journals and diaries of fur traders for full-length, close-up portraits of individual women—such as Captain William Clark has given us of Sacajawea—we are for the most part disappointed. From the writings of such traders and travelers as Jonathan Carver, Peter Skene Ogden, Zenas Leonard, Ross Cox, Osborne Russell, David Thompson, and Alexander Mackenzie, one might surmise a complete lack of personal interest on their part in the native women.

This uncommunicativeness may have been due to a puritanical sense of propriety; or it may have been based on a simple conviction that a man's private life in the *pays sauvage* was nobody's business but his own. White men on the fur trade frontiers, at any rate, had precious little to say about their own personal relations with the native girls; and intimate portraits of their "country wives" rarely appear in the pages of their journals.[15]

There were a few exceptions, however, and one of the most interesting has come down to us from Alexander Henry the

Younger. Henry the Younger—so called to distinguish him from
his famous uncle Alexander Henry of New Jersey—served the
North West Company for fifteen years, packing and canoeing
his way between Montreal and the Pacific. He had a compulsion
to record his life in the wilds. Every night, long after his brigade
was asleep, a candle glowed in Henry's tent as the *bourgeois*
wrote—sometimes until long past midnight—in his journal. Everything went in, adding up to thousands of pages; and Henry's
intimate experiences with the girls along his route were not left
out.

Among the more diverting passages of his journal is an account
of how he happened to collect a wife. At his post in what is now
northern Minnesota, Henry celebrated the advent of the year 1801
in the riotous Northwest manner. But not even a spectacular hang-
over could keep him away from his journal, and on January 1
he recorded the beginning of the New Year and his alliance with

LIARD'S DAUGHTER

Henry does not give us her name, but he does tell us that she was
the daughter of a Saulteur chief, Liard, i.e., Elm Tree; and
without a word of description, he proceeds to give us a very good
idea of just what sort of lass she was. The journal for New Year's
Day reports briefly and dourly:

Liard's daughter took possession of my room, and the devil himself
could not have got her out.

Next day, Henry went on a not very successful buffalo hunt,
from which he returned to make the querulous journal entry:

I was vexed to find my room still occupied and no sign of her budging.

A month passed with Liard's Daughter still in possession of
Henry's quarters, but on January 30 the *bourgeois*, now in high
spirits, was able to write:

I got rid of my bedfellow, who returned to her father with good grace.
Fine weather.

Two days later, however, the journal reports with an almost audible sigh of resignation:

The lady returned. A terrible snow storm.

How long this sort of thing went on is not clear. But ten years later, according to the roster of Fort Vermilion, Liard's Daughter seems still to have been secure in her role of *femme du bourgeois*. For the occupants of Henry's house are listed as: "1 man, 1 woman, 3 children."

What was her ultimate fate? We do not know. The journal of Alexander Henry the Younger does not bother to tell us. But she did not, at any rate, vanish without leaving behind her a wisp of memory. For how can anyone who has browsed through the pages of Henry's almost unremembered journal ever forget the wilful, unpredictable, and no doubt pretty Liard's Daughter? [16]

The women themselves are forever silent. In all the literature of the tribes, no Indian woman has ever spoken for her sisters or for herself. Yet the record is not totally blank. At least one feminine voice has come to us from the past, unconsciously revealing the depths of one Indian woman's soul.

It is a letter from an Aztec mother to her daughter, "the product," William H. Prescott calls it, "of the twilight of civilization." It is far too long to transcribe in full, but even a few passages are enough to give us, in her own words, the tender, poignant portrait of

AN AZTEC MOTHER

My beloved daughter, very dear little dove . . . I desire to say to you that I love you much, that you are my dear daughter. Remember that nine months I bore you in my womb, that you were born and brought up in my arms. I placed you in your cradle and in my lap, and with my milk I nursed you. This I tell you, in order that you may know that I and your father are the source of your being; it is we who now instruct you. See that you receive our words and treasure them in your breast. Take

care that your garments are such as are decent and proper; and observe
that you do not adorn yourself with much finery, since this is the mark of
vanity and folly. . . . When you speak, do not hurry your words from
uneasiness, but speak deliberately and calmly. Do not raise your voice
high, nor speak very low, but in a moderate tone. Neither mince, when
you speak, nor when you salute, nor speak through your nose . . .

In walking, my daughter, see that you behave becomingly, neither going
in haste, nor too slowly. . . . And when you may be obliged to jump over
a pool, do it with decency. . . . When you are in the street, do not
carry your head much inclined or your body bent; nor as little go with
your head very much raised, since it is a mark of ill-breeding; walk erect,
and with your head slightly inclined. Walk through the street quietly
and with propriety . . .

Another thing that you must attend to, my daughter, is that when you
are in the street, you do not go looking hither and thither, turning your
head to look at this and that: walk neither looking at the skies nor at the
ground. . . . See, my daughter, that you give yourself no concern about
the words you may hear in going through the streets.

See, likewise, my daughter, that you never paint your face, or stain it or
your lips with colors . . . since this is the mark of vile and unchaste
women. Paints and colorings are things which bad women use—the
immodest, who have lost all shame, and even sense, who are like fools
and drunkards, and are called rameras [prostitutes] . . .

Only one thing remains to be said, and I have done. If God shall give you
life, if you continue for some years upon this earth, see that you guard
yourself carefully, that no stain come upon you; should you forfeit your
chastity, and afterwards be asked in marriage and should marry anyone,
you will never be fortunate, nor have true love—he will always remember
that you were not a virgin . . . you will never be at peace, for your
husband will always be suspicious of you. O, my dearly beloved daughter,
see that no more than one man approaches you, and observe what I shall
now tell you as a strict command. . . .

Beware, that in no time or place, you commit the treason called adultery.
See that you give no favor to another; since this, my dear and beloved
daughter, is to fall into a pit without bottom, from which there is no
escape. According to the custom of the world, if it shall be known, for

this crime they will kill you, they will throw you into the street, for an example to all the people, where your head will be crushed and dragged upon the ground. . . . From this will arise a stain and dishonor upon our ancestors . . . your name will be forgotten and abhorred . . .

My dear daughter, whom I tenderly love, see that you live in the world in peace, tranquility, and contentment, all the days you shall live. . . . See that you honor me and your father, and reflect glory on us by your good life. . . .[17]

❧

They are only shadows. We can never really know them as they were. We can never say with assurance how the women of the tribes thought, and felt, and lived their inner lives. And least of all can we know their secret attitudes toward the white men who cohabited with them, enslaved them, bought and sold them, paid for their favors, took them by force, and sometimes married them. But from the codices, official reports, journals, private letters, and rambling reminiscences we can discern, at least, the outward appearance of this varied and complex relationship. And, since the simple record of events has a way of revealing the truth behind the events, we can detect the profound psychological impact of the white man's intrusion upon the Indian woman's primitive world. Indeed, even so elemental a phenomenon as rape—especially when practiced on the scale of the Spaniards' ravishments, or with the ferocity of American frontiersmen in near-modern times—is suffused with deep racial, religious, and psychological significance. . . . As the chronicle of the frontiers makes dreadfully clear.

PART TWO

Casual and Not So Casual Contacts

RAPES AND RAIDS

"In the royal baths, they found five thousand women, of whom they did not fail to take advantage, despite the fact that the women were sad and weary . . ."

Thus the historian Francisco López de Gómara concludes his description of the great massacre of Cajamarca, in which Pizarro's troops, "hurling themselves like thunderbolts at the Indians' squadrons, their lances at rest," killed more than five thousand of the Inca's warriors and some fifteen hundred old men, women, and children. The raping was the usual aftermath of a Spanish triumph.

Many Indian women first knew the white man as a violent creature who killed their menfolk and seized by force all young and good-looking females. It was the familiar pattern of war, all war perhaps, but the Spaniards seem to have outdone most soldiery in the sickening excesses of military victory. So horrible was their depravity, indeed, that chroniclers like Las Casas rarely mention simple rape; it is only the particularly atrocious cases—such as that of one soldier who cut off a mother's arms so that he might violate her daughter without interference—that receive notice in their histories.[1]

Spanish captains, as might be expected, ignored the incidence of rape in their official reports. Indian women, of course, had no souls and were rated unchaste besides, so there was really nothing amiss in a little ravishment; yet there were always spoilsports like Fray Don Bartolomé de las Casas around, and it was better, perhaps, to keep the dispatches clean.

Even the Cajamarca rape was not exceptional. Prescott, summing up the brutish behavior of Pizarro's *caballeros* in the rest of the country, says: "The most unbounded scope was given to licentiousness. The sacred houses of the Virgins of the Sun were broken open, and the cavalier swelled his harem with troops of Indian girls . . ." [2]

Prescott's passing reference hardly suggests, however, the enormity of the crimes perpetrated by the Spanish troops. Throughout the Inca's realm, girls chosen for their beauty and cleverness were housed in convents of the Virgins of the Sun. These girls, called *oklla-kone* (the chosen girls), were given a four-year course in weaving, spinning, the preparation of *chicha*, and other feminine arts. They then took an oath of chastity; and she who broke it was buried alive, her lover strangled, and her native village "sowed with stones." The oath did not, however, extend to relations with the Inca; any Virgin summoned to the Inca's bed hurried to Cuzco from the ends of the realm.

All these establishments were fair game for Pizarro's men, but the violation of the great convent at the capital surpassed in infamy anything they could boast of in the provinces. The Cuzco house was inhabited only by Virgins of royal blood—some fifteen hundred of them, with perhaps another five hundred young girls, also virgins, to serve them; one authority says that the total number of noblewomen living in the Cuzco convent may have been six thousand. Of this great number, all who were not killed after being raped by Pizarro's men were carried off as slave-concubines.

In Mexico the Spanish soldiery may have been under tighter control. Hernando Cortés once burned four hundred captives alive, forcing their wives and children to watch, but he is said to have been lenient in his treatment of women. During the bloody assault on the capital of the Aztecs he even detailed special guards to restrain the lust of his Indian allies. For this, at any rate, we have the word of a Spanish historian. Elsewhere, as in the Caribbean, the usual pattern seems to have held. When rape was not perpetrated directly, there was always a systematic distribution of female captives for more leisurely attention when the fighting was over.[3]

Bernal Díaz del Castillo, one of Hernando Cortés' little band of conquerors, glumly describes just how the allocation of captive girls was made:

When the girls had all been brought together and branded, the royal fifth was set aside when we were not expecting it, and then they quickly took another fifth for Cortés. In addition to this, after we had left the girls in the house they took away the best-looking ones. There seemed to be not a pretty one left, and when the time came for dividing them, they gave the old ones and the ruins to us.[4]

Girls were simply demanded of the Indians as the right of superior beings. As they progressed northward, however, the Spaniards sometimes ran into trouble from Indians with other ideas of racial status. When De Soto, for instance, made his customary demand for women, the Chickasaw (in what is today the state of Mississippi) fell on his party at dawn, killing eleven men and fifty horses, thus wiping out in blood the insult to their wives and daughters.[5] Coronado, Pedro Casteñada says, inherited the hatred of the Pueblos because of black Esteban's "weakness for rich gifts, including handsome women." The Cibolans, he says, killed Esteban because he had violated the girls who had guided him to their city. And it is not unlikely that, a hundred years later, the memory of Spanish mistreatment of their women—which succeeding Conquistadores managed to keep smoldering—was one of the resentments that flared forth in the great Pueblo revolt of 1680.

When a favorite wife of the young Inca was debauched by the Castilian officers, Las Casas could not refrain from writing of his own countrymen: "And they arrived at the height of impudence and unheard of boldness that a private Captain scrupled not to force the wife of the most potent king among them." [6] Las Casas says, too, that another soldier went about getting as many women as possible with child, "so that he might sell them for the more money." [7] And Casteñada, much later, cannot suppress his distaste for one of Coronado's officers "coolly calling to an Indian to hold his horse" while he violated his wife. [8]

Native women, however, were not always completely helpless victims. Sometimes they defended themselves, not only successfully, but to the vast embarrassment of their attackers. Indeed, they seem to have developed a special technique of defense, illustrated by the case of the unfortunate Francisco de Reynoso de Vaca in Florida. Francisco's advances to an Indian woman having been repulsed, he tried force and was promptly set upon by several of her friends. They rushed him and, "like mastiffs on a bull, seized him by the arms, legs, and neck; and one of them laid hold of his penis." Too chagrined to yell for help, Francisco was rescued only when his foot broke through the floor and a companion downstairs came to his aid. [9] There is also on record the case of a garrulous young blade named Herrera who was "fatigued, subdued, and nearly killed by a female savage who grabbed his genitals." [10] Jonathan Carver, several centuries later, describes the same mode of self-defense being employed by the Indian women of the North. [11]

But for every woman of the Indies who successfully fought off a Spanish rapist, countless thousands were their easy victims. It was part of the Spanish temper to mix a little cruel amusement with atrocities, and the violation of women was conducted in the same spirit as turning the dogs loose on native prisoners. Small wonder the Indians soon learned to hide their wives and daughters on the approach of white strangers.

As the years passed and conquerors turned into colonists, the racial contempt that gave rise to the earlier outrages continued to operate. With colonization came the great missions of California and the Southwest—and a problem of new complexity. Each mission housed hundreds of Indian women and girls, married and unmarried; and morality and discipline demanded that Spanish troops and civilians leave them strictly alone. Yet a great deal of illicit intercourse took place (as was proved by the spread of syphilis), and in 1777 strong disciplinary measures had to be taken at San Gabriel, San Juan, and Capistrano. Again in 1785, the officers and men at the presidios were cited for the vicious license with which they comported themselves at the missions. It seems to have been the sport of soldiers to "go by night to the nearby villages for the purpose of raping the native women." As late as 1823, Father Durán reported the situation still unimproved at San Luis Obispo and San Diego.[12]

All through the Kingdom of New Mexico (according to the clergy), Indian girls were the prey of licentious officials (and, according to the officials, of the dissolute friars). Thus Fray Carlos Delgado, writing in the year 1750:

The most grievous thing for the heathen Indians is that the alcaldes [mayors], and even some of the governors, mix with their wives and daughters, often violating them. . . . The shameless way in which the officials conduct themselves in this particular is proved by an occasion when a certain governor was in conversation with some missionaries, and an Indian woman came into their presence to charge him with the rape of her daughter, and he, without changing countenance, ordered that she should be paid by merely giving her a buffalo skin that he had at hand.[13]

One of the worst rapists in high office appears to have been Governor Don Diego de Peñalosa, whose specialty was little girls. Numerous declarations were made against him by both clerics and laymen. On the other hand, we have the accusation brought against Fray Diego de Parraga of "the rape of many of his women parishioners."[14] Declarations and accusations—usually by officials against the clergy or vice versa—were epidemic in New Mexico, and it is difficult to assess where the greater guilt lay. The general impression is that the lubricity of the whites met with little restraint in the Kingdom of New Mexico, and the persons of Indian girls with little protection.

The French met the Indians chiefly as traders and colonists rather than as conquerors, and there is no evidence of their having committed wholesale rape on the order of the Spanish outrages.

How they behaved as individuals is, of course, a matter for con-
jecture; the trader and bush ranger did not ordinarily record his
misdeeds in the shadow of the forest.[15]

The English did not come as conquerors either, but they fought
frequent and bloody wars with the Indians; and, although the
records are not explicit about it, the probability is that rape, as
usual, followed the fighting. One does not have to read very closely
between the lines to deduce the uses to which Indian women
prisoners were put. Here, for example, is one Captain Stoughton,
leader of the Massachusetts Bay Colony force against the Pequot
Indians, writing to the governor about the division of his women
captives:

> By this pinnace you shall receive forty-eight or fifty women and children,
> unless they stay here to be helpful, etc., concerning which there is one I
> formerly mentioned that is the fairest and largest that I saw among them,
> to whom I have given a cloak to clothe her. It is my desire to have her for
> a servant, if it may stand with your good liking, else not. There is a little
> squaw that Stewart Calient desireth, to whom he hath given a coat.
> Lieutenant Davenport also desireth one, to wit, a small one that hath
> three strokes upon the stomach.[16]

The English, in fact—and the Dutch even more so—were quite
the equals of the Spanish when it came to massacres, the torture
of prisoners, and the slaughter of women and children; and there
is little reason to believe that in the course of their righteous
bloodlettings, good-looking girls fared any better at their hands
than the women of Cuzco or Cajamarca did with the Spanish.

As for what went on in the English settlements, it was probably
no better or worse than could be expected in any rude community
short of women. The libertines and no-accounts who peopled the
Virginia colonies were not, as we have noted, insensitive to the
Indian girls' charms, and sexual drives occasionally got out of
hand. In Massachusetts, there were always a few colonists who
found it difficult to live up to the rigid moral code of New England,
and sexual offenses were occasionally among those tried by the
Puritan courts. Thus Peter Hunt was arraigned in Plymouth

for "having attempted the chastity of an Indian woman." William Makepeace, Sr., of Taunton River, was whipped at the post for "lascivious attempts toward an Indian woman." And Christopher Blake, who got drunk and was guilty of "unseemly carriages in his drunkenness with an Indian woman," was sentenced to sit in the stocks for two hours at Yarmouth on training day.[17]

But New England justice was even-handed, dealing out punishment to both whites and Indians. When Nathaniel Soule was caught trifling with an Indian woman, he was whipped at the post—but so was his partner. Colonial laws against adultery applied alike to Indians and whites, as is illustrated by the case of Mary Mendame, cited in the Plymouth Colony records:

Mary the wyfe of Robte Mendame, of Duxborrow, for using dallyance divers times with Tinsin, an Indian, and after committing the act of uncleanness with him . . . the Bench doth therefore censure the said Mary to be whipt at a cart tayle through the townes street and to bear a badge upon her left sleeve . . . and if she shall be found without it abroad, then to be burned in the face with a hot iron; and the said Tinsin, the Indian, to be whipt with a halter about his neck at the post; because it arose through the allurement and inticement of the said Mary that he was drawn thereto.[18]

English laws against sexual offenses also applied to crimes committed by Indians against Indians; or, in the case of adultery, between Indians. The penalty for rape was hanging, and juries trying such cases were composed of six Indians and six whites. Sometimes the death sentence was suspended and the guilty prisoner sold into slavery. Thus Twenty Rod, an Indian, having been convicted of raping a Praying Indian girl under nine years of age, was sold for life "to some of the Carib Indians," with a warning that if he showed up in the colony again, he would be executed.[19]

As the fur traders and beaver hunters—French, English, and then American—worked their way across the continent, the pattern of the white man's relations with the Indian woman changed. The crimes committed against the Indians by the whites are mostly unknown, the red men having no means of recording their wrongs or communicating them to posterity. But it seems quite safe to say that sexual violence against their women seldom occurred. And for a very practical reason.

The white trader who ventured among the wild and warlike tribes lived only so long as it pleased his savage hosts to suffer his presence—usually as long as he had guns, liquor, and blankets to trade. Almost always, the white man was exposed to the danger of instant extermination at the whim of his customers. And an Indian's resentment of a white man's attentions to his wife could easily lead to murder.

"It is extremely dangerous for a trader to be suspected," John Long moralized, after a harrowing experience of his own with an irate Indian husband at Nipigon, "for when the husband is intoxicated, his jealousy rises into madness; and revenge, whether the party suspected be innocent or guilty, is continually to be expected." [20] In such a climate, it is not surprising that the white man learned, as the Nor'wester Duncan M'Gillivray expressed it, "to exercise a certain degree of self control."

In some of the large, strong posts, it was possible for the trader to disregard the Indians' feelings. At Fort George, for example, M'Gillivray administered such a beating to a Cree chief that the *bourgeois* was afterwards able to write in his journal: "They even deliver up their women to the unlawful embraces of the men to purchase their lost favor—a custom hitherto held in some dishonor among the tribe." [21] Here a show of strength seems to have resulted in a sort of permissive rape.

Where a state of open hostility existed, as between the Blackfoot and the American mountain men, an attack on an Indian village was sometimes followed by the time-honored rape of the women after battle. Thus George Ruxton on the slave raids of the mountain men:

It is a fact that the mountaineers never lose an opportunity of slaughtering these miserable Diggers, and attacking their villages, often for the purpose of capturing women, whom they carry off and not infrequently sell to other tribes or to each other.[22]

But most traders, working alone or in small parties, treated the women of the tribes with the utmost circumspection. Any other course, indeed, would have been madness.

When the frontier of the fur trade gave way to the frontier of the settlers, there was yet another change. The character of Indian-white contacts on these two levels was wholly different. The trader wanted to preserve the *status quo*, to maintain the Indians as hunters, dependent on his guns, liquor, and woolen blankets; the settler wanted to change things about—even if it meant the Indian's extermination. And along with this divergence of view-point came a profound modification of the white man's attitude toward the women of the tribes.

In the early days of the fur trade, it was considered no "come-down" for a white man to marry an Indian girl. But that was before prolonged association with "civilized" whites had reduced the Indian to a level that could only be described as degenerate. By the time the sodbusters had begun to scatter the buffalo herds with the noisy progress of their wagon trains, the Indian woman had become a creature to be despised. A product of the white man's own rum, greed, and lubricity, she was held in contempt even by the plains' lowest form of human life—the buffalo hunter.

Many an American settler in the West reverted to the abysmal inhumanity of the Puritan colonists, who had not hesitated to exterminate Indian women and children as "the very seeds of increase." Between the 1850's and 1870's roughly, the sane and decent people of the covered wagons seem to have been swept by a sort of mob-acquiescence to the unmentionable crimes of vicious emigrants and gold seekers. These were the decades when the Indian man became a "buck" and the Indian woman a "squaw," and finally were thought of as "game to be shot, or as vermin to be destroyed." These were the decades when responsible politicians, clergymen, and upright citizens called for the extermination of all Indians in Oregon Territory, and native women were regularly hunted with dogs, clubbed to death, or shot with rifles.[23]

This was the time, too, when a group of stalwart citizens met at the Challenge Saloon in Silver City, Idaho, and adopted the following resolution:

RESOLVED, That three men be appointed to select twenty-five men to go Indian hunting. . . . That for every buck scalp be paid one hundred dollars, and for every squaw scalp fifty dollars, and twenty-five dollars for everything in the shape of an Indian under ten years of age.[24]

As for the armed forces of the United States, the country was only vaguely aware of their conduct on the remote frontier. After Captain William J. Fetterman's command of seventy-five men had been wiped out by the Sioux near Fort Phil Kearny, the eastern press blamed the massacre on "the soldiers' abuse of squaws and women of the country"; but Margaret Carrington, wife of the post's commander, loyally protested that no Indian woman ever set foot in the fort.[25] And, in fact, it would be difficult to find any reference to such abuse, at Fort Kearny or elsewhere, in the archives of the War Department.

The record, however, clearly reflects the savagery with which the military, from generals down to mule skinners, treated the wives and daughters of Indian fighting men.[26] ITEM: the pursuit and gunning down of some two hundred women and children in a dry ravine by the Seventh Cavalry at Wounded Knee. ITEM: Colonel John Chivington's "heroic" slaughter of helpless Cheyenne women and children at Sand Creek, described by young Robert Bent, a half-breed son of the famous trader William Bent:

I saw five squaws under a bank. When the troops came up to them they ran out and showed their persons to let the soldiers know they were squaws and begged for mercy but the soldiers shot them all. . . . Some thirty or forty squaws, collected in a hole for protection . . . sent out a little girl about six years old with a white flag on a stick. She was shot and killed . . . I saw one squaw cut open with an unborn child lying by her side . . . I saw one squaw whose privates had been cut out . . . I saw a little girl who had been hid in the sand. Two soldiers drew their pistols and shot her, then pulled her out of the sand by the arm. I saw quite a number of infants in arms killed by their mothers . . .[27]

But of the atrocities of American settlers in Oregon and California, and of our Indian-fighting army on the Great Plains, it is enough to say that they were possibly the most revolting in the history of Anglo-Saxon frontiers in the New World. And, as we observe force as one aspect of the sexual relationship between white men and Indian women, we must take into account this climate of hatred, contempt, and unrestrained viciousness. For it is hardly necessary to expand on the common occurrence, in such an environment, of gang rapes, murder by violation, and the almost casual ravishment of individual Indian women.

But what, it may be asked, of the many tales of the Indians' mistreatment of white women?

They were not imagined.

Before the coming of the whites, rape seems to have been almost unknown among the Indians themselves. Most tribes had plenty of women and few restraints against premarital intercourse; there was little reason for taking by force what could easily be had for the asking. Still, as in any primitive society, there were girls who fiercely treasured their chastity, and men who found little favor in feminine eyes; and a comely virgin, or even a married woman, was not always safe from assault.

In later times, Colonel Dodge says, a Cheyenne or Arapaho woman tied her legs together on going to bed at night when her husband was away. "Custom has made this an almost perfect protection against the brutality of the men. Without it she would not be safe for an instant, and even with it, an unmarried girl is not safe if found alone, away from the immediate protection of her lodge." Under the tribal governments, Colonel Dodge adds:

A man who outraged a girl was obliged to pay for and take her to wife, under penalty of death. . . . But the diminution of the power of the chiefs, and the failure of the United States Government to furnish any adequate substitute, work greatly to the injury and demoralization of the women. . . . Now there is no punishment. The only protection any woman has, is that derived from the custom of "roping" herself, and the fear lest the father or husband might execute his right of revenge on the perpetrator of an outrage on a woman so "roped." [28]

The Pottawatomie, Keating tells us, regarded rape in their own peculiar light. "Rape is considered as [being] visited by the anger of the Great Spirit, and is never practiced but on a female in a state of intoxication." [29] But there is no evidence that in other Indian communities such niceties were generally observed.

As for the Indians' treatment of white women captives, there is a division of opinion about the conduct of early eastern tribes, but none whatever when it comes to the fierce Plains Indians. The Iroquois and Huron may or may not have raped white women prisoners, but there is no doubt that the Sioux and Apache did, and in the most horrible of ways.

Mary Jemison, who was captured by the Shawnee in 1775 and lived among them for nearly fifty years, vouches for the correct conduct of the eastern Indians of her time. "I have been in the midst of these roaring lions and savage bears that feared neither God, nor man, nor the devil," she wrote (perhaps ironically) in later life, "by day and by night, alone and in company, sleeping all sorts together, and not one of them ever offered the least abuse or unchastity to me in word or action." [30]

In commenting on Mary's experiences in the twenty-second edition of *A Narrative of the Life of Mary Jemison* (stories of Indian captivity were very popular), Dr. James Everett Seaver concludes: "From all history and tradition, it would appear that neither seduction, prostitution, nor rape was known in the calendar of crimes of this rude and savage race, until the females were contaminated by the embrace of civilized man." The Indians often tomahawked, scalped, tortured, and otherwise barbarously mistreated female prisoners, Dr. Seaver points out, but rape—never.

This conclusion, improbable as it may seem, was supported by other writers—especially romantic novelists—of the eighteenth century. General James Clinton, in 1779, wrote: "Bad as the savages are, they never violate the chastity of any woman prisoner." And while Joseph Doddridge, in his *Notes on the Settlement and Indian Wars*, lists in lurid detail the tortures and barbarities suffered by captives of the Indians, he does not include rape among them.[31] Some of the early writers speculated on the reason for this odd forbearance and suggested that perhaps some sort of sex taboo was involved.

Not all of the early evidence, however, shows the Indian captor in so favorable a light. During King Philip's War, in which some eight hundred English were killed, the contemporary report was: "If they were women, they first forced them to satisfy their filthy lusts and then murdered them." During the French and Indian War, despite specific orders issued to the French field commanders to restrain their Indians, captured women suffered the ultimate indignity, as well as death. A Quebec priest, Father Claude Godfoy, wrote sorrowfully to his brother: "The Indians do not make any prisoners; they kill all they meet, men, women, and children. Every day they have some for their kettles, and after having abused the women and maidens, they slaughter and burn them." [32]

In any case, by the time the whites came into contact with the Sioux, Blackfoot, Apache, and other savage nations of the West, rape was the rule. Colonel Dodge, with his usual soldierly directness, says:

I believe I am perfectly safe in the assertion that there is not a single wild tribe of Indians in all the wide territory of the United States which does not regard the person of a female captive as the inherent right of the captor; and I venture to assert further that, with the single exception of the lady captured by the Nez Perces, under Joseph, in Yellowstone Park, no woman has, in the last thirty years, been taken by any wild Indians who did not, as soon as practicable, become a victim of the brutality of every one of the party of her captors.

After being raped by the whole war party for a few days, and tortured by the women, Dodge continues, the captive became the exclusive property of the Indian who captured her. In rare cases she was taken as a wife by her captor, but usually she was held by him as a slave "for the vilest purposes, being sold by her owner to anyone who wants her."[33]

Almost all the testimony is damning. Kit Carson finds two Mexican women, "their bodies very much mutilated and staked to the ground," victims of gang rape. After a Cheyenne attack on two emigrant wagon trains, troops from Fort Kearny came upon a woman "raped to death in relays," to avenge the loss of six warriors in a brush with the troops. Then there were the innumerable tales of horror brought back by white women from the Indian camps: the Oatman girls, one of whom died in captivity, the other living to become insane in later years; the Anderson girls, raped many times by the Sioux during the uprising of 1862 in Minnesota, until one of them finally died; the German girls, traded from brave to brave by the Cheyenne; and Mrs. White, who died shortly after her rescue, and whose death, Kit Carson said, "should never be regretted by her friends." So profound were the indignities suffered by female captives that many a ghost of what had once been a white woman was too ashamed to return home, and stubbornly refused to be ransomed.[34]

Except that Chief Joseph did not take white women as prisoners or suffer his Nez Perce braves to harm them, there is not much that can be said in defense of the Plains Indians' treatment of female captives. Perhaps the only reason they did not kill and rape women in such large numbers as the whites is that they did not have the opportunity. Otherwise, they were in every respect quite as cruel, brutal, and barbarous as their civilized white brothers.

The Indian woman who did not experience her first contact with white men in the form of simple rape, in the bush or after battle, quite possibly fell victim to what might be termed organized rape in the form of enslavement.

The abduction of women as concubines was perhaps the oldest form of human bondage, and it lasted down to quite recent times.[35] When the Spaniards began collecting women in the New World, it was largely with sleeping partners in mind. Later on, they hunted for slaves to work the mines and plantations, but at first it was for mistresses that they sent their gallant little bands into the interior. Many of their expeditions of discovery were, in fact, nothing more than slave raids, with the acquirement of Indian girls a primary objective.

Raiding Indian towns for women began almost immediately after the landing of Europeans on the shores of the New World and soon expanded into a full-fledged trade in Indian slaves. Columbus was a slave trader of prominence. In 1495 he sent back to Spain four ships whose lading was chiefly slaves. The hunting of slaves for home use was conducted so extensively in the Caribbean islands and on the mainland shore that by 1500 the supply of Indians was exhausted and Negroes began to be imported.[36]

The Indian woman captured by a Spanish Conquistador, either after battle or in a raid on her village, must expect to be branded with the King's iron. Then, after His Majesty had received his royal fifth, she and perhaps several hundred other women would be distributed among the soldiers. If she lacked something in youth and good looks, she might be put to work grinding corn and baking tortillas, or she might find herself condemned to killing labor in Cuba or Puerto Rico. But if she was young and handsome, she would almost certainly become the mistress—with perhaps several other girls—of a Conquistador. Technically, this may not have been rape, but it must have been difficult for a well-born Indian girl to see the difference.[37]

In 1538, Pope Paul III forbade all Indian enslavement; and a few years later, on the recommendation of the great defender of the Indians Fray Bartolomé de las Casas, Charles V promulgated the famous *Leyes Nueves* [New Laws], which recognized that the aborigines were, after all, really human beings, and as such entitled to the protection of the Crown. They were therefore declared vassals of His Majesty, with all the rights and duties of other vassals; and this, on paper at least, did away with Indian slavery.[38]

It cannot be said that the Crown was indifferent to the welfare of the Indians. Well-meaning *cédulas* were frequently issued from

Madrid for the protection and advancement of the natives. The
Leyes Nueves abolishing slavery were not, however, taken very seriously in the remote provinces. No sooner had Don Juan de Oñate
taken over as first Governor of New Mexico than he launched
a punitive attack on the sky city of Acoma. After scaling the
rock on which this great pueblo was perched, Oñate's men massacred half the inhabitants, cut one foot off the male survivors, and
marched all the women and children off to Santo Domingo as
slaves. From this bloody beginning, New Mexico swiftly developed
a slave economy. Navajo, Ute, and Apache villages were regularly
raided for slaves, and the Indians were encouraged to raid each
other and sell their captives to the Spaniards. By the middle 1560's
Indian slaves were so numerous that an Apache woman could be
purchased for 26 pesos, and Governor Peñalosa boasted that he
had given away a hundred girls as gifts.[39]

A vivid picture of the slave trade in early New Mexico, with
its lurid sexual overtones, has been left us in a report that the
Reverend Father Provincial, Fray Pedro Serrano, sent to the
Viceroy in 1761. After describing the great concourse of Comanche
and other Indians at Taos (as many as two hundred tents) to
trade with the Spaniards, the good Fray Pedro brings himself to
write:

Among many other infamies there is one of such a nature that if I did not
so desire a remedy I would remain silent, since it is so obscene and unfit
for chaste ears. It is the truth that when these barbarians bring a certain
number of Indian women to sell, among them many young maidens and
girls, before delivering them to the Christians who buy them, if they are
ten years old or over, they deflower and corrupt them in the sight of the
innumerable assemblies of barbarians and Catholics (neither more nor
less, as I say), without considering anything but their unbridled lust and
brutal shamelessness, and saying to those who buy them, with heathen
impudence: "Now you can take her—now she is good." [40]

Surplus slaves were disposed of at the great Chihuahua Fair,
with captive Navajo, Comanche, and Apache girls a distinctive
feature of the trading caravans that every spring set out from
Santa Fe. So oblivious were the New Mexicans of the New Laws

prohibiting slavery that when captives were auctioned off in Durango, the King's fifth was meticulously set aside before the sale began. In 1672, indeed, the Queen Mother, Maria Ana, found it necessary to sign her *Yo la Reyna* to a special communication tartly reminding the provincial governors that a law against slavery existed in New Spain and was still in force.[41]

That many Indian girls became mistresses of officials and the more important clergy is attested to by the *bandos* prohibiting concubinage, and by the many cases involving kept women that are scattered through the Spanish Archives.[42] However various the character of slavery, it has always retained an element of its oldest aspect, the sexual possession of women.

❦

The slave trade on the frontiers was facilitated by the fact that the Indians themselves had always been large slaveholders.[43]

"Before there were white women and children to scalp and mutilate," "Uncle Dick" Wootton remarked bitterly, "the Indian scalped, mutilated, and tortured women and children of their enemies of their own race. They made slaves of each other when there were no palefaces to be captured and sold for ransom." [44]

The Inca and Aztec, of course, had hordes of slaves, including a great many kept as mistresses and concubines. But the comparatively wild North American tribes were also in the slave business on a large scale. At first they acquired slaves as prisoners of war. From this it was but a step to the trade and barter of war captives. And finally, slaves even became a sort of currency, like furs or wampum, in intertribal trade.[45]

The Indians obtained their slaves, just as the Spaniards did, by raiding. Excursions against neighboring tribes for women and horses were a favorite sport of the Plains Indians. The Blackfoot raided the Assiniboin, the Assiniboin the Cree, and so it went. In these forays, Daniel Harmon said, "they make terrible havoc among the men; but they labor to take as many of their women and children alive as they possibly can, in order to carry them home as slaves." [46]

The Indians, particularly the Navajo, also raided the Spanish settlements for livestock, horses, and female slaves. During the Pueblo Revolt of 1680, one Fray Escalante reported that the Indians took the lives of eighteen friars and three hundred and eight Spaniards, but Popé, the leader of the revolt, reserved the most beautiful women for himself. Ogden says that in the Northwest, the Indians even raided white trapping parties and carried off women.[47]

Eastern tribes, such as the Huron and Ottawa, kept slaves as servants to perform household duties, care for the crops, and assist in hunting and fishing, but also to serve as mistresses to their owners. The Iroquois, despite statements to the contrary, were large slaveholders. One Iroquois woman was reported to have had twenty personal slaves. The Iroquois were, in addition, important middlemen in the slave traffic between East and West, sometimes bringing back as many as three or four hundred captives at a time from the Ohio country. In the very early days, the Pawnee frequently sold Apache women and children to the French on the Missouri and Platte; and from this trade perhaps, the French continued to call all Indian slaves *Panis* (i.e., Pawnee). It was a *Panis* woman who rescued Alexander Henry the Elder at the Michilimackinac massacre.[48]

The extent of the slave trade between the Indian tribes of North America is suggested by the fact that the Illinois had slaves brought from the East Coast and Florida; Eskimo slaves were to be found among the Great Lakes tribes; and the Jesuit Father Gulon reported that in Chinese Tartary he had seen a slave whom he recognized as a Huron woman he had met in Canada. The Comanche raided deep into Mexico for women.

Slavery, indeed, was universal among the Indian nations, but it was on the Pacific Coast that the traffic was most highly developed and the slaveholdings largest. It has been estimated that one-third of the entire Indian population between British Columbia and Alaska were slaves of the lowest condition. "Upon occasion," Clark Wissler says, "to show how wealthy he was, the Tlingit owner of slaves would club some of them to death in

public; in other words, he was rich enough to destroy property." [49]
Yet, contrary to usage in most slave societies, sexual relations
with female slaves were not tolerated by some of the West Coast
tribes, who held that intercourse with a slave woman disgraced
a free man.

The French in America developed a slave trade of their own
through their numerous *coureurs de bois*. These bush rangers,
scattered over the whole of Canada and much of what is now the
United States, lived on close terms with the natives, and were well
situated to obtain Indian slaves by trade or barter—often, incidentally, saving the Indians' lives in the process. Some they sold
to the military posts in the Interior, where they became servants
and mistresses of the officers and frontiersmen; and some they
brought back to the eastern settlements for domestic service.[50]
The Mackinac baptism records, for example, contain frequent
references to Indian slaves: "Marie, born a slave of Sieur Chevalier," "Marianne, about 20 years old, now the lawful wife of
Jean Baptiste, formerly a slave." [51] The *coureurs de bois* supply
was augmented by captives taken by troops in the wars the
French were incessantly fighting on their Indian frontiers.

Indian slavery in French America was sanctioned by the Royal
Council in 1745, and before that had been declared legal in Canada
by a royal edict of 1709; but it existed, particularly in the Illinois
country, long before it was authorized by law. Even the French
missionaries felt no scruples about owning a slave or two, usually
obtained as gifts and accepted as an end to saving their heathen
souls. On the whole, French slavery seems to have lacked the
harsh features of the Spanish institution. It was usually mild in
nature, and not infrequently led to some form of marriage; but
instances of cruelty were not wanting.[52]

Sex did not figure in Indian slavery among the French to the
extent that it did with the Spaniards. The supply of white women
was more adequate in New France, and in the remote wilderness
the French trader or trapper did not hesitate to take an Indian

woman as wife rather than slave. In the province of Louisiana, most of the slaves were Negro.[53]

In Louisiana, however, there appears to have been one pronounced, and rather disreputable, aspect of Indian slavery. Always short of white women, despite shipments of "casket girls" from France, the French in New Orleans and satellite settlements acquired large numbers of female Indian slaves for companionship, with results that became disturbing to the government. Life among both rich and poor, it was declared, became "quite licentious, and one of the means of fostering this life was the use of Indian women, slave and free." In 1709, the Governor of Louisiana sent an urgent plea for more girls to be sent from France as wives, "to prevent these disorders and debaucheries." [54]

The English colonists were by no means inactive in the Indian slave trade. As early as 1680, English slavers and traders organized and armed three hundred Creek, Cherokee, and Yuchi to raid Spanish missions on the Georgia coast. They burned and sacked towns and churches, and carried their prisoners back to South Carolina for enslavement. This activity reached its culmination in 1704, when Colonel Moore of Carolina, with fifty English volunteers and a thousand Creek warriors, descended on the Florida mission villages and bagged 3,600 captives, who were sold as slaves for the Carolina rice plantations and in the northern colonies.[55]

These northern colonies, however, had their own means of obtaining Indian slaves—principally war. In both the Pequot and King Philip's wars many slaves were taken; in the latter, so many that hundreds were shipped abroad. The English colonists also had a particularly despicable trick of accepting Indian boys and girls for adoption and education in European ways, then selling the children as slaves.

But Indian slavery, except in the very early days, was not of great importance in the English colonies. It never existed at all in Virginia, and by the early 1700's most of the northern colonies

had passed laws against it. Massachusetts decided that Indian
slaves were too "malicious, surly, and ungovernable" to work with;
and the other colonies gave their own reasons for discontinuing the
trade. In general, anti-slavery legislation was motivated more by
expediency than by ethics or humanitarianism. For one thing,
with the French poised on your northern flank, it was good to have
the Indians on your side. Even the Quakers (who abhorred war
but were not adverse to buying and selling a few war captives)
decided it was best not to give the Indians "occasion of discontent." [56]

There appears to have been little sexual involvement of the
English colonists with their female Indian slaves. Neither the
Cavaliers nor the Puritans were insensitive to the charms of many
of the Indian girls, as we have seen; and the doughty New England
soldiers took care to set aside a few choice females for their own
use before shipping the rest into slavery. But the capture and
purchase of Indian mistresses in the open Spanish and French
manner was not compatible with the English temperament apparently. Slaves were bought for work in the home and fields,
not as bed partners.

It is not until we come upon the British fur traders and our
own mountain men in the West and Southwest that we again
find the buying and selling of slave girls an important factor in
the relationships of white men and Indian women.

John Askin was a respected businessman responsible for forward-
ing supplies and liquor from Michilimackinac, the great depot
of the North West Company, to trading posts in the Interior.
In 1778 he wrote Monsieur Beausoleille at Grand Portage that
he was sending off a bark with goods, and informed him that he
would have an officer and several soldiers to pass the summer with
him at the Portage. What makes Askin's letter interesting is a
paragraph added as a sort of postscript:

I need two pretty Slave girls from 9 to 16 years old. Have the goodness to
ask the Gentlemen [at the Portage] to procure two for me.[57]

It isn't often that the fur trade's traffic in women—along with pelts, buffalo robes, and beat meat—is so explicitly mentioned in the traders' writings. But there are plenty of instances of white men buying Indian women, usually war captives, from friendly tribesmen, and there is not much to separate the condition of these women from enslavement. When, in 1798, David Thompson started home from his Mandan trip, his baggage consisted of "furs of wolves and foxes, with meal and corn; and two Sieux women which the Mandanes had taken prisoners and sold to the men, who, when they arrived at the trading house, would sell them to some other Canadians." [58] This was apparently a pattern of trade in Indian women that did not in the least disturb the conscience of even the saintly Thompson.

It is a pattern discernible in the early operations of the Hudson's Bay Company, when the traffic in women was important enough to attract Indians from the distant western plains. Female captives taken in slave raids by the Blackfoot were sold to the Cree or Assiniboin, who in turn disposed of them on the Bay. During the long journey from the Saskatchewan River to York Fort, the women were passed around the camp at night. On arrival at York they were traded, along with beaver pelts and buffalo robes, to the factors of "the Honourable Company." Those for whom there was no sale were said to have been destroyed.[59]

Thus Edwin Thompson Denig's statement that "no system of concubinage was tolerated" at Hudson's Bay Company posts seems hardly to square with the evidence. The factors and chief factors of the Concern, at any rate, appear to have paid little heed to the restrictions imposed on their sexual conduct by London. The notorious Governor Moses Norton maintained a rowdy harem of native girls—"five of the finest he could select," according to Samuel Hearne—at the same time lecturing his men piously on the impropriety, not to say dangers, of Englishmen having intercourse with the daughters of the country. Hearne himself, incidentally, seems to have not lacked an entourage of dusky maidens, although he sometimes grumbled about their quality and the price he was forced to pay for them.[60]

But if it is hard to deduce from the closemouthed journals and reports of the Hudson's Bay people just what went on in their remote posts, the *bourgeois* of the North West Company left little in doubt. There is no mistaking the fact that they carried on a lively, and no doubt profitable, trade in Indian girls.

Thus we have the autocratic Nor'wester Archibald Norman McLeod, at Fort Alexandria on the Upper Assiniboin, noting in his journal this routine transaction: "I gave the Chef de Canard's widow to the amount of 28 plus, & took the Slave Woman, whom next fall I shall sell for a good price to one of the men." And at Rainy Lake, Hugh Faries writes: "The Devil [an Indian hunter] set off. I gave him ½ keg of rum, & a few goods, with 45 plus that he owed me for his daughter. Jourdain arrived from the Long Sault with 200 plus. on his arrival I gave him the Devil's daughter for 500 lb. Grand Portage Currency." [61]

But it was up in the Department of Athabasca—the most remote, the loneliest, and yet the richest of all in the North West Company preserves—that the traffic in girls was carried on most openly, most cynically, and with utter disregard for the Indians' feelings. At Fort Chipewyan, for instance, the *bourgeois* of that vast department, James McKenzie, seizes the wife of one of his *engagés* for debt. He plans to sell her to the highest bidder, and he explains his scheme with gleeful satisfaction in his fort journal:

Two advantages may be reaped from this affair; the first is that it will assist to discharge the debts of a man unable to do it by any other means . . . the second is that it may be the means of thickling [*sic*] some lecherous miser to part with some of his hoard. I therefore kept the woman to be disposed of in the season when the Peace River bucks look out for women in the month of May . . .[62]

When McKenzie's Indians finally rebelled against his seizing and selling their women, he told them "we would do as we thought proper, for it was not their business to prescribe rules for us." This was mild; he usually threatened to chop off their heads.

While such traffic may not have been official Company policy, there is no evidence that it was ever officially proscribed. The ferocious James McKenzie, at any rate, was by no means alone among the Nor'westers in seizing women in payment of debts— i.e., goods advanced to Indian trappers against their anticipated catch of furs. Philip Turnor, a Hudson's Bay Company factor, and hence naturally antagonistic, probably spoke at least half the truth when he said that the Canadians, as the Nor'westers were called on the Bay, were heartily disliked by the Indians because of this practice. For each girl, Turnor informs us, the Nor'westers received "from five hundred to two thousand livres, and if the father or husband of any of them resist, the only satisfaction they get is a beating." [63]

As the Nor'westers pushed their forts and flying posts up the rivers toward the Rockies, they, like the Spaniards before them, found a source of female slaves in the wild Plains Indians. The Cree, Assiniboin, and other nearby tribes always had a good supply of captives traded from the more remote Crow, Mandan, Blackfoot, Apache, and even Navajo. And the Nor'westers were ready buyers. Thus, in his Red River journal, that highly respected *bourgeois* John ("the Priest") Macdonell notes casually: "Tranquille bought a slave women—i.e., taken in war—for two horses and 20 pluez of goods." [64] And Alexander Henry the Younger wryly reports the misfire of another transaction: "The Crows had a handsome slave girl, about 12 years of age, who was offered to us for a gun, 100 balls, and enough power to fire them; but those rascally Big Bellies would not allow us to purchase her, saying they wanted her for themselves." [65]

American mountain men, arriving in the Southwest about 1820, soon discovered that what the Spanish traders wanted most was horses and girls. The trade in these commodities centered around the New Mexican town of Taos, and it drew Indian trappers and free traders from all over the Southwest to dispose of their furs, hides, buckskins—and slaves.[66]

The girls were collected by the Indians in raids such as one described by James P. Beckwourth, who himself became a Crow chief and participated in that tribe's slave hunting. After scouting a large band of Blackfoot for two weeks, Beckwourth relates, he and his Crow warriors were apprised of a crowd of women approaching.

We were then in a forest of plum trees, bearing large red plums, which were fully ripe and very delicious. Feeling satisfied that the women were coming to gather fruit, we secreted ourselves, intending at a given signal to surround them while they were thus busily employed. Accordingly, we waited until they all set themselves about their task, they keeping up an incessant jabbor among themselves like so many blackbirds or bob-o-links, and having no suspicion that the Crows would soon come in for their share. At a sound from the whistle, they were entirely surrounded and their merry chatter was hushed in an instant. We marched them to an open piece of ground, made them form a line, and proceeded to make a selection. The aged and ill-favored, and the numerous matrons we withdrew from the body, telling them to return to the village and depart without clamor. They went away in sullenness, with their eyes flashing fire. The remainder, to the number of fifty-nine, very attractive looking young women, we carried along with us . . .[67]

Sometimes, to be sure, a band of slave hunters had to risk an attack on an Indian encampment or, even more unpleasant, meet the enemy in open battle, in order to gather a supply of girls for the Taos market. Beckwourth, again, recounts a sharp engagement between the Crow and Blackfoot in which the Crow came off best with 175 scalps, 150 women and children, besides "an abundance of weapons, baggage, and horses"—and, of course, not a single male prisoner.

On occasion, the Indians also raided the encampments of white traders, carried off their Indian wives, then resold them to other mountain men. Bending Reed, wife of the trapper La Bonté, was one of those thus captured by the Blackfoot and afterwards offered for sale at a trading post.[68]

In California and the Southwest, slave hunters plundered the missions for women. These great establishments housed thousands of nubile Indian girls, and the red slavers were not slow to make the most of such a rich and easy source of supply. Sometimes, however, the male mission Indians turned the tables, when they accompanied soldiers on raids into the Indian Country, and "went after the women."

The procurement of slaves for the Taos and Santa Fe markets thus evolved into a complicated business of Indians snatching girls from one another, Indians raiding white missions and settlements, and whites kidnaping women from Indian encampments. To add to the complexity of the picture, white traders like Beckwourth sometimes joined the Indians in collecting girl captives and selling them to the whites. Antoine Robidoux, a Frenchman with Mexican citizenship, carried on a side-line trade in slaves at Fort Wintey, sometimes called "Robidoux's Rendezvous." A visiting clergyman, the Reverend Joseph E. Williams, wrote aghast: "Mr. Robidoux has collected several of the Indian squaws and young Indians to take to New Mexico, and kept some of them for his own use. The Spaniards would buy them for wives." [69] To what extent this sort of slave trading "on the side" went on at established trading posts in the Southwest is a matter for speculation. How often was some handsome young Indian girl, supposedly ransomed from her Indian captors, more accurately bought for resale to a white trader or the Spaniards?

Between 1800 and 1850 the Spaniards carried on a flourishing slave trade of distinctive character north of Santa Fe. From their headquarters on the Chama, they went every spring into Ute and Navajo country. Here they traded whiskey, guns, blankets, and other trade goods for horses. They then drove the horses still farther north and traded them for Paiute slaves. Or, as early travelers observed, they simply captured the Paiute, weakened by a winter of near-starvation, fattened them up, and brought them down to Taos for auction. [70]

Some of these Indian slaves were bought by the New Mexicans for ranch hands and house servants; and some were purchased by traders and trappers who obviously had no need for either. The buyers' chief motivation can perhaps be gathered from the relative prices paid for male and female slaves. In 1850, the heyday of the mountain men, the first Indian agent in New Mexico reported:

"The value of captives depends on age, sex, beauty, and usefulness. Good females, not having passed the 'seer [*sic*] and yellow leaf,' are valued from fifty to a hundred and fifty dollars each. Males, as they may be useful, one half less, never more." [71]

Thus, in the mid-nineteenth century, slavery as a frontier institution heavily charged with sexual implications had not yet vanished. Enslavement and rape—which to countless native women must have amounted to the same thing—were not a major aspect of Indian-white contacts. But they did represent an attitude that left its grim impress on the relationships of the white man and the Indian woman. And that attitude continued operative down to almost modern times.

"LET YOUR WOMEN BE
KIND TO THEM"

On his first night in a Mandan village, Alexander Henry the Younger reported, with an air of boredom: "This evening we were plagued for some time by young women who came in and wanted to lie with us; but as we did not care to accept their kind offers, they retired very much displeased and muttering something we could not understand." [1]

Even seasoned traders like Henry could not understand many of the Indians' ways. And few tried. Few were as charitable as Father Charlevoix when he explained: "They [the Indians] have some usages in which no sort of regard is paid to modesty; but it appears that in this superstition has a much greater share than depravation of the heart." [2]

Yet, it is difficult to censure a fur trader for simply reporting what he saw and heard, without trying to draw any profound cultural conclusions. What, for example, could Peter Pond have read into his experience with the Puan women—except that liquor is not conducive to a high level of moral conduct?

Pond was one of the first American traders in the Northwest, that vast beaver country lying beyond Lake Superior. In 1773 he arrived at Lake Winnebago, in present-day Wisconsin, to find an Indian "wake" in progress. As the rum level in their "cag" sank, Pond recalled years later, the mourners grew more and more disconsolate. Then their grief took an odd turn, which Pond reports in straightforward fur trader style:

Rite wen they ware more than half drunk, the men began to approach the females and chat frelay and apearantly friendly. At length thay began to lean on each other, kis, and apeared varey amaras. I could clearly observe this bisiness was first pusht on by the women who made thare visit to the dead a verey pleasing one in thare way. One of them was quit drunk as I was by self seating on the ground observing thare saremones, cam to me and askt me to take a share in her bounty. But I thought it was time to quit and went about half a mile up the river to my canoes . . .[3]

The only untypical note in this little tale is Pond's flight from the Puan women. It was hardly regulation behavior. Usually, when a fur brigade arrived at an Indian encampment, little time was lost in getting acquainted with the female population. "Our young Canadians and Creoles who come here," Jean-Baptiste Trudeau wrote more characteristically from a Missouri Indian village, "are seen everywhere running at full speed like escaped horses into Venus' country." [4]

During much of their time, the Canadian trapper and American mountain man had little to think about but sex. "All their talk," Daniel Harmon said of the *voyageurs*, "is of dogs, horses, canoes, and women." Their boasts were of sexual prowess: *"Je suis un homme!* I had twelve wives in the country . . ."* Even their lovely paddle songs were sometimes too bawdy for print. They were men without women in a lonely land.

Nor did the American mountain man fare much better. Although he sometimes traveled with a trapping party, he was usually a loner who followed the creeks and valleys into country no white man before him may have ever seen. He wintered alone, worked his trap lines by himself, and sat at night before a solitary fire. What did he have to dream of except the coming of spring, the next rendezvous, whiskey by the keg—and women?

So, when at last he came to an Indian encampment, a trading post, or a rendezvous, nothing could have suited him better than the "obligingness" of the Indian women—and, from all accounts, not a few were always available and eager. "They beguile with gentle looks the hearts of passing strangers," one trader wrote romantically. They also teased and taunted new arrivals with jibes

and jests "of the most obscene nature." This raillery was encouraged and kept going by the older women, who delighted in observing its effect on the youthful members of a trading party. It
seems to have been the only preliminary—except, perhaps, for a
little gift-giving—to more intimate relations.[5]

"Of course," the Missouri trader Pierre-Antoine Tabeau con-
ceded, "there are a few prudes who greatly wish to pass for more
cautious ones, but who surrender themselves with discretion and
secrecy." Most of the girls, he added, were "hostile to ceremony"
and sought to avoid "the embarrassment of an intrigue."

In sex, as in most other things, the mountain man's wants were
simple; and it suited him fine that among the women he encountered there were always some willing and ready to meet him
without the delays and complications of civilized morality.

Sex, however, was not invariably that simple in the Indian
Country. A little casual dalliance with a native girl could enmesh
a trader in an affair of hideous complexity. Alexander Henry the
Younger, trading with the Saulteur in the Lake of the Woods
district, tells in great detail but with little relish the harrowing
story of his own experience of love *à la façon du pays*:

At night I was troubled by the visit of a young woman . . . which
nearly caused an ugly affair. About ten o'clock she came into my tent
without solicitation. I was asleep; she awoke me and asked for liquor. I
recognized her voice and knew that her husband, the greatest scoundrel
among them all, was exceedingly jealous. I therefore advised her to return
instantly, and not to let him know she had been here. She requested a
dram, although she was sober.

Henry was so anxious to be rid of his visitor that he gave her
a glass of his best French brandy, which he made her swallow at
a gulp. The result was alarming:

Whether it actually choked her or she was feigning, she fell down as if
senseless and lay like a corpse . . . it was totally dark, and I began to
believe her dead. I awoke my servant, whom I desired to assist me. I sent

him for a kettle of water, which I poured over her head while he held her up; a second was applied in the same manner, but to no purpose.

At this point, Henry became really "uneasy about her" and sent for a third kettle of water, which he dashed into her face with all his strength. She groaned and came to, and Henry lost no time in bundling her into a canoe and off to her people across the river. But his troubles were by no means over:

In half an hour she returned, having shifted her clothes and dressed very fine; her husband being an excellent hunter and without children, she had always plenty of finery. She told me in plain terms that she had left her husband and come to live with me. This was news I neither expected nor desired. I represented to her the impropriety of her doing so, her husband being fond of her and extremely jealous. Her answer was that she did not care for him or any other Indian, and was determined to stay with me at the risk of her life.

While Henry was pondering this, he was fired on from the other side of the river by the jealous husband, whereupon he had the lady carried kicking to a canoe and ferried over. So ended, at last, Henry's troubles, but the aftermath was a melancholy one:

On his wife's return, he asked her where she had been. She made no secret of the matter, but said she was determined to go with me. "Well, then," said the Indian, "if you are determined to leave me, I will at least have the satisfaction of spoiling your pretty face." He caught up a large firebrand, threw her on her back, and rubbed it in her face with all his might, until the fire was extinguished. Then, letting her up, "Now," he says, "go and see your beloved and ask him if he likes you as well as he did before."

Henry concludes: "Her face was in a horrid condition. I was sorry for it; she was really the handsomest woman on the river, and not more than 18 years of age." [6]

Most traders fought shy of full-scale affairs with native women. But sometimes it happened that a chance encounter at some Indian village or trading post led to a deadly serious infatuation. "Lacerte is almost mad for her," Roderic McKenzie said of one of his men who had fallen in love with a Cree girl at Fort Chipewyan.

And at Fort Sarpy on the Missouri, a trader named Chambers wrote with poor grace of his *bourgeois*: "Mr. Meldron [Meldrum] left for the Crow camp. He told me he was going for meat, yes it was meat but squaw meat and Meg's at that. Since she has gone away he has acted more like a crazy man than one possessed of sanity." [7]

When two white men became infatuated with the same girl, a feud of considerable proportions could erupt. A famous one was the fatal falling-out of the legendary frontiersman Mike Fink and his bosom friend Carpenter. Fink and Carpenter were in the habit of demonstrating their mutual trust by filling a cup full of whiskey and shooting it from each other's heads at seventy paces. Then they quarreled over a girl. They patched up the quarrel and agreed to seal the peace pact by repeating their familiar performance. Fink won the toss for first shot, and Carpenter—well aware that his rival's hatred still smoldered—prepared to die. He filled the cup and placed it on his head, his face impassive.

"Hold your noddle steady, Carpenter," Fink called out, "and don't spill the whiskey."

A trigger squeeze later, Carpenter was dead with a bullet hole in the center of his forehead and half an inch above his eyes.

"Carpenter," Fink said reproachfully, "you spilled the whiskey." [8]

Not many working *voyageurs* or mountain men, however, had the time or inclination for involved attachments, let alone for killing one another over Indian women. A few had a string of regular girls in various villages: the soldier-trader Captain Bonneville was said to have had a dozen. But mostly they depended on finding at each new stopping place what civilized men have always encountered in savage societies: sexual behavior innocent of civilized restraints.

"Come into my tent and dry your breeches before my fire," an Aricara girl invited the romantic painter Kurz. Wherever he went, the trader or mountain man found girls who, in Tabeau's words, were "eager to make the first advance in no equivocal manner."

In so genial a climate, sex on the Indian frontiers tended to become a perfunctory matter, routinely offered and casually accepted—and forgotten with the tightening of a pack-horse's cinch or the dip of a canoe paddle. In the entire roster of mountain men, only Jedediah Smith, a deeply religious trader, seems to have resisted the allurements of the Indian girls successfully. "There is no suggestion," Dale Morgan says, "that he ever admitted a squaw, however eager or lovely, to his bed." It is on record, however, that even Smith was intrigued by the topless costumes of the Mojave girls.[9]

Traders and mountain men were fond of the idea that Indian women found white men, especially blonds, irresistible. And, indeed, there may have been something in the belief. The ancient Mexican legend of the coming of a white god got Cortés' men off to a good start—until the Conquistadores' interest in the native women convinced the Indians that the bearded men in shining shirts were not so divine after all. And some of the old awe and fascination may have lingered on.

Traders, at any rate, were not backward in claiming for white men a special power over the native belles. "During all this time," says Pattie (he is describing a meeting with the Navajo), "we endured a sort of worship from them, particularly the women." Fair-haired men, Larpenteur says, were greatly admired by the Indian girls at Fort Union—so much so that Kenneth McKenzie, the *bourgeois*, tried to assassinate a young blond rival named Bourbonnais, who had been receiving too large a share of their affection.[10] The Crow women were notoriously fond of white men—but whether because of their sex appeal or their well-stocked packs is not clear.

The free trapper, it would appear, was especially admired. "[He] combines in the eye of the Indian girl," it was claimed for him, "all that is dashing and heroic in a warrior of her own race—whose gait, and garb, and bravery he imitates—with all that is gallant and glorious in a white man." [11]

The wide-eyed wonder of some California Indian women at the sight of a trader's white skin is graphically described by Pattie:

At length they made up to one of our companions, who was of a singularly light complexion, fair soft skin, and blue eyes. They wanted him to strip himself naked, that they might explore him thoroughly, for they seemed doubtful of his being alike in every part of his body. This, as mildly as possible, he refused to do.[12]

But the women brought the young man presents of dried fish, and out of gratitude he decided to "oblige these curious and good-natured women by giving them a full view of his body. . . . This delighted them, and they conversed and laughed among themselves, and then came one by one and stood beside him, so as to compare their bodies with his."

The fatal attraction of "fair soft skins" and towheads was supposed to be equally potent among the dark-eyed *mestizas* of the Southwest. According to Pattie, the sultry half-castes were easy conquests for the swaggering mountain men. After a New Mexican fandango, he smirks, "It seemed expected of us that we should escort a lady home, in whose company we passed the night, and none of us brought charges of severity against our fair companions."

But if Indian girls found white men fascinating, they appear to have been even fonder of Negroes. We have mentioned the fantastic Esteban, leading his parade of gaudy young women up to the walls of fabled Cibola. The Indians killed him when he arrived there, but whether it was because he had assaulted their women, as they claimed, or out of jealousy for the harem of girls he had collected along his way, we do not know.

In later times, the mulatto Beckwourth had "seven wives and a lodge for each." And Josiah Gregg was astonished and obviously piqued at the admiration of the *mestizas* for Negroes. He could never quite understand his own insignificance "in the eyes of these fair doñas, contrasted with the grandeur of my sable companion [a Negro servant called Don Jorge]." [13]

And, of course, there was the famous Negro York with the

Lewis and Clark expedition. The journals of the expedition recount his popularity with the Aricara women: "Two very handsome young squaws were sent aboard this evening and persecuted us with civilities. The black man York participated largely in these favors; for, instead of inspiring any prejudice, his color seemed to procure him additional advantages from the Indians." [14]

❦

One thing that puzzled traders was the ready acquiescence of fathers and husbands in their women's relations with white men.

The Aricara girls' wanton behavior, Tabeau says, all took place in the presence of, or even by order of, a husband who was offended only when the liaisons were secret. "What is more," Trudeau adds, "the fathers, brothers, even husbands offer and take the youngest and most beautiful daughters, sisters, and wives to the white men for their diversion in exchange for a few trifles." [15]

Practically all other traders concur on the generosity of the Indians with their wives and daughters. The Cree men, Henry says, were not only tolerant of their women's advances but "eagerly encourage them in this design." Of the Chipewyan he says:

Both themselves and their husbands for them are forward in seeking a loose intercourse with the Europeans. The former appeared vain of solicitation, and having first obtained consent of their husbands, afterward communicated to them their success. The men . . . were the first to speak in behalf of their wives on the subject; and were even in the practice of carrying them to Hudson Bay, a journey of many hundred miles, on no other errand. [16]

On the Lake of the Woods, Henry was alarmed by the zeal with which the Saulteur women, encouraged by their husbands, "abandoned themselves to my Canadians," and he lost no time in clearing out.

The Sioux braves were equally eager to surrender their wives and daughters to the whites. Tabeau tells of a Sioux who brought his young wife—"one of the prettiest in the village and reputed discreet"—to a French trader at the Isle of Cedars. She could be had, the Indian suggested, for a small price. The traders, feigning disinterest, offered a knife, some vermilion, and six inches of tobacco. The Sioux indignantly refused, and the haggling began. Suddenly the Indian pulled the robe from his wife's shoulders and soon afterwards a bargain was struck. The Sioux, Tabeau says, stood guard at the door of his lodge while his wife entertained the trader inside.[17]

It is hard to read into such behavior anything but the most sordid kind of commercialism. But as far back as 1709, John Lawson noted a curious fact. He wrote of the Indian women: "They are most of them mercenary, except the married women, who sometimes bestow their favors also on some other, in their husband's absence." [18] But, Lawson adds, as long as the husband was present, payment was demanded. This was a circumstance that puzzled white men almost as much as the Indians' openhandedness with their wives' favors.

"The husband will for a trifling present lend his wife for a night to a stranger," Captain Clark noted, "and the loan may be protracted by increasing the value of the present. Yet, strange as it may seem, notwithstanding this facility, any connection of this kind not authorized by the husband, is considered highly offensive and quite as disgraceful to his character as the same licentiousness in civilized societies." [19]

Alexander Henry the Younger points out, in the same connection, that the payment demanded by the husband might be nominal—"a mere trifle . . . even one single coat button." [20] But it was always demanded; and this, anthropologists speculate, may connote some ritualistic significance. Perhaps in this manner, it is suggested, the Indian husband eliminated any cause for jealousy on his part. There was no question of sexual attraction: the whole thing was purely a business transaction. Or so the husband of a pretty young wife kept telling himself.

But this, even the traders sensed, was only part of the answer to such improbable behavior. When the Spaniards first arrived in America, Gómara started on the quest for a more profound explanation. Of the lords of Tlaxcala he wrote: "Many offered their daughters as a token of friendship, so that they might bear children of such valorous men, and bring into the world a new warrior caste." Then, on second thought, he added, "Or perhaps they gave their daughters because it was the custom, or merely to please the Spanish." [21]

Traders long after Gómara's time were still guessing and speculating. In our own time, several theories have been evolved. The simplest is that the Indians were merely observing an old primitive custom in offering their women to strangers as a hospitality gesture. With primitive peoples it has always seemed the most natural thing in the world to offer a guest, or even a passing stranger, a girl for the night. It went along with food, drink, and a place by the fire.

When the first Europeans arrived in America, they found the provision of a bedfellow a universal expression of hospitality and good will. "The greatest token of friendship which they [the Indians] show us," Vespucci said, "is that they give you their wives and daughters; and when a father or mother brings you the daughter, although she may be a virgin, and you sleep with her, they esteem themselves highly favored; and in this way they practice the full extreme of hospitality."

A few centuries later, Jonathan Carver remarked that "complimenting a stranger with the company of their wives" was standard practice among the Indians of North America, even chiefs observing it. And still another two centuries after Carver, Sir George Simpson says, "The offer of their wives and daughters is the first token of their friendship and hospitality." [22]

So it was an ancient and widespread custom, and when the traders worked their way westward to the Missouri, they found it still being observed. The journal of Henry Marie Brackenridge describes how an Aricara chief played the perfect host:

Amongst others of their customs which appeared to me singular, I observed that it was part of their hospitality to offer the guest, who takes up his residence in their lodges, one of the females of the family as a bed-fellow; sometimes even one of their wives, daughters, or sisters, but most usually a maid-servant, according to the estimation in which the guest is held, and to decline such an offer is considered as treating the host with some disrespect.[23]

Rejection could also bring down on the head of a trader the simple fury of a woman scorned. But it was the man's reputation as a host that was chiefly involved, and how seriously he could take that responsibility was well expressed by the Sauk chief Wennebea. When Keating asked Wennebea what constituted a good man, the chief replied: "His hospitality ought to be boundless; his cabin, as well as all that he can procure, should be at the disposal of any one who visits him. . . . A good man should keep as many wives as he can support, for this will enable him to extend his hospitality more freely than if he have but one wife." [24]

When Keating inquired further, however, whether this meant that an Indian should offer his principal wife to strangers, "as practiced by the Missouri Indians," he received an indignant answer: "No man of any feeling could do such a thing; there could be no man so base as to be guilty of this."

Here Wennebea casts a little light on a confusion that seems to have existed in the minds of many traders, partly through vanity perhaps, partly through sheer ignorance of Indian mores. Were white men really offered the wives and daughters of Indian chiefs, as Vespucci and many after him supposed? Or was Brackenridge nearer the truth in saying that, even on the Missouri, the proffered bedfellow was usually a "maid-servant"? Was it a slave, or at best a second-string wife that the white man was given? Did the Mandan perhaps offer traders only female prisoners captured from other tribes, and never their own women? Were the traders deluding themselves? [25]

There can be little doubt that many an ordinary fur hunter flattered himself that he was sleeping with a chief's wife, when in fact he was sharing his buffalo robes with a slave or some other inferior member of the "family." On the other hand, the *bourgeois* or leader of a trapping party might indeed be honored by the company of the host's own wife or daughter. This—Wennebea's indignation to the contrary—seems to be well-established, at least among the Plains Indians, and the reasons for it go deep into the involutions of the primitive mind.

Gómara, attempting to rationalize the strange acquiescence of Indian husbands, theorized, it will be remembered, that the lords of Tlaxcala offered their daughters "so that they might bear children of such valorous men, and bring into the world a new warrior caste." And this, it has been suggested, may well have been the true reason why Indian men were willing, and even eager, for their wives to have intercourse with white men.

With all Indian tribes, the replenishment of fighting men was a serious problem. In some cases—as with the Iroquois—it could mean the difference between tribal survival and extinction. No warlike people could allow its reserve of warriors to dry up. And so sons and more sons were needed—even if they had to be captured and adopted, or sired by strangers. And of all male children, the sons of Indian mothers and white fathers were most wanted.

"Bolder warriors and better hunters," a Cree chief told Keating, were born of such unions. And this, in fact, was the universal belief. Whether or not it was true—and quite often it proved to be—the belief was quite enough to explain the Indian woman's eagerness to cohabit with a white man, and her husband's ready approval.

But another more complex and even mystical explanation has been suggested by anthropologists. When an Indian woman—a Mandan girl, for instance—offered herself to a man of her own tribe, it has been pointed out, the context was always sacred or ceremonial: in one of the fertility, hunting, or mourning rituals that the white trader gaped at but never understood. Similarly, a mystical belief was operative in the conduct of Mandan women toward white traders. It was a belief that through sexual intercourse the *power* of a white man could be transmitted to a woman, and from her to her husband.

Thus, it has been postulated, the young brave's desire to have his wife sleep with a white trader was rooted in a basic characteristic of Indian culture. Just as he shared her with those of his own people who had already accumulated power—his ceremonial fathers and the distinguished older men of the tribe—so he offered her to the "white chiefs." For the Indians were naive enough to believe that the fur traders were the most important men of their nation—with, no doubt, a lot of accumulated power.

The fur trader's notions about all this were hardly profound, and they may indeed have reflected a gross misunderstanding of Indian culture. Yet there were all sorts of Indians, just as there were all sorts of whites. And it can hardly be doubted that some Indians were actuated by motives somewhat less complex than a desire to accumulate power through the sexual intercourse of their wives with white men. Perhaps some, like Le Borgne, a powerful chief of the Big Bellies, were moved by nothing more complicated or mystical than a simple desire to curry favor with the white chiefs.[26]

Le Borgne was by all accounts a terrible man. A burly six-footer, with but one eye, a cavernous mouth, a huge aquiline nose, and "the aspect of a fierce, savage brute," he struck with awe everyone who crossed his path—including, it would seem, Alexander Henry the Younger, who has left us this chilling description:

His manners appeared pleasant; in conversation a perpetual smile played upon his countenance; when matters did not please him he still smiled, but it was then a ghastly grin. To his women he is a mere brute; he uses them more like slaves than wives. They appeared to be in continual dread of him, and not without cause, as he has butchered some of them with his own hands and with the greatest composure imaginable.[27]

Henry recounts Le Borgne's casual dispatch of one of his straying wives with an ax, then resumes his account of the great man:

It is extraordinary that he could with impunity resent an affront of this kind in such a harsh manner, as he had often been guilty of debauching young women, both maidens and wives. Some he has kept for his own use, and others he has returned to their friends or husbands when tired of their company; and still none have dared to avenge the affront. When any female strikes his fancy he makes no ceremony, but uses her as if she were his own.[28]

Le Borgne, it is clear, was not much in need of acquiring power from the white men, whom indeed he held in profound contempt. But he and his warriors did need the guns, ammunition, blankets, and other articles supplied by the traders. The whites, Le Borgne said, were a curious people. They loved beaver. What they did with the beaver, he had no idea; but they paid well for pelts, and that was enough. They were also fond of women. So, "Let your women be kind to them," Le Borgne enjoined. "They are generous and will pay you for your kindness." [29]

It would be difficult to detect any mystical overtones in this. For Le Borgne, supplying a trader with a girl was a simple matter of creating a favorable trading atmosphere. And the trader could not even preen himself on the seductive power of his white skin and blue eyes; his pretty bedfellow's co-operation was only a manifestation of commercial enterprise.

"TRADING GIRLS"
AND SUCH

"A canotee of prostitutes came here this morning, but were not allowed to land on pain of being put in irons; this threat, I hope, will keep them off." [1]

When Alexander Henry the Younger wrote this at Astoria, John Jacob Astor's fur trading post on the Columbia, he was talking about something quite different from the complex and even mystical relationships we have noted up to this point. Plain, ordinary prostitution had arrived in the Indian Country.

Henry referred frequently after this to the plague of Indian bawds at Astoria, and with increasing choler. But it was Ross Cox who left the best description of how bothersome the Chinook whores had become:

Numbers of women reside during certain periods of the year in small huts about the fort and from which it is difficult to keep the men . . . On the arrival of the spring and autumn brigades from the interior they pour in from all parts, and besiege our *voyageurs* much after the manner which their frail sisters at Portsmouth adopt when attacking the crews of a newly arrived India fleet. Mothers participate with their daughters in the proceeds arising from their prostitution; and in many instances husbands share with their wives the wages of infamy. Disease is the natural consequence of this state of general demoralization, and numbers of the unfortunate beings suffer dreadfully from the effects of their promiscuous intercourse.[2]

On the same spot, half a dozen years earlier, Lewis and Clark had experienced similar trouble. A Chinook chief's wife showed up with six female relations and "regular prices proportioned to the beauty of each female." Having made camp close to the fort, they set up for business, but apparently with poor success. "We warned the men," the journal entry reads, "of the dangers of intercourse with this frail society; and they cautiously abstained from connection with them." [3]

Commercialized vice of this kind was a new phenomenon in the North American Indian world. Prostitution, to be sure, had not been unknown in the Indies. And the thousands of virgins who lived in the great stone-walled convents of Peru, waiting for the Inca to summon them to his bed, were prostitutes of a sort. But as brides of the god, they more closely resembled the sacral harlots of ancient Asian and European civilizations; as such they were treated with esteem and even veneration. [4]

Side by side with this royal institution, which was actually concubinage on a magnificent scale, there existed in Peru the ordinary kind of prostitution. As Garcilaso describes it, there was nothing very glamorous about it:

I have yet to speak of the prostitutes, whose activities were authorized by the Inca in order to avoid worse catastrophes. They lived in the country in wretched thatched huts, each one separately, and they were forbidden to enter the towns and villages in order that no virtuous woman should ever encounter them. They were called *pampairuna*, a word containing both the place and the occupation, since *pampa* means any level place or country, and *runa* means people. The men treated these women with great contempt, and the women never spoke to them, under penalty of having their hair shorn in public, or of being repudiated by their husbands and treated like the others. The latter were never designated by their own names, but always by the common name of *pampairuna*. [5]

Among the North American Indians, concubinage was common. As we have seen, a powerful chief often maintained a string of "slave wives" for his own use, to accommodate his guests, and even to serve as a medium of exchange. In some of the fertility and hunting ceremonials, Indian girls, by publicly offering themselves to distinguished men of the tribe, assumed a role strikingly like that of the temple prostitutes of ancient civilizations. And there were, of course, always loose women who managed to turn their natural promiscuity to a profit. But none of this was prostitution on a professional basis.

Thompson gives us the rare instance of a "lady conjuress" at Rainy Lake[6] who had formerly been a whore, but, finding little demand for her services, had turned with better luck to magic:

She had set herself up for a prophetess, and gradually had gained by her shrewdness some influence among the natives as a dreamer and expounder of dreams. She recollected me before I did her, and gave me a haughty look of defiance, as much as to say, I am now out of your power. Some six years before this she was living with one of my men as his wife, but became so common that I had to send her to her relations; as all the Indians are married, a courtesan is neglected by the men and hated by the women.[7]

In his last sentence, Thompson perhaps sums up the reasons why the world's oldest profession was rare among the Indians of North America. In a war-directed society—which included most tribes—men were at a premium and women plentiful, polygamy was common and divorce was easy. To make the trade of the prostitute still less alluring, payment could be received only in goods or horses, a circumstance that made the maintenance of even one mistress apart from one's lodge awkward. The white traders with their small articles of commerce resolved this problem, of course, both for the women and themselves.

It is often difficult to tell from the traders' journals whether they are referring to intratribal prostitution or the procurement of Indian women for the whites. It seems clear that the Plains tribes, such as the Sioux, turned to native trollops only incidentally, if at all. The prostitution of wives was, however, common among the Crow, Russell says, and very rare with the Snakes (Shoshoni). The Apache warned loose women once, then spread-eagled them on an ant hill. The Mandan, according to Thompson's narrative, had prostitutes who danced and sang for the men's entertainment. The Beaver Indians, although very short of women, were not induced "to prostitute their wives among themselves, or to strangers, like other savage tribes inhabiting the North." And this statement by the Nor'wester W. F. Wentzel seems to indicate that such a practice *was* common among the northern tribes.[8]

According to Lahontan, there were rebellious Indian girls who refused to marry or remain in their villages, but attached themselves to any man who suited their fancy. These girls, he says, were called *ickoue ne kiouffa*, or "hunting women," because they accompanied the hunters on their expeditions. "The Jesuits," he adds, "do their utmost to prevent the lewd practices of these whores," but with no success.

The Assiniboin, according to Larpenteur, recognized three different grades or degrees of prostitution, one of which was looked upon as legal. "This," Larpenteur explains, "is when she is loaned with the consent of her parents, and then the larger the payment, the more honor is for the woman. When little quarrels arise among mothers in regard to the characters of their daughters, they will say, 'What have you to say against my daughter? What did yours get when you lent her? Look what mine got! You are making a *Wittico-Weeon* of your daughter.' "[9]

Wittico-weeon (fool woman), Larpenteur continues, was a term applied to the lowest degree of prostitute, i.e., "a regular prostitute who has no husband and goes about to lend herself for pay." Such women were considered lost beyond redemption.

Most of what we know about prostitution among the aboriginal Americans is obscured by faulty observation and ignorance. Wifelending, for example, seems to have been confused with pandering, concubinage with harlotry, slave trading with whoremongering, religious ritual with debauchery. But it may be repeated that before the coming of the whites, there appears to have been little prostitution in the sense of a woman "lending herself for pay."[10]

With the arrival of the white man, however, the whole picture changed swiftly.

It is uncertain who introduced prostitution to the Indians, but it was probably not the Spaniards, who took what they wanted without pay. Charges and countercharges of concubinage, rape, and other irregular relationships involving Indian women were not infrequent in the Spanish Archives, but it is difficult to find references to anything resembling commercialized vice. Military garrisons, government officials, and even the religious no doubt carried on an exchange of goods and trinkets for feminine complaisance, but on a private, unorganized level. The bordellos of Taos and Santa Fe were a later development.

During the French regime in Canada, however, the public exploitation of Indian women became a feature of frontier life. The *commandant* with his harem of native girls enlivened the dull isolation of the fur trading post, and the wild *coureur de bois* turned the mission villages into bedlam—or, as one distracted missionary expressed it, "so many taverns for drunkenness and Sodoms for iniquity."

The *coureurs de bois* exhibited traits not surprising in men a long time away from the delights of civilization. Lahontan describes their return to Montreal, after a year or eighteen months in the *pays d'en haut*:

You would be amazed if you saw how lewd these peddlers are when they return; how they feast and game, and how prodigal they are, not only in their clothes but upon women . . . the batchelors act just as our East-India men and pirates are wont to do; for they lavish, eat, drink, and play all away as long as the goods hold out; and when they are gone, they even sell their embroidery, their lace, and their clothes. This done, they are forced to go upon a new voyage for subsistence.[11]

The sudden influx of large numbers of such characters has never elevated the moral tone of a community, but when the military arrived on the scene, the situation became even worse.

The soldiers, Father Carheil wrote from Michilimackinac in 1702, had turned the fort into a brothel, and he goes into some detail about the swarms of Indian girls hired to spend their days and nights inside the palisades.[12] Of course, he may have been biased, for no love was lost between the Jesuits and the King's officers—and particularly between Father Carheil and La Mothe-Cadillac, *commandant* at Mackinac.

The distressing effect of such traffic on the Indian women is described by Charlevoix in one of his so-called letters to the Duchess of Lesdiguières:

Young people of both sexes abandon themselves, without either shame or remorse, to all kinds of dissoluteness, and it is chiefly among these that it was thought no crime for a girl to prostitute herself; their parents were the first to engage them in this vice, and husbands were seen to prostitute their wives for vile interest.[13]

The half-breed trader at La Pointe, William W. Warren, touches affectionately on another aspect of relations between the Indian girls and the French traders, hardly prostitution perhaps, but not without a certain commercial flavor:

The arrival of the French *bourgeois* with the flag of France flying at the stern of his canoe, was saluted with a volley of musketry. . . . The dark-eyed damsels, though they stood bashfully in the rear of those who thronged the beach to welcome the new-comers, yet with their faces partly hidden they darted glances of welcome, and waited in the wigwams impatiently for their white sweethearts to come in the darkness and silence of the night, to present the trinkets they had brought all the way from Quebec, to adorn their persons and please their fancy.[14]

A very different picture, as we shall see, from that of the raucous Missouri River women swooping down on the American traders and boatmen. But, then, the Ojibway girls were always known for their propriety and decorum.

What went on in the backwoods of the English colonies is not very well documented; but some of the early settlers' relationships with the neighborhood Indian women could scarcely be described as innocent gambols, even though they centered around a Maypole. William Bradford, of Plymouth Plantation, wrote of Thomas Morton and his friends at Merrymount:

They fell to a great licentiousness and led a dissolute life. . . . They also set up a Maypole, drinking and dancing about it many days together, inviting the Indian women for their consorts, dancing and frisking together like so many fairies, or furies, rather; and worse practices.[15]

This was certainly a bawdy business (if we may believe Bradford; Morton, in fact, was one of the few whites who refused to give liquor to the Indians), but it did not necessarily involve prostitution in the sense of sex for money. We come to that, however, and very explicitly, in John Lawson's *History of North Carolina*. Writing in 1709, Lawson says:

As for the Trading Girls, which are those designed to get money by their natural parts, these are discernible by the cut of their hair; their tonsure differing from all others of the nation who are not of their profession, which method is intended to prevent mistakes; for the savages of America are desirous (if possible) to keep their wives to themselves, as well as those in other parts of the world.[16]

The process of arranging for a night's diversion with one of these trading girls was, according to Lawson, a rather complicated and tedious one. First, the trader propositioned the girl, who took the matter up with her parents. The chief of the tribe (whom Lawson calls "the principal bawd of the nation") was next consulted. An extended debate, involving all the girl's relatives, then followed. And finally came the bargaining over the payment— if the trader, that is, was still interested.[17]

The results of the white man's willingness to pay for love were quickly apparent in the sexual behavior of the Indians. Even the Natchez, whose punishment for adultery on the part of either husband or wife was death, seem to have been completely demoralized. "I know of no nation on the continent," Charlevoix says, "where sex is more disorderly than in this. They are even forced by the grand chief and his subalterns to prostitute themselves to all comers, and a woman is not the less esteemed for being public." [18]

It is only fair to the aboriginal ladies of the Old South, however, that the voice of Robert Beverley be heard in their defense. After remarking in his *History and Present State of Virginia* that they are "generally beautiful, possessing an uncommon delicacy of shape and features, and wanting no charm but that of a fair complexion," Beverley says: "Though the young Indian women are said to prostitute their bodies for *wampum* . . . and other such fineries, yet I could never find any ground for the accusation, and believe it only to be an unjust scandal upon them." [19]

There were four points at which a *voyageur* or mountain man, in his continental quest for beaver, might meet Indian women: along his routes of travel, at Indian encampments, at trading posts, and at the great mountain rendezvous.

The only roads through the vast interior of North America were waterways. An interminable maze of rivers, lakes, and inland seas tied the remotest corners of the land together. From Montreal, a man's canoe might take him to Hudson Bay, the Arctic Ocean, the Pacific, or the Gulf of Mexico with only a few easy portages.

By the St. Lawrence River route, French traders, and after them the English, drove their big *canots du maître,* carrying five tons and a crew of ten, through Lake Superior to the Grand Portage. Here they changed to smaller "north canoes" and hurried ahead of the frost to their wintering stations in the *pays sauvage.* They pushed up the Assiniboin, the Saskatchewan, the Peace, the Athabasca, the Mackenzie to the farthest ends of the Canadian wilderness, and some crossed over the mountains and swept down the Columbia to the Pacific.

Other traders, French, English, and American, took to the Lower Lakes, scattering forts and trading posts along their way, and down the Ohio, Wabash, Illinois, and the Mississippi itself, and at last to Louisiana. Later, American traders took off from St. Louis in keel-boats and barges up the Missouri and its tributaries, the Platte, the Yellowstone, the Big Horn, and innumerable lesser streams to the high, solitary, hostile heart of the Rockies. Others struggled from the Pacific Coast up the Columbia and and Snake to posts beyond the mountains.

Where the rivers could not take them, they went with packhorses, wagon trains, and afoot. Sometimes they followed the

great caravan routes along the North Platte and through South
Pass, or the Santa Fe trail to the valley of the Rio Grande. And
sometimes they struck out on routes of their own finding through
country never before traversed. They traveled in mile-long supply
trains, or large trapping parties, or alone. But they were incessantly
on the move.

And wherever they went they found Indians and their women.
Or perhaps it would be more accurate to say the Indians found
them, for they were bringers of guns, blankets, kettles, knives, and
many other things that the red men soon discovered they must
possess or perish. The traders also brought liquor, foolish trinkets
for the women, and devastation in the form of drunkenness,
disease, and vice, but the Indians—at first—perceived only the
good things. So whenever word reached a band that the white
men were coming, they struck their tents and flocked to a camping
place along the traders' route. It was a great event, a gay holiday
time; as many as five or six thousand Indians might gather at the
white men's stopping place.[20]

In 1811, Brackenridge accompanied the famous trader Manuel
Lisa on his celebrated stern chase of Wilson Price Hunt's overland Astorians up the Missouri. Lisa's keel-boat, manned by
twenty-two boatmen, arrived at the Aricara villages about the
middle of June. Brackenridge has left us this description of what
happened when a swarm of fur traders met a large number of
friendly, or at least not openly hostile, Indians:

To these people, it seemed to me that the greater part of their females,
during our stay, had become mere articles of traffic; after dusk, the plain
behind our tents was crowded with these wretches, and shocking to
relate, fathers brought their daughters, husbands their wives, brothers
their sisters, to be offered for sale at this market of indecency and shame.
I was unable to account for this difference from any people I had ever
heard of; perhaps something may be attributed to the inordinate passion
which seized them for our merchandise. The silly boatmen, in spite of the
endeavors of the leaders of our parties, in a short time disposed of almost
every article they possessed, even their blankets and shirts. One of them
actually returned to camp one morning entirely naked, having disposed
of his last shirt—this might truly be called *la dernier chemise de l'amour*.[21]

At about the same time, John Bradbury painted a similar picture of the Osage braves traipsing down to the river with their chattering wives, daughters, and sisters, "anxious to meet with a market for them." Amid the bedlam of shrill laughter, ribald taunts, and multilingual haggling, Bradbury counted no fewer than eighty transactions in one evening. The Canadians, he says, were very good customers, keeping the leader of the party busy doling out beads and vermilion to them for payment. Vermilion paint in little paper packets and strings of blue glass beads, incidentally, became the accepted currency for the purchase of an Indian prostitute's favors.[22] A packet or two of vermilion and twenty strands of beads appears to have been the standard fee on the Missouri, with the price going up or down in ratio to the girl's charms and the white man's state of sobriety and lubricity.[23]

Other Indian tribes, it was often noted by traders, were by no means so liberal with their women. The Shoshoni, we learn from the Lewis and Clark journals, were "not so importunate in volunteering the services of their wives as we found the Sioux were; and indeed we observed among them some women who appeared to be held in more respect than those of any nation we had seen." [24]

At times, in fact, relations (even on the Missouri) were anything but cordial. Not long after the Aricara welcomed Lisa so openhandedly to their village and their women, General William H. Ashley appeared with a large party of his Rocky Mountain Fur Company men. During the night, one of the brigade—a youth named Aaron Stephens—stole out of camp to visit an Aricara trollop in the village. The result of this amorous escapade marked the worst disaster in fur trade history. The Indians killed Stephens and cut him into small pieces; then they used his visit to their woman as an excuse for an attack on Ashley's party in which they killed twelve men and wounded eleven, two of them fatally.[25]

In the other great fur country, the Canadian Northwest, the situation was somewhat different. The Indians inhabiting this

vast forested region were forced to break up into small hunting
parties in order to live on the scanty supply of game and fish. So
it was by the score rather than by the thousands that they came
to meet the traders' canoes on the waterways leading down from
Hudson Bay and up from Lake Superior.

The Canadian fur brigades were always in a frantic hurry to get
where they were going, and the men exhausted after paddling
sixteen hours, from three o'clock in the morning. So conditions
were somewhat less favorable to Indians who came to offer their
women at the portages. Nevertheless, as the journals of the traders
make clear, they did manage to do some business. Henry was not
the only *bourgeois* to complain of "a plague of women" at the
carrying places. The Cree and Chipewyan were notoriously forward. Even in the dim reaches of the Arctic, the Eskimo women
were on hand "with enticing gestures."

The *bourgeois* arranged matters for his own convenience while
on a long canoe voyage. Philip Turnor, a Hudson's Bay Company
man, observed enviously that a Nor'wester had "his feather bed
carried in the canoe, his tent, which is exceedingly good, pitched
for him, his bed made, and his girl carried in and out of the
canoe . . ." [26]

In the western fur country, trapping parties moving afoot and
with pack-trains encountered Indian panders on the mountain
trails. John Work recorded on his first trip as a brigade leader
that "as usual some women arrived for the night." The ladies
were paid in tobacco and buttons. Work estimated that there
were not two dozen buttons left among the mountain men by
morning.[27]

Much of the beaver ground, however, was controlled by hostiles,
such as the Blackfoot, and they and their ladies were not exactly
welcomed by lonely mountain men. If the larger parties had any
traffic with the Indian drabs except at the beginning and end of
their long trips, the journals of the leaders make no point of it.
Indeed, Zenas Leonard managed to cross the Rockies to California
with only one mention of Indian women—the offer of a good-
looking girl for an ox.[28]

On their long journeys across the Great Plains, the wagon caravans were more apt to receive visits from hostile Pawnee, Comanche, and Kiowa than from friendlies with girls for hire. But that they did occasionally encounter sizable parties of Indian prostitutes is indicated by Josiah Gregg's notation that his 1831 Santa Fe caravan was approached by thirty or forty women, "all of whom were summarily turned adrift without waiting to speculate upon the object of their visit." [29]

Even the supply ships of the fur trading companies were not immune to infiltration. John McLoughlin, writing from Fort Vancouver in 1830, was plainly upset by the news that a slave girl was aboard the Hudson's Bay Company's brig *Dryad.* "If so be the case," he wrote, "I request she be immediately sent on shore, and I hope no women on any pretense will be allowed to reside on the *Dryad* . . . P.S. I am informed there are three women residing on the *Dryad.*" [30]

Wherever they went, and whatever their mode of travel, traders, trappers, and mountain men were likely to find Indian women who were willing and eager to assuage their loneliness for a few baubles. And especially there was no lack of them at the big trading post, the rendezvous, or the trail-end settlement.

At any place where men gather in large numbers—at army camps, mining towns, seaports, logging camps, business conventions—there is, of course, bound to be an influx of gay ladies with nothing good in mind. And the large forts and rendezvous of the fur trading companies were no exception. Just as St. Louis had "the Hill" and Fort Kearny its "Dobeytown," every post of any importance and every field concourse of mountain men had its complement of tawny strumpets.

For most of the year, life at the big establishments was a rather dull routine of trading, cutting firewood, tending the kitchen garden, looking after the livestock, and clearing the fort of snow. But during the winter holidays, and when the fur brigades were on the move, a brand of drinking, fighting, and whoring such as was seldom seen in any cow town or mining camp broke out as regularly as the geese came north in March. And it was at these times that the dusky daughters of joy reaped their harvest of blue beads, vermilion, and silver crosses.

Throughout the Canadian fur country, there was a certain amount of merrymaking when the Indians came in with the fall and spring hunts, or when the canoes arrived with the new outfit from below. But the really Big Carouse was the one at Grand Portage.

Grand Portage was the North West Company's famous field headquarters at the western tip of Lake Superior. To the Portage came the big freight canoes from Montreal with trade goods for the Interior, and the fur-laden north canoes from Athabasca, the Saskatchewan, the Rocky Mountain posts. And here for a few fevered weeks each summer came a thousand half-wild North Men from the distant *pays sauvage*, and "porkeaters" from Lower Canada—and *les girls*.

"*Je suis un homme!*" The North Man's boast was a challenge to the porkeater—who seldom let it pass unanswered. Nor did the *bourgeois* mind a little mayhem. It developed the famous *esprit de corps* of the Nor'westers and kept them in condition for more serious battles with the Hudson's Bay people. No harm in a little drinking, either. A man had to blow off steam after a winter in the bush; besides, it helped to keep him in debt to the Company—and firmly anchored to his job. As for the girls . . .

No sooner had the *voyageur* lugged his prescribed quota of eight trade packs over the Grand Portage trail than he got ready to have himself a time. Decked out in his best short shirt, deer-skin leggings, and the gaudy sash that was his trademark, he tossed off his *régale* of a few gills of free rum and headed for the *cantine salope*. Here, at the "harlots' tavern," he could buy more rum (at eight dollars a quart), white bread, pork, butter, and the caresses of the Ojibway girls.

Morally, the Ojibway rated as high as any Indian tribe of North America; but every society has its fringe of light ladies, and some of the Grand Portage girls—as traders so often took time to note in their journals—had flashing eyes and sex appeal. Their pretty faces looked especially good to men who had spent a long, dreary winter among the unlovely females of the Far North; and so the *cantine salope* was undoubtedly the liveliest, loudest, and rowdiest spot inside the Grand Portage palisades.[31]

Its pleasures, however, were short-lived. A *voyageur* went broke quickly and was lucky if he did not wind up in the "butter tub," as the fort's calaboose was called. Well, no matter. He had something to take away with him from the rendezvous—something to remember in the long, dark, dismal days at his wintering station. "I spent all my earnings in the enjoyment of pleasure," one ancient *voyageur* exulted. "Now I have not a spare shirt to my back, nor a penny to buy one. Yet, were I young again, I should glory in commencing the same career. There is no life as happy as a voyageur's life, no place where a man can enjoy such freedom as in the Indian country. *Huzza! Huzza! pour le pays sauvage!*" [32]

The girls at the *cantine salope* had something to take away with them, too—that happy *voyageur*'s winter wages, and maybe even his shirt.

The permanent forts and posts of the fur traders were also the scene of "frolics" at certain set times—the Nor'westers, for example, celebrating Christmas, New Year's Eve, Twelfth Night, All Saints' Day, and St. Andrew's Day. On these occasions, the men were issued a holiday *régale* of rum. There was much ceremonial visiting back and forth, and a dance in the evening that invariably wound up in a round of battles. "Of all the people in the world," Daniel Harmon wrote in disgust after a particularly messy *boisson*, "I think the Canadians, when drunk, are the most disagreeable." [33]

These "frolics," as the Nor'westers quaintly called them, were characterized by the most flagrant sexual promiscuity, rape, and such orgiastic diversions as even the uninhibited Henry could not bring himself to describe fully. They were, of course, taken full advantage of by any loose women in the Indian camp that adjoined the fort; and even respectable tribal matrons surrendered themselves to completely unrestrained conduct under the influence of traders' rum. Just what a demoralizing effect liquor could have on the Indian woman is described by Duncan M'Gillivray, writing in his journal at Fort George in the Blackfoot country during the winter of 1795:

Men, women, and children promiscuously mingle together and join in one diabolical clamour of singing, crying, fighting, &c and to such excess do they indulge their love of drinking that all regard for decency or decorum is forgotten:—they expose themselves in the most indecent positions, leaving uncovered those parts which nature requires to be concealed—a circumstance which they carefully avoid in their sober moments, and the intercourse between the sexes, at any time but little restrained, is now indulged with the greatest freedom, for as chastity is not deemed a virtue among most of the tribes, they take very little pains to conceal their amours, especially when heated with liquor.[34]

At least some of the Indians seem to have resigned themselves to the evil power of rum over their women, and refrained from branding them as prostitutes for what they did when drunk. The Nipigon point of view is set forth by Duncan Cameron as follows:

They are pretty chaste when sober, but when the least in liquor, they indulge themselves in such sport as comes their way; when found out they will say they remember nothing about it, and they were senseless at the time, so that it was not they who misbehaved but the liquor. A woman, therefore, is never reckoned a prostitute for what she does when inebriate, provided she was never known to misbehave when sober . . .[35]

The men of other tribes kept a special watch over their women during a fête. "The ladies of His Majesty's Posts [i.e., the Montagnais]," James McKenzie says, "whether married or unmarried, young or old, are, it must be confessed, much inclined to gaiety. . . . The men, aware of this disposition, and naturally jealous, watch them very closely, particularly in drinking frolics . . ."[36]

Even by the Indians' own moral standards, one can hardly condone the sexual behavior that appears to have been typical of trading post "frolics"; and, in fact, it was a matter of grave concern to Indian leaders themselves. But one must go along with the

Nipigon in refusing to equate such conduct with prostitution. It was in another, more definitive, form that commercialized vice showed up at the trading posts as an everyday thing.

Henry the Younger's troubles with the Chinook ladies at Astoria was not an unusual experience for fur traders in the Far West. When the big posts of the Hudson's Bay Company and the North West Company began to move out of the forests and onto the prairies, they all ran into a plague of Indian panders and their women.

The Plains Indians, unlike those who lived in the woods, congregated in huge encampments of as many as two hundred lodges, and to have so many Indians trooping to his post with women for barter could be no small embarrassment to a trader. Henry the Younger gives us this anguished account of his own difficulties with the Gros Ventre at Rocky Mountain House on the Saskatchewan, in 1811:

In offering their women they surpass all other nations I have ever seen. They appear to be destitute or ignorant of all shame or modesty. In their visits to our establishments women are articles of temporary barter with our men. For a few inches of twist tobacco a Gros Ventre will barter the person of his wife or daughter with as much sang-froid as he would bargain for a horse. He has no equal in such an affair, though the Black-foot, Blood, or Piegan is now nearly as bad—in fact, all those tribes are a nuisance when they come to the forts with their women. They intrude upon every room and cabin in the place, and even though a trader may have a family of their [*sic*] own, they insist upon doing them the charity of accepting of the company of at least one woman for the night. It is sometimes with the greatest difficulty that we can get the fort clear of them in the evening and shut the gates . . .[37]

Henry closes his account with a gentle jibe at the Indians' claim that what they really wanted was children by white fathers. "And all for the sake of gain," he concludes, "not from any regard for us, though some of the men tell us it is with a view of having a white child—which frequently is the case."

What went on in the remote posts of the Hudson's Bay Company is not easy to ascertain. The masters were instructed to allow no women inside the forts; and concubinage, much less "frolics" with the native women, was strictly forbidden. But despite the Concern's stringent regulations, venereal disease was by no means rare at the Bayside posts or, later, at the western establishments. Fort journals reflect no hint of moral censure, nor any sense of the unaccustomed, when reporting men "lying in with the venereal complaint."

Hudson's Bay Company factors did not necessarily have to tell the governors in London everything, and a great deal may be read between the lines of their aseptic reports. Did Moose Factory, for example, burn down during a Christmas holiday revelry in 1737? The London Committee couldn't prove it—but only because everybody in the fort had been so drunk that no one was "left to impeach them." [38]

American posts in the Far West quite surely did not escape the same kind of harassment, but most of them appear to have resisted it more successfully. Fort Sarpy may have been somewhat of an exception. At Fort Sarpy, if we may believe a vitriolic American Fur Company trader named Samuel Chambers, the place was overrun by Crow prostitutes. "Fort full of loafers," Chambers noted in his journal, "feasting and lounging in the houses. Every pan, plate and cup is brought in requisition three or four times a day to feast brats and whores. . . . The women are all whores, the young bucks impudent scoundrels, the old rips thieves . . . I find this morning that Murrell [Meldrum], not being satisfied with one whorehouse, has converted the Store into another." [39]

As far as we know, conditions at Fort Sarpy—if indeed they actually obtained—were not duplicated at the other big American fur trading companies' forts. In his great mud castle on the Arkansas, William Bent kept a taut rein on his men and a close watch on their behavior; and the same could probably have been said for the *bourgeois* of Fort Union, Fort Pierre, Fort McKenzie, and the other key American posts. It certainly was true of such Canadian establishments as Fort Vancouver.

It was inevitable, however, that every trading post should have its "squaw town" and tipi brothels. And in some military posts, such as Fort Laramie, the fort sutler himself was accused of conducting a small bordello in his own quarters. Under its walls, every trading post had its little colony of heavily vermilioned girls, sitting in the doorways of their lodges and calling out soft ribaldries to passing white men. They were to be found in the raucous and unruly community outside the walls of Bent's Fort, and in its counterparts throughout the West. They were in business near the mission villages of the French and on the outskirts of the larger settlements and cities—Quebec, Montreal, St. Louis, New Orleans. And at the jumping-off points of the transcontinental supply routes, taverns like the Last Chance in Westport were thronged with "low women." Where the men were, the ladies were sure to be.

At a little later date, there sprang up around the western army posts and on the great caravan routes saloon-brothels known quaintly as "hog ranches," each with its little cemetery attached. In these unsavory oases, women known as "dance hall girls" or "sporting characters" were available to the troops, road agents, gamblers, trappers, and other colorful denizens of the Old West.[40]

In some cases, the "hog ranches" expanded into villages of ill repute. Such a place was Dobeytown, "a center of trade and entertainment" two miles outside Fort Kearny, which boasted six families and fourteen saloons. Nearby, in a cottonwood thicket, was Dirty Woman's Ranch, where "the meanest whiskey on earth" is said to have been sold. Its general character may be surmised from its inmates having hissed General Sherman and the fort's officers and their ladies on the occasion of a ceremonial visit.

The *filles de joie* of the "hog ranches," who usually dressed in soldiers' castoff clothing, were for the most part white women, while those in the Taos and Santa Fe bordellos were of mixed blood. It was at the fur trading posts or, in a purely amateur capacity, around the military reservations that the Indian girls were to be found. Usually they were from neighboring tribes, but at times—as on Hudson Bay—they were imported, perhaps from a considerable distance. The Hudson's Bay Company's Cumberland House journal for the winter of 1779 records that "in the evening an assinnee'poet [Assiniboin] man with 6 women arrived with a few Furrs and some Provisions to trade," and we need hardly ask what he was doing with so many women in tow.[41]

That supplying a trading post with women could be a profitable business is amply indicated by a Kwakiutl Indian who sent his wife twice a year as a prostitute to Victoria, a Hudson's Bay Company post near Fort Rupert. After each visit, he and his industrious mate returned home with a bale of at least fifty blankets, worth $125. The enormous potlatches for which the Indians of the Northwest were famous were not infrequently financed with the proceeds of this type of enterprise.[42]

When a trading post had strict rules against Indian women sleeping inside the palisades, traders could go to extreme lengths of ingenuity in circumventing the regulations. John Long tells of his own part in one such "whimsical Circumstance" at Michilimackinac:

I applied to two soldiers and asked them if they could spare time to roll a large hogshead of bottled porter from Chippeway Point to the Fort; they told me whenever it suited me they would be ready to assist. Having purchased the hogshead, and got it rolled down the hill whilst the officers were at dinner, I told the squaws of my plan, and having knocked out the head and bung, and bored several holes to admit as much air as possible, desired them to get in, which with some difficulty I persuaded them to do. I then replaced the head, and ran immediately to the soldiers to acquaint them that the porter was ready and desired their assistance without delay, as I was afraid some of the bottles were broken, and it would be proper to examine them as soon as possible. The soldiers immediately returned with me, and applying their shoulders to the cask, rolled it up the hill with great labor and fatigue, continually observing that it was very heavy . . .[43]

Long concludes this hilarious essay at frontier humor with one of the soldiers missing his footing, the hogshead breaking loose, and the girls spilling out at the bottom of the hill. The fort's commander was not without a *bon mot* to suit the occasion. He exclaimed, "Pretty bottled porter, indeed!" [44]

It was at the great rendezvous of the American mountain men, however, that the Indian prostitute and her pander hit the jackpot.

Rendezvous 1832 at Pierre's Hole, deep in the Rockies, was a good example of such a gathering. In the broad, flat, incredibly beautiful valley now known as Teton Basin, a great concourse of white men—ninety of the American Fur Company, a hundred of the Rocky Mountain Fur Company, and a multitude of free trappers—gathered to trade, gamble, lie, fight, drink, carouse, and play such merry jokes as setting one another afire. A little apart from the raucous din of the mountain men's camp rose two hundred white lodges of the Nez Perce and Flathead, glowing on the plain at night like lighted lanterns. The Indians had little to trade. But they had something even better than buffalo robes and beaver to offer the white men at this gay and festive occasion: their women. [45]

It was on the Indian girls—along with a lethal mixture of raw alcohol and plug tobacco called whiskey—that the mountain man squandered the proceeds of a long, cold winter in the beaver country. If he had enough plews left after paying his respects to the bottle and gaming blanket, he might buy himself a regular mountain wife. Plenty of dazzling girls were paraded in their snowy elkskins by fathers and brothers in the hope of entrapping some rum-dazed trapper in the coils of a prairie marriage. But a wife did not come cheap. First there was the bride-price to pay, then the cost of fofarraw. Joe Meek claimed that his Mountain Lamb's finery set him back $300 for her horse, $150 for her saddle, $50 for her bridle, $50 for her "musk-a-boots"—not to mention clothing, jewelry, blankets, and other adornments befitting a free trapper's lady. [46]

It is unlikely, however, that a free trapper often had enough plews left after his fling at the cards and bottle to invest in a bride of Mountain Lamb's class, or even a Paiute slave girl. Mostly, he had to content himself with whatever temporary happiness one of the camp's light ladies might offer him. So he staggered after an Indian brave and his drab to the outer edge of the rendezvous—if, indeed, he bothered to observe even that propriety.

As it does in the case of individuals, so in the case of the whole Indian people prostitution led to a lower and lower level of degradation. The nadir was reached in the gray later days of the fur trade, when the mountain men were on their way out and the buffalo hunters, settlers, soldiers, and railroad men were surging in. Thomas Fitzpatrick, a famous guide and frontiersman known to the Indians as Bad Hand, wrote sadly in 1835:

They [the Indians] are in abject want of food half the year. . . . Their women are pinched with want and their children constantly crying with hunger. . . . Already, under pressure of such hardships they are beginning to gather around a few licensed hunters . . . acting as herdsmen, runners and interpreters, living on their bounty; while others accept the most immoral methods with their families to eke out an existence.[47]

And the Sioux chief Strike-the-Ree complained in the toneless voice of despair:

Before the soldiers came we had good health; but once the soldiers came along they go to my squaws and want to sleep with them, and the squaws being hungry will sleep with them in order to get something to eat, and will get a bad disease, and then the squaws turn to their husbands and give them the bad disease.[48]

Whatever esoteric explanations anthropologists may offer for Indian prostitution in the early days of Indian-white relations, there can be no doubt about its springs in the dark closing days of the frontier: they were want, hunger, and desperation. And in a time when a squad of soldiers or a railroad gang could buy and share a woman for a bottle of whiskey, the voice of an Indian,

Lahontan's friend Adario, comes through with pathetic pride from an earlier day:

I know some husbands among you [white men] that consent as shamefully to the debauching of their wives as some mothers do to the prostituting of their daughters, and in such cases necessity obliges 'em to it. From hence it appears that 'tis a great happiness for the Hurons that they are not reduced to the practice of such mean actions as misery occasions among those who are not inur'd to it. We are at all times neither rich nor poor, and our happiness upon this score goes far beyond all your riches; for we are not forced to expose our wives and daughters to sale, in order to live upon their drudgery in the way of love.[49]

For the Indians of North America were by no means unaware of the destructive forces—aside from the rifle—that had brought them to the depths of degradation. They knew, as Clark Wissler has pointed out: "The deadliest weapons of the white man were his disease, his demoralizing vices, particularly prostitution and liquor. The first reduced the population to a fragment, the last tended to demoralize and incapacitate the survivors." [50]

But there was no compartmenting these forces of destruction; they acted and interacted to the same dreadful end. And none—not even the grisly killer of whole tribes, smallpox—were more devastating than the venereal diseases, which were closely related, of course, to the spread of prostitution on the Indian frontiers.

Whether or not Europeans brought syphilis to the Western Hemisphere, or vice versa, has not been settled to everyone's satisfaction, but the weight of evidence supports the view that Columbus' sailors added something new and dreadful to the New World's list of evils. From the West Indies, Cortés' men carried the disease to Mexico.[51] One of the prime urges to colonize Virginia and New England, ironically enough, was a search for a cure for syphilis, and sassafras—supposedly such a cure—was raised in Virginia before tobacco. The settlers brought with them the malady for which they were seeking a remedy, and soon transmitted it to the Indians. As early as 1612, the secretary of the Virginia colony noted the shocking spread of the disease among the natives. Only eleven years after the arrival of the *Mayflower*, Roger Williams wrote of the prevalence of syphilis among the Puritans' Indian neighbors.[52]

By the time the American and Canadian fur traders had made their way across the continent, venereal diseases seem to have spread to all the tribes. Alexander Mackenzie found them common among the Cree.[53] The Orkneymen contracted them in the early days of the Hudson's Bay Company.[54] Lewis and Clark had them communicated to their men by the Chinook women, and the explorers ascertained that they were not unknown among the Shoshoni.[55] But it was Alexander Henry the Younger who, writing at Astoria, gives us the best picture of the havoc these maladies could cause in a fur trading post:

By spring I fear at least half our men will be disabled by this disease; at present few are free from it, and some are far gone. This foul malady is so prevalent among our people and the women in this quarter that it may seriously affect our commerce. When the Americans first landed here in 1800 there was but little of it among the natives; but it was soon communicated to them by the whites, who brought it not only from New York, but also from the Sandwich Islands.[56]

The ravages of a loathsome new disease among a people already beset with almost unbearable burdens were bad enough from a purely physical standpoint, but they also had a profound psychological effect on the Indians. The sight of so much destruction, *and an awareness that the whites had brought it to them*, aroused the deepest feelings of hatred and despair. And especially depressing among people who so loved children was the knowledge that miscarriages and complete sterility were a common aftermath of venereal contagion.

Liquor and vice—and particularly the vice of prostitution—were indeed the white man's deadliest weapons. Even if the colonists had not killed off whole tribes, and the frontiersmen had not hunted Indians like game, and the U.S. Cavalry had not butchered Indian women and children en masse, liquor and prostitution would, in time, have done the work of extermination.[57]

PART THREE

Lasting and Not So Lasting Unions

I

AFTER THE FASHION OF
THE COUNTRY

There was always the problem of wives.

It worried the Spanish Crown so much that as early as 1505 a law was passed ordering all married men back to Spain to "renew relations with their wives," then fetch them to the Indies. A little later, no married man, even an official of the highest rank, was allowed to go to America without his spouse. And Spaniards already there were prohibited from living in Indian towns, i.e., with Indian women.[1]

At the same time, individuals were busy with their own private plans for "ennobling New Spain," as Cortés expressed it. To induce Spaniards in Mexico to send for their wives, Cortés gave money out of his own pocket "to bring maidens, ladies, and Old Christians" from Spain.[2] One Luis de Arriaga of Seville proposed to take two hundred Biscayans and their wives to Española, and actually got together more than forty married couples for the trip.

All this was designed, of course, to discourage white men from cohabiting with native girls. But, as might have been expected, the various *cédulas* and inducements were not very effective against the forces of human nature. Oddly enough, the Spanish Crown, unlike the French and British governments, did not favor the emigration of single women to the colonies. So the excess of white men in America—while not as disproportionate as De Soto's 1,500 men to one woman—continued. De Arriaga's colony, in Las Casas' words, "did not preserve its identity and soon merged into the heap." The mixed bloods, indeed, were presently so numerous that Ferdinand, finally acknowledging the facts of life, issued an ordinance approving marriages of Spaniards with Indian women.[3]

In New France, the Jesuits made similar efforts to keep white boys and Indian girls apart, while the government brought wives across the ocean by the shipload to counteract the tendency of young men to take to the woods and live with Indian women.

In some respects, the French policy toward intermarriage was quite contradictory. Champlain favored mixed marriages, and offered a dowry of 150 francs to each French-Canadian farmer who would marry an Indian girl—with, however, few takers. The Intendant Jean Talon, while unimpressed by the Indian women's reproductive abilities, thought that ways might be found to increase their fertility, and that a mixture of blood would be a good thing for New France.[4]

But what really bothered the French officials was the enticement of the Indian girls in the wilderness beyond the settlements. And it was to keep the *habitants* down on the farm that the "bride ships" began to arrive from France. Talon ruled that no man who remained a bachelor for more than fifteen days after the arrival of one of these ships could go to hunt with the Indians (i.e., live the life of a trapper in the *pays sauvage*). This kept some youngsters at home; others married French girls as required, then left them to go native anyhow.[5]

In some ways the government's program was a spectacular success. In one of his dispatches, the Intendant pridefully reported that two captains had married French damsels, and "four ensigns are in treaty with their mistresses, and are already half engaged." As for girls of the more common sort, the ships on which they arrived were stormed by the men, and marriages were celebrated "by thirties at a time." Not only that, the women proved astonishingly fertile in the climate of New France: in 1670 Talon reported to the Minister that most of the "King's girls" sent out during the summer were already pregnant, and a year later that six hundred to seven hundred babies had been born.[6]

If there was a sour note anywhere—aside from the fact that a few of the imported brides already had husbands—the Baron de Lahontan would surely have noted it. Failing in this, he seems to have invented a bit of lurid detail, which he incorporated in the second letter of his *New Voyages to North America* under the heading: "An Account of the Transportation of Whores from France to that Country [Canada], together with a view of its Climate and Soil":

Several ships were sent hither from France with a cargo of women of ordinary reputation, under the direction of some stale old nuns, who arranged them in three classes. The vestal virgins were heaped up (if I may so speak) one above another, in three different apartments, where the bridegrooms singled out their brides, just as a butcher does an ewe from amongst a flock of sheep. In these three seraglios there was such variety and change of diet as could satisfy the most whimsical appetites; for here were some big, some little, some fair, some brown, some fat, some meager. . . . And indeed the market had such a run that, in fifteen days time, they were all disposed of. . . . After the choice was determined, the marriage was concluded on the spot, in the presence of a priest and a public notary; and the next day the Governor-General bestowed upon the married couple a bull, a cow, a hog, a sow, a cock, a hen, two barrels of salt meat, and eleven crowns.[7]

So much for Lahontan's version of the King's girls, which deserves notice only because of the historic furor it aroused in Canada and the contempt in which the baron is held, to this very day, as a malicious slanderer.

But despite all efforts of church and state, there is no record that the drain of Canadian youths to the *pays sauvage* and the arms of the Indian girls was noticeably stemmed.

The early English colonists were remarkably free from race prejudice, as the marriage of John Rolfe to Pocahontas attests. Sons of famous families in Maryland and Virginia intermarried with the daughters of Indian chiefs, and from one such union, contracted in 1684, sprang a distinguished list of descendants— including, it is claimed, two Presidents of the United States, five generals, three Governors of Virginia, and two Justices of the U.S. Supreme Court.[8]

Bitter Indian wars in New England, Virginia, and the Carolinas aroused hatreds, however, that put a stop to mixed marriages, and there arose instead a determination to kill off all the Indians. In Virginia, the government tried to solve the wife problem by importing girls. On one ship ninety young women arrived and were sold to the settlers (with their consent) for the cost of their transportation—about $500 worth of tobacco. Similar cargoes of "this interesting merchandise" continued to supply the colony, at least in part, with marriageable maidens.[9]

In the northern colonies, settlers were generally married men who brought their wives with them or—like John Alden—found brides among the daughters of colonial families. But everywhere, from the Indies to Nova Scotia, the shortage of European women was a problem for governments as well as lonely men—just as it was in our own West when, as old-timers used to say, "We married anything that got off the stagecoach or railroad."

Marriage between white men and Indian women never took place on a large scale in colonial North America. Even race mixture was comparatively light in the settlements, except in New Spain. But as soon as a Frenchman, an Englishman—or, later, an American—"took to the woods" and became a fur trader, everything changed. Then the white man invariably found himself an Indian wife.

Aside from his simple biological needs, there were many reasons why a fur trader should take a native girl to live with him during his long years in the Indian Country. Of all these reasons, perhaps the most ingenious was the one rationalized by Philip Turnor in 1779. Turnor is explaining to the London Committee of the Hudson's Bay Company why, despite the rules, governors of the Company's forts usually kept Indian mistresses. With a fine disdain for commas, or even periods, he writes:

The masters of most of Your Honors Inland settlements particularly those belonging to York Fort would Labour under many difficulties was they not to keep a woman as above half the Indians that come to the House

Daughters of the Country

Early pictures of Indian women were by artists who had never seen one. Europeans believed that blond damsels, like this one by Theodore de Bry, were true to life.

This Theodore de Bry engraving, titled "A Renaissance Gentleman in America," shows Indian girls being offered to Amerigo Vespucci and his men in 1497.

Within the portrait:

MATOAKA NS REBECCA FILIA POTENTISS PRINC POWHATANI IMP. VIRGINIÆ

Ætatis suæ 21. Aº.1616.

Matoaks als Rebecka daughter to the mighty Prince
Powhatan Emperour of Attanoughkomouck als Virginia
converted and baptized in the Christian faith, and
Wife to the wor.ll Mr Tho: Rolff.

Courtesy of the Smithsonian Institution

Dressed in the latest court fashion, Pocahontas, then twenty-one, sat for
this portrait by an unknown English artist. She died a few months later.

SAUVAGE qui alume une ALUMETTE, pour aller trouver sa MAITRESSE.

SAUVAGE en conversation avec sa MAITRESSE étant assis sur le pied de son Lit.

SAUVAGE dont la MAITRESSE se cache dans sa couverture ne voulant pas le recevoir.

SAUVAGE dont la MAITRESSE éteint L'ALUMETTE pour le recevoir.

Here the French engraver Bernard Picart depicts the Indian custom of nocturnal courtship. The girl welcomes a suitor in her parents' lodge by blowing out his light.

In this famous painting, Alfred Jacob Miller depicts the marriage of an Indian girl to a white trapper — who, incidentally, paid $600 in trade goods for his bride.

This sultry teen-age beauty, named Wild Sage, was a Wichita captive of the Osage. She was painted by George Catlin in 1834.

In this painting of a frolicsome Shoshoni maiden, Alfred Jacob Miller reflects the romantic view that lonely mountain men sometimes took of Indian girls.

The Ojibway girls, a trader said, "have pretty black eyes, which they know well how to humor in a languishing and engaging manner." Eastman Johnson drew this one.

"Indian Maid at Stockade" was Charles Russell's title for his painting of this arrogant Plains Indian girl in a scarlet blanket and barbaric finery.

Traders took very young Indian wives. This wistful little girl, Navajo Annie Dodge, would have been considered old enough for marriage *à la façon du pays*.

In Nettie Lone Wolf, this Dakota girl, we sense a dignity and strength of character that traders remarked in the women of the proud, warlike Plains tribes.

Without exception, traders and mountain men agreed about the good looks and sexual attractiveness of the southwestern Indian women—such as this glamorous Navajo girl.

Like this Navajo woman serenely spinning wool for one of her tribe's beautiful blankets, all Indian girls were schooled "in the accomplishments of a feminine life."

Photo by James W. Manson

Indian women were voluble, fond of gossip and ribald stories, laughed a lot, and like this Seri girl flashed ready smiles that bewitched lonely traders.

Photo by James W. Manson

Like this modern Seri maiden, Indian girls loved to adorn themselves with paints, baubles, and pretty clothes—and traders were not unappreciative.

Traders and mountain men were impressed by the beautiful dresses worn by Indian girls—such as this one of buckskin, beads and silver on Shirley Bones, a pretty Apache lass.

would offer the Master their Wife the refusal of which would give great
offense to both the man and his Wife though he was to make the Indian
a present for his offer the Woman would think herself slighted and if the
Master was to accept the offer he would be expected to Cloath her and
by keeping a woman it makes one short ready answer (that he has a
Woman of his own and she would be offended) and very few Indians make
that offer when they know a Master keeps a Woman . . .[10]

Less complicated was the real reason why it was almost impossible for a white man in the *pays sauvage* to do without an
Indian wife: it was a simple matter of keeping alive.

It is hard to imagine a lonelier situation than that of a fur trader
in, for example, the North West Company's vast Athabasca
Department. To reach his wintering ground, the trader had to
travel three thousand miles from Montreal by canoe; and over
this entire distance he passed not one town or even a tiny settlement, only a few trading posts lost in the unbroken wilderness.
If he was lucky, he spent the winter at one of the Company's
larger posts—Chipewyan, for instance, which was headquarters
of the Department and even boasted a library of several hundred
books. More likely, he found himself holed up for the long sub-
arctic winter in a miserable outpost, with an illiterate French-
Canadian *engagé* or two as his only company. Possibly he spent
the winter alone.

Life at such a post was summed up by a partner of the North
West Company wintering at Athabasca in 1795: "We live on fish
and flesh, to which we sometimes add a few Canadian *douceurs* by
way of sauce. We take a glass of liquor perhaps once a week; and
get drunk perhaps once in seven years. We satisfy our other
appetites according to the dictates of nature or as best suits our
conveniency." [11]

Some traders went to fantastic lengths to escape the boredom—
ennui, they called it—of such an existence. At Chipewyan, Roderic
McKenzie busied himself with the preparation of an anthropological account of all the Indians in his territory, drawing an
analogy between their customs and those of ancient peoples. At
Fort Vermilion, Mr. Hallet, "a polite, sociable man, loving his

ease passably well and desirous of living in these wild countries
as people do in civilized lands," had a large *cariole,* a type of
Canadian sleigh, built in one of his houses; but the door was
found to be too narrow to take it through, so Mr. Hallet could
never drive out in his *cariole,* as people could in civilized lands.
While at Athabasca, Peter Pond spent his time preparing a map
showing a Northwest Passage from Great Slave Lake to the Pacific,
which he planned to lay before the Empress of Russia. But mostly
traders just succumbed to a routine as deadly as their unvarying
diet of frozen fish or buffalo meat.[12]

If he did not die of boredom, a fur trader stood a good chance
of being finished off by Indians. In the Canadian bush, traders
were in constant dread of swarms of natives demanding liquor.
Fort journals abound with such entries as: "The Indians threatened to destroy us. . . . But I soon convinced them that it would
prove a tough bone for them to gnaw." Sometimes the threat was
carried out. At a fort on the Saskatchewan, three terrified traders
spiked some belligerent Indians' liquor with laudanum, killing
one of them. The Indians in turn murdered the traders and seven
half-breeds, burned the fort, and tried to stir up a general massacre
of all whites on the river. At Portage la Prairie, the Assiniboin
killed eleven traders in two forts and laid siege to a third, scalping
three of those who attempted to flee. Many other posts were
attacked and sometimes sacked. At one point, a general plan to
wipe out all white traders in the Northwest seems to have been
well advanced when the great smallpox epidemic struck the tribes
from the Assiniboin to Churchill. This ended the threat to the
traders for a while, but by the time the American mountain men
appeared on the scene, sudden death at the hands of hostiles was
again a very real and constant possibility.[13]

Some tribes, such as the Crow and Flathead, were of a naturally
friendly disposition. But others—notably the Blackfoot, Comanche, and Apache—were so implacably hostile that their country
was carefully avoided by traders on the move. Even the so-called
"friendlies" were not to be wholly trusted; it was a fortunate
trapping party that could return from a hunt without having

given up some hair to the Indians. In the year 1829 alone, Jedediah Smith lost twenty-five men to the Umpqua and Mojave.[14] And aside from such massacres, individual trappers and traders were picked off continually by hostile bands roaming the mountains in search of loot. Sometimes they simply disappeared, singly or in pairs. And then a company casualty list might note: "The fate of these men is not known, but the conclusion is hardly doubtful." [15]

In this climate of peril and loneliness, there was one thing a trader or free trapper might do to lighten his boredom and save his skin: make a "country marriage." It was, in fact, almost a routine pattern, as Colonel Dodge describes it:

Taking advantage of the intervals of peace between the tribes, and steering clear of those tribes supposed to be specially hostile to whites, they [the trappers] arrived in the country they proposed to trap and immediately separated into small parties, many going off entirely alone. Each making his way to the village of Indians most convenient to his territory in which he wished to trap, proceeded to interview the chief whose friendship and protection were gained by generous presents. After a short sojourn, other presents purchased one or more squaws and a teepee. He thus became a member of the tribe, went where he pleased within the limits of its territory, and set his traps as suited his pleasure. His squaw did all the work, made and mended his clothing, cooked his food, skinned the animals he caught, and properly cared for the pelts. Within the limits of the territory of the tribe with which he was affiliated, he was as safe from harm as any other member of it . . .[16]

Without marriage, of course, a trader could smoke a pipe of peace and exchange a pledge of friendship with the headmen of a band, but it was always a shaky pact. Marriage into the tribe made it more binding. There was no scalp insurance quite so effective as a union with the daughter of a chief. Or, for the lone free trapper who could not aspire to such social heights, just any girl would do. Kinship at all levels was a potent force in the tribes, and loyalty a mandatory virtue.[17]

Personal safety, however, was not everything; and very early in the history of the fur trade, John Lawson of Carolina rounded

out the formula with: "These men [the traders] have commonly
their Indian wives, whereby they soon learn the Indian tongue,
keep a friendship with the savages, and besides the satisfaction of
a she-bedfellow." [18]

❦

Almost as important as retention of his scalp or possession of a
"she-bedfellow" was the advantage a white man gained in trade.
Shrewd Edwin Thompson Denig, at Fort Union in 1851, made
this point in his usual down-to-earth style:

Men in charge of trading posts like to marry into prominent Indian
families . . . by such connection they increase their adherents, their
patronage is extended, and they make correspondingly larger profits.
Their Indian relatives remain loyal and trade with no other company.
They have the further advantage of being constantly informed through
their association with the former as to the demands of the trade and the
village or even the tent where they can immediately find buffalo robes
stored away.[19]

Competition for the Indians' furs was always brisk—in fact it
was often murderous. Traders were not only killed by Indians,
they were also killed by one another. Wherever Indians were to be
found in large numbers—at strategic points on lakes and rivers,
near encampment sites—rival traders were almost certain to
build posts, and they were seldom friendly competitors.

This rivalry for the Indians' trade sometimes took on political significance. It was back of the Chevalier de Troyes' raid on
the British posts on James Bay in 1686. It figured strongly in the
efforts of James Adair and Lachlan McGillivray to line up the
Creek and Cherokee against the French. It motivated John Jacob
Astor's long dash around the Horn to head off the Nor'westers on
the Columbia. In such large-scale competitive operations, a diplomatic marriage to an Indian woman could be a factor of importance. But in the deep-bush struggle of small individual post
masters to win the favor of unpredictable, often fickle, and
always potentially dangerous Indians, possession of a native

wife could make the difference between success and failure—perhaps between life and death.

On a single Canadian lake, the North West Company, the Hudson's Bay Company, and Alexander Mackenzie's XY Company—plus a few free traders—might build posts within hailing distance of one another. Sometimes the rival traders lived in amity. Henry the Younger, out of sheer loneliness, struck up a friendship with his neighbor the Hudson's Bay trader at Pembina, and at one point recorded in his journal: "Played with J. McKenzie of the H.B. Co. with drums, fife, etc. and drank out of a ten-gallon keg of brandy." In a time of Indian trouble, competing companies might even enclose their posts in a common stockade for mutual defense.

But ordinarily the competition was bitter, brutal, and sometimes sordid. "Grande Gueule and myself had a serious dispute," Henry writes at Pembina; "he wanted to give his furs to the XY, which I prevented at the risk of my life; *he was advised by them to kill me.*" On another occasion, Henry descended to fighting with the Indian women for furs that rightfully belonged to the rival XY traders. "I got all they had," he recorded in somewhat shamefaced triumph, "but was vexed at having been obliged to fight with the women." [20] So ran the course of free enterprise in the *pays sauvage*.

The technique of trading was the same at all posts. In the fall and spring, the Indian was given a credit—figured in *plus* (plews) or beaver—against the furs he would bring in at the end of his hunt. In exchange for his pelts, he received such articles of trade as twist tobacco, point-blankets, vermilion paint, Spanish beads, guns, shot and balls, brass or iron kettles, axes, knives (butcher and scalping), printed cottons, flints and steels. And rum.

Rum—commonly brought into the beaver country in the form of unadulterated alcohol called "high wine"—was the trading factor of prime importance, whether given out as a "treat" or in exchange for pelts. A band of Indians might prefer French gunpowder to English, or Northwest guns to the Hudson's Bay *fusils*, but it was the trader's rum that often determined whether or not he got their furs. His generosity with it counted for more than the quality of his trade goods. And, of course, the more liberal he was, the more uncontrollable and chaotic became the trading.

Traders dreaded and feared the drinking matches that took place at the beginning and end of each hunt. Thus Alexander Henry the Younger, describing one:

> Indians having asked for liquor, and promised to decamp and hunt well all summer, I gave them some . . . Grande Gueule stabbed Capot Rouge, Le Boeuf stabbed his young wife in the arm, Little Shell almost beat his old mother's brains out with a club . . .[21]

And of another *boisson:*

> Men and women have been drinking a match for three days and nights, during which it has been drink, fight, drink, fight—drink and fight again— guns, axes, knives their weapons—very disagreeable.

Even when they were sober, the Indians could be disagreeable— crafty, bullying customers, burdening the trader with a constant sense of personal danger. Daniel Harmon was a peaceful man, but even he was driven to violence by an Indian who, to provoke a quarrel, insisted on inspecting piece after piece of cloth for a breechclout:

> I threw down the cloth and told him, if he would not have that, he should have this, (meaning a square yardstick which I had in my hand) with which I gave him a smart blow over the head, which cut it considerably. I then sprang over the counter and pelted him for about five minutes, during which time he continually called to his companions, all of whom had knives in their hands, to come and take me off. . . . It was happy for us that these Indians stood in such fear of us; for there were only four white men, at this time in the fort, and they could easily have murdered us.[22]

Under such conditions, a trader naturally sought to smooth his way by marrying the local chief's daughter. For, besides helping to control the Indians' drinking habits, his father-in-law could offer the protection of his chief's authority. He could see to it that his Indians paid their debts, and that they turned over their furs—or at least the best ones—to his son-in-law. He could also lend a hand in dealing with unruly hunters. All this an Indian father-in-law could do for a trader. It was only necessary for the white man to take his daughter to wife—for a while.

It was not the trader alone who benefited from such an alliance. An Indian girl who married a white man was the envy of all her sisters. Even marriage to a free trapper, if we may believe Captain Bonneville, brought her undreamed-of wealth and status:

[Observe] the indulgence with which he treats her, the finery in which he decks her out, the state in which she moves, the sway she enjoys over both his purse and person; instead of being a drudge and slave of an Indian husband, obliged to carry his pack and build his lodge, and make his fire, and bear his cross humors and dry blows. No, there is no comparison in the eyes of an aspiring belle of the wilderness between a free trapper and an Indian brave.[23]

But there were exceptions. Indian girls were not always overwhelmed by the prospect of marriage to a white man. That incurable romantic Rudolph Kurz learned this the hard way. Kurz was offered an Indian bride, a girl named Anene. Anene's mother told Kurz to sit down beside her daughter, "an exceedingly young but attractive girl," and made signs meaning "this is your wife." She began to outline her terms: for herself a pony and a new woolen blanket; for Anene a complete outfit of clothes, good food, and no beatings; for her relatives a seventy-pound sack of meal. At this point, Anene's sisters came in and broke up the transaction. All the girls fled, and Kurz waited in vain for his "bride" to return.

Later on, Kurz did succeed in marrying an Iowa girl. With some pride, he describes the trousseau he bought for her. It included a short skirt of red calico, a woolen undershirt and pantalettes, a red blanket, a string of large pearl beads, and many colored bands for her hair and costume. To all this he later added wool for knitting, and smaller beads for a girdle and garters.

Having paid his price, Kurz took home his bride, whose name was Witthae, and installed her in his quarters. He insisted that she dress in the Indian style, although Witthae preferred white women's clothes. All went well, however, until midwinter, when Witthae became homesick and sent for her mother and sisters to cheer her up. Then, of course, it happened. "Imagine my astonishment," Kurz wrote in his journal, "when I found that my bird had flown." Not only had the bird flown, but she and her relatives had taken all his goods and gear with them. "This," Kurz wrote sadly, "was the end of my romantic dream of love and marriage with an Indian!" [24]

Later, he generalized that Indian women stuck with their white husbands only long enough to get all they could out of them. "They know that women are in great demand," he commented wryly. But perhaps his point of view was colored by his unfortunate personal experience of native girls.[25] He seems, at the very least, to have lacked sex appeal. Other white men fared better, some of them forming unions with Indian women that rested on mutual loyalty, fidelity, and abiding love, and lasted for life.

Nevertheless, love or no love, most Indian girls stood to benefit from marriage—even a temporary marriage—with a white man. If she became the wife of a free trapper or *coureur de bois*, her life-style might not change greatly. Often she continued to live in her native village with her husband, who was perhaps more Indian than white in his way of life. She kept his house and reared his children in the Indian manner. But there was a difference. She was now the wife of a man who, however deeply acculturated to native ways, often retained some shadow of the European's respect for women. The Bayside English, the Scottish traders in the Northwest, the American mountain men, and many French *voyageurs* all persisted in treating their women as human beings. The mountain man, in particular, delighted in tricking out his dusky girl in barbaric finery. Ignoring the jeers of the Indians— and sometimes their resentment—he refused to consider his wife a slave. Although he may have shared the white man's generalized

contempt for Indians, he nevertheless gave his own wife a sense
of human dignity that few women enjoyed in a tribal environment.

And at times he loved her fiercely.

Such a man was John ("Liver Eating") Johnson, also known as
"the Crow Killer." Johnson was an obscure mountain man,
notable only for his flaming hair, huge frame and great strength—
and a seeming lack of interest in the native women. After a year
of successful trapping, however, young Johnson married a Flathead girl known as "the Swan." As a sign of respect for her, as
well as for practical reasons, he gave her a Tennessee rifle and
taught her to shoot.

Johnson built a cabin for himself and his new wife on the Little
Snake. He provided everything for her comfort during the winter,
then rode into the Uintahs for beaver and mink. Spring came and
the Swan, heavy now with child, looked for his return. But a party
of young Crow warriors arrived first. Johnson found only some
vulture-picked bones and two skulls, one of them very small. He
buried the bones and swore an oath of vengeance against the
entire Crow nation—an oath so terrible that it became legendary
throughout the West.

What is more, Johnson carried out his oath. Alone and unaided,
mountain men asserted, he tracked down and killed Crow until
that nation of valiant warriors appointed twenty braves to destroy
him or die in the attempt. Johnson killed them all, hand to hand.
Before his terrible thirst for revenge was satisfied, he had accounted for three hundred Crow warriors—and had eaten their
livers. Aside from how much credence may be given to the "Crow
Killer" legend, it does reflect the readiness of half-savage mountain
men to acknowledge the depth and power of a white man's love for
an Indian girl. Johnson's friends understood; the Indians thought
him divinely mad.[26]

A native girl who married an important trader vastly outranked
one who became attached to a simple mountain man like John
Johnson. And often she was inordinately conscious of her lofty

position. Henry the Younger, never one to miss a bit of human comedy, noted the status struggle between the Indian mistress of Duncan McDougall, *bourgeois* of Fort George (Astoria), and the wife of an ordinary *engagé:*

Battle between Mrs. McDougall and Ignace's woman regarding the latter's children, who were playing with some trifling things, when the former lady, who is haughty and imperious, took the playthings from them and set them bawling; the consequence was a slap from the mother. Royalty was offended, and a dreadful row ensued.[27]

On Hudson Bay particularly, class distinctions were very strong; and the wife of the chief factor was the "first lady" of the post. It made no difference whether she was Indian, half-Indian, or white; she met and entertained the aristocracy of the country, presided over a gentleman's house, and reared his children to their father's station in life. As recently as 1906, a visitor to Norway House reported that if the factor's wife had been a queen, she could not have been treated with more deference or ceremony.[28]

The classic description of an Indian girl in her exalted role of a free trapper's bride is given us by Washington Irving in *The Adventures of Captain Bonneville:*

The free trapper, while a bachelor, has no greater pet than his horse; but the moment he takes a wife (a sort of brevet rank in matrimony occasionally bestowed on some Indian fair one, like the heroes of ancient chivalry in the open field), he discovers that he has a still more fanciful and capricious animal on which to lavish his expenses.

No sooner does an Indian belle experience this promotion, than all her notions at once rise and expand to the dignity of her situation, and the purse of her lover, and his credit into the bargain, are taxed to the utmost to fit her out in becoming style. The wife of a free trapper to be equipped and arrayed like any ordinary and undistinguished squaw? Perish the groveling thought! In the first place, she must have a horse for her own riding: but no jaded, sorry, earth-spirited hack, such as is sometimes assigned by an Indian husband for the transportation of his squaw and her papooses: the wife of a free trapper must have the most beautiful animal she can lay eyes on. And then, as to his decoration; headstall, breast bands, saddle and crupper are lavishly embroidered with beads, and hung with thimbles, hawks' bells, and bunches of ribbons. From each side of the saddle hangs an esquimoot, a sort of pocket, in which she bestows the residue of her trinkets and knick-nacks, which cannot be crowded on the decoration of her horse and herself. Over this she folds, with great care, a drapery of scarlet and bright-colored calicoes, and now considers the caparison of her steed complete.

As to her own person, she is still more extravagant. Her hair, esteemed beautiful in proportion to its length, is carefully plaited, and made to fall with seeming negligence over either breast. Her riding hat is stuck full of parti-colored feathers; her robe, fashioned somewhat after that of the whites, is of red, green, and sometimes gray cloth, but always of the finest texture that can be procured. Her leggings and moccasins are of the most beautiful and expensive workmanship, and fitted neatly to the foot and ankle, which with the Indian women are generally well-formed and delicate. Then as to jewelry: in the way of finger-rings, ear-rings, necklaces, and other female glories, nothing within reach of the trapper's means is omitted that can tend to impress the beholder with an idea of the lady's high estate. To finish the whole, she selects from among her blankets of various dyes one of some glowing color, and throwing it over her shoulders with a native grace, vaults into the saddle of her gay, prancing steed, and is ready to follow her mountaineer "to the last gasp of love and loyalty." [29]

This is Bonneville's own description of his own bride (as quoted by Irving), and allowing for the fancy language, it is probably an accurate depiction of the social prominence to which an Indian girl was catapulted by marriage to a white man.[30]

But only young women of the best families, Catlin says, could aspire to such an elevation and "flounce and flirt about, the envied and tinselled belles of every tribe." To which Sir George Simpson, with his customary acerbity, adds that the Indian girl was not always much elevated by the relationship.[31] She had few standards by which to judge a white man—except for his wealth of blankets, beads, and scarlet cloth—and while she might become the wife of a Kit Carson or Charles MacKenzie, she might as easily find herself shackled, in all her finery, to a depraved wretch whom she hated and despised.

But usually just about everyone, it would seem, stood to gain from a marriage *à la façon du pays*. The white man acquired personal security and the adherence of his wife's people, not to mention the convenient satisfaction of his sexual needs. The bride won riches, security, social position. And the girl's family benefited, too. Her father's relationship to a powerful *bourgeois*, if she were fortunate enough to win one, could do much to further his tribal ambitions and, for that matter, those of her brothers, uncles, and numerous other male relatives.[32]

Finally, an Indian girl, having acquired different customs and standards of family life from her *bourgeois* husband, and living on a higher economic level, attained a position of influence among her own people. She could, and often did, promote cultural changes, especially in the use of the white man's textiles, tools, and utensils, and in new arts-and-crafts techniques.[33]

In marrying an Indian girl, the trader conformed to the custom of the tribe in which he happened to find his wife. Usually, he negotiated the match with the girl's parents, paid for her, and took her home. There were, of course, exceptions to this simple procedure; but an alliance with an Indian woman was generally formed without the bothersome complications of love or ceremony.

In its most elementary form, such an alliance involved only the capture of a girl or her purchase from a white or Indian slave trader. "Good females" brought as much as $150 in New Mexico. On the prairie, Henry the Younger says, the going price was one horse for one woman. "Livernois exchanged his mare for a young wife about eight years of age," his journal records in one place; "it is common in the North West to give a horse for a woman." The price, however, could be even lower. "There are a few freemen about this place," Henry reports in another journal entry, "who have actually disposed of their women to the H.B. Co's people in barter for beat meat." Very often, such sales were made by *voyageurs* who were returning to civilization and were forced to dispose of their wives—and families—at bargain prices. But some-

times, as Franklin noted at Cumberland House, they were negotiated by fathers who sold their half-breed daughters simply for
profit:

The girls at the forts, particularly the daughters of the Canadians, are
given in marriage very young; they are frequently wives at twelve years
of age, and mothers at fourteen. Nay, more than once, instance has come
under our observation of the master of a post having permitted a voyageur
to take to wife a poor child that had scarcely attained the age of ten years.
The masters of the posts and the wintering partners of the Companies
deemed this criminal indulgence to the vices of their servants necessary
to stimulate them to exertion for the interest of their respective concerns.[34]

Thus, even in so simple a thing as obtaining a little girl for a
wife, the "purposeful pursuit of profit," in the modern managerial
phrase, was a complicating factor.

The ordinary *voyageur* or mountain man often went directly
to the Indian parents of the girl who had taken his eye and asked
for her hand. (If he were a trader or leader of a trapping party,
however, the parents would be more likely to come to him.) There
then ensued very much the same kind of negotiating that took
place among the Indians themselves. Harmon has described the
basic procedure:

Payet, one of my interpreters, has taken one of the daughters of the
Natives for a wife; and to her parents he gave in rum, dry goods, &c. to
the value of two hundred dollars. No ceremonies attend the formation
of such connections . . . excepting that the bridegroom, at the time to
retire to rest, shows his bride where their common lodging place is; and
they continue to cohabit as long as both parties choose, but no longer.[35]

This easygoing attitude toward matrimony, Harmon pauses
to remark, at least made certain that the marriage, so long as it
lasted, would be a harmonious one—something "by no means
always found in the civilized world."

Even more casual, if possible, was the American mountain
man's acquirement of a wife, as in the case of Ruxton's hero
La Bonté:

Here La Bonté married a Snake squaw, with whom he crossed the mountains and proceeded to the Platte through the Bayou Salade, where he purchased of the Yutes a commodious lodge, with the necessary poles, &c.; and being now "rich" in mules and horses, and all things necessary for *otium cum dignitate*, he took unto himself another wife, as by mountain law allowed; and thus equipped, with both his better halves attired in all the glory of fofarraw, he went his way rejoicing.[36]

But on the Plains, as in the Canadian bush, a settlement must be made with the bride's parents, and this was not always such a simple matter as La Bonté's collecting a couple of wives on his way through the Bayou Salade might imply. There was first, according to Captain Bonneville, the formal step of going to the chief of the girl's tribe, asking for her hand, and settling on the bride-price. After a couple of days, the tricked-out maiden and her parents made their appearance, accompanied by half a dozen brothers and scores of cousins, at which point it would have been embarrassing indeed for the bridegroom to suffer a change of heart. With the girl seated beside her future husband, the pipe was then passed around and smoked very silently and solemnly. The chief lectured the girl on the duties of a wife. The presents were distributed. Then the girl at once assumed the style and dignity of a free trapper's bride and took possession of his lodge as if she had been his wife for years.[37]

On the West Coast, where tribal taste ran to flamboyancy, a good deal of pomp attended the wedding of a chief's daughter to a trader. When Koale-xoa, daughter of the Chinook chief Comcomly, was espoused to the Hudson's Bay Company factor Archibald McDonald, the ceremony was performed with full tribal rites on a beach at the mouth of the Columbia. Gentlemen from Fort Vancouver appeared in formal dress. A huge concourse of natives turned out on the bride's side. The bridegroom landed from his canoe and walked down a carpet of sea-otter skins, between two lines of impassive slaves, to where the chief, resplendent in a scarlet coat and silken cravat, awaited him with the bride.[38] The ceremony itself was simple and quiet, consisting of Comcomly's placing Koale-xoa's hand in McDonald's and pronouncing a brief blessing. But the potlatch after the wedding was another story.[39]

Marriages at trading posts were sometimes followed by an offensive ritual called a charivari. This, John Long says, consisted of "assembling old pots, kettles, &c. and beating them at the doors of the new married people . . . hallowing out very vociferously, until the man is obliged to obtain their silence by pecuniary contribution, or submit to be abused with the vilest language." American mountain men, as well as Canadian *voyageurs*, indulged in this sort of fun at the expense of newlyweds. At Bent's Fort, an *engagé* named Tessou was not amused. He planted a rifle ball a quarter of an inch from the skull of one of his tormentors.[40]

Although a white man in the Indian Country ordinarily bought and paid for his wife, there were departures from this rule, as when an American free trapper raided a New Mexican settlement and carried off, in Ruxton's words, "some dark-skinned beauty— with or without her own consent." But this method of avoiding payment was more romantic than practicable; most whites were content to arrange matters on a business basis.

From the amount of bride-money paid, we can infer a good deal about the character of a marriage *à la façon du pays*. You would not expect the *engagé* who bought his bride for a couple of sledge dogs to value her highly, or that the union would last very long. On the other hand, an Indian girl sold for less than the price of a horse probably did not regard herself as bound very securely to her husband. The scant respect in which such marriages were held may be surmised from two transactions—both on the same day!—recorded by one Michel Curot, a clerk of the XY Company on Lake Superior, in 1803:

David a pris une jeune fille de 9 à 10 ans pour femme: je lui ai vendu de la marchandise. Il l'a renvoyée pour en prendre une autre plus grande; je lui ai aussi vendu de quoi habiller cette seconde.

[David took a girl of 9 or 10 years of age for a wife: I sold him the merchandise. He then exchanged her for a larger one; for which I also sold
him the clothing.] [41]

Yet a still lower condition of conjugality was described by
Dr. John Richardson (with Sir John Franklin) at Fort Cumberland in 1819: "It is not very uncommon, amongst the Canadian
voyageurs, for one woman to be common to, and maintained at
the joint expense of two men; nor for a voyageur to sell his wife,
either for a season or altogether, for a sum of money proportioned
to her beauty and other good qualities, but always inferior to the
price of a team of dogs." [42]

While a girl's age, beauty, and social position were important,
other factors helped to determine her value to a trader or trapper.
White women—when they were available, as in the Southwest—
were not much wanted. "American women are valued at a low
figure in the mountains," Ruxton says. "They are too fine and
'fofarraw.' Neither can they make moccasins, or dress skins;
nor are they so schooled to perfect obedience to their lords and
masters as to stand a 'lodge poleing,' which the western lords of
creation not infrequently deem it their bounden duty to inflict
upon their squaws for some dereliction of domestic duty." [43]

Nor did fertility add anything to a native woman's value as
a wife. "Very few men wish to have any offspring by their Indian
wives," Ross Cox says; "a sterile woman is therefore invaluable.
They are, however, scarce, and happy is the man who succeeds
in obtaining one." [44]

Indian chiefs, well aware of the trading advantage gained from
marriage to their daughters, often drove a hard bargain in their
matrimonial deals with white men. This, however, resulted in
keeping whites below the grade of partner or factor out of the
market for well-born Indian girls. "For a clerk a woman of rank
is too expensive and brings him no advantage," Kurz says, "for
the reason that he is employed at a fixed salary and receives no
further profits [from marriage to a chief's daughter]." [45]

The well-heeled *bourgeois* who really wanted a particular Indian

girl—possibly for other reasons than just a trading advantage—
was often willing to pay a fantastic price for her. At Fort Sarpy,
the same diarist who recorded the post master's infatuation for
"Meg" in such revolting terms, was equally repulsive but inform-
ative in revealing what a white man would sometimes pay for
an Indian wife:

I find this morning that Murrell [Meldrum] took to himself another wife
last night, a dirty lousy slut that was offered to me last fall. I inquired
from her mother what she had received for her and was told One horse,
one gun, one chief's coat, one N.W. blanket, one Indigo Blue blanket,
two shirts, one pair leggings, six and a half yards of bed ticking, one
hundred loads of ammunition, twenty bunches of white beads, ten large
plugs of tobacco, and some sugar, coffee & flour.[46]

Yet Meldrum was a niggard in comparison with the *bourgeois*
Duncan McDougall when he contracted marriage with one of
Chief Comcomly's daughters. From what Lewis and Clark and
other whites have told us about the Chinook ladies, Comcomly's
daughter was probably no beauty. But McDougall was dealing
with a sharp negotiator who was fully aware of his powerful
bargaining position. And the price he exacted was enough to leave
even such a hard-bitten Nor'wester as Alexander Henry the
Younger reeling:

Mr. D. McDougall this afternoon completed the payment for his wife to
Comcomly, whose daughter she was; he gave 5 new guns, and 5 blankets,
2½ feet wide, which makes 15 guns and 15 blankets, besides a great deal
of other property, as the total cost of this precious lady. This Comcomly
is a mercenary brute, destitute of decency.[47]

Among Indian women—whom mountain men considered the
champion gossipers of all creation—the bride-price fetched by a
local girl must have been the topic of much lodge chatter and
rumor. Any mother could be forgiven a few airs over a fifteen-gun,
ten-blanket daughter. And who could blame the mother of a mere
one-gun, two-blanket, six-bunches-of-beads bride for a little dis-
appointment in her son-in-law?

II

HOME IS WHERE YOU HANG
YOUR HAWKEN

This is Killbuck (à la Ruxton) boasting of the wives he has had:

From the Red River, away up north amongst the Britishers, to Heely [Gila] in the Spanish country—from old Missoura to the sea of Californy, I've trapped and hunted. . . . For twenty years I packed a squaw along. Not one, but a many. First I had a Blackfoot—the derndest slut as ever cried for fofarraw. I lodge-poled her on Colter's Creek, and made her quit. My buffer hoss, as good as four packs of beaver, I gave for old Bull Tail's daughter . . . Thar wasn't enough scarlet cloth, nor beads, nor vermilion in Sublette's packs for her. Traps wouldn't buy her all the fofarraw she wanted; and in two years I sold her to Cross-Eagle for one of Jake Hawkin's guns—this very one I hold in my hands. Then I tried the Sioux, the Shian, and a Digger from the other side, who made the best moccasins as ever *I* wore. She was the best of all, and was rubbed out by the Yutas in the Bayou Salade. Bad was the best; and after she was gone under I tried no more.[1]

The life of a mountain man's wife was obviously no round of gaiety. It was hard and hungry and cruel, and apt to terminate suddenly with a lodge-poling at her husband's hands or the thud of an arrow out of nowhere. It took, one might think, some getting used to.

Yet its impact was probably not very unsettling to an Indian girl. She was, after all, a Stone Age woman, still leading a more-or-less Stone Age existence under her husband's lodge-pole. She continued to perform the ageless tasks of women—the cooking,

196

the fashioning of clothing, the bearing of burdens, the rearing of children—in the primitive ways she had been taught.

Her husband, on the other hand, might have some rigorous adjustments to make. Every mountain man was not a primitive like Killbuck. Often he was a man of good character and background, habituated to white culture and bound by the many inhibitions placed on him by his heritage. To him some of the customs of his wife's people were disgusting. Many of their ways were contrary to everything he had been taught was right and decent. If he succeeded in adapting himself to tribal life, it was often only because "white men found it easier to sink to the level of Indian customs," as Alexander Mackenzie said, "than to raise the Indians to theirs." One simply let down the bars and allowed oneself to become "Indianized." [2]

A modern anthropologist has expressed the same idea perhaps a little more profoundly: "Man is so fundamentally a social being that when he comes into contact with strange peoples, he tends to make such adjustments as are necessary to the enjoyment of normal human relationships. It seems to be more important to a man to enjoy such relationships than to maintain the standards of his former people." [3] Which seems to have been the way that many traders and mountain men felt about it.

Human relationships, however, are notoriously careless of general principles. Just as it does in civilized society, the kind of married life an Indian girl led depended largely on the type of husband she had collected. Was he a Frenchman, an Englishman, or an American? A lowly *engagé* or a *bourgeois*? An illiterate or a man of intelligence and education. A gentleman or a natural heel?

All such personal factors—including, of course, the wife's own character—had a direct bearing on the outcome of any individual "country marriage." Yet certain broad characteristics of the marital pattern are discernible in different areas and at different periods. History had a hand in shaping the style of married life on the frontiers of the fur trade.

In the early days, an English fur hunter or a French bush ranger usually settled down with his wife in her own village or at a trading

post such as Pickawillany on the Wabash or La Pointe on Lake
Superior. The French particularly had an empathy with the Indians. They cheerfully married into the tribes, lived as the Indians
did, spoke their language, took the warpath with them, and raised
a brood of half-breed children. And this to the dismay of church
and state, who labored hard but on the whole unsuccessfully to
bring them back to white ways and white women.

The British had a reputation for ineptness in dealing with the
Indians. They were not, in truth, loved as the French were. But
they did succeed—with the help of better liquor and better trade
goods—in seducing large numbers of Indians away from the
French. And they did mix their blood generously with that of the
natives. In the Chickasaw nation in 1792, a fourth of the thousand heads of Indian families were white men, mainly English.[4]
By 1825, almost a hundred and fifty white men had married into
the eastern Cherokee nation.[5] The British traders were obviously
not complete failures at integration.

The difference seems to have been in the ease with which
French traders, trappers, and soldiers adapted to Indian life. The
British had to make an effort. The French "acculturated" naturally. The French trapper, Captain Bonneville remarked, still
"must have his Indian wife, his lodge, and his petty conveniences."
Allowing for a dash of contempt, this probably summed things up.
It was not so much that the American and British fur hunters
were less interested in the native girls; their interest was simply
less domestic.

The *coureurs de bois*, who in their freewheeling, wide-ranging
operations closely resembled the American mountain men of a
later day, were followed by the licensed traders and *engagés* who
penetrated the Far West in the 1700's. In 1739, La Vérendrye's
men were making the first white contacts with the Indian women.
By 1779, French traders had settled down with Indian wives in
the Missouri villages.

One of these, René Jesseaume, was encountered by Alexander
Henry the Younger when he visited the Mandan in 1806. Henry's
portrait of Jesseaume, while hardly flattering, gives one an idea

of the degree of acculturation that resulted when a white man married an Indian woman and lived with her people:

We found in this village a Canadian named Jussaume [*sic*], who accompanied Captains Clark and Lewis the ensuing autumn to Washington on their return from their voyage to the Pacific Ocean, as interpreter for the Mandane chief, Gros Blanc. This man has resided among the Indians for upwards of 15 years, speaks their language tolerably well, and has a wife and family who dress and live like the natives. He retains the outward appearance of a Christian, but his principles, as far as I could observe, are much worse than those of the Mandane; he is possessed of every superstition natural to those people, nor is he different in every mean, dirty trick they have acquired from intercourse with the set of scoundrels who visit these parts . . .[6]

Other white men came to live with the Mandan and married into the tribe. One of the various Menards in the fur trade was apparently the first to settle down among them. Joseph Garreau was domiciled with the Aricara in 1793. And Toussaint Charbonneau—Sacajawea's husband—began in 1795 to live with the Hidatsa.[7]

These are the earliest known Frenchmen to take up life with the Indians in the West. They were followed by many others. There is a note of pathos in Franchère's description of one of them, a former guide of the North West Company named Antoine Dejarlais: "This man was married to an Indian woman, and lived with his family on the produce of his chase; he appeared quite contented with his lot. . . . He begged me to read for him two letters which he had had in his possession for two years, and of which he did not yet know the contents." [8]

These French-Canadian freemen on the Missouri differed from the *voyageurs* who later penetrated the West. They were of the same race and temperament, but unlike the *voyageurs*, who were bound by contract to the large fur concerns, Dejarlais and his breed were completely their own men. Most of them had once been indentured *engagés*, but had broken company ties to become free trappers, guides, or interpreters. Many were half-breeds who had

simply drifted back to the life of their Indian mothers. Their number was at no time large.

Among British fur hunters, individualists of the Jesseaume-
Dejarlais type were almost unheard of. The Englishmen, Scots,
and Orkneymen who served with the Hudson's Bay people and
the North West Company were all "organization men." They
drove into the Indian Country with energy and daring, but they
did it as regular employees of the great fur trading concerns.
Many of them married Indian women, to be sure, but they did
not live as Indians in Indian villages.

There were exceptions, of course. One was Jemmy Jock. He
was a Hudson's Bay man who, having been sent to live with the
Blackfoot and learn their language, fell in love with a chief's
daughter, married her, and remained with her tribe for thirty
years. The Blackfoot, who seem to have made chiefs out of white
men rather casually, elevated him to that dignity, and he acquired
great influence in the tribe.[9] But Jemmy Jock was an almost
unique case. It was not until the American mountain man appears
on the slopes of the Rockies that we again find a considerable
number of white men "going native" in the old *coureur de bois*
style.

The natural ease with which a mountain man, having married
an Indian girl, could himself become an Indian is illustrated by
the career of "Blackfoot" John Smith. "Blackfoot," a fugitive
tailor's apprentice from St. Louis, joined a trading party on its
way up the Missouri. He wintered with the usually hostile Blackfoot—until the roots of his hair began to stir under their contem-
plative stares. Then he joined and hunted with the Sioux, and next
with the Cheyenne. He learned to speak the Cheyenne tongue
fluently, and was so well liked by the Indians that he could laugh
out loud when a Governor of New Mexico—whose pumpkin traders
he had harassed—put a five-hundred-dollar bounty on his head.
He married a Cheyenne girl and kept his own lodge in her tribe,
a paleface tailor transformed completely into an Indian warrior.[10]

More spectacular than Smith—by his own account—was James
P. Beckwourth; in fact, they did not come more spectacular than

James P. Beckwourth. He first appears in the West with General William Henry Ashley's fur brigade in 1823. For several years he played a part (although possibly not so important a part as he later recalled) in the most colorful and momentous period of discoveries and adventures the West was ever to know. Then he, too, was adopted by the Crow. Offered the choice of a chief's three pretty daughters, Beckwourth selected one named Still Water. He settled down in Absaroka, as the Crow called their mountain paradise, hunting buffalo with his Indian relatives, fighting with them against their hereditary enemies the Blackfoot and Sioux. He acquired more wives, among whom was Red Cherry. "My new wife," Beckwourth said of her in later years, "was the perfection of symmetry. Few of the Caucasian race could boast of handsomer features, and nothing but the rich olive color of her skin betrayed her Indian origin." Finally, after many warlike and amatory adventures, he "rose to be a great man" among the Crow and became a chief.[11]

Another famous "white" Crow chief was Edward Rose. He had a bad reputation on the Mississippi as a river pirate, but Colonel Leavenworth spoke of him as "a brave and enterprising man." Rose, like Smith and Beckwourth, went to live with the Indians, first the Crow, then the Aricara. In addition to collecting wives for himself, he generously supplied women to other trappers along the Missouri.[12]

The famous scout Kit Carson, who seems to have been prone to involvement with Indian women, lived with at least two of them in their native villages. The first was an Arapaho girl, Singing Wind, over whom Kit dueled with (and probably killed) a French-Canadian. The second was a conceited Cheyenne belle, Making Out Road, who piled Kit's possessions outside their lodge not long after their marriage, thus divorcing him Indian-style. Finally, he fell deeply in love with and married Maria Josefa Jaramillo, who bore him seven children.[13]

William Bent, the famous builder of Bent's Fort on the Arkansas, married Owl Woman, the daughter of a Cheyenne chief, and divided his time between her lodge and his trading post. When

Owl Woman died, he followed the Indian custom of taking her younger sister Yellow Woman to fill her place and mother his children. We shall hear more about them later.

Other celebrated mountain men (outstanding among them Old Bill Williams, a half-mythical figure who shared his lodge with a succession of Osage and Ute women) hunted, trapped, and went on the warpath with the braves into whose tribe they had married. And hundreds more, with names unknown even in their own time, followed their example.

But despite the advantages, life in an Indian village sometimes so palled on a white man that he was quite willing to give up his wife and children in order to escape it. Such a case was described by the North West Company trader John Thomson, wintering at Rivière Rouge in 1798:

In the evening Vivier with all his family arrived; gave him a dram. I asked him what he meant by leaving the Indians. He says he cannot live with them any longer, and that all the devils in Hell cannot make him return. . . . He has made an offer of his wife and child to Demarrais who will take his place, but cannot get Madam to consent.[14]

In any case, white men in the fur country could not always settle down in an Indian village, even for a single trapping season. Many were forced to be forever on the move, either alone or in large trapping parties.

Under these circumstances, one could leave one's wife at home, as a sailor did when he went to sea or a soldier to the wars. The French traders who lived with their Indian wives in such settlements as La Pointe, La Baye, St. Joseph, and St. Ignace, did this regularly when they loaded up their trade canoes and pushed off for the *pays sauvage*. Later on, the *voyageurs* of the North West Company cached their wives at the big trading posts while they made the annual dash from their wintering stations to Rainy Lake Fort or Grand Portage. At Fort Cumberland, where both fish and wild rice were abundant, there was a big, and no doubt lively, gathering of wives and children of the *voyageurs* every spring.[15]

For the wife of a free trapper on the move, remaining behind in a mountain cabin her husband had built for her was not the best of arrangements. Charles Larpenteur, whose Indian wife and children stayed at home while he went into the mountains, recalled in his memoirs the uneasiness that must have hung over every mountain man—and then the tragic realization of his fears: "In September [of 1852] the news came that all of my children had died. I did not think this possible—some might have died, but not all." The Sioux later murdered his wife before his eyes.

Another way of solving the problem was to take one's wife, and even one's family, along. This was not always feasible, but in a surprisingly large number of cases it was done. Even the rather staid licensed French traders found a place in their canoes for their wives. One of them, Madeleine Framboise, a Chippewa woman, continued her husband's trading ventures after his death, and so successfully that she was able to send her daughter to school in Montreal. This daughter, incidentally, married the brother of President Franklin Pierce, thus gaining entree to the White House as well as the lodges of her mother's people.[16]

Large trading parties were commonly accompanied by the wives of French *voyageurs*. Thus, when Jean-Baptiste and Michel Cadotte led an expedition from Sault Ste. Marie in 1792, the sixty *voyageurs*, trappers, and a few Iroquois Indians comprising the party took along a large number of women. Michel Cadotte's widow recalled years later that "she and many other women of the party were left to winter at Fond du Lac, as their husbands were going into a dangerous region, and did not wish to be encumbered with women." As if the western tip of Lake Superior were the safest of havens in the year 1792![17]

Many years later, on their long journeys to and from their wintering stations, the Nor'westers found room in each canoe for a woman to do the cooking, mend gear, and otherwise make herself useful around the camp and on the portages. On a trip from Lake Superior to Fort Vermilion, each of Alexander Henry the Younger's eleven canoes was "manned by five men and one woman."

When, in the old French fashion, the Hudson's Bay Company

met the competition of the American mountain men with brigades
of trappers, the tradition of including women in such expeditions
was revived. Most of the men were French-Canadians; all of their
wives were Indian or half-breed women. It was John McLoughlin's policy to send the women with his trapping brigades "to act
as a restraint on the wilder spirits." [18]

These expeditions, sometimes afield for a year or two, resembled
one of those disorderly Indian tribal treks after the buffalo. In
Ogden's 1824–25 Snake-country expedition, the party out of Fort
Vancouver consisted of ten company *engagés*, fifty-three freemen,
thirty women, plus an unspecified number of Indian trappers. The
women, according to Ogden, played "a full and active part" in
skinning and dressing beaver, pitching and striking camp, cooking
food, and packing loads. But they also contributed a good deal
of turmoil and trouble.

The journal of William Kittson, a member of the party, is full of
painful instances: a Nez Perce kills his wife and then himself,
whereupon the supposedly dead wife comes to life; the expedition
is held up by sick women; children are frost-bitten; an Iroquois
is shot by his wife. Ogden himself adds to the roster of women
troubles: "Obichou's woman was delivered of a female child, in
consequence of her indisposition we had to stop in the rear." He
sends men in search of an Indian woman who had been sick for
some time and to his own knowledge hadn't eaten for eleven days;
she is found and returned to camp. Another woman and three
horses are missing, and Ogden suspects that she and the horses
have been stolen by the Snake Indians; but both are found. Yet,
in spite of all the delays and alarms, Ogden wrote, "It is a pleasure
to observe the ladies of the camp vieing with each other who will
produce the cleanest, best dressed beavers." [19]

Another Hudson's Bay Company trapping expedition was the
motley Snake-country brigade led by Alexander Ross from Flathead House in the winter of 1824. It consisted of Indians from
no fewer than a dozen different tribes, two Americans, seventeen
Canadians, five half-breeds, plus twenty-five women and sixty-four
children. It was a rough, unruly gang of savages, and one may

surmise that its female complement was not entirely out of place in such company.[20]

Some of the Canadian parties, however, drew the line at women fellow travelers. Finan McDonald's brigade, which joined Ogden's 1825 expedition, consisted of twenty-two *engagés*, two freemen, and four Indians, but "not one woman was allowed to accompany the party."

American trading expeditions sometimes included a woman or two. Captain J. C. Frémont, in his "Report of the Exploring Expedition to the Rocky Mountains," has left us this idyllic sketch of a camp of free trappers with their Indian families:

Seven miles further brought us to a camp of four or five whites (New Englanders, I believe), who had accompanied Captain Wyeth to the Columbia River, and were independent trappers. All had their squaws with them, and I was really surprised at the number of little fat buffalo-fed boys that were tumbling about the camp, all apparently of the same age, about three or four years old.[21]

When Jedediah Smith set out for San Francisco Bay in July, 1827, his party comprised eighteen men and two women (of whom ten of the men were killed by Indians and both of the women taken prisoner).[22] Ruxton observed two squaws tending the kettles in a camp of trappers on the Bijou in 1847. And "Uncle Dick" Wootton wrote that on one of his trips, two of his men were accompanied by their wives (Calvin Briggs and John Burroughs, whose wives were Shoshoni sisters); later, he added, all four went to California and got rich. The trader John Work's Nez Perce wife, Josette Legace, noted for her beauty and strength of character, scorned the safety of her husband's fort and marched with him at the head of his brigade. But despite such occasional instances, it is only rarely that the presence of women in an American trapping party is recorded.

Possibly the idea of attaching women and children to American brigades arose when, at Rendezvous 1825, a score or more deserters from the Hudson's Bay Company joined Ashley's men with their

women and children; for after that, Ashley's supplies began to
include combs, earrings, ribbons, sewing silk, and other feminine
articles.[23] But, while we know that the mountain men were beginning to acquire permanent wives, it is uncertain how many of them
accompanied their husbands on trapping expeditions. Ordinarily,
they seem to have been left behind.

Traders who traveled about a good deal sometimes kept a string
of wives along their customary routes of travel. This was the course
adopted by Michel Framboise, a celebrated French-Canadian
employed by John McLoughlin at Fort Vancouver. He was said
to have had a wife in practically every tribe along the Oregon
coast, an arrangement that not only provided him with the comforts of home at every stop, but acted powerfully to preserve his
hair in hostile territory.[24]

It was a famous governor of the Hudson's Bay Company, however, who made history in this respect. So enterprising was this
officer of the Honourable Company that, in his incessant jour-
neying through the fur country, he finally ran out of names for the
offspring he sired along the way. He is said to have had two daughters named Maria by different mothers, two sons named George
by different mothers, and two sons named James by different
mothers. It is not for nothing that his name is to this day a legend
in the Canadian bush.[25]

Indian women also accompanied the more formal expeditions of
discovery and exploration, many of which were led by fur traders.
On Alexander Mackenzie's journey to the Arctic Ocean in 1789,
two wives of his guide, "the English Chief," were taken along to
make moccasins.[26] Samuel Hearne, on his second attempt at
reaching the Arctic Ocean from Fort Prince of Wales, was less
well advised. Relying on Governor Norton's counsel, he set out
without a woman in his party.

"To avoid all encumbrances as much as possible," he explained,
"it was thought advisable not to take any women, that the
Indians might have fewer to provide for." He couldn't have been

more mistaken. Within a few months he was back at the fort in a sorry state, and quite ready to accept the Indian guide Matonab-bee's advice: "Next time, take some women with you." Matonab-bee, Hearne said, "attributed all our misfortunes . . . to the very plan we pursued, by the desire of the governor, in not taking any woman with us on this journey." [27] Hearne's next expedition was well supplied with woman-power. He reached the Coppermine River and the Arctic Ocean—where his Indians, incidentally, fell upon an encampment of sleeping Eskimo and murdered them all. Even the women this time; for Hearne tells of a writhing Eskimo girl, pierced by two Indian spears, clutching at his feet, and his Indians jeering at him while he begged them to kill her quickly.

From the earliest days of North American exploration, Indian women played a useful role as guides, interpreters, and peace-makers. Cabeza de Vaca was often succored and directed in his long wanderings by the women of the southwestern tribes.[28] La Vérendrye's search for the Western Sea was shared by Indian women who cooked, sewed, and carried for his men. One of Mackenzie's canoes on his Arctic Ocean trip was actually managed by a woman. David Thompson's wife Charlotte went with him on his hazardous quests for a pass through the Rockies and a portage to the Columbia.[29] Lewis and Clark, of course, had their Sacajawea.

But leaders of expeditions did not always bother to mention the wives of Indians in their parties, however useful they may have been. There were many, no doubt, whose names and deeds will never be known.[30] But in the dim background of American history the Indian woman with her deft fingers, quick intelligence and stout heart—and, one must add, her strong back—contributed not a little to the conquest of the wilderness. And she deserves to be remembered.

III

"EVERYONE ENTERED AND SETTLED"

In an Indian village, or even on the march with a trapping party, a white man and his Indian wife could raise children and lead something vaguely resembling family life. But it was much more usual to set up housekeeping at a trading post; and it is here that we may observe marriage *à la façon du pays* in its more typical aspects.

Trading posts were scattered by the hundreds over the continental wilderness. They were to be found hidden away on nameless lakes and sourceless rivers from the Arkansas to the Peace, from the Pacific to Hudson Bay. They rose, flourished, were abandoned, fell into ruins, were forgotten.

But each in its time was "home" to traders and their native wives and children, or perhaps to only a single couple. They were focal points which drew white men and Indians together—sometimes in great numbers—for trade. They also brought lonely trappers and traders into contact with the women of the tribes, often under circumstances (such as the riotous fort dances) highly conducive to intimate relationships. So the trading post was frequently the scene of a "country marriage"; and within its stockade, white men and their dusky brides settled down and proceeded to raise a family under approximately normal domestic conditions.

To understand the wilderness way of family life, it is necessary to know something about the nature of the fur trading posts that were home to so many white men and their Indian wives.

A few were impressive establishments by any standard. Fort

Prince of Wales, the Hudson's Bay Company post at the mouth of the Churchill River, had stone walls forty feet thick, and was defended by forty-two guns. It required more than thirty years to build, but Lapérouse, appearing suddenly with three French ships at the mouth of the river, took it in a few hours. He burned what he could, but the massive masonry walls still stand on the Bay, a monument to the vast importance of the fur trade at one stage of North American history.

On the whole continent, however, there was not another Fort Prince of Wales: it was unique in its size, strength, and fatuity. But other posts of a more practical design were almost as impressive. Fort William, for example. Fort William was the headquarters post of the North West Company on Lake Superior. Gabriel Franchère stopped there in 1814, on his way back to Montreal from the Columbia, and he was much impressed by what he saw:

Fort William has really the appearance of a fort, with its palisades fifteen feet high, and that of a pretty village from the number of edifices it encloses. In the middle of a spacious square rises a large building elegantly constructed, though of wood, with a long piazza or portico, raised about five feet from the ground and surmounted by a balcony extending along the whole front. In the center is a saloon or hall, sixty feet in length by thirty in width, decorated with several pieces of painting and some portraits of the leading partners. It is in this hall that agents, partners, clerks, interpreters, and guides, take their meals together at different tables. . . . On either side of this edifice is another of the same extent, but of less elevation; they are each divided by a corridor running through its length, and contain each a dozen pretty bed-rooms . . .[1]

In addition to these quarters for the elite, with their "pretty bed-rooms," Fort William had two "bachelor halls," a warehouse where furs were inspected and repacked, lodginghouses for the guides, another warehouse, a powder magazine, stores and workshops, canoeyards, a countinghouse, shops for the fort's various artisans, a house for its physician (at one time Dr. John McLoughlin), the *cantine salope*, and a jail. Add to all this the surrounding fields of barley, peas, and oats, the burying ground, a village of superannuated *voyageurs*, a wharf at which the Company's schooners from Sault Ste. Marie docked, and during the summer "a great encampment" of canoemen outside the walls, and you have an idea of the milieu in which an Indian girl—who had never known anything grander than her native village of smoky bark lodges—found herself as the wife of a Nor'wester at Fort William.

Just as imposing, and perhaps even more colorful, was that most famous of all American trading posts, Bent's Fort on the Arkansas. A great mud castle, with walls of sun-baked adobe brick rising fourteen feet above the plain, it enclosed a bewildering jumble of one- and two-story adobe buildings, including warehouses, a dining hall, shops, trading rooms, apartments for two hundred men and their Indian wives, even a billiard room. Bent's Fort, it has been said, was probably the most imposing work of man between the Mississippi and the Rio Grande.

Its Spanish-type *placita* and roof-top promenade were thronged with women, the Indian and half-breed wives of mountain men, Mexican *señoritas*, ransomed Comanche captives, an occasional white woman from the East. Here the "greenhorn" from New England gazed with an awed excitement at the Indian girls "tripping around the battlements in their glittering moccasins" and snowy deerskin shifts. Here a Cheyenne wife found herself plumped from her neolithic world into a never-never land that passed for civilization on the Indian frontier. And there was a lot that neither she nor the young New Englander could ever understand at Bent's famous fort.[2]

But not many fur trading posts were on the impressive order of Fort William or Bent's. Many a wintering station was no more than a log hut, a flimsy stockade, and perhaps a token warehouse, thrown together hastily in the face of danger and abandoned when the beaver—or the trader—gave out. Travelers seldom troubled to describe such posts, but Paul Kane did take disgusted note of Jasper House, one of the Hudson's Bay Company's less imposing stations, in the winter of 1846:

Jasper's House consists of three miserable log huts. The dwelling house is composed of two rooms, of about fourteen or fifteen feet square. One of them is used by all comers and goers: Indians, voyageurs, traders, men, women, and children being huddled together indiscriminately; the other room is devoted to the exclusive occupation of Collin [the trader] and his family, consisting of a Cree squaw and nine interesting half-breed children. One of the other huts is used for storing provisions in, when they can get any, and the other I would have thought a dog kennel had I seen any of the canine species about.[3]

Jasper House had its counterpart in many a tumbledown clutch of adobe huts on the sun-baked plains, but neither such miserable hovels nor the great establishments were typical of the posts in which most fur traders and their families made a home of sorts and raised a family.

Somewhere between Jasper House and Bent's Fort, there were hundreds of trading posts, neither very large nor very small, scattered from Hudson Bay to the Pacific. In them a trader and perhaps a score of men spent their lives. All of the men had their Indian wives; and these primitive women found life a little strange, perhaps, in the tight little enclaves of white civilization.

Fort Alexandria, a North West Company establishment on the Assiniboin River, was such a post. Young Daniel Harmon, less than a year up from Montreal, seemed pleased with it when he arrived there in the fall of 1800. Probably assuming that everyone knew what a fur trading post looked like, he wastes few words in describing it:

The fort is built on a small rise of ground, on the bank of the Assiniboine, or Upper Red River, that separates it from a beautiful prairie, about ten miles long and from one to four broad, which is as level as the floor of a house. At a little distance behind the fort, are small groves of birch, aspin, and pine. On the whole, the scenery around it is delightful. The fort is sixteen rods in length, by twelve in breadth; the houses, stores, &c. are well built, are plastered on the inside and outside, and are washed over with a white earth, which answers nearly as well as lime for white washing.[4]

The buildings, which consisted of the usual log dwelling houses, Indian Hall, warehouses, and shops, were arranged to form a hollow square, with their backs against the encircling stockade.

Bastions flanked the walls against Indian attack, and a blockhouse over the double gate further strengthened the post's defenses.

There was so much coming and going at Fort Alexandria, so many field trips and visits to other posts, that it is difficult to determine the exact number of families living there. Harmon says in the summer of 1803, "We now have thirty people in the fort." But Alexander Henry the Younger gives the population in 1805 as fifty-six men, fifty-two women, and eighty-two children.[5]

From Henry, too, we get a good idea of the housing arrangements at a typical North West Company trading post, in this case Fort Vermilion, on the Saskatchewan. In 1809, Henry arrived at Fort Vermilion to find it encircled by three hundred Blackfoot lodges. The Blackfoot were followed by large bands of Cree and Assiniboin, and Henry was busy for a month taking care of the trade and the colossal thirst the Indians had worked up during his absence at Fort William.

He then turned to the business of putting his post in order, and on October 20th was able to write in his fort journal: "My men finished repairing their houses, and this evening everyone was entered and settled." Then follows a roster of the fort's personnel which, because it gives such a clear idea of how the traders and their wives were housed, is worth printing in full:

HOUSE NO. 1

1. Parteneau	1 Man	1 Woman	5 Children	
2. Perain	1 "	1 "	1 Child	
3. Clement	1 "	1 "	2 Children	
4. Dubois	1 "	1 "	1 Child	17 Persons

HOUSE NO. 2

5. Cardinal	1 Man	1 Woman	5 Children	
6. Ladoucer	1 "	1 "		
7. Ottawa	1 "	1 "	3 "	
8. Pichette	1 "			15 Persons

HOUSE NO. 3

9. Crevier	1 Man	1 Woman	1 Child	
10. Thibault	1 "	1 "	1 "	
11. Dumont	2 Men	1 "	4 Children	
12. La Jeunesse	1 Man			14 Persons

HOUSE NO. 4
13. Guillon	1 Man	1 Woman	
14. Durand	1 "	1 "	1 Child
15. Carriere	1 "	1 "	2 Children
16. Martelle	1 "	1 "	4 "
17. Le Blanc's wife		1 "	2 "	18 Persons

HOUSE NO. 5
18. Faille	1 Man	1 Woman	4 Children
19. La Pierre	1 "	1 "	3 "
20. 21. Jussier	2 Men	1 "	1 Child
22. Gagnon	1 Man	1 "		17 Persons

HOUSE NO. 6
23. Parisien	1 Man	1 Woman	6 Children
24. Languedoc	1 "	1 "	1 Child
25. Croite	1 "	1 "	1 "
26. Beauvois	1 "			15 Persons

HOUSE NO. 7
27. Jerome	1 Man		4 Children
28. Rocque	1 "	1 Woman	1 Child
29. Rehelle	1 "		
30. Flemming	1 "			10 Persons

HOUSE NO. 8
31. Mr. Hamel	1 Man			1 Person

HOUSE NO. 9
32. Mr. Small	1 Man			1 Person

HOUSE NO. 10
33. Self [Henry]	1 Man	1 Woman	3 Children	5 Persons

TENT
34. F. Deschamps	1 Man	1 Woman	4 Children	
35. F. Deschamps, Jr.	1 "	1 "	1 Child	9 Persons

TENT
36. Martin	1 Man	1 Woman	6 Children	8 Persons
TOTALS	36	27	67	130 Persons

Twice, it will be noted, two men and a single woman are listed as one household. Several of Henry's men seem to have had no women; and one of them (Jerome) had four children but no wife, while "Le Blanc's wife" is listed with two children but no husband.[6]

By "house" Henry may mean a separate cabin, each in this case occupied by several families; or he may mean merely a partitioned-off space in a long building, perhaps occupying an entire side of the post. Ground plans for trading posts show that both arrangements were common. The *bourgeois*, however, as well as his clerks and interpreters, usually enjoyed the privacy of a separate cabin.

At Fort Union, at the forks of the Missouri and the Yellowstone, a building seventy-eight feet long and twenty-four wide extended along one side of the stockade. It had windows and a deep porch, and may have supplemented the men's bunkhouse as living quarters for married post personnel.[7] Fort Pierre, in what is now South Dakota, had a long building inside the enclosure, designated on Maximilian's drawing of the fort as "residences of clerks, interpreters, *engagés*, and their families." [8] And Parkman describes an "apartment block" of this type at adobe Fort Laramie:

Our arrangements made, we stepped out to the balcony to take a more leisurely survey of the long-looked-for haven at which we had arrived at last. Beneath us was a square area surrounded by little rooms, or rather cells, which opened upon it. These were devoted to various purposes, but served chiefly for the accommodation of the men employed at the fort, or the equally numerous squaws whom they were allowed to maintain in it . . .[9]

At a later, more effete period, toward the middle of the century, the evidence is that the families of *engagés* lived in their own separate cabins. This was probably true at Fort Vancouver, and Paul Kane says of Fort Edmonton, "All the Company's servants, with their wives and children, numbering about 130, live within the palings of the fort in comfortable log-houses, supplied with abundance of firewood." [10] At Fort William, retired *voyageurs* were similarly housed.

The irascible James McKenzie, master of Fort Chipewyan, gives us this picture of living arrangements and social life at one of his outposts:

In Labrie's house there are 5 men, a woman, and 3 children, in *La Becasse's* house there are 3 men and 3 women, and in *L'Espagnol's* house there are 2 men 2 women . . . They seem to owe a grudge to each other in the different houses; they never pay a visit to one another, and if their affairs oblige them sometimes to exchange a few words with one another, it must be without the doors.[11]

Even when, as at Fort Vermilion, each family enjoyed the luxury of separate bedrooms, sleeping arrangements in the fur country afforded precious little nocturnal privacy. It was customary for families, no matter how large, to sleep on the floor side by side, under shared blankets and robes. At best, this did not conceal much that went on during the night from all members of the family; and a communal bedchamber, occupied by as many as eighteen sleepers of both sexes and all ages, must have seemed a bit public even to a girl accustomed to the intimacy of an Indian lodge.

As in an Indian encampment, the children of a fur trading post learned the raw facts of life at a very early age. At Cumberland House, Franklin observed the effects of overcrowding and wholesale mingling of the sexes at night, and was not very encouraged by the moral outlook. The Orkneymen's children seemed to him a little less depraved than those of the *voyageurs*, "but all the good that can be said of the latter," he concludes, "is that they are not quite so licentious as their fathers are." The girls, he adds, were so inflamed by what they saw and heard on every hand that "they very early give up all pretentions to chastity." [12]

But Father Nicolas Point, speaking of the half-breed girls in Westport, the staging point for trading and trapping expeditions to the Missouri and the Rockies, has this to say: "The fact is that among the twenty-three families in that community, there was not a single girl of immoral character." Which, he says, was "an admirable thing in a country where dissolute men are common." [13]

Among the advantages supposedly gained by an Indian girl from marriage to a white man was the luxury of living in a tight,

weatherproof house, with a roof overhead and a floor underfoot.
But a leather tipi or bark-and-rush lodge, however cold and smoky,
could hardly have been more uncomfortable than a house built
of logs or adobe bricks.[14]

From Isham Jones's account of life at well-built York Fort, we
get an idea of what a Canadian winter in a log house was like:

> In 4 or 5 hours after the fire is out . . . the inside of the wall of our houses
> are 6 to 8 inches thick with Ice, which is Every Day cutt away with
> Hatchetts,—three or 4 times of a Day we make Iron shott of 24 lb. weight
> hott in the fire, and hang up at the windows of our apartments, yet will
> not hinder a 2 Gallon Bottle of water freezing by the fire side . . .[15]

The cold on the open plains of North Dakota and Montana, or
even in the densely wooded Interior, could hardly have been much
less ferocious; for astounding amounts of firewood were required
to keep the rude fireplaces going. At his small Park River post in
northern Minnesota, Henry the Younger estimated that 120 cords
of oak "would suffice" for four fireplaces, "since we shall leave
early in the spring."

In the heavy winter air, chimneys often smoked so insufferably
as to drive people out of their houses, and even out of the post
enclosure. Sometimes, like Henry's, they collapsed: "At daybreak
I heard a crash in my kitchen, and found the chimney had fallen
from top to bottom; it was lying on the floor and the fire blazing
on . . ."[16]

All in all, a Flying Crane or Morning Moon, shivering through
the night in a trader's drafty cabin, might well have longed for
her father's lodge, where she could lie in her warm buffalo robes
and watch the firelight flicker on the tipi walls.

The wife of a *bourgeois* lived far more comfortably, of course,
than the mate of a common *engagé*. She had a whole house to herself, and naturally the finest in the post. It usually consisted of a
living-sleeping room and a kitchen, and it boasted at least a few
pieces of furniture—a table, bed, some chests perhaps, which
served for storage and as seats. In some of the big posts, indeed,
a *bourgeois*'s wife might be chatelaine of an almost luxurious

ménage, with servants and nursemaids to help her keep house, rear the children, and entertain distinguished guests. Such was her position, for example, at York Fort on Hudson Bay. In the key American trading posts, the *bourgeois*'s house was the most pretentious building on the post; and its mistress, whether white or Indian, enjoyed every luxury the establishment could offer. At Fort Vancouver, Dr. John McLoughlin's house was a comfortable French-Canadian cottage, weather-boarded and painted white; vines grew around the piazza, and two flights of stairs led up to the front door.[17]

Even the wife of a trader in charge of a small post was several cuts above the girl of an ordinary *engagé*. She, too, lived in her own house at least, and was accorded the respect due the wife of any *bourgeois*.[18]

Given half a chance, the Indian girl probably made a good home for her white husband. From earliest childhood, she was schooled in the household tasks she would be called on to perform as a woman. She was also trained, as Frances Densmore charmingly puts it, in "the accomplishments of a feminine life." From her mother she learned how to be a good housekeeper, whether in a lodge or a trader's cabin, and how to make her husband comfortable and happy. Jeanny, the Cree wife of the Hudson's Bay trader John Sutherland, was one such example.

The Nor'wester Archibald Norman McLeod did not relish what he called, in curiously modern idiom, "the super-stupid conversation" of his neighbor Sutherland. But he did find the company of Sutherland's wife Jeanny very agreeable. "I slept at Mr. Sutherland's," he says at one point in his fort journal, "and had the honor of playing cribbage with Jeanny, his wife." And young Daniel Harmon, homesick for his family in Vermont, was also fond of visiting Jeanny. "I was pleased to find she could speak the English language tolerably well," he wrote of her. "She appears to possess natural good sense, and is far from being deficient in acquired knowledge." [19]

In feeding her man, an Indian wife had little new to learn. The food was what the country afforded—to Indian and white man alike. And the techniques of preparing it did not differ much between Indian village and trading post.

Meals in a fur trading post were eaten twice a day, as was the Indian custom. The men, at least those above the rank of *engagé*, seem never to have eaten with the women and children. So rarely did a wife sit at table with her husband, that John Henry Le Froy, at Fort Simpson in 1844, took special note of such an instance as "the first time in which I have seen a woman at table." [20] This segregation, of course, was also an Indian custom, and one to which a trader's wife conformed naturally.

The *engagés* were routed out at daybreak to perform their assigned tasks, and at midmorning were given breakfast by the *bourgeois* at a common mess. In some posts the men may also have eaten dinner together and apart from their families. But where rations were issued to each family individually, as at Fort Vancouver, the wife probably prepared the evening meal for her husband and children in the family living quarters. Although the pattern was basically the same everywhere, eating customs varied in accordance with the character and activities of individual posts.

At Fort William, for example, where a great many transient *voyageurs* congregated each summer, the high-ranking traders, from agents down to guides, dined very well indeed. They feasted in the great dining hall on bread, salt pork, beef, smoked ham, whitefish, venison, butter, peas, Indian corn puddings, potatoes, tea, brandy, and wine—and even milk supplied by the post's two milch cows. In their tent encampment outside the palisades, on the other hand, the ordinary canoemen had to be content with a mess of boiled Indian corn and tallow.

The standing rules and regulations of the Hudson's Bay Company prohibited guides and interpreters, let alone common "laborers," from eating with the "Commissioned Gentlemen and Clerks" in charge of the posts. Officers of the key posts made an elaborate show of observing the amenities of civilized living;

wine was served and toasts drunk, even when the post was on starvation rations.[21]

American mountain men, like their Canadian fellow traders and trappers, subsisted on monotonous and often scanty fare when deep in the fur country. But on the Missouri and its tributaries, with steamboats and wagon trains to bring in supplies, traders enjoyed a style of dining that fur hunters in their lonely mountain camps or Indian villages had almost forgotten. When Rudolph Kurz dined with Denig at Fort Union, he seems to have been quite overcome with the sumptuousness of the post's board:

A bell summoned me to the first table with Mr. Denig and the clerks [lower ranks apparently ate at later messes]. My eyes almost ran over with tears! There was chocolate, milk, butter, omelet, fresh meat, hot bread—what a magnificent spread! [22]

The part played by women in the preparation of meals for hungry trappers, traders, and canoemen in the larger posts is not altogether clear. The *pays sauvage* had a way of imposing its stamp on white patterns of living; and no tribal law was more inviolable than the one interdicting men from the performance of domestic tasks. One would assume, therefore, that in most posts the wives of the *engagés* did the cooking. There is, however, James McKenzie's unusually ebullient account of his post's preparations for New Year's Day, in which the men appear to have taken over the kitchen:

Great preparations going on here this night for tomorrow, which is New Year's Day. Dusablon, with hands which have not seen a drop of water since last New Year's Day, made a kettle full of *boulettes* of fish, each as big and as ill-shaped as his own head. Lambert made fish cakes, *alias* "*pétes*," boiled for an hour with dried meat. *Masquaro* made the fire, drew water and cleaned shoes, &c. Mr. Wentzel and I were continually running from the shop to the *hangard*, from the *hangard* to the garret, and thence to the kitchen; in short, every body in the house had a finger in the pie and were as busy all night as *une queue de veau*.[23]

But one suspects that the exuberant *engagés* at Fort Chipewyan were merely showing off on a grand occasion, and were glad to relinquish the routine preparation of meals to the women. In the Indian Country it would have been odd indeed if men were drafted for what was so obviously a woman's work.

It was not light work, even for an Indian woman. The cooking itself was simple. How many ways can you serve whitefish, without even a seasoning of salt? Or buffalo meat, day after day, without bread or vegetables? Yet in many a trading post the fare was that unvaried. At Fort Alexandria, a prairie establishment, the unchanging diet was one of buffalo, boiled, roasted, or as pemmican. In the forest belt, moose meat and venison took the place of hump rib and back fat. Sometimes fish was the sole food throughout the winter, sometimes rabbits.

Flour in small quantities and perhaps a little sugar were usually available, but they were very special treats, doled out with a few gills of rum as a *régale* on festive occasions. At the Hudson's Bay posts, the flour was made into little cakes of exactly uniform size, one of which was placed beside each gentleman's plate at dinner. The Nor'westers shaped the unleavened dough into *galettes*, small loaves baked in the ashes. At a few posts, such as Bas de la Rivière, wild rice was plentiful. And many of the older posts had kitchen gardens and potato patches, which yielded a sometimes astonishing harvest of vegetables and greens. Even on the unfriendly shores of Hudson Bay, such gardens were hopefully planted.[24]

In addition, the *bourgeois* and clerks received an allowance, according to rank, of tea, coffee, chocolate, brandy, and wine. But such luxuries did not last long, and most posts soon settled down to a straight diet of flesh or fish. It became a little monotonous by the end of a long winter. Angus Shaw wrote to Roderic McKenzie from Lac d'Orignal in 1789:

I arise with the sun and, after *debarlouilling mon visage*, I take a walk to my traps, return to the house and eat *Tollibees* [whitefish] (2) about nine; then take another walk or work all day at something or other. About 7 p.m., I again eat *tollibee* boiled or roasted and pass the rest of the evening in reading and writing. . . . Indeed, my dear man, I find time very long . . .[25]

Even the usually uncomplaining *voyageur* had eaten enough fish by spring, and moaned, *"Toujours le poisson!"*

But what was lacking in variety was made up in quantity, and even though she cooked only for her own family, a fur trader's wife must have been a very busy person at mealtime. Prodigious amounts of food were required to sustain a man in the fur country. At the prairie posts, eight pounds of buffalo meat was the daily ration; in the northern departments, two whole geese were no more than a meal for a single diner. An isolated trader and his family, plus a man or two, could put away thirty or forty rabbits a day, or as many whitefish of from four to six pounds each. Harmon's people in British Columbia each consumed four large salmon daily; elsewhere eight whitefish a person was the usual ration.

In the aggregate, the amount of flesh or fish required to provision even a small trading post was staggering. In one winter at Alexander Henry the Younger's Pembina post, seventeen men, ten women, and fourteen children "destroyed," to use Henry's own phrase, 63,000 pounds of buffalo meat, 1,150 fish of different kinds, some miscellaneous game, and 325 bushels of vegetables from the garden. It added up to about a ton of meat and fish apiece for every man, woman, and child at Pembina.[26]

Much of this huge volume of food was doubtless prepared by native women for their husbands and children. The evening meal in most posts was probably taken *en famille*, with the Indian mother, of course, cooking the food over an open fire. At Fort Edmonton, where each *engagé*'s family was housed in a separate cabin, preparations for Christmas dinner, as described by Paul Kane, bear out this supposition: "Toward noon every chimney gave evidence of being in full blast, while savory steams of cooking pervaded the atmosphere in all directions."[27]

At Fort Vancouver the *engagés* received weekly food rations to be prepared at home. At many of the larger posts, a kind of "officers' mess" was maintained, but there are occasional references in the journals to the *bourgeois* depending on his wife's cooking. The references are not always complimentary. Thus Alexander Henry the Younger on the occasion of a visit to one of his outposts: "Madame Desjarlaix contrived to get intoxicated, and in her endeavors to show her art of cooking, came near poisoning us." At Fort Alexander, incidentally, the still unmarried Daniel Harmon hired a half-breed son of a Saulteur woman "to serve me as cook, &c."

Mealtime at an American trading post, in this instance Fort Laramie at the fork of the North Platte and Laramie rivers, has been described by Parkman:

The discordant jingling of a bell, rung by a Canadian in the area, summoned us to supper. The repast was served on a rough table in one of the lower apartments of the fort, and consisted of cakes of bread and dried buffalo meat—an excellent thing for strengthening the teeth. At this meal were seated the *bourgeois* and superior dignitaries of the establishment, among whom Henry Chatillon was worthily included. No sooner was it finished, then the table was spread a second time (the luxury of bread being now, however, omitted) for the benefit of certain hunters and trappers of an inferior standing; while the ordinary Canadian *engagés* were regaled on dried meat in one of their lodging rooms.[28]

Parkman does not tell us how the wives and children of the fort were fed, but apparently they took their meals in their rooms, and probably apart from the men.

White men in the New World quickly accustomed themselves to the native cuisine, and the fur trader soon learned to accept a distinctly Indian bias in his wife's cooking. He finally came to relish the tail of the beaver, the snout of the moose, and the sweet marrow in roasted buffalo bones. He could accept a mess of wild rice cooked up with bear's grease and sugar. He even learned to eat dog and like it. Kane gives us an idea—perhaps a little exaggerated—of how thoroughly white traders became accustomed to Indian food when he describes a Christmas dinner at Fort Edmonton. It included boiled buffalo hump: boiled unborn calf, dried moose nose, whitefish browned in buffalo marrow, beaver tails, and roast wild goose.[29]

A trader's wife naturally fed her half-breed children in the way that she herself had been reared. For a long time—usually two or three years—she nursed her child, as was the Indian custom. Then, between breast-feeding and solid food, she prepared a pap made of Indian corn and milk—if her husband's post happened to boast a milch cow. Or she pounded wild rice fine and boiled it with maple sugar to make a thin gruel. She also gave her child the broth of fish and meat, and a pap made of *toquo* root. The trader John Long, who contributes these interesting details on child-feeding, adds that the *toquo* root was also baked into a kind of cake for infants to chew on.[30]

On the whole, it is doubtful that an Indian woman's kitchen labors were much lightened by marriage to a white man. Perhaps the chief difference was that she was not obliged to go out and gather firewood with which to cook the family's dinner. Less frequently, too, she was without food to cook; starvation did not come quite so often to a trading post as to an Indian village. And if she were so fortunate as to marry a *bourgeois*, there were those fabulous luxuries for her table—fine white flour, glistening cones of sugar, cakes of chocolate, little canisters of tea and coffee, the choice of the game and fish brought in by the post's hunters, and perhaps even an occasional bottle of sweet Madeira wine—what more could a woman ask?

At Fort Chipewyan, in the winter of 1786, Alexander Mackenzie is writing a letter to his cousin Roderic. Mackenzie is in deep trouble.

"See what it is," he writes, "to have no wives!"

What bothered Mackenzie was a lack of women to make snowshoes. "I have no one at the fort," he wailed, "that can make *raquettes*. I do not know what to do without these articles. See what it is to have no wives! Try and get *raquettes*, there is no stirring without them." He was, in other words, immobilized. As a fur trader, he was out of business.[31]

Thus, in a few anguished words, Mackenzie underscored the

immensely important role of the Indian woman in the operation
of a fur trading post—and indeed of the fur trade as a whole. For
her usefulness extended far beyond keeping house, preparing food,
and rearing children. It is hard to see, in fact, how a trading post
could have got along without her cheerful industry and skillful
hands.

Like the men, Indian women were assigned certain definite
tasks by the *bourgeois*. As in an Indian camp, there was an accepted
division of labor between the sexes. The men built the post's
canoes, the women sewed and pitched them. While the men trapped
beaver, the women cleaned and dressed the skins. This system of
sharing the work was deeply implanted by the Indian girl's tribal
training; it was one of the things that helped to make her a good
wife to a fur trader—and an invaluable asset to a trading post's
operation.

Some of the jobs performed by women called for very special
skills. One of these, as Mackenzie has so eloquently told us, was
netting snowshoes. Another was fashioning moccasins. Like snowshoes, moccasins were a vital necessity in bush travel. Since they
wore out quickly—sometimes in only one day—vast quantities
of them were needed. The Lewis and Clark party of twenty-eight
men required four hundred pairs for its homeward journey. And
only the women knew how to make them.[32]

In general, the work an Indian woman did in her native village
she also performed at a trading post. As soon as the sap began to
rise in the maple trees, off she went to the sugar bush and made
sugar for the whole post. She gathered gum from pine trees with
which to pitch the post's canoes. She tended the garden and
watched over it at night, lest the horses or her own kinsmen steal
the turnips and new potatoes. Every trader's journal is a record
of her ceaseless industry:

The women continue to cut up buffalo to make tallow. . . . Women
making sugar. . . . Women gathering rat tails [a kind of root] to eat. . . .
The women gathered great quantities of hazlenuts. . . . Women all busy
stretching buffalo hides to make pemmican bags and pack cords. . . .
Sent women for gum to daub the covering of the house. . . . Women

drying meat. . . . Women raising wattap—33 women, 8 bundles each.
. . . The women bring in great quantities of poires, raspberries, and
strawberries. . . . Women all off on horseback for berries.[33]

These excerpts from the journal of a single trader give one a
faint idea of how the women of a fur trading post spent their
leisure time. Their tasks were endless, and varied according to the
location of the post in which they lived. There were no canoes to
gum and sew at a prairie post, for instance, but there were innumerable bags of pemmican to prepare.

So important was pemmican to the fur trade that large posts,
such as Fort Vermilion and Fort George, were built and maintained
chiefly to produce it. And its manufacture in astounding quantities
was the special province of the post women. When the hunters
brought in buffalo meat from the prairie, the women cut the lean
parts into thin slices and hung them up to dry in the sun or over
a smoky fire. When the meat was thoroughly dry, they pounded
it fine between hides with stones. Then they melted down buffalo
fat and mixed it, half and half, with the "beat meat." Sometimes
they added huckleberries, serviceberries, or cranberries "to cut the
grease," or sweetened it with maple sugar. After it was thoroughly
blended—and not without a certain increment of dog hairs and
small pebbles—they poured the mixture into bags of buffalo hide
called *taureaux*, always exactly ninety pounds to a bag. And this
was pemmican.

Properly stored, pemmican would keep for years. It could be
eaten in its natural state, or boiled up with flour and water to
make a nourishing and not unpalatable soup called *rubbaboo*.
Pemmican, David Thompson says, "affords the most nourishment
in the least space and weight, even the gluttonous french canadian
that devours eight pounds of fresh meat every day is contented
with one and a half pounds per day." This, of course, was a factor
of the utmost importance in canoe travel, saving space in a north
canoe for trade goods and rum. And often, in a famine-beleaguered
post, the trader found pemmican his last defense against starvation. It is difficult to see how the fur trade could have got along
without pemmican—or the women to make it.[34]

When spring came and the meat could be dried in the sun, life at a "pemmican post" was a busy one for every *femme du pays*. At Duncan M'Gillivray's Fort George, on the Saskatchewan, 8,900 pounds of beat meat and an equal quantity of fat were on hand in January for making pemmican, 200 bags of which were produced in April. Henry the Younger reported 334 bags (30,000 pounds of pemmican) as the output of his Pembina River post in 1807.[35] It was hard, heavy work, and there was probably a collective sigh of relief when the last shaggy *taureau* was stowed in a departing north canoe and a woman could turn to more enjoyable tasks, such as gathering the first wild strawberries.

But while she was pouring the melted fat into the shredded meat, she knew at least where the next meal was coming from. There were times when this was not so. To every post, sooner or later, came the day when the last scrap of meat had been devoured, the day when you began to eat the post's dogs and then—but only at the last—the hunters' horses; and after that, after the last, you ate your moccasins, and the parchment out of the windows, and hunted through last winter's refuse heaps for bones of fish the dogs had overlooked. Then, if you were a woman, you were sent out on the prairie or into the woods to search for food: swan potatoes, flagroot, trout herb, *choux gras*, even the nauseous lichen the *voyageurs* called *tripe de roche*, or any sort of root or plant that would sustain life a little longer.

Yet this was what it meant to be an Indian. Far better than the white man, his Indian wife was conditioned by training—and perhaps by nature—to starve today and feast tomorrow, and accept it all as part of living.[36] Besides, starvation was not an everyday or even an every-year thing; between the times of hunger, there was plenty around a fur trading post to divert, and amuse, and make an Indian girl laugh.

The idea has got around that Indian girls did not laugh much—that all Indians, including their women, were terribly impassive and, except for an occasional grunt, very uncommunicative. This may have been true at trading and treaty-making times, but otherwise all the evidence is to the contrary. As every trader soon learned, the red men had a wry and ribald sense of humor—often at the white man's expense. And some tribes, notably the Crow, were famous for their special brand of drollery.

Indian women laughed a lot, and Indian girls giggled like any teen-agers. Far from being the taciturn creatures that tradition has made them, they were often voluble, fun-loving, and full of the devil. John Bradbury had a taste of their gaiety when three young Minetaree girls stripped, jumped into the river, and swam around his canoe, pulling the frail craft out of course, seizing the stern and holding it back, and making a laughing nuisance out of themselves generally. He was rescued by an Indian who held the girls' heads under water until they escaped by diving and swimming in different directions; and on his return to shore, he revenged himself by seizing his tormentors' clothing. "This," his journal concludes, with a sedate chuckle, "occasioned much laughter." [37]

William H. Keating, trading on the banks of what is now the Minnesota River with an ancient Ojibway squaw, had the old woman's two granddaughters as an audience, and he has left us this charming impression of the girls:

They were as handsome and as good-looking as Indian females can probably be; they were young, about fifteen or sixteen; their complexion was so light that we could scarcely credit the assertion of our guide that they were full-blooded Indians; their features were regular; the large dark eye which distinguished the elder would have been deemed beautiful anywhere; their forms, which were good, were perhaps taller than those which we usually found among Indian women. But what added most to their charms, was the gay, good-humored appearance which brightened their eyes and animated their features. While the old hag was muttering her discontent, they were smiling, and when she extended her bony hand to receive the present offered her, the damsels burst out into laughter which displayed a beautiful set of teeth. Their observations upon our party seemed to afford them as much gratification as we derived from the examination of theirs, and the merriment which it occasioned them was displayed in the most unreserved manner.[38]

Most traders and early travelers seem to agree with Bradbury and Keating, not only on the natural gaiety of Indian women but on their loquacity and love of gossip.[39] In an Indian encampment of several hundred lodges, there must certainly have been much to interest, amuse, and scandalize such women; and one must wonder whether a Cree or Crow girl, suddenly immured in a small fur trading outpost, might not have found life rather dull. The Fort Dunvegan journal, kept by the Nor'wester A. N. McLeod, suggests that she did—and that she sometimes attempted to escape that boredom:

Two of the women of the fort asked for a canoe to cross the river, and as soon as they had crossed and were no longer watched, they went down the river. A man was sent after them and brought them back . . .[40]

Many another Indian girl in an isolated flying post must have felt the same compelling urge to "go down the river," and occasionally acted on it. But at the large establishments a woman's life could be not altogether uninteresting. Much of her work was in the company of other women. Even the hard work—scraping skins, making pemmican, sewing *taureaux*—was shared by the wives of the *engagés*. They worked together, with the chatter and laughter, the droll stories and gossip, and the occasional hair-pulling, that gave it all a pleasant social turn.

The women especially enjoyed the tasks that came with the turn of the seasons. The annual excursion to the sugar bush, before the snow had melted in March or April, was a gala holiday. While the men scattered to hunt for game, the women gathered sap, kept the great kettles boiling, and saw the bubbling liquid turn to tawny sugar under the swirl of their long paddles. Some of it they threw on the snow, to harden into candy for the children; and some they poured into ducks' bills, to make "lollipops" for the little ones. What fun, after the long, dark winter's confinement in the snow-bound post!

Then came the exodus of the women to the berry patches, first to gather wild strawberries, then raspberries, blueberries, and the luscious *poires*, in the sunny fire-swept clearings, each woman with her little basket slung from her beaded belt, and the big birchbark *makuks* filling swiftly as the chattering berrypickers vied with one another in stripping the bushes of their sun-warmed fruit.

With summer, too, came the excitement of the new outfit's arrival—the return of the *bourgeois* and his canoes, filled with trade goods and feminine finery; and then the influx of the Indian hunters and their families from the beaver grounds, eager to trade and taste the trader's "new milk," as they called his rum. All at once, so many people! For a little while the northern posts were almost as populous as the big Missouri River and Plains establishments, where men of many races—Americans, French-Canadians, Mexicans—and their wives from every tribe—Blackfoot, Crow, Aricara, Sioux, Arapaho, Cheyenne, Pawnee, Snake, Assiniboin, even Chinook—turned the sprawling posts into a bedlam of warring tongues.

And where so many people came together, there was sure to be plenty of diversion—dances, racing, gambling, "frolics," battles, intrigues, and usually a few murders—to enliven post life.

While the journals of American trappers and travelers in the Southwest tell us a good deal about the fandangos so fondly remembered by mountain men after a visit to Taos or Santa Fe, they have little to say about the social life at the adobe forts on the dry Plains or on the Upper Missouri and other rivers of the West. But most of these American posts had their complement of French-Canadian *voyageurs* and Mexican horse drovers, and *fiesta* was in their blood. Dancing, racing, gambling, and wenching were their way of life, although they also took a childlike pleasure in more innocent pastimes. While the Reverend Joseph Williams was shocked at what he called "debaucheries," [41] we are told that taffy-pulling frolics were a favorite winter diversion at Bent's Fort, with the laborers and teamsters sharing the fun with the Indian women of the fort. The white men and native women of that famous post were pictured by George Bird Grinnell as "a happy, contented family." [42]

In the North, the passionate love of both *voyageurs* and Indian women for dancing was satisfied by balls to celebrate almost any occasion—a holiday, the arrival of a canoe brigade, visitors from another post, or just Sunday. At some forts a dance was held practically every weekend, and a not uncommon Monday entry in the journal of a *bourgeois* was: "Dance lasted all night. Very little work done today."

The music at one of these affairs, a bored white spectator wrote, was "a very bad performance of one vile, unvarying tune, upon a worse old fiddle, accompanied by a brilliant accompaniment on a large tin pan." [43] Well, no matter. The women of the post—always in short supply as partners—were all belles of the ball, and every dance a great success.

But it was on the high winter feast days that the *voyageurs* and their Indian wives and daughters put on their holiday best and made their serious bid for a brief Dionysian escape from the gloom of winter in the *pays sauvage*. Mostly it was a matter of getting as drunk as possible at the expense of the *bourgeois*.

Festivities led off with a celebration of All Saints' Day, the French-Canadian special holiday, on November 1. A month later came St. Andrew's Day, an important Scottish fête, which, since most of the *bourgeois* were Scots, the *voyageurs* observed enthusiastically. Presentation of a cross to the *bourgeois*, and a few volleys of musketry in his honor, were always good for a generous issue of rum and a dance in the Indian Hall. The dancing began in a mood of light-hearted gaiety, but was likely to end on the sour note recorded by Harmon in his Fort Alexander journal: "They behaved with considerable propriety until about eleven o'clock . . . then some of them became quarrelsome, as the Canadians generally are when intoxicated, and to high words blows soon succeeded; and finally two battles were fought, which put an end to this truly genteel North Western ball." [44]

By Christmas and New Year's, it was not unusual for a post to be starving, but however hungry they might be, its *engagés* never allowed two such important holidays to pass unobserved. No matter how short the food rations, there was generally enough rum to get the whole post properly drunk—much to the disgust of young Harmon again, who wrote of his first Christmas in the *pays sauvage:* "This day being Christmas, our people spent it as usual, in drinking and fighting." [45]

New Year's Day, in the French tradition, was somewhat the more important of the two holidays, and hence the drunks were bigger and longer. There was much visiting back and forth, the *voyageurs* making ceremonial calls on one another and on their *bourgeois,* kissing the ladies, and extending felicitations of the season. Even the traders of rival posts dropped their animosities and became brothers for the duration of the festivities. The scale of these New Year's Day celebrations is suggested by several successive entries in the Fort Vermilion journal for 1810:

Jan. 1st. I gave a dance to which all hands were invited, including my neighbor [the Hudson's Bay Company trader] and his family.

Jan. 2nd. My men all drinking and carousing.

Jan. 3rd. Men and women all drinking pell-mell.

It was not until January 4th that the *bourgeois* finally was able to write in his journal: "I got the fort cleared out and everything in as good order as before the boisson." [46]

Henry the Younger shrinks from describing in detail what went on during some of these holiday frolics (a reticence not at all characteristic of him), but he does say at one point: "My hunters and other men have been drinking and rioting since yesterday; they make more d——n noise and trouble than a hundred Black-feet." [47]

As time passed in the *pays sauvage,* however, the tone of trading-post holiday festivities seems to have improved—or perhaps it was only that the Hudson's Bay Company people were a little better behaved than the Nor'westers. At any rate, Paul Kane's description of a Christmas ball at Fort Edmonton sounds almost sedate:

In the evening the hall was prepared for the dance to which Mr. Harriett had invited all the inmates of the fort, and was early filled by the gaily dressed guests. Indians, whose chief ornament consisted in the paint on

their faces, voyageurs with bright sashes and neatly ornamented moccasins, half-breeds glittering in every ornament they could lay their hands
on; whether civilized or savage, all were laughing, and jabbering in as
many different languages as there were styles of dress. . . . The dancing
was most picturesque of all, and almost all joined in it. . . . After enjoying ourselves with such boisterous vigor for several hours, we all gladly
retired to rest about twelve o'clock, the guests separating in great good
humor.[48]

On this occasion Kane seems to have been much impressed by
the charms of one of his dancing partners, a Cree girl with the won-
derful name of One That Looks at the Stars. "I was so much struck
by her beauty," he wrote afterwards, "that I prevailed upon her
to promise to sit for her likeness." He painted her portrait in a
beautiful beaded dress, holding her swan's-wing fan coquettishly
across her forehead.

However heavy the work a woman must do at a fur trading
post, at least it ended at dusk. When the light failed, all activity
stopped (as in an Indian village) and every woman's evenings were
"free." Kane, again, describes night life at Fort Edmonton:

The evenings are spent round their large fires in eternal gossiping and
smoking. The sole musician of the establishment, a fiddler, is now in great
requisition amongst the French part of the inmates, who give full vent
to their national vivacity, whilst the more sedate Indian looks on with
solemn enjoyment.[49]

But even during the daylight hours, while at work with her
neighbors, putting up pemmican or sewing fur pack covers, a
woman could pass the time pleasantly at one of her favorite indoor
diversions: gossip and scandal. With a hundred or more men and
women fenced in for a whole winter behind the stockades of a
snowbound fort, there was sure to be no lack of material. In every
trader's journal such items as these recur frequently:

Sat up to deal out spirits to the Indians. One of them has his own daughter
for a wife, and her mother at the same time.[50]

One of my men having beaten his woman, she went in the woods with a
piece of rope and attempted to hang herself.[51]

My blacksmith's woman ran away with Charlo.[52]

Piche has made the wife of one of my hunter's desert, and she is lurking
in the woods near the fort.[53]

Working together around the drying racks or a lodge cover,
Indian women, from all accounts, did not fail to make the most of
the post's juicy matter for gossip. Colonel Dodge gives us this
good-natured but incisive appraisal of their native bent for scandal-
mongering:

Where no one can commit a moral wrong, there would appear to be no
opportunity for what we call *scandal*, yet every act, every incident,
accident, or condition is common talk for the whole band, to be discussed
broadly, and without reservation, by old and young, male and female.
The broad caricatures of the tattle of a New England village are merely
faint conceptions of the capabilities in this direction of an Indian encampment.[54]

Scandal and gossip, however, were not a woman's sole source of
diversion in a winter-bound trading post. Besides sharing the
dances and other entertainments (including gambling) with the
men, she had games that were exclusively her own. One of these
was a feminine version of the violent game of lacrosse. As the
ladies played it, according to the Nor'wester Peter Grant, it was
not exactly a genteel sport:

The game is begun and continues in the same manner as hurdle [lacrosse],
with the same impetuosity, but seldom with the same good order and
good humor, for it is common for these ladies, before the game is decided,
to quarrel and fight with their cudgels in good earnest, and to the no small
diversion of the men.[55]

During the winter, women and children joined their husbands
in such sports as those described by Henry the Younger:

My winter stock of provisions is complete—all good, fat buffalo meat,
and my men have little to do. They, therefore, amuse themselves by sliding

down the bank on sleighs from the S. gate. The Indian women join them
and they have excellent sport.

And a few days later:

This is delightful weather for the Indian women to play their favorite
game of coullion on the ice; they generally keep it up till dark, whilst
the men are at their game of platter, and others beat the drum to their
wabbano songs . . .[56]

Other games were played indoors, sometimes with the men.
Among these were the dicelike game of "platter," the "moccasin
game," and the game of "sticks"—at all of which the women as
well as their husbands gambled. And there was one game, "bones,"
which was the women's and children's own.

Another *divertissement* for Indian women was the care of their
children. Little girls especially were the object of fond attention,
and mothers spent much of their free time on their adornment.
At Fort Dearborn, Mrs. Kinzie watched delightedly as an Indian
woman did up her daughters' hair with scarlet ribbon, "tying a
piece to each of the little clubs into which their hair was knotted
at the temples," laughing and exclaiming *"Saum!"*

An Indian mother devoted a great deal of time to her children,
devising many games for their amusement: the new-tooth charm,
how to call butterflies, how to speak with the "spirit of the woods,"
how to stop a snowstorm. She told them endless stories, about
Mother Wren, the raccoon and the crawfish, often acting them
out. She taught them how to make little "snowshoes" from the
needles of the pine tree, miniature tipi covers, tiny birchbark utensils. She showed them how to amuse themselves with the leaves
of the pitcher plant, and how to string red berries on nettle fiber.[57]

"The little girls are very fond of dolls," Colonel Dodge says of
the Cheyenne, "which their mothers make and dress with considerable skill and taste. Their baby houses are miniature teepees, and
they spend as much time and take as much pleasure in such play
as the white girls." [58]

A little girl was given her first lesson in beadwork by sewing
beads on her doll's dress. Later on came instruction in the other

womanly arts: quillwork, moccasin-making, snowshoe-netting, sugar-making, rice-harvesting, cooking, and keeping the lodge clean and neat. A woman who had been taught these things by an Indian mother could never forget them, and even in the alien environment of a fur trading post, she made them part of her own children's amusement and training.

But in bringing up her daughters to be virtuous, competent, respected women, the Indian wife of a fur trader was, of course, faced with a complex and perhaps insoluble problem. As an Indian child, she herself had been taught to observe a well-defined set of tribal usages, but her daughters were "marginal women," living between two worlds and torn by conflicting ideas of what was proper feminine behavior. The result—especially when the Indian population of a post had, sometimes for generations, received repeated infusions of white blood—could be disastrous. Occasionally a *métis*, or half-breed, girl won esteem and even eminence in the white world. But the seeds of tragedy were always present, and many an Indian mother must have spent sleepless nights as well as crowded days in bringing her daughter to womanhood.

Then, of course, there were "happenings"—some funny, some tragic, some exciting, some marvelous, some catastrophic. They repeated themselves with the seasons, or exploded suddenly in the quiet milieu of a stockaded post, or were the casual pranks of fate and human nature.

About the worst thing that could happen was a successful attack by hostiles. It did not occur often, but sometimes, as at a Hudson's Bay Company post on the Saskatchewan in 1794, the savages succeeded in breaking in and butchering everyone, including all the women and their children. And even if it did not actually come off, there was frequently the dread of imminent attack, so that fort journals often carried such items as: "This night the House was filled with women & children who were afraid to sleep in their lodges, on account of the rumors spread abroad about the Fall Indians." [59]

Next to being butchered by a mob of howling demons, death by
smallpox was the worst of ends. Perhaps the smallpox was even
more to be dreaded; it killed many more (as many as three-fifths
of some tribes) and in crueler ways. From Hudson House on the
Saskatchewan, factor William Walker wrote to tell how cruel:

The Indians all Dying by this Distemper . . . lying Dead about the
Barren Ground like rotten sheep, their tents left standing & the Wild
Beasts Devouring them.[60]

No trader's wife after the great epidemic of the late 1700's
could ever rest easy in the assurance that the dreadful scourge,
or something equally as horrible (measles was nearly as bad),
would not return to carry off her family and herself.

Disease and starvation were the great catastrophic happenings
against which the highest stockade was no defense, with massacre
always a background threat. But in each post minor dramas of
love and hatred, despair and delight, played themselves out and
were part of life in the *pays sauvage.*

Through the laconic, often illiterate, pages of the traders' journals, sandwiched between accounts of furs traded and debts given
out, are strewn brief memoranda of human suffering, violence, and
death. Here, for instance, is Henry the Younger making note of
the melancholy end of his Indian hunter Charlo:

Charlo died early this morning. Since last August his two eldest daughters,
two sons, their mother, and now their father, have died. . . . Their
complaint was a cough which soon killed them. They were all in good
health when they arrived at the Forks last summer.[61]

And here, in another vein, is the *bourgeois* Archibald Norman
McLeod playing "the Law" west of the Athabasca at Fort Dunvegan:

The only one known to be guilty [of stealing some meat] is Martineau,
whom Mr. McLeod spoke to, and in order to punish him took his wife
away and gave her to M. Cadieu, who is more able to maintain her.[62]

Sometimes the daily drama was so *outré* as to stagger even so
case-hardened a trader as Alexander Henry the Younger. At Pem-

bina he records what, with considerable understatement, he describes as "an extraordinary affair":

One of Mr. Heney's Orkney lads, apparently indisposed, requested me to
allow him to remain in my house for a short time. I was surprised at the
fellow's demand; however, I told him to sit down and warm himself.
I returned to my own room, where I had not been long before he sent
one of my people, requesting the favor of speaking with me. Accordingly,
I stepped down to him, and was much surprised to find him extended on
the hearth, uttering dreadful lamentations; he stretched out his hands
toward me, and in piteous tones begged me to be kind to a poor, helpless,
abandoned wretch, who was not of the sex I had supposed, but an unfortunate Orkney girl, pregnant and actually in childbirth. In saying this
she opened her jacket and displayed a pair of beautiful, round, white
breasts. . . . In about an hour she was safely delivered of a fine boy . . .[63]

Improbable things were always happening to Henry, however.
Perhaps the only event in fur trade history to compete with the
Orkney girl incident was the arrival of the Portsmouth barmaid
Jane Barnes at Astor's post on the Columbia, an affair in which
Henry was also involved.

Miss Barnes appeared at Astoria in the company of Donald
McTavish, a partner of the North West Company, who had picked
her up in England on his way from New York. He had promised
to take her to Montreal by a somewhat circuitous route around
the Horn and across the continent of North America; and Miss
Barnes, whose ideas of geography were not very well-defined, had
cheerfully accepted.

"A flaxen-haired, blue-eyed daughter of Albion," Ross Cox
called her, with great restraint. "She had a rather extravagant
wardrobe, and each day exhibited her in a new dress, which she
always managed in a way to display her figure to the best advantage." [64]

She created havoc, needless to say, not only among the whites
at Astoria, but even more among the Chinook. The Indians were
so enchanted by her blond beauty that they laid plans to abduct
her; and McTavish and Henry—as a measure of protection—made
an agreement to share her charms.[65]

But it was not often that a Jane Barnes, or even an Orkney girl, showed up at a trading post. For the most part, life inside the stockade was punctuated only by the less exotic events recorded monotonously in every trader's fort journal:

The Indians continued drinking. About ten o'clock I was informed that old Crooked Legs had killed his young wife.

Two of my men had a boxing match, or rather a rough and tumble fight.

My neighbors came visiting, and before sunrise both sexes of all parties were intoxicated and more troublesome than double their number of Saulteurs; the men were quarreling and fighting all night.

January 1, 1803. Plagued with the ceremonies of the day—men and women drinking and fighting, pell mell.

A man gave a large, stout dog a kick in the side, of which the poor beast died instantly.

Le Boeuf quarreled with his wife and knocked her senseless with a club, which opened a gash on her head six inches long and down to the bone.

Charles Hesse cut an ugly gash in his woman's head with a cutlass this morning, through jealousy.

Grande Gueule stabbed Pedrix Blanche with a knife in six places; and later, in fighting with his wife, fell in the fire and was almost roasted, but had enough strength left, notwithstanding his wounds, to bite her nose off.[66]

In such sordid ways was existence enlivened at a typical post of the North West Company in what is now North Dakota. Things may have been better at the Hudson's Bay Company establishments, where liquor—in theory, at least—was dispensed less freely. And there is no record of any such drunkenness, mayhem, and debauchery at the posts of the American fur trading companies—possibly because they were unreported.

What with fort balls and "frolics," holiday fiestas, arrivals of new outfits, threats of hostile attack, and the drab interruptions of everyday violence and passion, life, at the larger establishments at least, must not have been altogether dull. But it was not the same as life in a big Indian encampment. And perhaps a trader's Indian wife may sometimes have missed the primitive, blood-stirring throb of the drums and the return of a war party with captives for her to torture and scalps for her to dance. For she was, after all, a "woman savage."

IV

I TAKE THIS WOMAN . . .

What passed for marriage in the Indian Country was commonly known as "marriage *à la façon du pays*" ("marriage in the fashion of the country"), a "mountain marriage," a "prairie marriage," and often simply as an "Indian marriage."

All these terms carried the connotation of an extended relationship with an Indian or half-breed woman, but just as implicitly they signified marriage of a nonpermanent nature. For, by whatever name it was called, the marriage of a white man and a native woman was a one-sided bargain.

The trader or mountain man could set his wife adrift whenever his fancy moved him, send her back to her parents, or sell her to another man when he returned to civilization. The Indian girl had no such rights. Unless she eloped with a lover, there was no practical way she could escape the tyranny of a brutal or bestial husband. Except by hanging herself—which she sometimes did.

Yet Indian girls were usually not just willing but eager to form such a liaison. And, as we have already observed, mountain men and *voyageurs* found it hard to get along without a woman in the *pays sauvage*. The fur trading companies fostered the idea of "country marriages" for business reasons. The result was a proliferation of such unions at every trading post.

To some extent, the character of marriage *à la façon du pays* was influenced by the official attitudes of the dominant fur trading concerns—the Hudson's Bay Company, the North West Company, and such large American organizations as the Missouri

Fur Company, the Rocky Mountain Fur Company, and the American Fur Company.

Despite the original Hudson's Bay Company order forbidding its men to take concubines, or even to admit Indian women to the forts, the rule was little observed by either officers or "laborers" in later years. But in 1690 it was still on the books, and it took the audacious challenge of a twenty-year-old boy to upset the over-stuffed London Committee's ideas on proper sexual conduct for men in the Canadian wilds.

Henry Kelsey, who is still famous for his explorations (he was the first white man to see the musk ox, first to see the buffalo on the Canadian plains), set out from York Fort in the spring of 1690 to investigate the country inland. He pushed westward for more than a thousand miles, farther than anyone had ever gone before, and when he returned to York he brought with him an Indian bride.

The governor of York Fort met the situation squarely: he refused Kelsey's wife admission to the post. Hundreds of miles from home, the girl stood before the great double gates of the fort and waited for her white husband to speak. Kelsey answered the governor with admirable directness. The gist of what he said was: "Either my wife comes in with me, or I'll go and live with her people." Mrs. Kelsey was allowed to enter.[1]

That was the first crack in the dike. Before long, the moralistic directives of the London Committee were almost forgotten. And finally, more than a century later—for the wheels of change turned slowly in the Great Company—a situation that had long existed in fact was recognized and even approved. From the Mackenzie River District we find Sir George Simpson writing:

Connubial alliances are the best security we can have of the good will of the natives. I have therefore recommended the Gentlemen to form con-nections with the principal Families immediately on their arrival, which is no difficult matter, as the offer of their Wives and Daughters is the first token of their friendship and hospitality.[2]

True to its love of form and convention, the Company worked out a marriage contract to cover such "connubial alliances."

Even the fort Indians cemented their unions with native women by making their mark on some such agreement as this:

I, George Ross, Native Indian of the Albany District, but now of Rupert's House, Hudson's Bay, personally appearing before Rob't. Miles—Chief Trader at Rupert's House, do hereby form a Marriage Contract and expressly agree to take unto myself as my Lawful Wife, by the same Laws as if I had been legally married by a Clergyman of the Church of England, Sally, daughter of Commutchaupai deceased (now a widow having survived her two former husbands Eschocaupe and Coapaun), whom I hereby declare and acknowledge in every respect, from the date herein expressed, to be my legal and Lawful Wife, as if I had passed through the Ceremony of the Church—and hereafter bind and oblige myself to support her as long as the Almighty may be pleased to sustain me in life.[3]

Sworn and subscribed by his mark and her mark, witnessed by three witnesses, and sealed with the seals of the chief trader, this formidable document would seem to have amply secured the rights of an Indian wife. There was a catch, however: the agreement was binding "only in the country." When he returned to England, a trader was free to leave his wife behind—which he usually did.

Yet, despite the official formality, the attitude of some H.B.C. factors could only be described as casual, not to say facetious, toward their men marrying native women. Thus we find chief factor Duncan Finlayson of York Fort deriving great sport from promising the same Indian girl to two different men as a reward for their labor, then forcing her to marry a third.[4]

By the time the Hudson's Bay Company had established posts west of the Rockies, however, "service marriages" were so general that their observance was regarded as evidence of a post's permanence and respectability. A report by Jedediah Smith, David E. Jackson, and W. L. Sublette to the Secretary of War in 1829, for instance, includes this paragraph:

No English or white women are at the Fort [Fort Vancouver], but a great number of mixed blood Indian extraction, such as belong to the British fur trading establishments, who are treated as wives, and their families and children taken care of accordingly. So that everything seemed to combine to prove that this fort was a *permanent establishment*.[5]

At Fort Vancouver, in fact, marriage *à la façon du pays* probably reached its highest level, thanks to the influence of two great men, Dr. John McLoughlin and James Douglas. Robert C. Johnson, in his short but admirable biography of McLoughlin, describes the sort of women who married the officers and men at this important post on the Columbia:

Some of these wives had been educated in Canada. They had a natural aptitude for the life of a trader and often accompanied their husbands on long and dangerous journeys. They were daughters of chief traders and factors and native mothers of superior birth and comeliness. While they dressed in the English fashion, all retained as a mark of their class, the embroidered leggings made of richly colored cloth of good material. Other wives were of full blood, daughters of leading chiefs, and married by full tribal rites . . .

Outside the officers' quarters was the more common life of the hunter, trapper, and laborer. The lower servants married native women, usually from the upper river tribes, who did not flatten the heads of their children as a sign of noble birth, and who were of cleaner personal habits than the coast Indians. These native women never failed to make good wives and to learn household arts.[6]

There are no statistics on the number of Indian women at the Hudson's Bay Company forts. Simpson's roster of people at Fort Wedderburn (Athabasca Department, 1821) lists Orkney fishermen, Canadian *voyageurs*, and others, but no Indian women or children. Yet Wedderburn, like all other H.B.C. forts, undoubtedly had its full complement of native wives and their offspring. The Orkneymen, coming from their dour islands where life was hard and women scarce (since they emigrated to England and Scotland, where husbands were easier to get), were by no means proof against the charms of the Indian girls; and, as soon as they went inland, they fell readily into the French-Canadian pattern of taking native wives.[7] The H.B.C. forts in the Interior, Franklin implies, supported as many Indian women and children as those of the North West Company.

It was not long before the partners of the North West Company
—most of whom had at least one Indian wife—were pointing with
alarm to the large number of native women and half-breed children
cluttering up the Concern's posts.

By 1805, one *engagé* in four had taken an Indian wife. At some
posts, such as White Earth House, the women actually out-
numbered the men. In the whole Northwest, from a thousand to
fifteen hundred Indian women and children were living in the
North West Company's forts.[8]

"Some remedy ought to be applied to check so great an evil,"
the *bourgeois* complained.

During the 1806 Rendezvous at Kaministiquia, they even got
around to passing a resolution against it—perhaps as half-hearted
a resolution as ever a board of directors adopted:

It was suggested that the number of women and children in the country
was a heavy burden to the Concern, and that some remedy ought to be
applied to check so great an evil, at least if nothing effectual could be done
to suppress it entirely. It was therefore resolved that every practicable
means should be used throughout the Country to reduce by degrees the
number of women maintained by the Company, that for this purpose no
Man whatever, either Partner, Clerk, or Engagé, belonging to the Concern
shall henceforth take or suffer to be taken under any pretense whatsoever,
any woman or maid from any of the tribes of Indians now known or who
may hereafter become known in this Country to live with him after the
fashion of the North West, that is to say, to live with him within the
Company's Houses or Forts and be maintained at the Expense of the
Concern.[9]

Along with fines for drunkenness and the senseless racing of
canoes, the penalty for transgressing this regulation was fixed at a
stiff 100 pounds Halifax currency. Then—possibly because there
was not a *bourgeois* present who was not himself a transgressor—
this paragraph was somewhat sheepishly added:

It is however understood that taken the Daughter of a white man
[i.e., a half-breed girl] after the fashion of the Country shall be considered
no violation of this resolve.

That left most of the *bourgeois* off the hook, since their wives were generally of mixed blood. As for the ordinary *engagés* and canoehands, there is no evidence that they ever heard of the Kaministiquia resolution. In any case, the Northwest had by this time so numerous a population of half-breed girls that no man wanting a wife would have had much trouble in complying with the interdiction against marrying a full-blooded girl. Indeed, it might have been difficult for him to find one in the vicinity of his trading post.

While marriage tended to become regularized, even to the point of legal recognition, under the aegis of the great Canadian companies, nothing of the sort happened on the American fur trade frontier.

Among American mountain men, taking a wife was usually no weightier a matter than buying a horse, and getting rid of her no more complicated. There were exceptions, of course—instances of trappers and traders who showed their Indian wives the honor and respect they would have received among their own people. But the attitude of most might be described as one of cheerful irresponsibility. Or, less charitably, something not much better than the criminal indifference attributed by Colonel Dodge to the "squaw man" of a later era. "These men," Dodge wrote, "purchase and abandon women at pleasure, debasing and prostituting them."

How things stood at some of the American trading posts is suggested by Rudolph Kurz's ironic description of family life at Fort Berthold:

The young priest, Father Charles Lacombe, began to preach. He found at once much with which to reproach us. Mr. Kipp living here with squaw and children while he had a family in the States. His half-breed son not baptized . . . P. Garceau, living here with two squaws, was sire of several children equally unregenerate . . . Bellange has a troop of half-breed offspring not yet baptized. . . . Things are in a bad state.[10]

"But," Kurz adds, "conditions under which a man has to live in this region, he [the priest] was told, were not his concern; white women would not live here."

In the Southwest, *mestizas* from the Spanish settlements were an important element in the trading-post population. John C. Frémont reported that Fort Pueblo was inhabited by American mountain men with Spanish wives. But Ruxton particularized with: "Three or four Taos women and as many squaws of every nation comprised the female society of the Upper Arkansas, giving good promise of peopling the River with a sturdy race of half-breeds." [11]

In view of the rampant individualism of the mountain man, it would be surprising to find anything even remotely resembling a pattern of "country marriages." And there seems to have been none. Hundreds of nameless fur hunters and Indian traders merely bought, seized, or loaned a woman for a season or two, begot children, moved on to fresh beaver grounds and a new domestic setup. Others like Charles Larpenteur traveled about with a large family, sometimes depositing them at a settlement while they went into unexplored and possibly dangerous territory. Old Bill Williams, James P. Beckwourth, and numerous other mountain men took on a succession of wives, or up to half a dozen concurrently. Not a few, like James Kipp and Peter Sarpy, maintained two ménages simultaneously, one presided over by an Indian woman, the other by a white wife.

And some, like Marcellin St. Vrain, managed to get themselves into a matrimonial tangle that was remarkable even by fur trade frontier standards. Marcellin, having acquired two wives, one a Sioux, the other a Pawnee, was unfortunate enough to kill an Indian in a wrestling match, which forced him to flee Bent's Fort, leaving his wives and children behind. The Pawnee, mother of two boys, drifted to Pueblo, where, David Lavender surmises, she may have married a hanger-on. But the Sioux woman, for whom Marcellin had a deep attachment, was taken to Mora by Marcellin's brother Ceran, who promised to care for her while Marcellin was away. Each day, according to legend, the Sioux

woman climbed a hill and looked toward the east for her husband's
return. But Marcellin had met Elizabeth Jane Murphey in Missouri, and had married her. When he did return, it was only to
take his two sons from his Sioux wife, who, refusing to believe
that he would not someday come back to her, still kept her hilltop
vigil. Finally, she yielded to the wooing of William Bransford, a
celebrated mountain man, and married him. It all turned out
well for her. The marriage lasted till her death, more than thirty
years later, and she bore Bransford seven children.[12]

Marriage on the American fur trade frontier ran a course as
unpredictable as the mountain men themselves. Perhaps there
was somewhat more conformity to a pattern among the *bourgeois*
and *voyageurs* of the Canadian companies. But not even under
the quasi-legal "service marriage" contracts of the Hudson's Bay
Company could an Indian girl really hope that her white husband
would be hers forever. Sometimes it happened; but if anything
was basic to marriage *à la façon du pays,* it was the husband's
acknowledged right to make an end to it at any time, for any
reason—or none.

Occasionally, an Indian wife was brave, or strong, or desperate
enough to take matters into her own hands and leave her white
husband without excuse or explanation. But most often her
escape was through elopement with another man, something
that native women were no strangers to in tribal life. Larocque
speaks of the prairie women deserting en masse in the spring to go
with their lovers in the mountains. And James McKenzie fulmi-
nates characteristically when he discovers a tendency on the part of
his *voyageurs'* wives to leave Fort Chipewyan with Indian hunters.
He threatened:

. . . if any d——nd rascal of them [the Indians] deserted this summer
with any of the Frenchmen's women, he and she both would lose their
heads, were we to give 200 skins as a reward to such as would choose to
search for them and cut off their head.[13]

To say the least, the problem appears to have been a real one at Chipewyan, and it is not unlikely that other post masters had similar trouble—although most of them probably shrugged it off. Kurz says that Denig was of the opinion that, with wives so easy to come by, it wasn't worthwhile to try and get back an erring mate; better to buy another at once.[14]

At Fort Vancouver, John McLoughlin, who insisted on his men living up to their obligations as husbands of Indian women, was also concerned about the faithfulness of some native wives. He writes to the master of Fort Nisqually:

There is an Indian woman lawfully married to one Tetreau, but who ran away and left him. This woman has lived with Vizeau here, but if she goes to Nisqually, you will not allow her to live with him.[15]

Alexander Henry the Younger was not, of course, without defections to report, although they do not seem to have troubled him overmuch. At his White Earth post he notes in his fort journal:

Piche and other lads came in from my hunters' tents on a visit. Piche had made the wife of one of my hunters desert, and she is lurking in the woods near the fort. . . . [next day] Piche off with his fair deserter.[16]

In many cases, it is obvious that these elopements were motivated, as they often are in civilized society, by jealousy, infatuations, or just plain promiscuity. In others, Kurz maintains, the women had no intention of staying hitched in the first place; they remained with their husbands "just long enough to get all they could give them." But in still others, escape from a husband's mistreatment was the sole objective; the woman fled not with another man, but simply back to her own people. Mrs. Kinzie, in *Wau-Bun*, tells of a Potawatami woman named Madeline, married to "a surly, ill-tempered Canadian," who did just that—with Mrs. Kinzie's frank approval.[17]

The other escape route was self-destruction, and not infrequently it was taken. Entries like this one in Henry the Younger's journal are by no means rare:

One of my men having beaten his woman, she went into the woods with a piece of rope and attempted to hang herself, which she actually would have done, had she not been discovered as she was climbing the tree to throw herself off. Instances of this sort are not uncommon among the Saulteur women.[18]

Everywhere, separation was comparatively simple for the man, more difficult for the woman. But human emotions—affection, loyalty, guilt, sympathy, even love—sometimes intervened to complicate matters.

Even a lowly *engagé*—and some of them seem to have been pretty lowly—might have a few qualms about casting off a wife and children with whom he had shared years in the *pays sauvage*. *Voyageurs* and mountain men often developed a deep affection for the girl they had once bought casually, perhaps for a horse or a few yards of scarlet cloth.

With these men there was always the problem of what to do with their wives and families when they left the Indian Country. To take them back to their native villages along the St. Lawrence was not easy. Often the women did not want to go. And often, when they did, they received a cruel reception from the white men and women—especially the women—of Lower Canada.

The *voyageur* knew this and, if what Gabriel Franchère surmised was true, he was also a little ashamed of showing up in Terrebonne or Chateauguay with a dusky wife and a troop of half-savage children. The answer sometimes was to remain in the Indian Country. Franchère describes some who did, at Fort William:

There are also on the opposite bank of the river a certain number of log houses, all inhabited by old Canadian *voyageurs*, worn out in the service of the company, without having enriched themselves. Married to women of the country, and encumbered with large families of half-breed children, these men prefer to cultivate a little Indian corn and potatoes, and to fish, for their subsistence, rather than to return to their native districts, to give their relatives and former acquaintance certain proofs of their misconduct and imprudence.[19]

After the conquest of Canada by the British, many French-Canadians who had married Indian women still clung to the fur country in such half-breed settlements as Michilimackinac rather than leave their families behind. One French trader, Jean-Baptiste Cadotte, with his Ojibway wife, Anastasie, continued to fly the fleur-de-lis over their trading post long after it had been lowered on the ramparts of Quebec.

But if the time for departure could pose problems for the *voyageur* or mountain man, it could bring stark tragedy to his Indian wife. While she was young and good-looking, it may have been, as John Lawson said early in the history of Indian-white relationships, that "she was as ready to untie the knot at one end as you are at the other." But aside from matters of the heart, there was always the question of survival, alone and in a hostile world. For an Indian woman—especially if she was along in years and burdened with children—was not welcomed back by her own people.

The plight of an Indian wife discarded by her man is pictured by the early Superintendent of Indian Trade, Colonel Thomas L. McKenney:

It is true, uncles sometimes sell their nieces for money or merchandise, to traders and engagés. Marriages thus contracted frequently produce a state of great connubial happiness; but if the purchaser abandon his purchase, she is discarded, and is never taken for a wife by a brave, but is left to perform all the drudgery of the lodge and the field, and is treated as an outcast.[20]

The irony of the Indians' complaints about the number of women and children thus left on their hands by white men is pointed out by Colonel Dodge:

A father can get for his daughter possibly twice as much from a white man as an Indian would pay, and he sells at the highest price. . . . Having sold and got his price, he feels himself relieved of all responsibility regarding her. She should henceforth be supported by her husband; and the father regards it as a hardship, an outrage, a real cause for complaint, to be obliged, even partially, to assist in the support of a woman, his own daughter, sacrificed by his cupidity to a man whom he knew would abandon her sooner or later.[21]

To be protected from outrage and insult, hunger and want, it was imperative for an Indian woman to have a man. Even widows much preferred the abuse of a brutal husband to the horrors of being left alone; and a widow's life was soft and secure compared with that of a woman thrown back on the mercies of the tribe by a vanishing white husband.

To be turned adrift in a white settlement or trading post was perhaps even worse. It could lead only to prostitution, degradation, and a tragic, lingering death. Yet this could happen to any Indian girl who found herself sold to a white man; it was only the lucky ones who escaped.[22]

In some ways the children may have suffered most. They suffered the panic, fear, dismay, and perhaps bewildered anger that little ones must always feel when parents separate, no less in the *pays sauvage* than in civilized environments. Henry the Younger, never too busy to record the small dramas of his post, sets this one down in his fort journal:

Duford quarreled and parted from his wife; he wished to detain his son, a boy about nine years of age; but the little fellow preferred to go with his mother, and on leaving the house fired three arrows at his father, but missed him . . .[23]

In addition to the usual "broken home" trauma, the abandoned children of white men became the victims of cruel interracial tensions. Neither white nor Indian, they were destined to grow up as "marginal" men and women, lost between two worlds, in neither of which were they liked or wanted.[24] Just as their mothers regarded themselves as superior to other Indian women because of their alliances with white men, these half-breed offspring often took an overbearing pride in their white blood. Their airs offended the pure-blooded Indians, and the whites regarded them with contempt.[25]

Half-breed children whose fathers remained in the Indian Country were protected, to a degree at least, from hunger and want. But those left behind with an abandoned mother, to shift for themselves among resentful and hostile adults, could hardly have drawn a more bitter fate.

Some of the fur trading companies made halfhearted attempts to alleviate what even the hard-nosed *bourgeois* must have recognized as a deplorable situation. But it is difficult to find evidence that any American trader ever showed much interest in the problem; anything done west of the Mississippi must be credited to the feeble efforts of the missionaries. The Nor'westers, who were forever complaining about "the burden" of half-breed children to the Company, did not, at least, leave them and their mothers to starve. As the Reverend Daniel Haskell righteously points out in his preface to Daniel Harmon's journal, "These women and children, with a humanity which deserves commendation, are not turned over to the savages; but they are fed, if not clothed, by the Company." At one time the North West Company contemplated a settlement on Rainy Lake River, where such people would not encumber the trading posts. Company officers even subscribed several thousand dollars for a school at Rainy Lake Fort or Fort William. But union with the Hudson's Bay Company overtook both plans—if, in fact, they were ever seriously considered.[26]

The Hudson's Bay Company displayed what at first glance might seem to have been an enlightened concern for the women and children of its "servants." In a set of forty-two "Standing Rules and Regulations," the last deals with the matter thus:

RESOLVED that all Officers and Servants of the Company having women and children, and wishing to leave the same in the country on their retirement therefrom, be required to make such provisions for their future maintenance, more particularly for that of the children, as circumstances may reasonably warrant and the means of the individual permit; that all those desirous of withdrawing the same from the country be allowed every facility for that purpose; and that none hereafter be allowed to take a woman without binding himself to such reasonable provision and maintenance of her and children, in the event of issue, as on a fair and equitable principle may be considered necessary, not only during his residence in the country, but after his departure therefrom.[27]

This, of course, was as full of holes as a Cree snowshoe, and how much it benefited the wife and children of a departing trader may be doubted.

The Company was also piously concerned about the moral condition of its servants and their wives and children. Another set of regulations—this for the promotion of moral and religious improvement—directs chief factors and chief traders to see to it that divine service be read every Sunday to everyone, including Indians "who may be at hand, and whom it may be proper to invite." Women and children were to be furnished regular and useful occupations "best calculated to suppress vicious and promote virtuous habits." Fathers were always to address their wives and children in English or French, and to devote part of their leisure hours to teaching their children the ABC's, catechism, and other elementary instruction.[28]

Harmon says that his friend Jeanny Sutherland learned to read and write at a school on the Bay. And Letitia Hargrave tells of an Indian woman at York Fort whose children attended the important missionary school in the Red River settlement. She was not allowed to see them, Letitia says, because, as the Reverend John McCallum so reasonably pointed out, she had never been legally wed to her Indian husband.[29]

After an odd disappearance of some seventy-five years' duration, Roman Catholic missionaries began to rebuild churches and open schools in the old French settlements—Michilimackinac, La Pointe, Sault Ste. Marie—and the Presbyterians were soon hard on their heels. Between the 1820's and 1830's a lively competition for souls was waged between Protestants and Catholics, and schools were provided for Indian and half-breed children in fur trading settlements as far west as Vancouver. In 1844, Grey Nuns from Montreal traveled to Fort Garry on the Red River of the North, a wilderness journey of two months, to teach in the school founded by Angelique Nolin, daughter of a North West Company trader, at St. Boniface.[30] Incidentally, daughters of prominent traders, including the half-breed daughter of Ramsay Crooks, quite often devoted their lives to the education of women and children of their tribes.

Bourgeois who wished to give their sons the advantages of a higher education than the rudimentary instruction offered by the missionary schools sent them to Montreal, St. Louis, and sometimes even to Europe. Some deep psychological compulsion seems to have moved successful traders to try and make educated "white men" out of their sons by Indian mothers. In rare instances, the attempt was successful; more often it ended in disaster.[31]

❧

With the *bourgeois*, many of whom were cultivated men of honor and sensitivity, leaving behind a wife and children was often a more complicated and painful matter than it was with the ordinary *engagé* or mountain man. But most of them brought themselves somehow to abandon their families, perhaps after making some provision for their support.

The early French traders were often an exception to what became the general rule. Not only did most of them take Indian wives, but also, since there was usually a black robe near at hand, they frequently had their marriage legitimized by the church. Many ended their days with their legal Indian spouses in some trading settlement such as Sault Ste. Marie or La Pointe.

While the evidence points to almost all the officers of the Hudson's Bay Company having married Indian women *à la façon du pays*, it is obvious that such unions were regarded as mere stopgaps—something with which to make do until the time for return to England, and marriage to a white woman, rolled around. It is painful, for instance, to have to report that young Henry Kelsey, who so manfully demanded admittance to York Fort for his new Indian bride, appears ten years later in English marriage records as the husband of Elizabeth Dix of East Greenwich. On his death, he left his property to her, and there is no mention in his will of the Cree girl who stood with him on that anxious day before the great gates of York.[32] Later on, as we shall see, chief traders and chief factors of the Great Company remained in Canada and the pattern changed. Then Indian wives were often cherished, honored, and defended against white prejudice through life. And sometimes they became titled ladies.[33]

Among the Nor'westers, a few like Alexander Henry the Younger were frank enough to document their relationships with Indian women; but most of the personal diaries, let alone fort journals, are stiffly silent on the subject, and it is only from collateral evidence in court records, registry offices, and other official sources that we learn how individual *bourgeois* married, then left native girls in the *pays sauvage*.

Even Henry, after his entertaining account of how he happened to acquire the Liard's daughter as a wife, has little to say about her. There is only an occasional journal mention of "Her Lady-ship's" being indisposed or bearing him another child. We never learn her name or what happened to her when Henry left for the Columbia and the fascinating company of blond Jane Barnes. Of his children, it may be surmised that one Robert Henry, who for a time served the North West Company and the Hudson's Bay Company, then returned to Lower Canada and "henceforth disappears from view," was possibly his son.

Henry's more famous uncle, Alexander Henry of the Province of New Jersey, says nothing in his detailed *Travels and Adventures* about his having had an Indian wife. But the Catholic Church baptismal records at La Pointe show that a Jean-Baptiste Henry, Jr., was born to Jean-Baptiste Henry and Theresa Kebeweke Henry in 1840; and the discoverer of this obscure vital statistic asks, "Did Alexander Henry leave behind some *bois brulés?*" Through this kind of detective work the ghostly wives of the *bourgeois* emerge from the past.[34]

Alexander Mackenzie, the greatest of the Nor'westers, had a native wife. Mackenzie not only became the most powerful of the *bourgeois*, but he also immortalized himself as an explorer by two daring expeditions. On the first, he discovered the great river that bears his name and followed it to the Arctic Ocean. On the second, he crossed the continent, the first man ever to accomplish the feat, twelve years ahead of Lewis and Clark. He wrote his famous memoirs, was knighted, returned to Scotland and married a celebrated beauty, his cousin Geddes Mackenzie. That this illustrious man, somewhere during the course of his vast adventures, took an Indian girl as a wife is revealed by a passage in Harmon's journal:

Mr. A. R. McLeod and company have just arrived from Encampment Island; and they bring the melancholy intelligence of the death of Mr. Andrew McKenzie, natural son of Sir Alexander Mackenzie. He expired at Fort Vermilion on the 1st inst. The death of this amiable young man is regretted by all who knew him.[35]

We know from other sources that Andrew was employed as a clerk by the North West Company in the Athabasca district, but there is no record of what became of his mother, the Indian girl who was the famous explorer's wife before he married the beautiful Geddes Mackenzie and became the Laird of Avoch.

The list of Nor'westers who took "Indian wives," begat half-breed children, and left both the children and their mothers behind them in the *pays sauvage* is a long one. Again in Harmon's journal, we find this charmingly oblique reference to the "country marriage" of the powerful *bourgeois* Archibald Norman McLeod:

Mr. A. N. McLeod has a son here [Fort Vermilion] named Alexander, who is nearly five years of age, and whose mother is of the tribe of the Rapid Indians. In my leisure time I am teaching him the rudiments of the English language. The boy speaks the Sauteaux and Cree fluently, for a child; and makes himself understood tolerably well in the Assiniboin and French languages. In short, he is like most children of this country blessed with a retentive memory and learns very readily.[36]

McLeod, after rising to great prominence in the hierarchy of the North West Company, retired to Scotland and married a white wife. What happened to the Rapid Indian mother of his precocious little son Alexander, we shall never know.[37]

Among the Nor'westers, Patrick Small stands out as a man enjoying something like civilized home life in the *pays sauvage*.

The journals of several *bourgeois* pause to comment on his pleasant household, presided over by his Cree wife, at Isle à la Crosse. The Smalls had three children. Patrick became a successful trader. Charlotte married the great David Thompson. Nancy became the wife of colorful John McDonald of Garth. But the records are silent on what became of their attractive Cree mother after Small retired from the fur trade and returned to England.[38]

A Frenchman, Charles Chaboillez, sprung from a line of prominent traders, was college-educated in Montreal, and traded on the Red and Assiniboin rivers. Enigmatically, he brought back with him from the West four half-breed children, who were properly baptized at Terrebonne, in Lower Canada. The same year, he married Jessy Dunbar Selby Bruyères. Of the half-breed children's mother, nothing, not even her name, is known.[39]

Hugh McGillis became rich enough in the fur trade to buy Sir John Johnson's large estate at Williamstown in Upper Canada, where there is a tablet in the Catholic church to his memory. He married an Indian wife in the West, but sent her back to her own people when he settled in Williamstown. And that is all we know of her.[40]

Duncan M'Gillivray, along with William and Simon, a nephew of the great Simon McTavish, was proprietor of Upper Fort des Prairies. He wrote a well-known journal of trading-post life and, after rising to a high place in the councils of the Nor'westers, retired and became a respected resident of Montreal. He never took a white wife, but he was survived by a half-breed son William, whose Indian mother remains, like so many of her sisters, nameless.[41]

Among the American *bourgeois* along the Missouri River and westward into the Rockies, there were few—perhaps none—who did not have "Indian connections."

Ramsay Crooks, John Jacob Astor's right-hand man and, after Astor himself, the most powerful figure in the American Fur Trading Company, may be taken as an example of how these *bourgeois* managed their liaisons with native women. At the age of thirty, Crooks married an Ojibway girl, who bore him a daughter at Michilimackinac. The next we hear, he has become interested—possibly for reasons of policy—in the teen-age daughter of General Bernard Pratte, a prominent St. Louis fur merchant. In 1825 we find him married to her, although he is twice her age, and the following year a daughter is born to them.

It can be said of Crooks that he did not abandon his first child by his Indian wife. He gave this daughter—whom he called Hester—his own name, visited her, and placed her in a missionary school at Michilimackinac. Years later, we find him visiting Hester at Fond du Lac, where she taught school, and frequently sending letters and dolls to his granddaughter, and gifts for her little half-breed schoolmates. But we are not told what became of the Ojibway girl who was Hester's mother.[42]

Next to Crooks, perhaps the most compelling figure in the American Fur Company was Kenneth McKenzie, head of the Upper Missouri Outfit and builder of Fort Union. McKenzie was a Scot by birth and a relative of Sir Alexander Mackenzie. Wearing a military uniform and dealing out directives, discipline, and hospitality with the assurance and arrogance of a born commander, he was universally respected and feared—and "the ablest trader the American Fur Company ever had." Even the veteran trader Charles Larpenteur was impressed by him: "Imagine my surprise . . . to find myself in the presence of Mr. McKenzie, who was at that time considered king of the Missouri: and from the style in which he was dressed, I really thought he was a king." While he reigned at Fort Union, McKenzie married an Indian woman, by whom he had a son, Owen McKenzie. With that, our knowledge of his marital relationships in the Indian Country ends. Except for the usual denouement: after returning to St. Louis, he married a white woman, by whom he had two children. About the King of the River's Indian queen—nothing more.[43]

And so it went, along a line that seldom deviated, ending with the return of the *bourgeois* to civilization and his Indian wife's disappearance in the silence of the *pays sauvage*. It was no different on the bleak shores of Hudson Bay, on the Missouri River, in the defiles of the Rockies, or on the sun-baked plains of the American

Southwest. In this, as in most other respects, the relationships of white men and Indian women had a curious way of shaping up to the same pattern on all frontiers—or, for that matter, at any place in the world where civilized men and primitive women came together.

But there are exceptions to every rule of human behavior, and sometimes a *bourgeois* broke the stereotype.

Some wanted to have it both ways. Reluctant to leave their Indian wives and half-breed children, yet drawn by irresistible racial attraction to marriage with a white woman, they tried to keep the old along with the new; and occasionally, after a fashion, they succeeded.

One who did was the great William McGillivray, chief of the Nor'westers, after whom Fort William on Lake Superior was named. Born and educated in Scotland, McGillivray came to Canada as a youth, entered the North West Company and spent five or six years in the Interior before becoming a partner of the Concern. During these years, he married a Cree girl named Susan. He left her behind when he returned temporarily to Montreal, but rejoined her at Isle à la Crosse in 1790. Susan gave birth to twin boys at that remote post; and the baptismal records of Christ Church, Montreal, show that "Simon and Joseph, twin sons of William McGillivray in the Indian Country," were christened there, with the illustrious Nor'westers Alexander Mackenzie and Joseph Frobisher as godfathers.

Not long after this, McGillivray married Magdelein McDonald, sister of John McDonald of Garth, in London; but he continued to maintain his Indian family, which now included a daughter Elizabeth and another son, Peter, at La Crosse. He gave all his *métis* children his name and probably sent the twins to boarding school in Montreal. Susan, however, was "kept out of mind." She was brought to Fort William in 1807, where she may have been married "to some honest man," in the fashion of the Northwest. In 1817 she died, and a marker was erected on her grave at Fort

William, it is not recorded by whom. It reads: "To the memory of Susan, the mother of Simon, Joseph, and Peter McGillivray . . ." [44]

Alexander Fraser was also a two-family Nor'wester. A partner of the Company and proprietor of important posts in the Interior, he bought the seigniory of Rivière du Loup on his retirement, and settled in with two wives—one Indian, the other white. In the *pays d'en haut*, Fraser had married a native girl named Angelique Meadows, and by her he had a son and three daughters. While his Indian wife and children were still living Indian fashion at Rivière du Loup, he married Pauline Michaud, by whom he also had several children. We do not know exactly how Fraser's marital plan worked out, but it seems to have functioned fairly well. On his death, at any rate, his half-breed progeny were still on hand to claim a share of his estate—and, what is more, to win their case when the courts adjudged his "country marriage" to his Indian wife valid and binding. [45]

The marital history of William Conolly, a celebrated Nor'wester, was somewhat similar, although Conolly, whom Ross Cox called *un véritable bon garçon*, did not attempt to maintain his two wives as neighbors. During his thirty years in the Indian Country, Conolly married a Cree woman named Susanne, who bore him six children, one of whom became Lady Douglas. After twenty years, however, he repudiated his Indian wife, having been advised by the church that the marriage was not valid. He sent Susanne to a convent on the far-off Red River of the North and married Julia Woolrich, the daughter of a wealthy Montreal merchant. He continued to support his Indian wife; and after his death, his white wife assumed that responsibility. As in Fraser's case, his half-breed children sued to obtain a share of his estate, and once again the Canadian courts ruled the Indian marriage valid. [46]

The American Fur Company trader Peter Sarpy was another of those who maintained a kind of dual matrimonial establishment such as could have existed only on the bizarre frontiers of the fur trade. Having married a beautiful Omaha-Iowa girl, Nicomi, the widow of Dr. John Gale, physician and surgeon of the Sixth

Infantry at Fort Atkinson, Sarpy raised a family of eight half-breed children, including Gale's daughter Mary. With promises that she would be allowed to visit her tribe at least once a year, Nicomi was persuaded to live in St. Louis, where Mary had been placed in school. But the pull of her Indian blood was too strong for her. She begged to be taken back to her people. So Sarpy built a comfortable house for her near his post; and here, the respected wife of a *bourgeois*, she passed her later days close to the scenes of her Indian girlhood. At the same time, Sarpy's white wife lived across the river at St. Mary's, Iowa.[47]

Yet another prominent American *bourgeois* who maintained a white wife and family in the East while living with an Indian spouse at his trading post was James Kipp, a trader on the Missouri for four decades. When John Palliser met "the hardy old veteran" in 1846, he was living on his farm near Independence, Missouri, with a white wife and family. But when Rudolph Kurz visited him at Fort Berthold five years later, he was entertained by Kipp and a Mandan wife.[48]

Of the polygamous Indian trader toward the end of the fur trading era, Colonel Dodge paints this unflattering portrait:

These men frequently become very wealthy, building great outfitting stores and depots in favorable locations, and gain great influence, not only with the Indians, but sufficient among the magnates at Washington to secure the passage of laws for the benefit of themselves and their half-breed children. Their red wives, being only property, are no impediment to their possession of white wives and families in the States. As they grow old, some retire from business, return to their families in the States, and not infrequently take a prominent position in society and public affairs, and are looked up to as authority on all Indian questions. Others pass the winter of their days in their Western homes, surrounded in a patriarchal manner by a crowd of admiring wives, children, and dependents.[49]

How much of love, heartbreak, hatred, and torment beyond the ken of civilized women sometimes attended a trader's "country marriage," one can only guess. But in some cases, as in the marriage of Manuel Lisa, it was tragically clear.

Of all the Indian traders who sent their fur brigades up the Missouri from St. Louis, Manuel Lisa was the most daring, the most active, and—his ubiquitous enemies would have added—the most ruthless. Concentrating every ounce of his prodigious energy on his own aggrandizement and that of his Missouri Fur Company, he was also one of the most successful of traders.

Lisa made the sort of Indian marriage one would expect of such a man. Purely to ingratiate himself with the powerful Omaha tribe, and thus gain a trading edge over his rivals, he negotiated marriage with the beautiful daughter of one of that nation's principal families. The girl, Mitain—possibly repulsed by Lisa's dark intensity—was not very enthusiastic. The fact that Lisa was already married to a white woman may also have dampened her interest, although in the Indian view it was no bar to a second alliance. The marriage, however, was celebrated *à la façon du pays*, and Mitain took her wifely place in Lisa's quarters.

Then Lisa went down to St. Louis with the winter catch of furs; and when he returned in the fall, Mitain joyfully brought her first-born, a daughter, down to the boat landing. The following autumn, Mitain presented Lisa with another child, this time a son; and what had begun as a frank marriage of policy gave every sign of having developed into a tender marital relationship. Mitain, it has been suggested, had even fallen deeply in love with her husband.

But Lisa, seized with the same odd compulsion that gripped so many white men when they became the father of a child by an Indian woman, could not let matters be. On his return to St. Louis, he insisted on taking his daughter Rosalie with him. Mitain, wilting before his white inflexibility, consented. Indianlike, she stoically concealed her grief as she watched her husband and first-born child start down the muddy Missouri; then, Indianlike, she burst into a terrible paroxysm of weeping as they disappeared.

But Lisa was not yet through. That same fall, his first white wife having died, he married Mary Hempstead Keeney, from a promi-

nent St. Louis family. In the fall of 1819, he planned to take his
new wife up the Missouri with him, to Fort Lisa, and such was the
"sensitiveness" of his nature that he sent word ahead to have
Mitain removed from the vicinity of the post. Mitain, however,
sent their second child, Raymond, to him from her people's
encampment. Lisa received his son affectionately, sent the mother
some presents, and ordered her to remain away.

In the spring of 1820, Lisa pushed Mitain a little closer to the
brink of despair. He sent for her and broke the news that he
intended to take Raymond to St. Louis with him. That evening,
Mitain fled with her child across the river, but the next morning,
surrendering to the inevitable, she returned, to beg only that
Lisa take her with him also. Any little corner in the strange world
downriver would do; she would keep out of his way, make herself
as nothing, just so that she might be near her children. Then, in the
face of his obdurateness, she flew into a fierce, taunting, berating
defense of her right to remain his wife and the mother of his little
ones. Lisa remained inflexible.

It says something for human compassion, perhaps, that the
Indian agent at Fort Lisa stepped in at this point and forbade
Lisa to take the child away from his mother. And something for the
even-handedness of fate that all of Manuel Lisa's white children
died without issue; if any of his blood still flows in human veins,
it is mixed with that of his rejected Indian wife.[50]

V

"TO HAVE AND TO HOLD"

Sometimes it happened that a *bourgeois* fell in love with his Indian wife. Perhaps at first sight something jumped the gap of centuries and forever afterwards "the small roots of their hearts entangled," as the Ojibway so poetically expressed it. Or perhaps love came slowly, almost reluctantly, through years together in the *pays sauvage*, but all the more enduring because of its subtle, imperceptible unfolding in the long sharing of danger, privations, suffering, and affection for their children.

Nor were the lower ranks of the fur trade—the *engagés*, *voyageurs*, trappers, and freemen—always content to accept sex where they could find it and ask no more of a woman. Many discovered that having a new wife each time one shifted to a new tribe was not the same as coming home from a dreary trap line to one girl whose sole interest was to feed him and see to his comfort and make much of him with a complete singleness of affection. So it was that both *bourgeois* and lowly *engagé* sometimes made alliances with native women which, despite *pays sauvage* custom, and notwithstanding the frowns and sneers of missionaries' wives and other pillars of white Christian society, endured till death.

Where a priest or minister of the Gospel was available, these unions were often celebrated in proper form. The "Mackinac Register of Marriages" records scores of very early marriages performed by missionary fathers. A typical entry:

October 13, 1749, I received the mutual marriage consent of joseph victor Couvret, a former voyageur, and of marie charlotte, a woman savage, after one publication of bans, having granted dispensation from the others for valid reasons . . .

P. Du Jaunay, miss. of the society of Jesus.[1]

At times such marriages were merely a confirmation of vows taken before witnesses in the *pays d'en haut*; occasionally they validated marriages performed by a justice of the peace or the commander of a military post. It was all rather complicated, and some of the good missionary fathers worried about it. Thus Father Sevère Joseph Nicolas Dumoulin, writing from Pembina to his bishop in Quebec:

Some of the Indian women have been taught, and would be ready for baptism and marriage if they were not already married, according to the custom of the land, to drunken Canadians. What shall be done with these women? Must we wait until their husbands are converted, or advise them to abandon them?[2]

It was customary, when married by a priest, for the husband to acknowledge paternity of any children he and his bride may have already produced, and for the offspring to be baptized.[3] A certain quaintness attaches to a marriage certificate that reads:

July 22, 1747. I received the mutual marriage consent of jean Baptiste Tellier de la fortune and of marie josephe, a nepissingue woman Baptized this morning, by which marriage were legitimized Antoine, 19 years old; francois xavier, 14 years old; Ann, ten years old; ignace, 6 years old; Joseph, 3 years old; and marie joseph, 6 months old, their children . . .[4]

In settlements without a priest, an interval of several years might separate the visits of a missionary father; in this case, something like a mass celebration of marriages and baptisms took place. This happened as a matter of course on the more remote frontiers, as is indicated by Father De Smet's activities among the Flathead Indians,[5] and those of Protestant clergymen in Rupert's Land and Oregon. Garry mentions a Reverend John West's having married twenty-five couples and christened 121 children at the Hudson's Bay Company's Norway House;[6] and the same Reverend West is described as being fully occupied after his arrival at the Red River settlement "in marrying many who had formerly lived as man and wife, though already married after the Indian fashion, and in baptizing the children." [7]

Some couples, however, were unwilling to wait for a clergyman to come to them, and traveled long distances to have their marriages legitimized. Thus, when the trader Michel Cadotte fell in love with Traveling Woman, daughter of the famous Ojibway chief White Crane, and there was no priest to marry them, they journeyed from La Pointe to the Sault, a distance of some five hundred miles, for a church marriage. Traveling Woman was christened Madeleine at the Sault, and when the newlyweds returned home, La Pointe was renamed Madeleine Island in her honor. [8]

On Hudson Bay no Christian clergyman or visiting missionary was to be found for a hundred and fifty years after the first supply ship arrived. Nor did the French priests who accompanied La Vérendrye to the Missouri leave behind them any missions. After the conquest of Canada by the British, the French traders withdrew from the Northwest, leaving no trace of Christianity in their wake. And in the vast beaver country stretching westward from the Missouri and into the Rockies, the Cross was not to be seen anywhere before the Spanish settlements were reached. Hence, it was not until the revival of missionary activity in the early nineteenth century that religious ceremonies began to figure in the marriages of white men and Indian women. And even then, traders often had their "country marriages" validated only because such troublesome matters as inheritance rights cropped up. Some, like tough old Peter Skene Ogden, the famous Hudson's Bay Company trader, held out against convention to the end. At the point of death, Ogden stubbornly refused to remarry his native wife according to church rites. If all their years together were not proof enough of the depth and integrity of their relationship, he said, a few words intoned by a man of God would not make it sacred. [9]

It was not always easy for a *bourgeois* to face the ordeal of returning home with an Indian wife and a brood of half-breed children. Sometimes, indeed, the step was taken only after a long and agonizing struggle of love and conscience with inbred racial attitudes. One trader has left us a record of his ordeal of self-torment: Daniel Williams Harmon, of Vermont.

Harmon was twenty-two years old when, on April 29, 1800, he left Lachine with a brigade of Nor'westers for the Indian Country. "For the first time in my life," he wrote in his journal, "I am to pass the night in a tent."

At first, Harmon was to find life in the *pays sauvage* quite trying. The way people behaved, for instance, was scandalous. Take "Mr. P.", of whom Harmon wrote on his second week out from Montreal:

I have had a little conversation with my fellow-traveler respecting his conduct the last evening, while I was absent. When I departed for the Fort, I gave him the keys to our traveling box and basket; and, on my return, I was not a little surprised at finding not only him, but several of the common laborers, much intoxicated. I reprimanded Mr. P. with considerable severity, today, and told him, that if I should ever again find him in the like shameful condition, I should be under the disagreeable necessity of informing our employers of his conduct . . . He promised that he would not again be guilty of such conduct, but I should place more reliance on his promise, had not his mother been a *squaw*.

The italics are Harmon's own, and they underscore an attitude that must have generated a good deal of puzzlement, and perhaps a few raised eyebrows, among the Nor'westers. For young Daniel Harmon brought with him into the Indian Country a fanatical contempt for—and perhaps fear of—the native women that not even the celebrated charms of the Ojibway girls could break down. Against all the temptations of the *pays sauvage*, he raised the defences of his strict New England Puritanism; and for several years he held out successfully, although at times he was perilously near to surrender.

On one of these occasions, Harmon was at Swan River Fort, Manitoba, and eighteen months had passed since he had left home

and civilization. A Cree chief called on him and offered him one of
his pretty daughters. Harmon declined the offer, but only after
a terrific struggle with his natural inclination; and it was characteristic of him that, in reporting the incident, he should write:

He almost persuaded me to keep her, for I was sure that while I had the
daughter I should not only have the father's furs but those of all his band.
This would have been for the interest of the Company, and would therefore turn to my own advantage in some measure; so that a regard to
interest well nigh made me consent to an act, which would have been
unwise and improper. But, happily for me, I escaped the snare.

The daughters of the Cree were often comely and sometimes
beautiful, but Harmon, it seems, thought only of the Company's
interest. He managed to maintain this improbable posture for
another three years, in the face of temptations we can only surmise.
Then, far up the Saskatchewan, he sat down before his fort
journal one night and wrote:

This day a Canadian's daughter, a girl of about fourteen years of age, was
offered to me; and after mature consideration, concerning the step which I
ought to take, I have finally concluded to accept her, as it is customary
for all gentlemen who remain for any length of time in this part of the
world to have a female companion with whom they can pass their time
more socially and agreeably than to live a lonely life, as they must do if
single.

So far, so good. Harmon has at last dropped the old "interest of
the Company" pose and is speaking in almost human terms. But
now comes an insufferable paragraph about how, if they can live
together in harmony, he intends to keep his new wife until he
returns to his native land. Then, of course, he will endeavor to
place her under the protection "of some honest man." After all,
she would find it very difficult to accustom herself to the language,
manners, and customs of the civilized world. She would be much
better off——

Poor Harmon—still battling with his Puritan's conscience, even
into the distant future. But, as if aware of the chill detachment of
what he has just written, he adds:

Her mother is of the tribe of Snare Indians, whose country lies along the Rocky Mountains. The girl is said to have a mild disposition and an even temper, which are qualities very necessary to make an agreeable woman and an affectionate partner.

Harmon's journal thereafter traces his travels to corners of the continent "where no white man has ever been before," and his steady rise to eminence as a Nor'wester. We almost never glimpse him at home with Elisabeth—for that was her name, although the journal does not tell us. But three years after their marriage *à la façon du pays* we come across this laconic entry:

Early this morning, the woman whom I have taken to reside with me became the mother of a boy, whom I name George Harmon.

Then, at Fort Dunvegan, on the icebound Peace River, a brief recording of a shared tragedy:

On the evening of the 15th ist. my woman was delivered of two living boys. They appear, however, to have been prematurely born; and from the first, little hope was entertained that they would long survive. One of them died on the morning of the 22nd, and the other last night; and today they were both buried in the same coffin.

In 1811, Harmon was stationed at a fort on the western slope of the Rockies, in what is now British Columbia. In April of that year, he sent his small son on an almost incredible journey from that remote post to the State of Vermont. The journal explains why:

Tomorrow I shall leave this place with Mr. Quesnel and others, for McLeod's Lake. I shall take with me my little son George, who was three years old last December, for the purpose of sending him to my friends in the United States, in order that he may receive an English education.

In the autumn of the following year, word reached Harmon that his son had arrived safely in the United States. A daughter, whom he named Polly, was born. Then, by the winter express, came the devastating word of George's death. And now, for the first time, Elisabeth appears as a woman of flesh and blood in her husband's journal, as Harmon clumsily tries to break the news to her:

I endeavored, by some introductory remarks, on the uncertainty of earthly things, to prepare her mind for the disclosure I was about to make. Her fears were alarmed . . . and probably she discovered in my countenance something to confirm them. When I informed her that our beloved son George was dead, she looked at me with a wild stare of agony and immediately threw herself upon the bed, where she continued in a state of delirium, during the succeeding night.

There can be no doubt that the death of his son was a heavy blow to Harmon, and a reality hard for him to accept. In one of the journal's most touching passages, written more than a year after George's death, he actually writes as though the little boy were still alive:

I now pass a short time every day, very pleasantly, in teaching my little daughter Polly to read and spell words in the English language, in which she makes good progress, though she knows not the meaning of one of them. In conversing with my children, I use entirely the Cree Indian language; with their mother I more frequently employ the French. Her native tongue, however, is more familiar to her, which is the reason why our children have been taught to speak it in preference to the French language.

It is not difficult to detect here an almost but not quite expressed change in Harmon's feelings toward the Cree girl whom he had, more than ten years before, taken with the intention of keeping "as long as I remain in this part of the world." She is the mother of his children now; they must be taught her language—her Indian tongue—as a mark of respect for her. Soon the same note of tenderness repeats itself in another journal entry:

This evening the mother of my children was delivered of a daughter, whom I name Sally Harmon.

Almost exactly two years later, Daniel Harmon, having spent seventeen years in the *pays sauvage*, prepared to return to civilization. The time of decision had at last arrived; and Harmon, groping for words, still half resisting, wrote out in his journal what, whether he realized it or not, was his testament of love for Elisabeth, his wife:

Saturday, February 28, 1819. . . . I am going to McLeod's Lake to prepare for my departure for Head Quarters; and my intention is, during the next summer, to visit my native land. I design, also, to take my family with me, and leave them there, that they may be educated in a civilized and christian manner. The mother of my children will accompany me; and, if she shall be satisfied to remain in that part of the world, I design to make her regularly my wife by a formal marriage . . .

Harmon pauses to make some comments on his change of attitude during his seventeen years in the *pays sauvage*, to acknowledge his moral obligations, and to set down the reasons why he has arrived at this "weighty decision." His coldly logical explanation is interrupted, however, by a rush of words in which he comes as close as Harmon ever could, perhaps, to declaring his deep and abiding love for the Indian woman he took as his wife *à la façon du pays* so many years ago:

The union which has been formed between us, in the providence of God, has not only been cemented by a long and mutual performance of kind offices, but also by a more sacred consideration. . . . We have wept together over the departure of several children, and especially over the death of our beloved son George. We have children still living who are equally dear to both of us. How could I spend my days in the civilized world, and leave my beloved children in the wilderness? How could I tear them from a mother's love and leave her to mourn over their absence to the day of her death? How could I think of her in such circumstances without anguish?

In late summer, Harmon and his family arrived at Fort William, and he recorded the arrival in the last entry of his journal:

I have at length arrived at headquarters. In coming from New Caledonia to this place, which is a distance of at least three thousand miles, nothing uncommon has occurred.

At Fort William, Elisabeth gave birth to a boy, whom Harmon named John. The rest of the journey to Canada, and then by the regular Lake Champlain route to Vermont, was uneventful. But the homecoming was not all what Harmon—and, no doubt, Elisabeth—had dreamed it would be.

It is not known exactly what happened, but the family tradition is that Daniel's Indian wife and half-breed children did not receive a friendly welcome in his native village of Vergennes, or later in Burlington. So Daniel and his brother Argalus founded a town of their own, Coventry, Vermont, where they would be safe from racial intolerance. After prosperous years in Coventry, during which they reared a large family, Daniel and Elisabeth fell on evil days and were forced by adversity to move to a tiny Canadian village near Montreal. And there, like so many other once affluent fur traders, Daniel Harmon died in poverty.[10]

There is a story still current in Canada that reflects the situation facing a *bourgeois* who brought his Indian family back to civilization with him. Finan McKenzie returned to his native village after many years in the beaver country, and the rumor quickly spread that he had brought an Indian wife with him. The women of the village, bursting with curiosity, delegated their husbands to engage Finan in conversation and, as diplomatically as possible, find out if the rumor was true. Cornering Finan in the local tavern, the men gradually worked the talk around to the point of their mission.

"Finan, we hear that ye have brought a wife home with ye from the West."

"Aye, that I have."

"And what might her nationality be, Finan?"

"She is a daughter of the country."

"Och, Finan, 'tis a great relief to hear ye say it. We feared she might be a squaw." [11]

Among the Nor'westers, however, there were not a few who, without Harmon's agonizing, did bring their Indian wives and children home, and settled into their native communities with no apparent difficulty. One of these was John ("The Priest") Macdonell.

There were so many Macdonells and McDonalds in the fur trade that the *voyageurs* gave them nicknames by which they could be told apart. Thus there was McDonald le Grand, McDonald le Borgne, McDonald of Garth, and John Macdonell (sometimes spelled McDonald) who, because of his reputation for piety, was called "Le Prêtre."

In 1793 Macdonell signed up with the North West Company and spent most of the next nineteen years in the Indian Country, where he married Magdeleine Poitras, the half-breed daughter of a trader on the Qu'Appelle River. When he returned to Lower Canada in 1812, he brought Magdeleine and their children with him and settled down to a patriarchal life at his "Poplar Villa" on the Ottawa River. Although a devoted Roman Catholic, he seems to have felt a church marriage unnecessary, and it was not until 1835 that he and Magdeleine, then the mother of his eight children, were legally united in wedlock.[12]

Equally faithful to his Indian wife, but in a different and tragic fashion, was Charles MacKenzie. After becoming an apprentice clerk of the North West Company in 1803, MacKenzie had the bad luck to be stationed during his whole career in the poorest fur districts in Canada. Without much hope of advancement, he married an Indian woman, raised a family, and resisted his friends' urgings to leave the Indian Country. MacKenzie battled fiercely for his half-breed children against the bias of the whites. When his son, an intelligent youngster who had completed a full course of studies at the Red River Seminary, was refused a position by the Hudson's Bay Company, he wrote hotly: "It appears that the present Concern has stamped the Cain mark upon all born in this country." He raged against missionary work among the natives of Africa and Asia while the American Indians were neglected. He cursed the British government for having sold the red men to a "monopoly," i.e., the Hudson's Bay Company. Charles MacKenzie was not the only Nor'wester who married an Indian girl and remained true to her for life, but he may be remembered as one of

the few who waged an unremitting—and, of course, futile—
crusade on behalf of his wife and her people.[13]

🌸

That white men of the highest intelligence and accomplishment
could find happiness in marriage to an Indian woman, and that
such a union could endure through a lifetime of mutual respect
and affection, is nowhere better illustrated than by the marriage
of David Thompson and Charlotte Small.

"The greatest land geographer the world has ever known," J. B.
Tyrrell, the eminent editor of *Thompson's Narrative*, has called
Thompson. And it is indeed difficult to follow, even in the imagi-
nation, this remarkable man's peregrinations over half a continent.

David Thompson served his apprenticeship with the Hudson's
Bay Company. At the age of nineteen he struck inland from the
Bay and reached a point farther west on the Saskatchewan than
any white man had yet ventured. About this time perhaps, his big
dream was already forming: the dream of a "Great Map of the
West." During the next two years, he was endlessly on the move,
making traverses, observing for longitude and latitude, taking
notes, performing singlehanded almost incredible feats of geodetic
surveying.

Then, receiving little support or encouragement in his work
from the Hudson's Bay Company, he joined the Nor'westers. His
first assignment was: (1) to determine the Forty-ninth Parallel,
the new boundary between the United States and Canada; (2) to
visit the Mandan Indians; (3) to search for fossil bones of large
animals, i.e., mammoths; (4) to fix the positions of the North
West Company's trading posts. Freed of all other responsibilities,
Thompson made a tremendous 4,000-mile swing through totally
unmapped territory—a one-man survey that took him far up the
Assiniboin, to the Mandan villages, and back through Grand
Portage and Sault Ste. Marie. The Great Map of the West was
taking shape; and succeeding surveys, even longer and more
hazardous, pinpointed lakes, rivers, mountains, and trading posts
so accurately that their locations remain fixed to this day.

In the midst of all this, Thompson married Charlotte Small. Charlotte was the daughter of Patrick Small, whom we have already observed leading a pleasant domestic life at Isle à la Crosse. Her oldest sister, Nancy, had become the "Indian wife" of John McDonald of Garth; and Charlotte was fourteen when Thompson dropped in at Isle à la Crosse, fell in love with her, and asked Patrick Small for her hand. Married "after the fashion of the Northwest," Charlotte immediately set out with her husband on his epic journeyings.

Almost everywhere that Thompson went thereafter, Charlotte went with him. On his most perilous voyages, such as the one on which he discovered Athabasca Pass and followed the Columbia to the Pacific, he left her behind with friends or relatives. But on the others—even when he went into the dangerous Piegan country—he was accompanied by his "little family." They were with him at Rocky Mountain House, the westernmost post of the North West Company, in 1804, and on the long journey in the spring of that year to Fort William. In 1807, they were with him when he made his first great leap over the mountains and built Kutenai House on the Columbia. When Alexander Henry the Younger met Thompson on Lake Winnipeg in the spring of 1808, Charlotte had borne her peripatetic husband three children and was waiting for a fourth at a post called Boggy Hall, on the Saskatchewan; in October they were off again for Kutenai House, 3,000 miles away.[14]

Trading, building forts, taking observations, Thompson continued for twelve years to cross and recross the abysmal wilderness of the Canadian Northwest, traveling between Fort William on Lake Superior and Spokane House (ten miles from the present city of Spokane, Washington) as casually as a vacationist might set out on a trip by automobile over superhighways. Typical entries in Thompson's journal read: "Passed Grand Rapids into Lake Winnipeg; walked the portage with my family" . . . "Here [at Winnipeg House] I left my little family with her sister-in-law to the care of good Providence."

But even such indefatigable journeyings as David Thompson's

must come to an end, and in 1812 the great cartographer retired
to prepare his Great Map of the West—"the basis of all subsequent
maps" of the area, W. Stewart Wallace says. He and Charlotte
settled down with their children (there were sixteen in all) at
Terrebonne, Lower Canada. Their last days were passed in extreme
penury, which Thompson tried to relieve by writing his now
famous *Narrative*—and, at last, by pawning his beloved surveying
instruments, and even his coat. Charlotte died two months
after his own death in 1857, their marriage having endured for
fifty-eight years.[15]

❧

Much married among the Indians of the Lake Superior region
were the Cadottes. The first member of this celebrated family
of traders to appear in the country of the Ojibway was a Frenchman who spelled his name "Cadeau." He arrived at Sault Ste.
Marie in 1671, in the train of Simon-Francis Daumont, Sieur de
St. Lusson. Settling at the Sault, he wisely made it his first
business to marry an Indian girl.

Cadeau's son, Jean-Baptiste Cadotte, also took a daughter of
the Ojibway to live with him, then had the marriage legitimized
by the Jesuit Father Le France at Mackinac in 1756. His Indian
wife, Anastasie, appears to have been a remarkable woman. She
took an active part in her husband's business, went with him on
long and dangerous journeys into the *pays d'en haut*, and on occasion even commanded his fur brigades. She was, Alexander Henry
said, "very generally respected." And it is quite possible that
Anastasie's influence among her people was the chief reason why
Henry formed a partnership with Jean-Baptiste. Henry had other
reasons, too, for admiring Anastasie: at one point in his precarious
career, she had talked a band of hostile Indians out of doing him
in.[16]

How an Indian wife of Anastasie's caliber lived at home,
raised her family, and helped to conduct her husband's business
is reflected in Jean-Baptiste Cadotte's account book for his Sault
Ste. Marie post. At times indeed the book seems to have been less

Jean-Baptiste's than Anastasie's, who no doubt kept it for her husband. Some of the items were:

Paid to Sieur de Serre, and charged to Mme. Cadotte, £500 for 8 months at boarding school in Montreal [for Jean-Baptiste, Jr., age 12].

What Mme. Cadotte received: 1 pair silk gloves; 3¼ yards Valencienne [lace]: 1 dozen little buttons; 13 ells narrow braid; 1 pair shoes, double strong; 1 pair black silk gloves; 1½ ells cotton for lining trousers; paid for making redingotes, trousers, etc. £15; 6 pairs of shoes; 2 hats; 4 pairs trousers; 4 pairs stockings; 12 shirts . . . 1 cloak "devilishly strong."

Madame Cadotte apparently bought her husband's trousers and shirts, as well as her own gloves, stockings, and redingotes. Of special interest is an account of "provisions made to Mme. Cadotte for her and her children by Sieur Caseau":

Cotton thread for making stockings for the children; one quire of paper for Jean-Baptiste [age 11]; 3 ells Indienne [printed] calico; 4 ells royal Swiss linen; 2 packages silk fringe; 2 ells flowered carizee; taffeta cape of 9 ells; 2 balls of cotton to finish the stockings; 4½ ells fine blue cloth [broadcloth]; 100 needles; 5½ ells fine cotty to make beds for the children; 4 ells very strong linen for the straw mattresses.[17]

There is also an unspecified amount charged to "Mme. Cadotte's servant."

Life for an Indian wife and mother in the wild interior of the continent could apparently be almost as civilized as at the big Missouri River posts, or the extensive establishments of the H.B.C. on the Columbia. Some of the young Cadottes seem to have gone to school in Lower Canada. One of them, Jean-Baptiste, who cost Madame Cadotte £500 "for 8 months at boarding school in Montreal," spoke Latin, French, English, and Nipissing fluently, it was said. But he was also a drunkard who threw away his brilliant chances in the North West Company and was finally expelled. He was widely remembered in the *pays d'en haut* for having had an Indian murderer stabbed to death in the presence of "a vast concourse of people" at Fond du Lac.[18]

One of the sons of Anastasie and Jean-Baptiste was Michel

Cadotte, whose marriage to Traveling Woman (Madeleine) we have already noted. Among the many children of Michel and Madeleine was Marie, who married a trader named Lyman Warren, later chief factor of the American Fur Company at La Pointe. Another daughter, Charlotte, also married a Warren, a brother of Lyman's named Truman. And from this crossruffing of white and Indian blood there evolved a numerous family of traders, settlers, legislators, and writers, many of whom became eminent in the Northwest, and all of whom remained proud of and deeply loyal to their Indian heritage. The extent to which the genes of a single white trader could proliferate in an Indian population is indicated by the 1850 census of La Pointe: out of a total of 485 persons, no fewer than forty were descendants of Michel and Marie Cadotte, and so of the Frenchman Cadeau.[19]

When an Indian girl married a white man of rank and distinction, she had thrust upon her the fearful responsibility of directing his household, not just competently but with a touch of elegance; of entertaining his guests with charm and tact; and of rearing his children for their father's station in life. If her husband was master of a large post, whether on Hudson Bay, Lake Superior, or the Missouri, her social position was that of "first lady," the gentlemen she met were the aristocracy of the country, and much of her husband's success depended on her skill and diplomacy as a hostess.

Quite an order, one might think, for a "woman savage"! Yet, it was often the Indian wife who contributed the atmosphere of gracious hospitality, elegant living—and sometimes the intellectual tone—to a distinguished white man's establishment. And often she passed her own talents on to her daughters.

Shagowashcodawaqua ("the Woman of the Green Glades") was one such woman. When John Johnston, the son of a "highly connected" Irish family, came to La Pointe in 1791, he immediately fell in love with her. It must have been a little difficult for young Johnston to court a girl with a name like Shagowashcodawaqua, but he made out somehow, and Shagowashcodawaqua was quite willing to change all that to Mrs. Johnston. However, her father, Chief White Fisher, was not enthusiastic about a hasty marriage with a white man. In the way that Indian chiefs apparently had of talking, he is supposed to have said: "Englishman, my daughter is yet young, and you cannot take her, as white men have too often taken our daughters. It will be time enough to think of complying with your request when you return again to this lake. My daughter is my favorite child, and I cannot part with her, unless you promise to acknowledge her by such ceremonies as the white men use. You must ever keep her, and never forsake her."

Business called Johnston back to Montreal, but when he returned to La Pointe the following spring, he was still in love with White Fisher's beautiful daughter and she with him. So the protégé of Lord Dorchester was married to the daughter of an Ojibway chief, and the newlyweds moved to Sault Ste. Marie. Here they lived until Johnston died, thirty-seven years later.[20]

During these years, Johnston and his Indian wife reared a family of four girls and four boys, all of whom were well educated and acquitted themselves creditably in adult life. At the Sault, the Johnstons maintained a large domestic establishment that offered guests most of the amenities, including a library of a thousand "well-bound, well-selected" books in English and French; and here they welcomed such distinguished visitors as Governor Lewis Cass, Ramsay Crooks, Count Paolo Andreani, Commissioner Thomas McKenney—and a young man with Cass's party named Henry Rowe Schoolcraft.

Schoolcraft is best remembered today for having provided Longfellow with the background material for *Hiawatha*. But he was an enthusiastic—if rather pompous and pedantic—amateur of many disciplines, including geology, mineralogy, ethnology, linguistics, exploration, and literary composition. His chief interest, however, was in the language and customs of the Ojibway, and it was not long after his arrival at the Sault that this interest was transferred to Jane, the charming and accomplished young daughter of the Johnstons. After a brief courtship, they were married; and Jane, like her mother, became the chatelaine of an elegant ménage, famous for its warm and open hospitality. It seems likely, in view of Schoolcraft's brusque and egotistical personality, that Jane was in no small measure responsible for her husband's success as a host and man of affairs; it has even been suggested that some of the best in his voluminous writings was strongly influenced by the style and grace of his gifted, Irish-educated wife.[21]

When John Johnston died, White Fisher's daughter carried on his work, taking his fishing fleet into Lake Superior for the fall harvest of whitefish and overseeing the spring exodus to his personal "sugar bush." She never lost the simple dignity of her race or failed to meet the challenge of a white man's world on even terms.[22]

"Your people are not my people; your ways are not my ways. I must return to my own country."

This is the conventional—and convenient—way in which to end a novel depicting the love of an Indian girl and a white man of important rank. And, in fact, the outcome of such an attraction could be grim and tragic. Even Colin Robertson, a personage of considerable prominence among H.B.C. officers, was not strong enough to defend his *métis* wife's position in Red River Settlement society. The matter of his marriage to Theresa Chalifoux became a bitter issue between Robertson and Governor Simpson; and the fiery little governor fairly crowed in triumph when he wrote:

Robertson brought his bit of Brown with him to the settlement this spring in hopes that she would pick up a few English manners before visiting the civilized world; but it would not do—I told him distinctly that the thing was impossible, which mortified him exceedingly—he takes his departure, I understand, tomorrow, mortified and chagrined beyond description.[23]

A woman knew how to be even more cruel in fewer words. Thus Letitia Hargrave, writing of the Indian wife of Peter Warren

Dease, one of the Hudson's Bay Company's most illustrious chief factors, a famous explorer, and a man devoted to music and literature: "She is a very black squaw, and will make a curious lady." [24]

But the history of the fur trade does not want for instances of Indian women who did fit handsomely into civilized society, keeping the respect of their white neighbors and the love of their white husbands through a long lifetime. As we have seen, Shagowashcodawaqua was such a woman, and her daughter Jane another. And so, also, were the Indian wives of two great and famous men of the Hudson's Bay Company, Dr. John McLoughlin and Sir James Douglas.

It was rumored that young John McLoughlin decided to go west while practicing medicine in Quebec—and that his having pitched a drunken British officer into the muddy street, thus insulting His Majesty's uniform, had some bearing on the decision. He was nineteen at the time.[25]

In the summer of 1807, at any rate, he was at the North West Company's post on Sturgeon Lake, and for some years afterwards in the Rainy Lake district. Here he took an Indian girl as wife, but lost her at the birth of their first child. He then married Margaret Bruce, the half-Ojibway widow of Alexander McKay, who had accompanied Mackenzie on his overland journey to the Pacific.[26]

Margaret had received some education in the convent of the Ursuline nuns in Quebec. She was reputedly "a woman of physical charm and calm temperament," and she seemed to be just what "the Big Doctor" needed. McLoughlin himself had an outsize temper to go with his gigantic six-foot-three frame. He was constantly embroiled with antagonists ranging from the missionaries at Vancouver to Sir George Simpson. Margaret's placid disposition, in fact, seems to have been all that kept him within bounds during some of his famous tantrums.

McLoughlin's talents as trader and administrator eventually became more valuable to the Company than his skill as a physician and surgeon. After the North West Company and the Hudson's

Bay Company amalgamated in 1821, Governor Simpson chose him to command the Columbia Department, with the rank of chief factor. In 1823, he and his family set out from York Fort, traversed Lake Winnipeg, ascended the Saskatchewan and Athabasca rivers to Athabasca Pass, crossed the Rockies, and descended the Columbia to Astor's old post, Astoria, now called Fort George. Not long afterwards, McLoughlin began to build Fort Vancouver. In the spring of 1825, the new headquarters was completed, and Governor Simpson cracked a bottle of rum on the flagstaff, proclaiming in a loud voice to the assembled whites and Indians, "In behalf of the Honourable Hudson's Bay Company, I hereby name this establishment Fort Vancouver. God save King George the Fourth." And here, in perhaps the most enchanting setting that ever blessed a trading post, McLoughlin, with Margaret and their children, spent the next twenty years.

They were magnificent, stormy, frustrating, joyful, and finally tragic years. They were years filled with the vision of life in a Promised Land of unbelievably fertile valleys and a soft, pleasing climate. McLoughlin settled his retired French-Canadians and their Indian wives in the lovely Willamette Valley, where their children could be raised among white people, refusing to let them live near the tribes of their native wives. Although a devout Roman Catholic, he welcomed Protestant missionaries, and the miserable survivors of American fur trading operations in the West—mountain men with their Indian wives and children. "The Big Doctor" was kind and helpful to them all, supplying the newcomers with farming equipment, buildings, seeds, cattle, and food until they could stand on their own feet. And at the end, they turned on him and destroyed him.[27]

But in the years between, McLoughlin ruled his mountain empire benevolently, autocratically, and with a viceregal display of pomp and ceremony when the occasion seemed to require it. Toward Margaret he always showed a respect and deference that made her the envy of every American wife at Vancouver. When he accompanied one of his fur brigades as far as the Willamette Valley settlement, Margaret sometimes rode beside him on a silver-mounted saddle, with strings of silver bells tinkling on the bridle reins. In the florid idiom of the day, a trader's journal thus described "the Lady of Fort Vancouver":

Arrayed in brilliant colors, she wore a smile which might cause to blush and hang its head the broadest, warmest, and most fragrant sunflower. By her side rode the lord, the king of the Columbia, and every inch a king, attended by a train of trappers, under a chief trader, each upon his best behavior.[28]

Even in the halcyon days, however, there were troublesome interludes: for instance, McLoughlin's difficulties with the missionaries over his "country marriage." The most tolerant of men, welcoming people and pastors of all faiths, "the Big Doctor" nevertheless fell victim to the worst brand of bigotry and racial prejudice—the sanctimonious wrath of the clergy. American missionaries were beginning to arrive, Presbyterians and Methodists, and McLoughlin felt that the Hudson's Bay Company should be represented by a Church of England chaplain at Fort Vancouver. He accordingly put in a request for a clergyman of that faith, and the Company sent him the Reverend Herbert Beaver.

"Amongst the many good things their honours sent us this summer," Peter Skene Ogden wrote with gentle irony, "was a clergyman and with him his wife, the Reverend Mr. Beaver, a very appropriate name for the fur trade." The new chaplain soon proved himself to be no joking matter. A small man with a high, feminine voice, he was unimpressive in the pulpit, but he assailed the prevalence of "country marriages" and mixed blood with great vigor and venom, and soon reduced the well-ordered life of Fort Vancouver to chaos. The focus of his attack was the marital status of McLoughlin, Douglas, Ogden, and other officers, all of whom had Indian wives. When he charged them publicly with living in sin, McLoughlin was so incensed that he took after the Reverend Beaver with his famous gold-headed cane.

In the end, however, virtue triumphed. To save the women from further harassment, McLoughlin agreed to a proper marriage—but not by Beaver. The ceremony was performed by Douglas in his

capacity of justice of the peace. Later he and Margaret were re-
married by Bishop Francis Norbet Blanchet. The Douglases, in
the meantime, were legally united in a double wedding participated
in by McLoughlin's youngest daughter, Marie Eloise, and a handsome young Scot, William Allen Rae.[29]

James Douglas, who shared McLoughlin's matrimonial troubles
at Fort Vancouver, and later succeeded him in command, met his
Indian wife, Nellie, while stationed at Fort St. James, a Hudson's
Bay Company post near the summit of the Rocky Mountains.
She was sixteen, the daughter of William Conolly and the Cree
woman Susanne, whom we have seen repudiated by Conolly in
favor of the wealthy Julia Woolrich. But Nellie was more fortunate
than her Indian mother. Throughout the years of his steady climb
to the rank of chief factor and then Crown governor, James Douglas honored and loved the *métis* girl he had married *à la façon du
pays*. When, thirty-five years after their marriage, he was knighted,
Nellie became Lady Douglas. And when he died, fourteen years
later, she survived him as the great lady of the Crown colony he
had founded on Victoria Island.[30]

Like Nellie Douglas, another "daughter of the country," this
time the child of a fur trader in remote Labrador, lived to wear a
coronet. She was Isabella Hardisty, whom a young Scot named
Donald A. Smith met at her father's lonely post in 1835. Smith
fell in love with Isabella, and a few months later they were married.
From then on, Smith's rise—at first slow, then with whirlwind
velocity—was spectacular. From apprentice clerk in one of the
dreariest departments of the fur trade, he climbed to the dizzy
levels of chief factor, governor of the Hudson's Bay Company,
empire builder, elder statesman, philanthropist, and one of the
richest and most powerful men in Canada. And when, forty-three
years after their marriage in frozen Labrador, Smith was raised
to the peerage, Isabella was still at his side as Baroness Strathcona
and Mount Royal.[31]

Visiting nobility—some spurious, some genuine—was not unknown on the American end of the fur trade frontier. But the real
peerage of the Missouri and the Great Plains was not the titled

kind. There was no lack of duchesses and baronesses, but instead of tiaras they wore scarlet dresses and silver armlets. Their lords were the masters of the lofty, heavy-gated trading posts, the *bourgeois* of the fur brigades. They themselves were mostly chiefs' daughters, and often beautiful.

It is hardly remarkable that these superior, comely, spirited women should become the wives of the fur trade's elite. What is remarkable perhaps was the constancy of so many of their marriages, despite the almost insurmountable barriers of time, race, and culture. "Till death do us part," was not included in the marriage ritual *à la façon du pays.* But quite often it was a promise understood—and fulfilled.

Not much is known about the personal lives of many important American traders, and their relations with Indian women are especially obscure. Some, like Francis A. Chardon, seem to have maintained a complex ménage of regular, semi-regular, and irregular wives, perhaps from several different tribes. But not a few took one Indian girl in what was a true marriage by all but legal standards.

One of those who remained faithful through life to his bride of a "country marriage" was Thomas Fitzpatrick, whom the Indians called "Bad Hand." Fitzpatrick, "one of the best men the mountains ever produced," was a famous guide, partner of Ashley's in the Rocky Mountain Fur Company, and a staunch friend of the Indians on a blood-drenched frontier. At the age of fifty-one he married the teen-age daughter of an Arapaho chief's sister, and was loyal to her until he died.[32]

Another was William Laidlaw, master of Fort Pierre. George Catlin visited him at his Fort Pierre headquarters and was much taken with his wife, "a fine looking, modest, and dignified Sioux woman, the kind and affectionate mother of his little flock of pretty and interesting children." Laidlaw educated his sons and daughters at eastern academies, and when he retired from the fur trade he took his wife and family with him to Missouri.[33]

Still another was Philip F. Thompson, *bourgeois* of Fort Davy Crockett. When Thompson left the fur trade and moved to Oregon in 1842, it was largely to give his half-breed daughter a proper education in a missionary school. The girl's Indian mother, however, could not bring herself to leave her tribe and become "a white woman." And it was only after following her husband and children for days on their march to Oregon that she finally found the courage to brave the terrors of civilization with them. In the end, legally married to Thompson, she was affectionately known in the Willamette Valley as "the most careful of housewives." [34]

And a word should be said for Robert Meldrum, whom we have seen handled so roughly by the diarist Chambers at Fort Sarpy. Meldrum was, in fact, "a man of gentle but courageous character." He spent some thirty years in the Crow country, lived among the Indians much of the time, and was said to have spoken the Crow tongue better than English. When Father De Smet visited Fort Union, Meldrum was married to his Blackfoot wife aboard the steamer Yellowstone. [35]

At times the white man's adjustment to such a permanent commitment was not an easy one. We find one young trader, Lancaster P. Lupton, concealing from his family for years the fact that he had married the daughter of a Cheyenne chief. When he at last confessed his alliance, it received the blessing of understanding parents; and Lupton ended his days happily with his Indian wife and their eight children in California. [36]

Sometimes traders married to native women joined forces to oppose the prejudices of white society. Thus Caleb Wilkins, Robert Newell, and Joe Meek, all married to daughters of a Nez Perce chief, made a pact among themselves to move with their wives and children to Oregon, and to live together there in a kind of defensive alliance against the bigotry of white settlers. [37] Sometimes, to spare their Indian wives the slights of white women on the frontier, trappers like John J. Burroughs and Calvin Briggs (married to Shoshoni sisters) simply remained together with their families in the wilderness, where race hatreds could not touch them. [38]

Among "mountain marriages" that endured as lifelong unions
were those of the highly respected traders Fontenelle, Drips, and
Larpenteur. Lucien Fontenelle was of French descent, and rumored
to be of royal lineage. At the age of fifteen he ran away from New
Orleans and the banking house in which he was a clerk. In St.
Louis he joined the American Fur Company and was soon leading
its mountain brigades. He went into partnership with Andrew
Drips, another celebrated mountain man, and later joined the
legendary Fitzpatrick, Sublette, and Bridger combination. Fontenelle was married to an Omaha woman by Father De Smet. They
had four children.[39]

Andrew Drips, along with Fontenelle, was a member of another
famous trio of mountain men, Fontenelle, Drips, and Vanden-
burgh. Like his partners, he spent many years leading trapping
parties of the American Fur Company into the remotest canyons
of the Rockies. At Bellevue, headquarters for his expeditions, he
married a woman of the Oto nation, and by her had several children—one of whom was born at Pierre's Hole on the day of the
storied battle between the mountain men and the Gros Ventre.[40]

Charles Larpenteur, born in Fontainebleau, France, never
achieved the success that came to his fellow mountaineers; in
fact, bad luck seems to have dogged all his undertakings. But
through everything, he remained pathetically loyal to his Indian
wife—who, in an ultimate stroke of cruel fate, was murdered before
his eyes by the Sioux. Larpenteur kept a daily journal which he
worked up as a biography. It is a valuable source of fur trade
history, but, more than that, a touching record of one mountain
man's devotion to his Indian wife and their children.[41]

There were quite a few others, most of them a credit to the
character and integrity of the *bourgeois* commanding rude posts
in the heart of remote and completely savage country. Some were
men of remarkable intellectual power and strong personal views;
and one might expect the "country marriages" of such individualists to possess elements of the unexpected—as, indeed, those of
Edwin Thompson Denig did.

Denig, as we have already observed, was the energetic, intellec-
tually active, hard-drinking *bourgeois* of Fort Union, "the principal
and handsomest trading post on the Missouri." According to Kurz,
he was "a small hard featured man wearing a straw hat, the brim
of which was turned back. . . . He impressed me as a very prosy
fellow."

Prosy or not, Denig ran his big post with style and iron-fisted
authority, and had the respect of the toughest Indian tribes in the
West, as well as his own lawless crew of trappers and *engagés*. He
was friend and faithful correspondent of such notables as Father
De Smet, Henry Schoolcraft, and James Audubon. He played the
fiddle at the post dances, collected specimens for the Smithsonian
Institution, held palaver with the Indians in their own languages,
and married two of their women.

That is, he kept two of them as wives at the same time. His
first marriage to an Indian girl, of whom we know little, was probably not a love match. Denig's views on romantic love were
rather dim, not to say violent. Kurz has him exploding: "Love—
damn the word—is a madness of the brain; a contagious disease,
like smallpox or measles." So when he did marry a native woman,
who bore him a child but otherwise remains a vague figure, it was
probably for political reasons.

The same could be said, no doubt, of his second marriage to
Deer Little Woman, the daughter of a prominent Assiniboin chief
named Iron Arrow Point. She was also the sister of two very important chiefs: The Light, first Assiniboin Indian to visit the Great
White Father in Washington; and First to Fly, second-ranking
chief of the tribe. So Denig's alliance with Deer Little Woman
furthered the fortunes of both her husband and her male relatives;
but it also—despite Denig's jaundiced views on love—seems to
have developed into a relationship of deep mutual respect and
affection.

Denig's having two wives was perfectly proper and normal, of
course, from the Indian viewpoint. To himself and other whites,
he justified the arrangement on the grounds that his first wife
was sickly. Yet he could not put her away. She was the mother of

his first child, for one thing, and she afforded Deer Little Woman company, after all. So he kept them both.

Although he understood the Indians better than any other trader on the Missouri, Denig did not make the mistake of trying to be one of them. He conducted himself as a first-class white man, not a second-class Indian. And he encouraged his wives to live like white women. He imported fine clothes for them from St. Louis, accustomed them to the food of the whites, even provided white children's toys for his own half-breed brood. He sent his oldest son, Robert, all the way to Chicago to be educated.

So Denig and Deer Little Woman lived a civilized life, as far as was possible on the Upper Missouri, in the big house at Fort Union. Then, quite suddenly it seems, they decided to leave the Indian Country. The time had come to move to civilized parts, where their children could go to school. Accordingly, in the summer of 1855 they embarked on a trip to Columbus, Ohio, to visit Denig's relatives, and at St. Louis, on the way out, they stopped to be formally married.

Whether or not Denig sensed a problem in establishing himself with his Indian wife and children in the East can only be conjectured. He himself gave the summer heat as his rather lame reason for deciding not to settle in Columbus. In any event, the Denigs went north to the *métis* Red River Settlement in Canada; and there, in 1858, Denig died, leaving a considerable estate to Deer Little Woman and their children.[42]

Despite its somewhat unorthodox features, Denig's married life had been a successful and happy one. Not every trader was as fortunate as he; not every white man escaped the dark consequences that, in the fateful pattern of a Greek tragedy, might attend union with an Indian woman. Sometimes it took years for the bitter fruits of such a union to ripen, but when they did, they were all the more bitter. As William Bent, for one, was to learn.

William Bent, with his brother Charles and their partner Ceran St. Vrain, built Bent's Fort, the huge adobe post on the Arkansas

that dominated the fur trade of the Southwest. While Charles
handled the business of Bent, St. Vrain & Company in Taos and
Santa Fe, William looked after the trade at the fort. And there
he paid court, in the Indian fashion, to Owl Woman, the daughter
of Painted Thunder, a very big man among the Cheyenne and
keeper of the Medicine Arrows. In 1835, William and Owl Woman
were married.

Perhaps as a matter of policy, possibly to satisfy his wife's
longing to be near her people, William maintained a lodge in
Painted Thunder's village; and, although they usually lived in
the fort, Owl Woman often visited with her Cheyenne relations.
It was a deeply perceptive step on William's part. Not only did
it further his purpose as a trader, but it must have helped a primitive girl immeasurably in adjusting to the strange ways of civilized
life.[43]

During the years that followed their prairie marriage, William
was busy building additional posts on the South Platte and
Canadian rivers, extending the firm's trade to the Arapaho, Kiowa,
and Apache—ancient enemies of the Cheyenne—and consolidating
Fort Bent's position as the great crossroads station of the Southwest. He was often away, and Owl Woman spent a great deal of
time in her own nomadic village, but there is no hint that their
marriage was anything but a happy one. In 1838, their first child
was born, a girl, and William named her Mary, after his sister.
Other children—Robert and George—followed Mary; and then,
in 1847, Owl Woman died giving birth to Charles.

During the more than ten years of their married life, Owl
Woman's younger sister Yellow Woman had spent a great deal of
time in William's Cheyenne lodge, keeping Owl Woman company
during William's long absences, helping to care for the children.
In most ways—except perhaps sexually—she was very like the
second wife that many Indians of wealth and position possessed.
And now, with Owl Woman's beautifully adorned body still
resting, Cheyenne fashion, on its burial scaffold, Yellow Woman
became William Bent's wife in fact.

It was a logical and, in Indian practice, a natural thing. Yellow

Woman had always been a sort of "second mother" to the children. When Owl Woman died, she no doubt took over automatically in the desolated lodge, filled her sister's place as best she could with the little ones, and at William's side as his wife. She bore William another child, a daughter Julia, and their marriage endured for almost twenty years—until, in what William Bent himself described as "the desperate war of starvation and extinction" that was to reach its climax in the horrible slaughter at Sand Creek in 1864, Yellow Woman died under the lances of the Pawnee.

William, for reasons best known to himself, had destroyed his fort on the Arkansas in 1849, and in 1852 had begun building a new post down the river, at a place called Big Timbers. During the next two years, while work on the new fort went forward, William lived with Yellow Woman and his children in a lodge under the huge cottonwoods along the stream. Robert was twelve then, George ten, Charles six, and baby Julia (Yellow Woman's child) two; Mary was grown up at fifteen, and probably giving her parents the vague misgivings familiar to all parents of teenagers. But the younger members of the brood were no problem. Julia played with dolls, the boys with the Indian children.

Sharing the long days of childhood with little savages, the Bent boys naturally turned into something very close to savages themselves. How deeply they became imbued with Indian ways, Indian thoughts, Indian instincts, William Bent was to realize only later, and then in unbelieving horror. But he could see, at least, that Big Timbers was no place to raise a family of white children—especially sons of the distinguished Bents of Missouri. So he took Mary, Robert, and George to Westport, where his old friend Albert Boone, Daniel's grandson, agreed to look after them while they attended school there. Then he returned to his fort and resumed his trading, easier in his mind about his young; telling himself, no doubt, that Bent blood would tell and all would be well.

But it was the blood of Owl Woman and Yellow Woman that proved the stronger . . . their Indian blood and perhaps an upsurge of instincts older, deeper, darker, and more powerful than all the canons of white civilization. When Chivington's cavalry rode down the women and children at Sand Creek, three of William's sons were present at that butchery. But not on the side of the whites. Two of them, Charles and George, were in the paint and feathers of Cheyenne warriors. Charles was captured and saved from instant death only by the intervention of a half-breed scout. George, fighting desperately from a sand pit, had his hip shattered by a rifle ball. Robert was with Chivington's troops, but only because he had been forced by threats of death and torture to show the way to the Cheyenne village. It was he who later wrote: "I saw five squaws under a bank. When the troops came up to them, they ran out and showed their persons to let the soldiers know they were squaws and begged for mercy but the soldiers shot them all . . ." Julia was there, too, as the wife of a half-breed living in the Indian camp; she was one of the few who escaped the slaughter.

The Indians wailed for their dead, while Chivington celebrated a victor's triumph in Denver. Then, joined by the Sioux, the Cheyenne struck back. They sacked lonely little towns in Colorado, burned ranches along the Platte, attacked wagon trains, murdered settlers, and carried off women; and the Bent boys, Charles and George, rode with their war bands.

William Bent, with his old friend Kit Carson, labored desperately to stem the flood of red horror, to head off the Indian-killers and calm the panicky reaction of the tribesmen. He did not censure his sons for their part in the savagery of Indian warfare. He had hoped, of course, that his children would grow up to be Bents— white Bents. He had planned on it, on their all being together again when the troubles were over. Yet if in their half-Indian hearts they chose to follow the ways of their mothers' people . . . well, there was no disgrace in that. There was no disgrace even in his sons fighting with the Cheyenne against the people of their father's race. So long as it was a clean fight.

But young Charles Bent, twisted and tortured by torments known only to himself, was not fighting that kind of fight. While his father and Kit Carson were struggling vainly to bring some sort of peace to the Plains, he led a band of Cheyenne raiders against a stage station, lured the white defenders into the open with false promises, then fell on them with a fury that not even the Cheyenne Dog Soldiers could match. While the remaining whites, forted up in a buffalo wallow, watched, Charles's Indians spread-eagled one of their captives on the ground, cut out his tongue, "substituted another portion of his body in its place," and built a fire on his stomach . . .

Suddenly all became too much for William Bent. As Charles's savageries plumbed new depths of treachery and horror—including even an attempt on his father's life—it was too much for George, too. William disowned his youngest son; George broke with his brother.

The end was confused and unhappy. The Cheyenne fought on hopelessly, and Charles with them until, wounded in a skirmish with the Pawnee, he died in an Indian camp. George remained with his mother's people, but occasionally came home for a visit. Robert and Mary's husband took up ranching on the Purgatory River. Julia lived as an Indian with her half-breed husband.

After the fury had abated, William Bent carried on his work in a desultory fashion. He went to Washington and tried vainly to collect back rent on Big Timbers from the government. He led his caravans over the old routes, deep-rutted now, and returned from one trip to learn that his long-time friend Kit Carson had died in sorrow. He married Adalina Harvey, daughter of a Blackfoot woman and a notorious riverman, took her to his ranch, and that is the last we hear of her.[44]

Nothing had come out as he had planned. He had done everything that had to be done, but somewhere along the line, a force he could not grapple with had taken over—a fury in his children's blood that could not be stilled. A man and a woman could work things out together somehow . . . but with the children it was different. William Bent died at sixty, a wealthy but a sad and bewildered man.

"CHILD OF A WOMAN
SAVAGE"

It is the middle of the nineteenth century; four hundred years and more have passed since "a small girl, naked" came out in a dugout canoe to welcome Christopher Columbus to the New World. And at Locust Grove, Medicine Snake Woman moves in elegance and dignity through her magnificently furnished house, entertaining distinguished guests, living in the grand manner, "every inch an Indian Princess," John James Audubon calls her.

Four centuries have wrought vast changes in the lives of thousands of native American women, have bridged the chasm between savagery and civilization, have sometimes made primitive scalp-dancing girls into great ladies. . . . Or have they?

Perhaps Medicine Snake Woman best knew the answer.

When "Major" Alexander Culbertson became *bourgeois* of Fort Union, the American Fur Company's key post on the Missouri, he felt the need of a wife to cement relations with the Indians and to act as hostess at the post's social affairs. He decided that Medicine Snake Woman, a sister of the Blood chief Seen from Afar, would serve nicely. She was young, beautiful, vivacious, and very fair, as Father Point's portrait of her proves; yet, although only fifteen years old, she was capable of assuming a mature dignity that befitted the wife of the most important *bourgeois* in the West. Besides, Culbertson may have fallen a little in love with her.

So the Major selected nine horses from the post's herd and sent them to be tied in front of Seen from Afar's lodge. Before long, the chief returned nine equally fine mounts—and Medicine Snake

Woman. In the Blackfoot book of etiquette, this amounted to a marriage.

For the next twenty-five years, Medicine Snake Woman was all that Culbertson could have asked in a wife—and sometimes more. She did not lose her beauty, like most Indian women, as she grew older. White men who visited Fort Union agreed unanimously with the artist Rudolph Kurz when he described her as "one of the most beautiful of Indian women . . . an excellent model for Venus." She loved silks and satins, and Culbertson imported the latest fashions for her to wear at the post balls and parties. She had a fondness for jewelry, too—especially the colored gems, rubies and emeralds. She could speak no English, but so vivid was her personality and so direct her charm that she never failed to fascinate the most sophisticated of Fort Union's white guests.

All the while, Medicine Snake Woman, in subtle, feminine ways, was furthering the fortunes of her husband and relations. She gaily accompanied Culbertson on long trips to outposts and Indian villages, visiting with her kinswomen, keeping them in stitches with droll stories about the whites and their absurd ways. Thanks largely to Medicine Snake Woman and her powerful, gift-dispensing husband, her brother Seen from Afar waxed more powerful as a chief of the Blood tribe, and her cousin Little Dog became head man of the Piegan.

Medicine Snake Woman was also a potent influence for peace on the always restless river. Her people, the Blackfoot, gave place to no tribe in their hatred of the whites. But she was their blood-sister, as well as a consummate diplomat; so she succeeded where perhaps anyone else would have failed in winning them over to a peaceful, if not friendly, attitude toward the traders. And when, in 1853, the Pacific Railway survey hesitated to enter the country of "the most blood-thirsty Indians on the Upper Missouri," it was Medicine Snake Woman who opened the way through Blackfoot territory.

During these active, exciting, sometimes dangerous years, Medicine Snake Woman bore Alexander Culbertson five children. Like William Bent's youngsters at Big Timbers, the small Culbertsons grew up like little savages, swimming with the half-breed post children in the river, riding Indian ponies across the wide prairies, chattering in the tongue of their Blackfoot mother. Whether this caused Medicine Snake Woman any disquiet may be questioned, but it surely must have made Alexander Culbertson think some long and hard thoughts. At any rate, when the second child was drowned while swimming in the Missouri, the others were quickly sent to school downriver. Eventually, in 1858, Culbertson decided to retire from the Indian trade and take Medicine Snake Woman with him to civilization.

Twenty-five years as a trader, during which he had been in charge of the American Fur Company's most important posts on the Upper Missouri and Yellowstone, had made Alexander Culbertson a wealthy man. Now that he was through with the trade, he proceeded to spend his fortune on the good things denied him during his long hitch in the Indian Country. Near Peoria, on the Illinois, he bought a tract of farm land, and on it built a house whose size and magnificence were the pride of the countryside.

"Locust Grove," Culbertson called his mansion, and he furnished it with the most elegant furniture, the richest rugs, and the finest plate, china, and crystal his amassed plews could buy. On the walls hung pictures painted especially for him by the eminent artist John Mix Stanley. An imported English gardener cared for the beautifully landscaped grounds. The latest and finest in stables was filled with blooded horses.

Here Major Culbertson and Medicine Snake Woman lived on a scale required by their glittering environment. No expense was spared in educating the children. The boys attended a military academy, the girls a finishing school in the East, where they were taught the fashionable feminine accomplishments—drawing, music, French, dancing. Lavish entertainments were attended by notables from New York, New Orleans, St. Louis, even Europe.

And here, after sixteen or seventeen years of life together as man and wife in the Indian Country, Alexander Culbertson and Medicine Snake Woman were married according to the rites of the

Roman Catholic Church—with, no doubt, the festivities appropriate to such an important event.

Medicine Snake Woman took all this in stride, just as she had fitted into the scheme of her husband's life as a trader on the Upper Missouri. She had beauty, style, intelligence, sex appeal, and she made the most of all of them. She wore the latest fashions with a flair, entertained with the ease of a hostess born to charm, and made Locust Grove a byword for elegant living and gracious hospitality.

But there was something strange, even a little disturbing, about Medicine Snake Woman.

Audubon mentioned that at Fort Union she had presented him with six mallard ducks, not in itself an unusual gift—except that Medicine Snake Woman had caught them herself by swimming after them.

Other visitors at the post told of her riding across the prairie in her beautiful beaded doeskins, hair flying, and of her racing the best men riders on the Missouri—and frequently beating them.

At Locust Grove, her conduct was singular. For most of the year, she lived as the lady of a great house, acting the hostess in her chic gowns and jewels, mistress of all the manners and graces of civilized life. But when the haze of Indian summer drifted across the Illinois bluffs and the cottonwoods along the river turned to shimmering gold, a change came over her.

Then Medicine Snake Woman took off her white woman's clothes and pitched a tipi on the spacious lawns of Locust Grove. And here she lived as she had when a girl . . . as her people lived. Old friends from the Missouri country came to visit her. She entertained them with tales, wondrous and ribald, of white fatuity. For a brief interval, she escaped to her beginnings, answering a call of the blood too strong to be denied. Then, when the first skim of ice appeared in the kettle at her tipi door, she returned to the great house, put on her white woman's fine clothes, and welcomed famous men who came to visit her husband from distant cities.

Then, after ten years of lavish living, Major Culbertson suddenly found himself beset by some thirty-three creditors, with nothing to stand them off. Locust Grove and all its rich furnishings went under the auctioneer's hammer, and Culbertson returned with Medicine Snake Woman to the Missouri. There he traded in a small way, served as interpreter for various agencies, scratched out a living however he could. His two sons remained with their father in the West. His highly educated daughters went east.

And Medicine Snake Woman left him to go and live with her people.

She had no home of her own, no tall tipi scoured white and shining in the prairie sunlight, so she was glad to live in the log house of her nephew Chief Old Moon on a Canadian reservation. For a while she shared with her Blackfoot kinsmen the dwindling life-support of the buffalo. Then, when the herds had vanished, she drew the regular Indian ration on the Blood Reserve in Alberta. And there, about seventy years of age, she died and was buried in the Indian cemetery. At a place called—perhaps not inappropriately—Standoff.[1]

What mysterious force, one must wonder, drew Medicine Snake Woman with such irresistible attraction back to her savage beginnings?

Was it a kind of nostalgia—a homesickness for familiar surroundings, a longing to relive the time of her girlhood, perhaps even a vague desire to die among her own people?

Or was it something still deeper, more elemental, reaching farther back into the occult shadows of racial origin? Was Medicine Snake Woman, in the language of the early fathers, simply the "child of a woman savage"? A Stone Age creature who never had, and never could, really bridge the gulf of some thirty millennia?

Or was she simply a deeply disillusioned Blackfoot woman?

We can never finally know what she or any other Indian woman thought or felt. Chiefs and warriors made noble orations, many of which were written down and may still be read in books. But the women of the tribes are forever silent.

Yet one suspects that Medicine Snake Woman, amid all the magnificence of Locust Grove, was never happy. The novelty of all that splendid living finally wore off. As the years passed, she saw more and more clearly, and with a growing distaste, the meanness of the white man's scrabble for plews—his greed for money and power, and more money and more power.

She had witnessed, too, the degradation of her people—the drunkenness, vice, and disease, which were the price exacted from a once proud nation for her own husband's wealth and position. And it must have depressed her profoundly.

So, when a white woman's way of living became too much for her to bear, she pitched her tipi on the lawns of Locust Grove and strove to return not just to the manners and customs of a primitive society, but to a truer range of human values. The values of a savage people, to be sure, but values closer to the center of truth than the power-hungry, money-grubbing code of the whites.

"An Indian woman who marries a white man," a frontier army officer observed smugly, "is better fed, better clothed, and better cared for."

True, no doubt. But there were other things, Medicine Snake Woman saw, that mattered even more than silk dresses and jewels, imported foods, and the amused adulation of a husband's distinguished friends. . . . Things that only the "child of a woman savage" could know about.

The fur trade, like every other calling, had its argot. Some of the terms appearing in the present work were in common use by either Canadian or American traders, some by both. The American terms often derived from French-Canadian usage.

Bayside: the Hudson's Bay Company posts located on Hudson Bay.

beat meat: dried meat pounded fine for use in making pemmican.

beaver: the value of one prime beaver pelt, a unit of currency in the fur country.

boisson: drinking match.

bois brulé: French-Indian mixed-blood.

bourgeois: commander of a trading post or trapping party; on the American fur trade frontier often "bushway."

brigade: a party of trappers or a flotilla of traders' canoes.

cache: store of food or furs concealed for later recovery.

canot du maître: large freight canoe with a crew of ten and carrying a cargo of five tons; also called Grand River canoe and Montreal canoe.

cantine salope: the "harlot's tavern" at Grand Portage.

cédula: royal decree.

clerk: officer of the North West Company, ranking next to partner.

coup (to count coup): brilliant stroke, such as touching an enemy and escaping unscathed.

coureur de bois: unlicensed French trader; also "bush ranger," "woods runner."

dope: a lure prepared from the excretion of the beaver's perineal glands and smeared on traps.

engagé: indentured employee of a fur trading company, usually a French-Canadian canoehand; also Hudson's Bay Company "laborer."

express canoe: a canoe light-loaded and strong-handed for fast traveling or carrying mail.

factor: officer of the Hudson's Bay Company, in charge of a trading post.

femme du pays: Indian or mixed-blood woman; a "daughter of the country."

fofarraw: gewgaws and finery with which a mountain man decked out his Indian girl.

fort: any fur trading post, but usually defended by a stockade and bastions.

flying post: small outpost attached to a principal trading establishment.

freeman: independent trapper; i.e., "free trapper."

frolic: drinking bout.

Hawken: gun made by gunsmiths Jake and Samuel Hawken, the most prized weapon on the American fur trade frontier.

high wine: concentrated alcohol, mixed in the field with water to produce "trader's rum." The more remote the tribe, the more water in the mixture.

march: any wilderness trip, whether by land or water.

makuk: birchbark container in which maple sugar, wild rice, etc., was stored.

marriage *à la façon du pays:* marriage without benefit of clergy, "after the fashion of the country"; also "Indian marriage," "country marriage," "marriage in the fashion of the Northwest."

mountain man: American trader or trapper in the Rockies; often called "mountaineer" by himself.

métis: French-Canadian mixed-blood: *cf.* Spanish *mestizo.*

north canoe: canoe half the size of the *canot du maître,* used beyond Grand Portage.

North Men: *voyageurs* of the North West Company who wintered in the northern posts; also *hommes du nord.* (The elite of the fur trade.)

Northwest: the country north and west of Lake Superior.

Nor'wester: a North West Company trader, especially a partner.

partner: officer of North West Company, usually in charge of a department; also "wintering partner."

pays d'en haut: "the Up Country," same as the Northwest.

pays sauvage: the Indian Country.

plus: the value of one prime beaver pelt, a unit of exchange in the fur country; in the United States, "plew."

porkeater: tenderfoot, North West Company canoeman from Montreal who did not go beyond Grand Portage or Rainy Lake.

possibles: the mountain man's odds-and-ends, kept in his "possible sack."

régale: treat (usually rum, bread, and butter) on arrival at a post or on holidays.

rendezvous: annual meeting of trappers, traders, and Indians at designated site in mountains. At Grand Portage, annual meeting of partners.

road: the route of a trading or trapping party, by land or water.

rum: mixture of high wine and water, sometimes with the addition of red pepper and plug tobacco.

taureaux: buffalo-hide bags containing pemmican.

trading post: sometimes called "house," as Brandon House; or "factory," as York Factory; or "hall," as Boggy Hall.

voyageur: French-Canadian canoehand, but sometimes applied to partners of the North West Company.

winterer: trader who spent winter in the Northwest.

TRIBAL DISTRIBUTION

The Indians moved about a great deal. Tribal boundaries were blurred by wars, economic pressures, and finally the inroads of the whites. But during the fur trade era the approximate habitats of the tribes mentioned in this work were as follows:

APACHE. In Spanish times, the Apache roamed the plains of New Mexico and west Texas, from which they harassed the Pueblo and Spanish settlements. Later they moved into Arizona and raided as far south as Jalisco, Mexico.

ARICARA. Like their relatives the Mandan and Hidatsa, the Aricara moved up and down the Missouri, but their principal villages were perched on the bluffs at the mouth of the Cheyenne River in South Dakota.

ASSINIBOIN. This Siouan tribe trended westward from Lake Winnipeg to the Saskatchewan and Assiniboin headwaters. During the fur trade period, they were almost wholly nomadic, ranging as far west as the Rockies.

BLACKFOOT. Inflexibly hostile to the whites, the confederacy of Siksika tribes (Piegan, Blood, and Blackfoot), commonly known as the Blackfoot, occupied an immense territory between the headwaters of the Saskatchewan in Canada and those of the Missouri in Montana. Their hunting grounds extended westward to the mountains.

CHEYENNE. Forced out of Minnesota by the Sioux, the Cheyenne took to the horse and buffalo hunting on the plains west of the Mississippi. Lewis and Clark found them in the Black Hills of South Dakota, from which they drifted still farther west.

CHIPEWYAN. This numerous but not very advanced people claimed a great triangle of forest enclosed by lines running from Churchill on Hudson Bay to a point north of Great Slave Lake, then south to the eastern end of Lake Athabaska, then back to Hudson Bay near Fort Prince of Wales.

CHIPPEWA. A far-flung tribe, the Chippewa (called Ojibway by themselves) once occupied territory along both shores of Lake Huron and
Lake Superior. At one time their council fires burned from the Ottawa
to the Red River of the North and Lake Winnipeg.

CREE. The Cree (called Kinistineaux by the French) occupied a vast
territory, originally the wilderness between Hudson Bay and Lake
Superior, but later including the plains south of the Saskatchewan.
Eventually, the Cree overcame Sioux and Blackfoot hostility to estab-
lish themselves on the upper Saskatchewan and in the valley of the
Missouri. They remained both a forest and Plains tribe.

CROW. This talented and virile tribe appears first on the Missouri (they
were probably related to the Hidatsa), then successively on the Bighorn River, the Yellowstone, and the eastern slope of the Rockies.
In general, their territory was near the sources of the Powder, Wind,
and Bighorn rivers, and along the south side of the Yellowstone as
far as the Laramie fork on the Platte.

HIDATSA. This Siouan tribe, closely related to the Aricara and Mandan,
maintained their villages of earth-covered lodges at the junction of
the Missouri and Knife rivers in what is now North Dakota, a few
miles above the Mandan towns.

IROQUOIS. The Confederacy of Iroquoian Tribes, including the Cayuga,
Mohawk, Oneida, Onondaga, and Seneca, defended territory from the
east watershed of Lake Champlain to the west watershed of the Genesee River, and from the Adirondacks south to the territory of the
Conestoga in central Pennsylvania. Later on, conquest of neighboring
tribes extended Iroquois dominion from the Ottawa River to Tennessee, and from the Kennebeck to the Illinois and Lake Michigan. Individual Iroquois frequently appeared as fur trade *engagés* as far west
as the Rockies.

MANDAN. At one time the Mandan had nine large villages at the mouth
of the Heart River, near present-day Bismarck, North Dakota. But
when Lewis and Clark visited them, they were reduced to two villages
on the Missouri, at the junction of that river and the Knife. Smallpox
finally destroyed them.

SIOUX. Pushed out of Minnesota by the Chippewa armed with French
guns, the Sioux (properly the Dakota) broke up into many splinter
tribes. The main body ranged from the west bank of the Mississippi,
north of the Arkansas, almost to the Rockies—except where chal-
lenged by the Pawnee, Aricara, Cheyenne, Arapaho, Blackfoot, Comanche, and Kiowa. The Santee Sioux occupied southern Minnesota,
the Yankton Sioux part of South Dakota; other remnants of the
tribe remained east of the Mississippi, in Minnesota and Wisconsin.

SHOSHONI. This colorful and far-ranging tribe occupied an immense swath of country from California, through Nevada, Utah, and Idaho, to the heart of the Rockies in Wyoming. And from Wyoming the Shoshoni, mounted on Spanish horses, rode eastward, spreading destruction across the high plains.

Some of the tribes mentioned briefly were distributed roughly as follows: Arapaho, northeastern Colorado; Cherokee, Georgia; Chinook, Columbia River; Creek, Alabama and Georgia; Flathead, western Montana; Huron, the wedge between Lakes Huron, Erie, and Ontario; Illinois, Illinois and Indiana; Navajo, northern New Mexico; Nez Perce, Idaho; Pawnee, along the Platte; Paiute, northwestern Nevada; Ute, northeastern Utah. The southwestern tribes, including the Pueblo Indians, the Pima, Papago, and Maricopa, were located principally on the Rio Grande, Colorado, and Gila rivers, in New Mexico and Arizona.

NOTES AND REFERENCES

INTRODUCTION

1. Louis R. Masson, *Les Bourgeois de la Compagnie du Nord-Ouest*, I, 348.
2. In the early colonial period of the fur trade, however, American beaver was not used in Europe for hats, but went to the fur auctions in Moscow. "American beaver was in little demand among hatters in the early period, since European beaver—until its extinction—was the preferred material for felting into hats." (John Witthoft, "Archeology As a Key to the Colonial Fur Trade," *Aspects of the Fur Trade*, p. 60.)
3. Unlike the fur of other animals, the soft, downy underhair of the beaver is covered with tiny barbs. When this underhair is sheared from the hide and processed into felt, the microscopic barbs bind the fibers tightly together, producing a smoother, silkier, more lustrous felt than can be made from the fur of any other animal.
4. On Lake Superior the French had in fact pursued a policy not unlike that of the Hudson's Bay Company's. While making occasional excursions into the interior, their traders had for the most part waited for the Indians to come down with their furs to posts at La Pointe, Le Pic, Fond du Lac, and other strategic spots. (*The Journal of Duncan M'Gillivray*, ed. Arthur Morton, p. xxii.)
5. General works pertaining to the fur trade include: Hiram Martin Chittenden, *The American Fur Trade of the Far West;* Paul Chrisler Phillips, *The Fur Trade;* Gordon C. Davidson, *The North West Company;* Marjorie Wilkins Campbell, *The North West Company;* George Bryce, *The Remarkable History of the Hudson's Bay Company;* Douglas McKay, *The Honourable Company;* and LeRoy R. Hafen's fine introduction, "A Brief History of the Fur Trade," to *The Mountain Men and the Fur Trade of the Far West*, of which he is general editor.

PART ONE

SEX ON THE AMERICAN INDIAN FRONTIERS

I MEN WITHOUT WOMEN

1. Julius Olson, "The Voyages of the Northmen," *The Northmen, Columbus and Cabot, 985–1503*, p. 61, p. 64.
2. *Journal of Christopher Columbus*, trans. and ed. Cecil Jane, p. 23, p. 24.
3. This and all other Vespucci quotations are from *Amerigo Vespucci's Account of His Third Voyage*, trans. and ed. Clements R. Markham.
4. *Early English and French Voyages*, ed. Henry S. Burrage, p. 23.
5. *Ibid.*, p. 298, p. 300.
6. William Christie MacLeod, *The American Indian Frontier*, f.n. p. 359.
7. *David Thompson's Narrative, 1784–1812*, ed. Richard Glover, p. 177.
8. Henry Marie Brackenridge, *Journal of a Voyage up the River Missouri* (*Early Western Travels*, ed. Reuben Gold Thwaites, Vol. VI), p. 130.
9. *New Light on the Early History of the Greater Northwest: the Manuscript Journals of Alexander Henry the Younger and David Thompson*, ed. Elliott Coues (cited hereafter as Coues, *New Light*), I, 235.
10. *Ibid.*, I, 206.
11. Francisco López de Gómara, *Cortés: The Life of the Conqueror by His Secretary*, trans. and ed. Leslie Byrd Simpson, p. 149.
12. Thomas James, *Three Years Among the Indians and Mexicans*, p. 156.
13. Coues, *New Light*, I, 282.

II THE LADIES OF THE AMERICAS

1. Columbus, *Journal*, p. 96.
2. Victor W. von Hagen, *The World of the Maya*, p. 40.
3. Pedro de Cieza de Leon, *The Travels of Pedro de Cieza . . .*, ed. and trans. Clements R. Markham, *passim*.
4. Gómara, *Cortés*, p. 140, p. 387.
5. Bernal Díaz del Castillo, *The Bernal Díaz Chronicles*, trans. and ed. Albert Idell, p. 50.
6. Von Hagen, *World of the Maya*, p. 40.
7. Gómara, *Cortés*, p. 21, p. 49.
8. John Lawson, *History of North Carolina . . .*, p. 299.
9. This section is based on John C. Ewers, "An Anthropologist Looks at Early Pictures of North American Indians," *The New-York Historical Society Quarterly*, October, 1949, pp. 223–35; Frank Weitenkampf, "How the Indians Were Pictured in Earlier Days," *The*

New-York Historical Society Quarterly, October, 1949, pp. 213–21; and George Catlin, *North American Indians . . . , passim.*

10. Thomas McKenney and James Hall, *The Indian Tribes of North America . . .* , I, xxxii-xlvi.

11. *Journal of Rudolph Friedrich Kurz*, trans. Myrtis Jarrell, ed. J. N. B. Hewitt, Bureau of American Ethnology Bulletin 115, p. 38.

12. Aleš Hrdlička, *"Beauty Among the American Indians," Anthropological Papers, Boas Anniversary Volume*, August, 1906, pp. 38–42.

13. George Catlin, *North American Indians*, I, 106. But Kurz disagrees with Catlin. "What Catlin calls blonde hair among the Mandan," he says, "is nothing more than sunburned hair . . . I may mention also that the lighter color of some Indians' skin (not only the Mandan) is easily traced to the whites." (Kurz, *Journal*, p. 100.)

14. *The Indian and the White Man*, ed. Wilcomb E. Washburn, p. 284.

15. *Thompson's Narrative*, p. 176.

16. Alexander Mackenzie, *Voyages from Montreal . . . through the Continent of North America . . . (Master-Works of Canadian Authors,* ed. John W. Garvin, Vol. III), p. 100.

17. *Thompson's Narrative*, p. 73.

18. Masson, *Bourgeois*, II, 247.

19. Alexander Henry, *Travels and Adventures in Canada and the Indian Territories . . .* , p. 190.

20. Masson, *Bourgeois*, II, 315.

21. Daniel Williams Harmon, *A Journal of Voyages and Travels in the Interior of North America*, ed. Daniel Haskell, p. 17.

22. "Diary of Nicholas Garry . . . ," *Proceedings and Transactions of the Royal Society of Canada*, Ser. 2, VI, 104.

23. Mackenzie, *Voyages*, p. 123.

24. Samuel Hearne, *A Journey from Prince of Wales's Fort . . .* , ed. J. B. Tyrrell, Champlain Society Publication 6, p. 299.

25. Royal B. Hassrick, *The Sioux: Life and Customs of a Warrior Society*, p. 339.

26. William H. Keating, *Narrative of an Expedition to the Source of St. Peter's River . . .* , I, 384.

27. "The French Regime in Wisconsin—II," ed. Reuben Gold Thwaites, *Wisconsin Historical Society Collections*, XVII, 28.

28. Catlin, *North American Indians*, I, 212.

29. Edwin Thompson Denig, *Five Indian Tribes of the Upper Missouri*, ed. John C. Ewers, p. 155.

30. Masson, *Bourgeois*, I, 349.

31. Brackenridge, *Journal*, p. 121.

32. *The Journals of the Expedition under the Command of Capts. Lewis and Clark*, ed. Nicholas Biddle, I, 65.
33. Kurz, *Journal*, p. 93.
34. Ross Cox, *The Columbia River*, p. 135.
35. Henry, *Travels*, p. 295.
36. *De Smet's Letters and Sketches* . . . (Thwaites, *Early Western Travels*, Vol. XXVII), pp. 299–300.
37. *Thompson's Narrative*, p. 335.
38. Biddle, *Journals of Lewis and Clark*, II, 319.
39. *Pattie's Personal Narrative, 1824–1830*, ed. Timothy Flint (Thwaites, *Early Western Travels*, Vol. XVIII), p. 166.
40. Howard L. Conard, *"Uncle Dick" Wootton*, ed. Milo M. Quaife, p. 262.
41. *On the Trail of a Spanish Pioneer: Diary and Itinerary of Francisco Garcés in His Travels through Sonora, Arizona, and California, 1775–1776*, ed. Elliott Coues, p. 282.
42. James, *Three Years Among the Indians and Mexicans*, p. 158.
43. *Spanish Archives of New Mexico* . . . , ed. Ralph Emerson Twitchell, II, 284.
44. Adair, however, mentions that the Choctaw flattened their heads, "which gives them a hideous appearance." (James Adair, *History of the American Indians*, ed. Samuel Cole Williams, p. 10.)

III THEIR LIVES . . .

1. *Dictionary of Canadian Biography*, ed. George W. Brown, I, 351–59.
2. Harold L. Peterson, *American Indian Tomahawks*, pp. 5–6.
3. *Bradbury's Travels in the Interior of America* . . . (Thwaites, *Early Western Travels*, Vol. V), p. 109.
4. Frances Densmore, *Chippewa Customs*, Bureau of American Ethnology Bulletin 86, pp. 61–62.
5. Hassrick, *The Sioux*, p. 42.
6. Catlin, *North American Indians*, I, 58.
7. As one example of Indian feminine dress, we may take the costume of the Sioux women. It consisted of two elkskins sewn together, unadorned for everyday wear but heavily embellished with rows of elk teeth or quillwork for formal occasions. Leggings and moccasins were ornamented with colored quill embroidery, later with beads. Leather belts around the waist were decorated with geometric designs. Young girls wore their hair in braids down the back but over the breasts after reaching puberty. Styles changed slowly in the Indian world of fashion, but the women of most tribes prided them-

selves on their workmanship and the individuality of their costumes. Hassrick, *The Sioux*, p. 194.

8. Walter O'Meara, *The Last Portage*, pp. 90–91.

9. Edward D. Neill, "Dakota Land and Dakota Life," *Minnesota Historical Society Collections*, I, 284.

10. Osborne Russell, *Journal of a Trapper, or Nine Years in the Rocky Mountains, 1834–1843*, p. 113.

11. Paul Kane, *Wanderings of an Artist among the Indians of North America . . . (Master-Works of Canadian Writers*, ed. John W. Garvin, Vol. VII), p. 242.

12. Juliette A. Kinzie, *Wau-Bun, the "Early Days" in the Northwest*, ed. Milo M. Quaife, p. 194. In Tennessee, a Mrs. Bean is said to have been carried off by the Cherokee so that she could "teach their womenfolk how to make butter and cheese." (Harriette Simpson Arnow, *Seedtime on the Cumberland*, p. 302).

13. Col. Richard I. Dodge, *Our Wild Indians*, p. 205.

14. Primitive women were the carriers of burdens, the "pack animals," following behind their mates on the trail, anthropologists suggest, for a very good reason. The man, as hunter and protector, must be unencumbered and always in a position to respond instantly to signs of game or threat of danger.

15. Hearne, *Journey*, pp. 101–2.

16. J. G. Kohl, *Kitchi-Gami*, p. 125.

17. Denig, *Five Indian Tribes*, p. 195.

18. *The Life and Adventures of James P. Beckwourth*, ed. T. D. Bonner, pp. 133–38.

19. Alfred Barnaby Thomas, *The Plains Indians and New Mexico, 1751–1778 . . . (Coronado Cuarto Centennial Publications, 1540–1940*, ed. G. P. Hammond, Vol. XI), p. 53.

20. Twitchell, *Spanish Archives*, II, 58.

21. In some tribes, however, the men prized their women and tried to make life easier for them. Thus, Harmon tells us, the Carrier Indians were remarkably fond of their wives, the men doing most of the drudgery about the house, such as cutting wood and bringing water. (Harmon, *Journal*, p. 249.)

22. Alice Clark, *Working Life of Women in the Seventeenth Century*, p. 47.

23. *A Narrative of the Captivity and Adventures of John Tanner . . .*, ed. Edwin James, p. 223.

24. Walter McClintock, *Old Indian Trails*, p. 69.

25. David Lavender, *Bent's Fort*, p. 172.

26. *Franchère's Narrative of a Voyage to the Northwest Coast, 1811–1814*, trans. and ed. J. V. Huntington (Thwaites, *Early Western Travels*, Vol. VI), p. 227.

27. Conard, *"Uncle Dick" Wootton*, p. 112.

28. Hassrick, *The Sioux*, pp. 123–24.

29. *Ibid.*, pp. 125–26.

30. Cox, *Columbia River*, p. 266.

31. Biddle, *Journals of Lewis and Clark*, II, 371.

32. Ralph Linton, "Analysis of Comanche Culture," in Abram Kardiner and collaborators, *The Psychological Frontiers of Society*, p. 83.

33. George Simpson, *Journal of Occurrences in the Athabasca Department, 1820–1821*, Champlain Society Publication, Hudson's Bay Company Series, I, 311.

34. *Thompson's Narrative*, p. 106.

35. Sir John Franklin, *Narrative of a Journey to the Shores of the Polar Sea in the Years 1819–20–21–22*, p. 65.

36. One of Catlin's drawings in the American Museum of Natural History, however, depicts a man "of Herculean strength" holding his terrified nude wife so that the artist could paint her picture.

37. *Tabeau's Narrative of Loisel's Expedition to the Upper Missouri*, ed. Annie H. Abel, p. 149.

38. Harmon, *Journal*, p. 298. If we may believe the Spanish chroniclers, the Panama Indians held some sort of record for the degradation of their women. Cieza relates that when he went to visit a Panamanian chief, he found him reclining on a bed formed by the bodies of two of his wives, with a third lying crosswise as a pillow. The chief explained to the astonished *fray* that he had a fourth wife whom he would eat before retiring.

39. Alvin M. Josephy, Jr., *The Patriot Chiefs*, pp. 13–14.

40. Pierre François Xavier de Charlevoix, *Journal of a Voyage to North America . . .*, ed. Louise Phelps Kellogg, II, 106.

41. Martha Champion Randle, "Iroquois Women Then and Now," Bureau of American Ethnology Bulletin 149, pp. 169–80.

42. Charlevoix, *Journal*, II, 244.

43. Masson, *Bourgeois*, II, 361.

44. Masson, *Bourgeois*, II, 107; Diamond Jenness, *The Indians of Canada*, National Museum of Canada, Anthropological Series No. 15, Bulletin 65, p. 156; Hearne, *Journey*, p. 142.

45. Conard, *"Uncle Dick" Wootton*, p. 116. In ancient Peru, so-called "fertility races" were conducted on a very literal level. Men and women ran naked, "and every man violated every woman he overtook." (Ruth Benedict, *Patterns of Culture*, p. 114.)

46. Charles Larpenteur, *Forty Years a Fur Trader on the Upper Missouri*, ed. Elliott Coues, II, 399.

47. Hassrick, *The Sioux*, p. 115.

48. "Night wooing" was not peculiar to the Indians. "All the emigrants to North America," Sumner says, "were familiar with the custom." In Massachusetts, it was called "tarrying" and was prevalent until after the Revolution. (William Graham Sumner, *Folkways* . . . , p. 528.)

49. H. A. Innis, *Peter Pond, Fur Trader and Adventurer*, p. 37.

50. Henry, *Travels*, p. 290.

51. Baron de Lahontan, *New Voyages to North America*, ed. Reuben Gold Thwaites, II, 454.

52. Keating, *Narrative*, II, 166. Alexander Henry the Younger noted a departure from the general custom in the Mandan villages. "Love is not made by entering the tent at night, as it is among other nations I have seen. The custom here is to barricade the doors of the huts during the night and not to admit the young men. The latter therefore employ the night in addressing love songs to their mistresses, who either come out immediately, or wait until day-break, when they repair to the cornfields and are soon followed by the young men, who enjoy their company and take every liberty." (Coues, *New Light*, II, 327.)

53. Masson, *Bourgeois*, II, 319–20; Conard, *"Uncle Dick" Wootton*, p. 115.

54. Lawson, *History*, p. 306.

55. Densmore, *Chippewa Customs*, p. 108; W. Vernon Kinietz, *Chippewa Village, the Story of Katikitegon*, Cranbrook Institute of Science Bulletin 25, p. 128.

56. Densmore, *Chippewa Customs*, p. 72.

57. John Long, *Voyages and Travels of an Indian Interpreter* . . . (Thwaites, *Early Western Travels*, Vol. II), p. 173.

58. In John Lawson's time, a young Indian who was not wealthy enough to buy a wife outright could purchase one on the installment plan. After a price had been agreed on and a small down payment made, the girl went home with her husband and shared his blankets. But she was "to remain the same as when she first came to him" until the final payment was made. Lawson volunteers the opinion that no European could have stood the strain. (Lawson, *History*, pp. 301–3.)

59. *The Voyages and Explorations of Samuel de Champlain (1604–1616) Narrated by Himself*, ed. A. N. and E. G. Bourne, I, 143, 319.

60. Kurz, *Journal*, p. 155.

61. *De Smet's Letters and Sketches*, p. 311.

62. Hearne, *Journey*, p. 303.

63. Kurz, *Journal*, p. 155.

64. James Everett Seaver, *A Narrative of the Life of Mary Jemison, the White Woman of the Genesee*, f.n., p. 423.
65. Larpenteur, *Forty Years a Fur Trader*, II, 401.
66. White men self-righteously blamed the Indian husband for his wife's drudgery, but it was the trader's demand for more and more pelts— the dressing of which was woman's work—that added intolerably to her burden.
67. Catlin tells of a young Indian, about eighteen years of age, who took four wives on one day. "This extraordinary and unprecedented freak of his," Catlin comments, "was just the thing to make him the greatest sort of *medicine* in the eyes of his people; and probably he may date much of his success and greatness through life to this bold and original step, which suddenly raised him into notice and importance." (Catlin, *North American Indians*, I, 239.)
68. Polygamy posed a special housing problem in most Indian tribes. A man with six wives would require at least two tipis to accommodate them and their children. (Hassrick, *The Sioux*, p. 120.)
69. In 1731 the French Minister Maurepas proposed to Beauharnois, Governor of Canada, that white children be left in Indian villages to learn the natives' language, and that Indian children live among the whites for the same purpose. This early effort at desegregation was declared in every way impracticable by Beauharnois. "Their [the Indians'] love for their children," he pointed out, "would never permit them to send them away to a distance and abandon them to strangers. There are no children in any village that have no father or mother, either natural or adoptive, the latter tie being quite as strong in their communities as the former; and the children are so dear to their parents . . . that you cannot get them to part with them." (*Journals and Letters of Pierre Gaultier de Varennes de la Vérendrye and his Sons* . . . , ed. Lawrence J. Burpee, Champlain Society Publication 16, p. 90.)
70. McClintock, *Old Indian Trails*, p. 75.
71. Tanner, *Narrative*, p. 218.
72. Franklin, *Journey*, p. 225.
73. Hassrick, *The Sioux*, p. 39.
74. Cox, *Columbia River*, p. 115, p. 135.

IV AND LOVES . . .

1. Lahontan has his Indian friend Adario, in comparing the sexual appeal of the whites with that of the red men, say: "This is a truth that

our young Women can vouch for. They tell you that when a young *French-man* obliges 'em six times a night, a young *Huron* do's not rise to half the number. . . . This intelligence given in by our good Girles, who are better pleased with your young men's over-doing, than with the Moderation of our Youths . . ." (Lahontan, *New Voyages*, II, 599.)

2. Biddle, *Journals of Lewis and Clark*, II, 371; *Bradbury's Travels*, p. 62; *Tabeau's Narrative*, p. 181; Dodge, *Our Wild Indians*, p. 63. Of the Indian women's well-known ribaldry, which William Clark says was almost too general to be called obscene, Lahontan gives a specific example. When a *coureur de bois* brought some magnifying glasses to Michilimackinac, all the Indians marveled. "But what was most comical, there was among the rest of the Spectators a *Huronese* Girl who told the Pedlar in a jokose way, That if the Glas had the Vertue of Magnifying the Objects really, as it did in appearance, all her Companions would give him in exchange as many Beaver Skins as would make his Fortune." (*New Voyages*, II, 430.)

3. Keating, *Narrative*, II, 166.

4. Charlevoix, *Journal*, II, 74.

5. Lahontan, *New Voyages*, II, 453.

6. To the missionaries, the Indians' practice of sexual freedom was, of course, the worst kind of viciousness; and the control of sex among neophytes, and of neophytes with outsiders, one of their gravest problems. The missionary priests, and later the Protestant clergy, faced almost insuperable difficulties as guardians of female virtue among their converts. There is a revealing note of pathos in a report by Father Allouez that "the young people's debauches are no longer as frequent; and the girls who formerly did not blush at the most shameless acts, hold themselves in restraint . . ." (*Early Narratives of the Northwest, 1634–1699*, ed. Louise Phelps Kellogg, p. 116.)

7. Denig, *Five Indian Tribes*, pp. 152–53.

8. "Journal of Jean-Baptiste Trudeau Among the Arikara Indians in 1795," *Missouri Historical Society Collections*, IV, 31.

9. Russell, *Journal*, p. 146.

10. *Tabeau's Narrative*, p. 181.

11. Harmon, *Journal*, p. 295. It is remarkable how often traders' journals and the writings of travelers in the Indian Country mention the Indian women's mode of sitting. Catlin says: "The position in which women sit at their meals and on other occasions is different from that of the men, and one which they take and rise from again, with

great ease and much grace, by merely bending the knees together, inclining the body back and the head and shoulders forward, they squat entirely down to the ground, inclining both feet either to the right or left. In this position they always rest while eating, and it is both modest and graceful, for they seem, with apparent ease to assume the position and rise out of it, without using their hands in any way to assist them." Almost all white men, from La Vérendrye on, commented on the Indian women's practice of sitting "with their knees close together," as evidence of modesty and decorum. (Hassrick, *The Sioux*, p. 47; Catlin, *North American Indians*, I, 138; Masson, *Bourgeois*, II, 255, 328; Jonathan Carver, *Three Years Travel Throughout the Interior Parts of North America*, p. 136.)

12. Brackenridge, *Journal*, pp. 131–32.

13. John D. Hunter, *Manners and Customs of Several Indian Tribes Located West of the Mississippi*, p. 24.

14. Lahontan, *New Voyages*, II, 460.

15. *Thompson's Narrative*, p. 107.

16. Hassrick, *The Sioux*, p. 44.

17. Larpenteur, *Forty Years a Fur Trader*, II, 397–98.

18. Mackenzie, *Voyages*, p. 261.

19. Dodge, *Our Wild Indians*, p. 80.

20. Hearne, *Journey*, p. 140.

21. *Peter Skene Ogden's Snake Country Journals, 1824–1825 and 1825–1826*, ed. E. E. Rich, p. 70.

22. Kurz, *Journal*, p. 86.

23. *The Leading Facts of New Mexican History*, ed. Ralph Emerson Twitchell, I, 182.

24. Washington Irving, *The Adventures of Captain Bonneville . . .*, III, 241–48.

25. *The Journal of Duncan M'Gillivray . . . 1794–1795*, ed. Arthur S. Morton, p. 60.

26. Winthrop Sargent, *History of an Expedition Against Fort Duquesne . . .* (includes so-called "Seaman's Journal"), p. 376.

27. *Thompson's Narrative*, p. 177.

28. Coues, *New Light*, I, 327.

29. Maximilian, Prince of Wied, *Travels in the Interior of North America* (Thwaites, *Early Western Travels*, Vols. XXIII, XXIV, XXV), XXV, 30.

30. Biddle, *Journals of Lewis and Clark*, I, 94.

31. George Catlin, *O-kee-pa, a Religious Ceremony and Other Customs of the Mandans*, ed. John C. Ewers, p. 71.

32. Henry, *Travels*, p. 241.

33. Masson, *Bourgeois*, II, 69.

34. Hearne, *Journey*, p. 161.

35. Mackenzie, *Voyages*, p. 259.

36. Edward Moffat Weyer, *The Eskimos, Their Environment and Folkways*, p. 140.

37. Garcilaso de la Vega, *The Incas; the Royal Commentaries of the Inca*, trans. Maria Jolas and ed. Alain Gheerbrant, p. 328.

38. Catlin, *North American Indians*, II, 243, 462; Hassrick, *The Sioux*, p. 121; Benedict, *Patterns of Culture*, p. 243; Keating, *Narrative*, I, 227; Lahontan, *New Voyages*, II, 462; Tanner, *Narrative*, p. 90; Coues, *New Light*, I, 163.

39. Tanner, *Narrative*, 90. Henry the Younger says that Yellow Head was a renowned warrior, on one occasion standing off a whole war party of Sioux singlehanded, while his own people escaped to the safety of a trading post. (Coues, *New Light*, I, 163.)

40. Catlin, *North American Indians*, II, 243.

41. Coues, *New Light*, I, 399.

42. *Thompson's Narrative*, p. 366.

43. Except where otherwise noted, the following section is based principally on Clellan S. Ford and Frank A. Beach, *Patterns of Sexual Behavior*, and on anthropological data in the Human Relations Area Files at Yale University Library.

44. Hassrick, *The Sioux*, p. 36.

45. Lahontan, *New Voyages*, II, 600.

46. Denig, *Five Indian Tribes*, p. 186; Hubert Howe Bancroft, *History of Arizona and New Mexico, 1530–1888* (*The Works of Hubert Howe Bancroft*, Vol. XVII), p. 306; Sumner, *Folkways*, p. 315.

47. Samuel Hearne, quoted in *Thompson's Narrative*, p. xxi.

48. Edward M. Bruner, "Mandan," in *Perspectives in American Indian Culture Change*, ed. Edward H. Spicer, p. 217.

49. One source of misinformation on the Indians was the deliberate garbling of reports. As dispatches from the field reached headquarters, they were often redacted for transmittal to higher authority, and in the process grossly distorted. Thus, compare La Vérendrye's report on Mandan dress to Governor Beauharnois with the same information passed on by Beauharnois to the Minister Maurepas. (La Vérendrye, *Letters*, p. 342, p. 370.)

V AND INFINITE VARIETY

1. John C. Ewers, *Artists of the Old West*, p. 104.

2. John Knight, *Indian Atrocities: Narratives of the Perils and Sufferings*

of Dr. Knight and John Slover among the Indians during the Revolutionary War, pp. 19–26.

3. Masson, *Bourgeois*, I, 364.
4. Henday quoted in Agnes C. Laut, *The Conquest of the Great Northwest*, I, 348.
5. Tanner, *Narrative*, p. 10.
6. Mary Rowlandson, "Narrative of the Captivity of Mrs. Mary Rowlandson," *Narratives of the Indian Wars, 1675–1699*, ed. Charles H. Lincoln, p. 137.
7. Franklin, *Narrative*, p. 260.
8. "They did their best in such close quarters," Gómara says of this slaughter, "and within two hours had killed 6,000 or more. Cortés ordered them to spare the women and children." But he adds, "the city was put to sack," and one's imagination may supply the rest. (Gómara, *Cortés*, p. 129.)
9. Díaz, *Chronicles*, p. 51 *et seq.*; William H. Prescott, *History of the Conquest of Mexico*, II, 30; III, 180, 249; Gómara, *Cortés*, p. 56.
10. MacLeod, *American Indian Frontier*, f.n., p. 260.
11. *Narratives of Early Virginia, 1606–1625*, ed. L. G. Tyler, pp. 239–44; Washburn, *The Indian and the White Man*, pp. 21–25; Oliver La Farge, *Pictorial History of the American Indian*, p. 76; MacLeod, *American Indian Frontier*, pp. 182–85.
12. McKenney and Hall, *Indian Tribes of North America*, I, 353 *et seq.*
13. Charles MacKenzie has left us the following description of Sacajawea and her role in the complicated business of interpreting for Lewis and Clark: ". . . the woman who answered the purpose of wife to Charbonneau, was of the Serpent [Snake] nation and lately taken as a prisoner by a war party. She understood a little Gros Ventre, in which she had to converse with her husband, who was a Canadian and did not understand English. A mulatto, who spoke bad French and worse English, served as interpreter to the Captains, so that a single word to be understood by the party required to pass from the Natives to the woman, from the woman to her husband, from her husband to the mulatto, from the mulatto to the captains." (Masson, *Bourgeois*, II, 336.)
14. John C. Ewers, "Mothers of the Mixed Bloods," *Probing the American West*, pp. 64–69; Biddle, *Journals of Lewis and Clark, passim;* Brackenridge, *Journal*, p. 32; Wissler, *Indians of the United States*, p. 232.
15. A notable exception, of course, was James P. Beckwourth, who was anything but reticent about his Indian wives.
16. Coues, *New Light*, I, 162–63.

17. Prescott, *Conquest of Mexico*, III, 353–57, trans. from Bernardino de Sahagures, *Historia de Nueva Espana, Lib. VI, Cap. XIX.*

PART TWO

CASUAL AND NOT SO CASUAL CONTACTS

I RAPES AND RAIDS

1. Don Bartolomé de las Casas, *An Account of the First Voyages and Discoveries Made by the Spaniards in America, passim.*
2. Prescott, *History of the Conquest of Peru*, II, 178.
3. See Gómara, *Cortés;* Las Casas, *Account;* Prescott, *Conquest of Peru; passim.*
4. Díaz, *Chronicles*, p. 277.
5. Herbert E. Bolton, *The Spanish Borderlands*, p. 64.
6. Quoted in Washburn, *The Indian and the White Man*, p. 226.
7. Las Casas, *Account*, p. 55.
8. Quoted in Herbert E. Bolton, *Coronado on the Turquoise Trail*, p. 202.
9. Garcilaso de la Vega, *The Florida of the Inca*, ed. and trans. John Grier Varner and Jeanette Johnson Varner, p. 445.
10. *Ibid.*, p. 445.
11. Carver, *Travels*, pp. 25–26.
12. Sherburne F. Cook, "The Conflict Between the California Indian and White Civilization," *Ibero-Americana: 21*, pp. 105–6.
13. *Historical Documents Relating to New Mexico, Nueva Vizcaya, and Approaches Thereto, to 1773*, ed. Charles Wilson Hackett, III, 427.
14. *Ibid.*, p. 214.
15. Lahontan does quote Adario as asking: "Do we not see every day that your youths pursue our daughters and wives, even to the very fields, with a design to envigle 'em with presents? Do they not roll every night from hut to hut in our villages, in order to debauch 'em? And dost thou not know how many adventurers are among thy own soldiers? (Lahontan, *New Voyages*, II, 536.)
16. MacLeod, *American Indian Frontier*, p. 296.
17. *Records of the Colony of New Plymouth in New England*, ed. Nathaniel B. Shurtleff, V, 27, 107.
18. *Ibid.*, I, 132.
19. *Records of the Governor and Company of the Massachusetts Bay . . . ,* ed. Nathaniel B. Shurtleff, Vol. IV, Part III, 216–17.
20. Long, *Voyages*, p. 130.

21. M'Gillivray, *Journal*, p. 46.
22. George Frederick Ruxton, *Life in the Far West*, ed. LeRoy R. Hafen, p. 87. Hafen adds the footnote, "The trade in Indian captives was a long established business in New Mexico, and was conducted in the Utah country as late as the eighteen fifties."
23. MacLeod, *American Indian Frontier*, p. 485, p. 487.
24. *Idaho State Historical Society Reference Series No. 86*. This resolution was not, as is sometimes stated, adopted by the Idaho Territorial Legislature.
25. Margaret Carrington, *Absaraka, Home of the Crows*, p. 255.
26. Among the Indian killers were some of tender sensibilities, such as one Kinsey who "could not bear to kill children with his 56-caliber rifle. 'It tore them up so bad.' So he did it with his 38-caliber Smith and Wesson revolver." (T. T. Waterman, *The Yana*, quoted in MacLeod, *American Indian Frontier*, p. 487.) On the credit side of the white man's ledger was the Mormon Jacob Hamblin's stout defense of two Paiute women traveling with his party. When a band of Navajo marauders demanded the women, Hamblin bluntly refused. The refusal cost the life of one of his party in the ensuing attack, but the others escaped—with the Paiute women. (Frank McNitt, *The Indian Traders*, p. 90.)
27. Quoted in Ralph K. Andrist, *The Long Death*, pp. 90–91. Before the "battle," two of Chivington's officers later testified, he exhorted his troops: "Now, boys, I shan't say who you shall kill, but remember our murdered women and children."
28. Dodge, *Our Wild Indians*, p. 203, pp. 212–13. A team of modern anthropologists found that matters have not much improved in modern times—at least among the abject remnant of the Ojibway under their investigation. The girls, they report, are taught to fear almost every man. No woman should risk the danger of being alone in the bush. Girls especially fear rape by men in their own households, particularly stepfathers. (Ruth Landes, *The Ojibwa Woman*, p. 30.)
29. Keating, *Narrative*, I, 126.
30. Seaver, *Life of Mary Jemison*, p. 161.
31. Joseph Doddridge, *Notes on the Settlement and Indian Wars of the Western Parts of Virginia and Pennsylvania*, ed. A. Williams, *passim*.
32. Walter O'Meara, *Guns at the Forks*, p. 161.
33. Dodge, *Our Wild Indians*, pp. 529–32. James P. Beckwourth, however, says that a Crow could not marry a female captive. While himself a member of the tribe, he "took a very pretty young woman prisoner, but was obliged to give her to one of the braves. . . . When

a warrior takes a woman prisoner, she is considered his sister, and he can never marry her. If she marries, her husband is brother-in-law to her captor." (Beckwourth, *Life and Adventures*, p. 139.)

34. *Kit Carson's Autobiography*, ed. Milo M. Quaife, p. 85, p. 134; Lavender, *Bent's Fort*, p. 354; Royal B. Stratton, *Life Among the Indians; or the Captivity of the Oatman Girls* . . . , *passim;* Kenneth Carley, *The Sioux Uprising of 1862*, p. 29; Andrist, *The Long Death*, p. 198; Josiah Gregg, *Gregg's Commerce of the Prairies, 1831–1839* (Thwaites, *Early Western Travels*, Vols. XIX, XX) XIX, 208.

35. See Alan Moorehead, *The White Nile*, pp. 196–97, for excerpt from George Melly, *Khartoum and the Blue and White Niles,* describing a party of Abyssinian girls, varying in age from twelve to sixteen, destined for the Turkish harems.

36. Philip Ainsworth Means, *The Spanish Main*, p. 29.

37. Almon Wheeler Lauber, "Indian Slavery in Colonial Times within the Present Limits of the United States," *Studies in History, Economics, and Public Law*, p. 55; Gómara, *Cortés*, p. 293.

38. MacLeod, *American Indian Frontier*, p. 124; Twitchell, *Leading Facts*, I, 110; Garcilaso, *Commentaries*, p. xv, pp. 291–92. Fray Bartolomé de las Casas, known as "the Apostle to the Indians," came to America with Columbus on his first voyage, and made seven round trips in all to the New World. He was the first priest ordained in the Indies. Las Casas is remembered for his massive protest against Spanish cruelty to the Indians and his largely futile efforts to obtain justice for them. In about four decades, Las Casas claimed, the Spaniards killed twelve million natives. Some authorities regard Las Casas' charges as "vehemently exaggerated" and largely responsible for the unpleasant reputation borne by the Spaniards in the New World. (Means, *Spanish Main*, p. 17, p. 70.)

39. Lauber, "Indian Slavery," pp. 57–58; McNitt, *Indian Traders*, p. 156; Hackett, *Historical Documents*, II, 34–35.

40. Hackett, *Historical Documents*, III, 487.

41. *Ibid.*, II, 135, 207. According to L. R. Bailey, between 1700 and 1760, nearly eight hundred Apache women and children were held as slaves in New Mexico. Since they were baptized as Catholics, the term *esclavas* (slaves) was avoided, however, in ecclesiastical records. (L. R. Bailey, *Indian Slave Trade in the Southwest*, p. 19.)

42. Twitchell, *Spanish Archives, passim;* Prescott, *Conquest of Mexico*, II, 115.

43. But after about 1830, it may be noted, the Indians no longer sold or traded women captives. With the demand for furs now so urgent, they needed all the women they could round up to dress skins for

the white traders. (Oscar Lewis, *Effects of White Contact upon Black-foot Culture*, Monographs of the American Ethnological Society, VI.)

44. Conard, *"Uncle Dick" Wootton*, p. 102.
45. Lauber, "Indian Slavery," p. 37. The Creek Indians were also large holders of Negro slaves. (MacLeod, *American Indian Frontier*, p. 305.)
46. Laut, *Conquest*, I, 348; Harmon, *Journal*, p. 308.
47. On one occasion, a Cheyenne chief demanded payment of "one thousand white women for wives" as a condition of peace with the whites. (Remi Nadeau, *Fort Laramie and the Sioux Indians*, p. 111.)
48. Lauber, "Indian Slavery," p. 28, p. 29; *After Coronado*, trans. and ed. Alfred Barnaby Thomas, p. 204; Henry, *Travels*, p. 81.
49. Clark Wissler, *Indians of the United States*, p. 199.
50. Lauber, "Indian Slavery," p. 65, p. 75.
51. "Mackinac Register of Baptisms and Interments, 1695–1821," *Wisconsin Historical Society Collections*, XIX, 1–162, *passim*.
52. Lauber, "Indian Slavery," p. 67; Long, *Voyages*, p. 117.
53. MacLeod, *American Indian Frontier*, p. 258.
54. Lauber, "Indian Slavery," p. 83.
55. MacLeod, *American Indian Frontier*, pp. 106–8.
56. *Ibid.*, pp. 302–3.
57. "Fur Trade on the Upper Lakes," *Wisconsin Historical Society Collections*, XIX, 240.
58. *Thompson's Narrative*, p. 179.
59. Lewis, *Effects of White Contacts*, p. 50; Laut, *Conquest*, I, 348.
60. *Thompson's Narrative*, p. xxii; Laut, *Conquest*, I, 366; Hearne, *Journey*, p. 108; Constance Lindsay Skinner, *Beaver, Kings, and Cabins*, p. 163. Harsh things have been said about Governor Moses Norton's relations with the Indian women on Hudson Bay. But to his credit, it might be noted that in his will, after leaving his savings to his white wife, he directed her to set aside £10 yearly to provide clothes for his Indian wives at Churchill. (Laut, *Conquest*, I, 374.)
61. *Five Fur Traders of the Northwest* . . . , ed. Charles M. Gates, p. 179, p. 240.
62. Masson, *Bourgeois*, II, 384–85.
63. *Thompson's Narrative*, p. xix.
64. Masson, *Bourgeois*, I, 288.
65. Coues, *New Light*, I, 399.
66. McNitt, *Indian Traders*, p. 17; La Farge, *Pictorial History*, p. 143.
67. Beckwourth, *Life and Adventures*, p. 146.
68. Ruxton, *Life in the Far West*, p. 107.

69. McNitt, *Indian Traders*, p. 23.

70. *Ibid.*, p. 18.

71. James S. Calhoun to C. I. A. Orlando Brown, March 15, 1850, quoted in McNitt, *Indian Traders*, p. 18.

II "LET YOUR WOMEN BE KIND TO THEM"

1. Coues, *New Light*, I, 326.

2. Charlevoix, *Journal*, II, 106–7.

3. Gates, *Five Fur Traders*, p. 32.

4. Trudeau, "Journal," p. 31.

5. *Tabeau's Narrative*, p. 90.

6. Coues, *New Light*, I, 71 *et seq.*

7. "The Fort Sarpy Journal, 1855–1856," ed. Anne McDonnell, *Contributions to the Historical Society of Montana*, X, 99.

8. Chittenden, *Fur Trade*, II, 701.

9. Dale L. Morgan, *Jedediah Smith and the Opening of the West*, p. 200, p. 312.

10. Larpenteur, *Forty Years a Fur Trader*, I, 120.

11. Irving, *Captain Bonneville*, III, 228.

12. *Pattie's Personal Narrative*, p. 209.

13. *Gregg's Commerce*, XIX, 258.

14. Biddle, *Journals of Lewis and Clark*, I, 65.

15. Trudeau, "Journal," p. 31.

16. Henry, *Travels*, p. 241, p. 314.

17. *Tabeau's Narrative*, p. 180.

18. Lawson, *History*, p. 299.

19. Biddle, *Journals of Lewis and Clark*, II, 256.

20. The Aricara women, Bradbury recalls, offered Donald McKenzie their favors for a snippet of the handsome green surtout he was wearing. This, Bradbury, says, occasioned much mirth among the Indians. (*Bradbury's Travels*, p. 141.)

21. Gómara, *Cortés*, p. 118.

22. Campbell, *The North West Company*, p. 262.

23. Brackenridge, *Journal*, pp. 129–30.

24. Keating, *Narrative*, I, 226, 227.

25. Bruner, "Mandan," *Perspectives*, p. 217.

26. Colonel Dodge stated his own views on this complex matter with his usual forthrightness: "There is no dirty act, from bearing false witness to prostituting his favorite wife, that an Indian will not commit when whiskey is held out as an incentive." (Dodge, *Our Wild Indians*, p. 334.)

27. Coues, *New Light*, I, 380.
28. *Ibid.*, I, 381.
29. Masson, *Bourgeois*, I, 348.

III "TRADING GIRLS" AND SUCH

1. Coues, *New Light*, II, 890.
2. Cox, *Columbia River*, p. 166.
3. Biddle, *Journals of Lewis and Clark*, II, 370, 377.
4. John Howland Rowe, "Inca Culture at the Time of the Spanish Conquest," Bureau of American Ethnology Bulletin 143 (*Handbook of
   South American Indians*, ed. Julian Haynes Steward, Vol. II), p. 269.
5. Garcilaso, *Commentaries*, p. 139.
6. This was the same "prophetess" that Thompson and Franchère encountered, dressed in a man's clothing and "married to a young
   woman, west of the mountains."
7. *Thompson's Narrative*, p. 314.
8. Masson, *Bourgeois*, I, 86.
9. Larpenteur, *Forty Years a Fur Trader*, II, 397.
10. Indian women were said to have sometimes expressed grief by turning
    to promiscuity. "Nice, quiet girls" might go on the loose after an
    emotional shock, such as the loss of a baby. (Margaret Mead, *The
    Changing Culture of an Indian Tribe*, p. 142.)
11. Lahontan, *New Voyages*, II, 54. Lahontan, on the other hand, says
    that Indians visiting Montreal with furs to sell were welcomed by
    white prostitutes. "These merry companions, who know the brisk
    She-merchants as well as we, are not wanting in making an Offer,
    which is sometimes accepted of, when the present is of good mettle.
    If we may credit the common report, there are more than one or
    two of the Ladies of this Country, whose Constancy and Vertue has
    held out against the Attacks of several Officers, and at the same
    time vouchsaf'd a free access to these nasty Lechers. 'Tis presumed
    their Compliance was the Effect of Curiosity, rather than any nice
    Relish." (Lahontan, *New Voyages*, I, 95.)
12. Francis Parkman, *The Old Regime in Canada*, p. 384, p. 506.
13. Charlevoix, *Journal*, II, 107.
14. William Warren, "History of the Ojibways," *Minnesota Historical
    Society Collections*, V, 134.
15. William Bradford, *History of Plymouth Plantation, Collections of the
    Massachusetts Historical Society*, Series 4, Vol. III, p. 237.
16. Lawson, *History*, p. 299.

17. Lawson says that after several years of life as a prostitute, the trading girls married and "neither does their having been common to so many in any way lessen their fortunes, but rather augments them." (Lawson, *History*, p. 300.)
18. Charlevoix, *Journal*, II, 248.
19. Robert Beverley, *The History and Present State of Virginia*, ed. Louis B. Wright, p. 159, pp. 170–71.
20. Catlin, *North American Indians*, II, 214.
21. Brackenridge, *Journal*, p. 130.
22. Contrary to the general impression that red was the Indians' favorite color, white or blue beads were preferred by Indian women, and red beads least desired. (McNitt, *Indian Traders*, p. 37.) Henry the Younger reported that a trading crisis arose because of a scarcity of blue Canton beads, "which is the only kind they the Indians will have," at Astoria.
23. Trudeau, "Journal," p. 31; *Tabeau's Narrative*, p. 178.
24. Biddle, *Journals of Lewis and Clark*, II, 256.
25. Morgan, *Jedediah Smith*, pp. 50–55; Chittenden, *Fur Trade*, II, 264–65.
26. *Thompson's Narrative*, p. xliii.
27. Ray M. Reeder, "John Work," *The Mountain Men and the Fur Trade of the Far West*, ed. LeRoy R. Hafen, II, 367.
28. Zenas Leonard, *Leonard's Narrative, passim*.
29. *Gregg's Commerce*, XIX, 67.
30. *Letters of Dr. John McLoughlin, Written at Fort Vancouver, 1829–1832*, ed. Burt Brown Barker, p. 130.
31. Harmon, *Journal*, p. 14; Mackenzie, *Voyages*, p. 52.
32. Skinner, *Beaver, Kings, and Cabins*, p. 266.
33. Harmon, *Journal*, p. 73.
34. M'Gillivray, *Journal*, p. 72.
35. Masson, *Bourgeois*, II, 263.
36. *Ibid.*, p. 424.
37. Coues, *New Light*, II, 735.
38. *Letters from Hudson Bay, 1730–1740*, Hudson's Bay Record Society Publication 25, ed. K. G. Davies, p. xlvi.
39. McDonnell, "Fort Sarpy Journal," p. 108, p. 113, p. 159.
40. J. W. Vaughn, "The Fort Laramie Hog Ranches," *The Westerners Brand Book* (New York), Vol. XIII, No. 2, pp. 39–41.
41. *Cumberland and Hudson House Journals and Inland Journal, 1775–82*, ed. E. E. Rich, Hudson's Bay Record Society Publication 15, p. 78.
42. Bruner, "Mandan," *Perspectives*, p. 459, p. 466.
43. Long, *Voyages*, pp. 179–80.

44. From colonial times on, commanders were faced with the age-old
    problems raised by the presence of female camp followers in the
    vicinity of the troops. Braddock's troubles with the Indian women
    are described by Winthrop Sargent in his narrative of the British
    expedition against Fort Duquesne: "Another reason he had for
    wishing the Indian women removed from the neighborhood of his
    troops, was the licentiousness their presence introduced into the
    camp. An eye witness (Peters, the Secretary of Pennsylvania) par-
    ticularly states . . . there were constant and high quarrels among
    the Indians on account of the amours of the royal officers with their
    squaws and the *largesses* the latter received. These gentlemen were
    'so scandalously fond' of their swarthy lovers that an order was
    issued forbidding their admission into camp." (Sargent, *History
    of an Expedition*, p. 172.)
45. Chittenden, *Fur Trade*, I, 298; Don Berry, *A Majority of Scoundrels*,
    pp. 259 *et seq.*
46. But it is quite possible, as Don Berry suggests, that Joe Meek was
    stretching the truth a little. Meek, it was said, "could outlie the
    Crow."
47. Lavender, *Bent's Fort*, p. 349.
48. Remi Nadeau, *Fort Laramie*, p. 161.
49. Lahontan, *New Voyages*, II, 611.
50. Wissler, *Indians of the United States*, p. 64.
51. Egon Friedell, in *A Cultural History of the Modern Age*, expresses the
    belief that syphilis was exported to Europe from the New World.
    (Washburn, *The Indian and the White Man*, p. 460.)
52. MacLeod, *American Indian Frontier*, p. 42.
53. *Ibid.*, f.n., p. 42.
54. Davies, *Letters from Hudson Bay*, p. xliv.
55. Biddle, *Journals of Lewis and Clark*, II, 263, 370.
56. Coues, *New Light*, II, 836.
57. Wissler, *Indians of the United States*, p. 64.

PART THREE

LASTING AND NOT SO LASTING UNIONS

I AFTER THE FASHION OF THE COUNTRY

1. Hackett, *Historical Documents*, II, 87; f.n., 464.
2. Gómara, *Cortés*, p. 325.

3. *Ibid.*, p. 216.
4. Parkman, *Old Regime in Canada*, f.n., p. 289.
5. Skinner, *Beaver, Kings, and Cabins*, p. 94.
6. Parkman, *Old Regime in Canada*, pp. 289–90.
7. Lahontan, *New Voyages*, I, 36–37.
8. MacLeod, *American Indian Frontier*, p. 550.
9. Tyler, *Narratives of Early Virginia*, p. 339.
10. Davies, *Letters from Hudson Bay*, p. xxv.
11. Davidson, *North West Company*, p. 233.
12. Roderic McKenzie, "Masson Papers," Nos. 32–36, Canadian Archives; *Franchère's Narrative*, p. 371; Gates, *Five Fur Traders*, p. 147.
13. Mackenzie, *Voyages*, p. 21; Davidson, *North West Company*, p. 46; M'Gillivray, *Journal*, p. xxxiii.
14. Morgan, *Jedediah Smith*, pp. 344–45.
15. Don Berry, *A Majority of Scoundrels*, pp. 208–9. The mortality rate among mountain men may be judged from a memorandum written by Smith, Sublette and Jackson (The Rocky Mountain Fur Company) to John H. Eaton, Secretary of War, in 1829. Although the firm employed only 80 to 180 men, the list of those killed by Indians in a six-year period added up to 94. (Morgan, *Jedediah Smith*, pp. 344–45.)
16. Dodge, *Our Wild Indians*, p. 266.
17. James P. Beckwourth, having been offered a chief's daughter as a wife, expressed the trader's view: "Considering an alliance that would guarantee my life as well as enlarge my trade, I accepted the offer, and without any superfluous ceremony became the son-in-law of As-as-to." (Beckwourth, *Life and Adventures*, p. 75.)
18. Lawson, *History*, p. 301.
19. Quoted in Kurz, *Journal*, p. 156.
20. Coues, *New Light*, I, 239.
21. *Ibid.*, I, 243.
22. Harmon, *Journal*, p. 174.
23. Irving, *Captain Bonneville*, III, 228.
24. Kurz, *Journal*, p. 44, pp. 51–52.
25. In justice to the Iowa, it should be said that the women of that tribe had a prairie reputation for chastity. It was reported "on unquestioned authority" that an illegitimate child had never been born among them. The saintly Female Flying Pigeon was an Iowa. (McKenney and Hall, *Indian Tribes of North America*, I, 296–98.)
26. Raymond W. Thorp and Robert Bunker, *Crow Killer, passim.*
27. Coues, *New Light*, II, 891.

28. Letitia Hargrave, *Letters,* ed. Margaret Arnett Macleod, Champlain Society Publication 28, p. lvi.

29. Irving, *Captain Bonneville,* I, 235–37.

30. His wife's display of fofarraw was something of a status symbol for the free trapper himself, and he took an inordinate pride in decking her out. This, coupled with the women's striving to outdo one another in dress and adornment at the rendezvous, did more than liquor perhaps to keep the free trapper broke.

31. *Ogden's Snake Country Journals, 1824–25 and 1825–26,* ed. E. E. Rich, p. xi.

32. Offsetting a trader's gains from marriage to a native girl was his sudden acquisition of numerous hungry and importunate relations. A white man who took an Indian wife, it was said, did not marry a woman, he married a whole tribe.

33. Ewers, "Mothers of the Mixed Bloods," *Probing the American West,* p. 69; *Race Culture and Contacts,* ed. E. B. Reuter, p. 118.

34. Franklin, *Narrative,* p. 80. "The ages of these young brides," George Catlin notes, in speaking of the Upper Missouri Indians, "were probably between twelve and fifteen years, the season of life in which most of the girls in this wild country contract marriage. It is a surprising fact that women mature in these regions at an early age, and there have been some instances where marriage has taken place at eleven; and the juvenile mother blest with her first offspring at the age of twelve!" (Catlin, *North American Indians,* I, 241.)

35. Harmon, *Journal,* p. 57.

36. Ruxton, *Life,* p. 93.

37. Irving, *Captain Bonneville,* I, 232–34.

38. Comcomly was hardly putting himself out here. On other occasions, he was known to have provided distinguished visitors with a carpet of prone slaves.

39. Robert C. Johnson, *John McLoughlin, Patriarch of the Northwest,* p. 62; Benedict, *Patterns of Culture,* p. 162; Cook, "Conflict Between the California Indian and White Civilization," *Ibero-Americana; 21,* p. 104.

40. McNitt, *Indian Traders,* p. 37.

41. Masson, *Bourgeois,* II, 114. While *"la marchandise"* might possibly refer to the bride herself, it is more probable that it is a reference to the Canadian dress and other articles of clothing that were usually part of the bride-price in the Northwest.

42. Franklin, *Narrative,* p. 80.

43. Ruxton, *Life,* p. 96.

44. Cox, *Columbia River,* p. 362.

45. Kurz, *Journal*, p. 156.
46. McDonnell, "Fort Sarpy Journal," p. 109.
47. Coues, *New Light*, II, 901.

II HOME IS WHERE YOU HANG YOUR HAWKEN

1. Ruxton, *Life*, pp. 191–92.
2. Mackenzie, *Voyages*, p. 9.
3. Reuter, *Race Culture*, p. 153.
4. Herbert E. Bolton, *Wider Horizons of American History*, p. 10.
5. Wissler, *Indians of the United States*, p. 128.
6. Coues, *New Light*, I, 333.
7. Ewers, "Mothers of the Mixed Bloods," *Probing the American West*, p. 63.
8. *Franchère's Narrative*, p. 367.
9. Kane, *Wanderings of an Artist*, p. 288.
10. McNitt, *Indian Traders*, p. 38; Lavender, *Bent's Fort*, p. 198.
11. Beckwourth, *Life and Adventures, passim;* Chittenden, *Fur Trade*, II, 679.
12. Chittenden, *Fur Trade*, II, 675; Lavender, *Bent's Fort*, p. 39.
13. *Carson's Autobiography, passim;* Lavender, *Bent's Fort*, p. 196, p. 220. When Carson fell madly in love with Josefa Jaramillo, he was faced with the problem of what to do with his half-breed daughter by Singing Wind. Don Francisco Jaramillo coldly rejected the idea of his daughter foster-mothering the child of an Arapaho squaw. Kit just as firmly refused to send the little girl back to her Indian relations. The matter was solved by Carson's taking Adaline to Missouri and placing her in a convent school. "When she was older, and the Indian stain was washed away," Lavender comments ironically, "she could return." (Lavender, *Bent's Fort*, p. 220.)
14. Davidson, *North West Company*, f.n., p. 232.
15. *Franchère's Narrative*, p. 376. If his Indian wife's tribe was carrying on a traditional feud, as in the case of the Ojibway and the Sioux, it was dangerous for a *voyageur* to venture into the territory of her enemies with his wife. This, as well as logistic and economic reasons, may have accounted for the common practice of "caching" wives while a fur brigade was on the move. (Grace Lee Nute, in Gates, *Five Fur Traders*, p. 8.)
16. "Mackinac Register," *Wisconsin Historical Society Collections*, XIX, f.n., p. 109.
17. Warren, "History of the Ojibways," p. 282.

18. Johnson, *McLoughlin*, p. 48.
19. *Ogden's Snake Country Journals, 1824–25 and 1825–26, passim.*
20. Berry, *Majority of Scoundrels*, p. 79.
21. Janet Lecompte, "John J. Burroughs," *The Mountain Men*, ed. Le-Roy R. Hafen, III, 68.
22. Morgan, *Jedediah Smith*, p. 337.
23. Berry, *Majority of Scoundrels*, p. 110.
24. Morgan, *Jedediah Smith*, p. 274.
25. Hargrave, *Letters*, f.n., p. 205.
26. Mackenzie, *Voyages*, p. 135.
27. Hearne, *Journey*, p. 70, pp. 101–2.
28. Twitchell, *Leading Facts*, II, 101.
29. *Thompson's Narrative, passim.*
30. Pierre Dorian's Indian wife was one of the great heroines of the fur trade. After the breakup of Astoria, John Reed and a large party built a trading post in the Snake River country. Three of them, Dorian, Giles Leclerc, and Jacob Rezner, were killed by the Indians while trapping about five miles from Reed's post. When the mortally wounded Leclerc brought the news to Dorian's wife, she caught two horses and fled with her two small boys to the shelter of Reed's stockade. When she arrived five days later, she found that Reed and the rest of his party had also been murdered. There was nothing left to bury, and no time to mourn. Dorian's wife set off at once for the Columbia River. She forded the Snake and reached the Blue Mountains, where winter pinned her down. During the winter, she killed both of her horses for food, but was driven by hunger to move on as soon as the snow melted. After incredible suffering, she crossed the mountains and reached the Columbia, where some Walla Walla Indians gave her refuge. In April, a North West Company brigade ascending the river from Astoria was startled to hear a child's voice calling out in French, "Stop! Stop!" It was Pierre Dorian's wife and her two boys. (*Franchère's Narrative*, p. 343; Cox, *Columbia River*, p. 152; Chittenden, *Fur Trade*, I, 225; Irving, *Astoria*, p. 197.)

III "EVERYONE ENTERED AND SETTLED"

1. *Franchère's Narrative*, pp. 386–87.
2. Lavender, *Bent's Fort*, pp. 145–47; Chittenden, *Fur Trade*, I, 50–51.
3. Kane, *Wanderings*, p. 105.
4. Harmon, *Journal*, p. 33.

5. Coues, *New Light*, I, 282.
6. *Ibid.*, II, 553–55.
7. Lavender, *The Fist in the Wilderness*, p. 385.
8. Phillips, *Fur Trade*, I, 518.
9. Francis Parkman, *The Oregon Trail*, p. 96.
10. Kane, *Wanderings*, p. 255.
11. Masson, *Bourgeois*, II, 374.
12. Franklin, *Narrative*, p. 80. Under circumstances in which marital intercourse must inevitably be a public affair, some primitive peoples seek a secluded place in the bush or a neighboring cornfield. The Indians, we know, did this on ceremonial occasions and perhaps to some extent in private love-making. But there is no evidence that this was the case under crowded trading-post conditions. (Ford and Beach, *Patterns of Sexual Behavior*, pp. 68–71.)
13. Nicolas Point, *Wilderness Kingdom, Indian Life in the Rocky Mountains, 1840–1847*, trans. and intro. Joseph P. Donnelly, S.J., appreciation by John C. Ewers, p. 22.
14. Throughout the northern fur country, buildings were constructed in the French "post-in-sill" fashion, rather than in the familiar notched-corner style of log cabin. To a heavy frame, or "sill," the builders morticed squared and grooved uprights. Horizontal logs, tongued at each end, were then dropped into place between the uprights, thus building up the external walls. Roofs were covered with planks or cedar bark, floors laid of adzed poles, windows of scraped parchment installed, and the whole plastered inside and out with white clay. For the American trans-Mississippi posts, adobe brick was used when wood could not be obtained.
15. James Isham, *James Isham's Observations on Hudsons Bay, 1743*, ed. E. E. Rich and A. M. Johnson, Champlain Society Publication, Hudson's Bay Company Series XII, p. 173.
16. Coues, *New Light*, I, 163.
17. Johnson, *McLoughlin*, p. 58.
18. We have almost no information on how the *bourgeois* of the North West Company lived at home in the wilderness. But they were fully as caste-conscious as their Hudson's Bay Company rivals, and their wives and families undoubtedly enjoyed the comforts and privileges attaching to rank.
19. Harmon, *Journal*, p. 39.
20. John Henry Le Froy, *In Search of the Magnetic North* . . . , ed. George F. G. Stanley, p. 119.
21. McKay, *Honourable Company*, p. 362.
22. Denig, *Five Indian Tribes*, p. xx.

23. Masson, *Bourgeois*, II, 377–78.
24. Davies, *Letters from Hudson Bay*, p. xxi.
25. Masson, *Bourgeois*, I, 33.
26. Coues, *New Light*, I, 252.
27. Kane, *Wanderings*, p. 261.
28. Parkman, *Oregon Trail*, p. 101.
29. Kane, *Wanderings*, p. 262.
30. Long, *Voyages*, p. 98.
31. Masson, *Bourgeois*, I, 16.
32. Biddle, *Journals of Lewis and Clark*, II, 410.
33. Coues, *New Light*, II, *passim.*
34. *Franchère's Narrative*, p. 380; *Thompson's Narrative*, p. 312.
35. Coues, *New Light*, I, 440.
36. There were times indeed when the courage and resourcefulness of Indian women were all that saved a fur trading post from extermination in time of famine. Letitia Hargrave tells of chief factor John McDougald Cameron's young Indian wife who, during his absence, kept the people of his starving post alive with soup made from every living thing she could find or snare, even mice. She grew to be a woman of finesse and dignity, Letitia says, and after her husband's retirement she traveled with him and lived happily among his people. (Hargrave, *Letters*, p. lii.)
37. *Bradbury's Travels*, p. 165.
38. Keating, *Narrative*, I, 341.
39. Colonel Dodge cites an odd case of unseemly feminine hilarity on the part of two Apache girls held under guard in an army camp, while a third girl was forced to lead the troops to the Indian *rancheria.* "Just at daylight next morning, the two girls began a most animated conversation, laughing heartily and sometimes positively screaming with delight. They were talking over the attack on their own camp, and fancying how their fathers, mothers, and lovers, terrified almost out of their wits, were scurrying away from the bullets." This, Dodge adds, was an excess of heartlessness unusual even among the Indians. (Dodge, *Our Wild Indians*, pp. 539–40.)
40. J. N. Wallace, *The Wintering Partners on the Peace River* . . . , p. 131.
41. McNitt, *Indian Traders*, p. 23.
42. George Bird Grinnell, *Pawnee, Blackfoot, and Cheyenne*, pp. 272–76.
43. Grace Lee Nute, *The Voyageur*, p. 84 (quoting Robert Kennicott).
44. Harmon, *Journal*, pp. 36–37.
45. *Ibid.*, p. 73.
46. Coues, *New Light*, II, 579.
47. Harmon gives us an idea of how the *boissons* of the *engagés* impressed

the yet innocent Indians of British Columbia. "This being the first day of another year, our people have passed it, according to the custom of the Canadians, in drinking and fighting. Some of the principal Indians of this place [Fraser's Lake] desired us to allow them to remain in the fort, that they might see our people drink. As soon as they began to be a little intoxicated and to quarrel among themselves, the Natives began to be apprehensive, that something unpleasant might befal them also. They therefore hid themselves under beds and elsewhere, saying that they thought the white people had run mad." The Indians, Harmon adds, were a little surprised to see that "those who were the most beastly in the early part of the day, became the most quiet in the later part." (Harmon, *Journal*, p. 162.)

48. Kane, *Wanderings*, p. 263.
49. *Ibid.*, p. 261.
50. Harmon, *Journal*, p. 46.
51. Coues, *New Light*, I, 252.
52. *Ibid.*, I, 274.
53. *Ibid.*, II, 609.
54. Dodge, *Our Wild Indians*, p. 344.
55. Masson, *Bourgeois*, II, 339.
56. Coues, *New Light*, I, 168.
57. Densmore, *Chippewa Customs, passim.*
58. Dodge, *Our Wild Indians*, p. 190.
59. Gates, *Five Fur Traders*, p. 177.
60. Rich, *Cumberland and Hudson House Journals*, p. 226.
61. Coues, *New Light*, I, 167.
62. J. N. Wallace, *Wintering Partners*, p. 124.
63. Coues, *New Light*, I, 426. According to the Abbé Dugas, Marie Gaboury was the first white woman in the Northwest and first to give birth to an all-white child in the Red River country. Henry's journal, however, seems definitely to give that honor to the Orkney girl. She is said to have been sent home to the Orkneys, where she and her daughter "became public characters, and were known as vagrants, under the name of the Nor-westers."
64. Cox, *Columbia River*, p. 158.
65. Coues, *New Light*, II, 908. Cox says that Jane eventually became the mistress of an East India Company nabob, but actually she married a Captain Robson, of the ship *Columbia*. (See Mary W. Avery, "An Additional Chapter on Jane Barnes," *Pacific Northwest Quarterly*, XLIV, pp. 330–32.)
66. Coues, *New Light*, I, *passim.*

IV I TAKE THIS WOMAN . . .

1. McKay, *Honourable Company,* pp. 58–64; Skinner, *Beaver, Kings, and Cabins,* p. 157.
2. Simpson, [*Athabasca*] *Journal,* p. 392.
3. Hargrave, *Letters,* p. 286 (Appendix).
4. *Ibid.,* p. 87.
5. Morgan, *Jedediah Smith,* Appendix A, p. 347.
6. Johnson, *McLoughlin,* pp. 62–63.
7. Rich, *Cumberland and Hudson House Journals,* p. xxxvi, p. xliv.
8. Coues, *New Light,* I, 282.
9. W. S. Wallace, *Documents,* pp. 210–11.
10. Kurz, *Journal,* p. 83.
11. Clyde and Mae Reed Porter, *Ruxton of the Rockies,* ed. LeRoy R. Hafen, p. 266; Conard, *"Uncle Dick" Wootton,* pp. 90–91.
12. Lavender, *Bent's Fort,* pp. 332–33.
13. Masson, *Bourgeois,* II, 388.
14. Kurz, *Journal,* p. 208. Many traders, however, testified to the fidelity of Indian wives to their white husbands. Cox, after recounting the unfaithfulness of a trader's wife at Fort William, says: "Instances of this nature are, however, rare among the half-breed women; and taking their number and want of education into consideration, perhaps fewer cases of infidelity occur among them than among an equal portion of females in the civilized world." (Cox, *Columbia River,* p. 361.)
15. McLoughlin, *Letters,* p. 80.
16. Coues, *New Light,* II, 609.
17. Kinzie, *Wau-Bun,* p. 179. A rather extraordinary case of husband-and-family abandonment was afforded by Mrs. Mary Campbell, a full-blooded Ojibway woman who, babe in arms, left her white husband and nine children at Sault Ste. Marie to accompany a Presbyterian minister and his wife to La Pointe. (Hamilton Nelson Ross, *La Pointe, Village Outpost,* p. 75.)
18. Coues, *New Light,* I, 252.
19. *Franchère's Narrative,* p. 388.
20. McKenney and Hall, *Indian Tribes,* I, pp. 297–98.
21. Dodge, *Our Wild Indians,* p. 218.
22. On the Red River of the North, John Macdonell says, the Indians esteemed daughters no less than sons, because "they bring them much greater emoluments." With the coming of the white men and their generous payments for wives, the market value of girls increased even higher. (Masson, *Bourgeois,* I, 278.)
23. Coues, *New Light,* I, 197.

24. Nicholas Garry tells of "a very nice boy, moitié noir et moitié blanc [i.e., a half-breed]," who showed up at his party's tent and asked to see Mr. William McGillivray. When the great chief of the Nor'-westers appeared and asked the lad what he wanted, Garry reports, "After a short preface, the boy said, 'Monsieur, vous êtes mon Père.'" This struck Garry and Simon McGillivray as so funny that "I thought we should never have ceased laughing." (Garry, "Diary," p. 93.)

25. John Spargo, *Two Bennington-born Explorers and Makers of Modern Canada*, p. 48.

26. Harmon, *Journal*, p. xiv (Daniel Haskell, preface).

27. McKay, *Honourable Company*, Appendix I, pp. 370–71.

28. *Ibid.*, p. 371.

29. Hargrave, *Letters*, p. 177.

30. *Minnesota History*, Vol. 40, No. 6, p. 313.

31. Even after he had left his Indian wife, or had been separated from her by death, a trader sometimes sought anxiously to have his children reared in white ways. Thus Joe Meek asked the missionary Marcus Whitman and his wife to care for his infant half-breed daughter, Helen Mar. The little girl died in the massacre of the Whitmans by the Cayuse. (Alvin M. Josephy, Jr., *The Nez Perce Indians and the Opening of the Northwest*, p. 208, p. 252.)

32. Davies, *Letters from Hudson Bay*, p. 394.

33. Rich, *Cumberland and Hudson House Journals*, p. xxxv.

34. Ross, *La Pointe*, p. 72.

35. Harmon, *Journal*, p. 143.

36. *Ibid.*, p. 54.

37. W. S. Wallace, *Documents*, p. 480.

38. *Ibid.*, p. 498.

39. *Ibid.*, p. 432.

40. *Ibid.*, p. 468.

41. *Ibid.*, p. 469.

42. Lavender, *Fist in the Wilderness*, p. 249, *passim;* Nute, *Lake Superior*, p. 108.

43. Chittenden, *Fur Trade*, I, 384 *et seq.*; Larpenteur, *Forty Years a Fur Trader*, I, 65.

44. W. S. Wallace, *Documents*, p. 47; Campbell, *North West Company, passim.*; Marjorie Wilkins Campbell, *William McGillivray, Lord of the Nor'Westers, passim.*

45. W. S. Wallace, *Documents*, pp. 443–44.

46. *Ibid.*, p. 433.

47. Mari Sandoz, *Love Song to the Plains*, p. 76.

48. Ray H. Mattison, "James Kipp," *Mountain Men*, ed. LeRoy R. Hafen, II, 201–5.
49. Dodge, *Our Wild Indians*, p. 600.
50. Chittenden, *Fur Trade*, I, 126–34.

V "TO HAVE AND TO HOLD"

1. "Mackinac Register," *Wisconsin Historical Society Collections*, XVIII, 476.
2. Washburn, *The Indian and the White Man*, p. 214 (excerpt).
3. Occasionally no father came forward to acknowledge his child at baptism, and the record then would read, "of a French father not yet declared," or "child of a father she would not name." ("Mackinac Register," *Wisconsin Historical Society Collections*, XIX, 18, 26, 30, 85, 86.)
4. "Mackinac Register," *Wisconsin Historical Society Collections*, XVIII, 474.
5. Father De Smet performed many baptisms and marriages among the Flathead Indians, to whom he was devoted. His assistant, Father Point, married twenty-four couples and Father De Smet many more. He believed, incidentally, that the Virgin Mary had appeared to one of his young converts, a little orphan named Paul. (*De Smet's Letters and Sketches*, p. 311, p. 347.)
6. Garry, "Diary," p. 180.
7. George Bryce, *The Remarkable History of the Hudson's Bay Company*, p. 420.
8. Ross, *La Pointe*, p. 65.
9. Johnson, *McLoughlin*, pp. 116–17; Laut, *Conquest*, II, 323.
10. Harmon, *Journal, passim;* John Spargo, *Two Bennington-born Explorers*, pp. 31 *et seq.;* Walter O'Meara, "Adventure in Local History," *Minnesota History*, Vol. 31, No. 1, pp. 1–10.
11. For this bit of fur trade lore, I am indebted to Mr. Hugh P. MacMillan, Archives Liaison Officer, Department of Public Records and Archives, Ontario, Canada.
12. W. S. Wallace, *Documents*, pp. 465–66; Gates, *Five Fur Traders*, pp. 63–66.
13. Masson, *Bourgeois*, II, 317 *et seq.*
14. Coues, *New Light*, II, 459; W. S. Wallace, *Documents*, p. lxxiii, p. cii.
15. *Thompson's Narrative*, p. lxv.
16. W. S. Wallace, *Documents*, p. 428; Henry, *Travels*, p. 154; Ross, *La Pointe*, p. 59; Warren, "History of the Ojibways," p. 10, p. 11, f.n., p. 448.

17. Jean-Baptiste Cadotte, Account Book, trans. Evan A. Hart and Elizabeth Bennett Hart, *passim*. (Manuscript.)

18. W. S. Wallace, *Documents*, p. 428; Warren, "History of the Ojibways," pp. 294–97.

19. Ross, *La Pointe*, p. 114; Warren, "History of the Ojibways," p. 449, *passim*.

20. Ross, *La Pointe*, p. 64; Thomas L. McKenney, *Tour to the Lakes*, pp. 181–4.

21. "Fur Trade on the Upper Lakes," *Wisconsin Historical Society Collections*, XIX, 361; Walter Havighurst, *Three Flags at the Straits: the Forts of Mackinac*, pp. 164 *et seq.*; Nute, *Lake Superior*, pp. 230–33, *Franchère's Narrative*, f.n., p. 394; Bryce, *Remarkable History*, p. 181.

22. Nute, *Lake Superior*, p. 230.

23. McLoughlin, *Letters*, Appendix, p. 300.

24. Hargrave, *Letters*, p. 78. Contrast Letitia's acerb comment with Juliette Kinzie's description of "Mrs. W" at Michilimackinac: "Mrs. W. was an extremely pretty, delicate woman, part French and part Sioux. . . . She had been a great belle among the officers at Fort Crawford; so much so, indeed, that the suicide of the post surgeon was attributed to an unsuccessful attachment he had conceived for her. I was greatly struck with her soft and gentle manners, and the musical intonation of her voice, which I soon learned was a distinguishing peculiarity of those women in whom are united the French and Indian blood." (Kinzie, *Wau-Bun*, p. 18.)

25. Laut, *Conquest*, II, 12; Johnson, *McLoughlin*, p. 27.

26. McKay was murdered when the Indians massacred the crew of John Jacob Astor's supply ship *Tonquin*, on its way to Astoria in the summer of 1811.

27. Johnson, *McLoughlin*, *passim*; McKay, *Honourable Company*, pp. 208–9.

28. Johnson, *McLoughlin*, p. 120.

29. *Ibid.*, pp. 116–18.

30. Bryce, *Remarkable History*, p. 400.

31. McKay, *Honourable Company*, pp. 288–303; Beckles Willson, *The Life of Lord Strathcona and Mount Royal*, *passim*.

32. Lavender, *Bent's Fort*, p. 340.

33. Ray H. Mattison, "William Laidlaw," *Mountain Men*, ed. LeRoy R. Hafen, III, 167–72.

34. LeRoy R. Hafen, "Philip F. Thompson," *Mountain Men*, III, 339–47.

35. McDonnell, "Fort Sarpy Journal," p. 153, p. 284.

36. Ann W. Hafen, "Lancaster P. Lupton," *Mountain Men*, ed. LeRoy R. Hafen, II, 207–16.

37. Harvey E. Tobie, "Caleb Wilkins," *Mountain Men*, ed. LeRoy R. Hafen, III, 387–88.
38. Janet Lecompte, "John J. Burroughs," *Mountain Men*, ed. LeRoy R. Hafen, III, 67–68.
39. Chittenden, *Fur Trade*, I, 389.
40. *Ibid.*, I, 389–90.
41. *Ibid.*, I, 391; Larpenteur, *Forty Years a Fur Trader*, *passim*.
42. The foregoing sketch of Edwin Thompson Denig is based primarily on John C. Ewers' introduction to Denig's *Five Indian Tribes of the Upper Missouri*, and his "Mothers of the Mixed Bloods" in *Probing the American West*, pp. 62–70.
43. Colonel Dodge attributed much of the Indians' ill health to home-sickness, and suggested that "the extraordinary and unnatural diminution in the numbers of certain tribes is due to nostalgia more than any other cause." (Dodge, *Our Wild Indians*, p. 311.)
44. The story of William Bent is derived chiefly from David Lavender's *Bent's Fort*, with material also extracted from Twitchell's *Leading Facts*, II, 120 and notes 87 and 254; Andrist, *The Long Death*, p. 88, p. 96; and Chittenden, *Fur Trade*, II, 539.

VI "CHILD OF A WOMAN SAVAGE"

1. Ewers, "Mothers of the Mixed Bloods," *Probing the American West*, pp. 65–67; McDonnell, "Fort Sarpy Journal," note 2, pp. 240–46; Kurz, *Journal*, p. 213.

BIBLIOGRAPHY

Adair, James. *History of the American Indians,* ed. Samuel Cole Williams. Nashville, Tenn., 1930.

Allier, Raoul. *The Mind of the Savage,* trans. Fred Rothwell. New York, 1929.

Anderson, Capt. Thomas G. "Narrative of Capt. Thomas G. Anderson," *Wisconsin Historical Society Collections,* IX, 137–43. Madison, 1909.

Andrews, Ralph W. *Indians as the Westerners Saw Them.* Seattle, 1963.

Andrist, Ralph K. *The Long Death.* New York, 1964.

Arnow, Harriette Simpson. *Seedtime on the Cumberland.* New York, 1960.

Aspects of the Fur Trade. Selected Papers of the 1965 North American Fur Trade Conference, ed. Russell W. Fridley. St. Paul, 1967.

Bailey, L. R. *Indian Slave Trade in the Southwest.* Los Angeles, 1966.

Ballantyne, Robert Michael. *Hudson Bay.* London, 1876.

Bancroft, Hubert Howe. *History of Arizona and New Mexico, 1530–1888.* (*The Works of Hubert Howe Bancroft,* Vol. XVII.) San Francisco, 1889.

Barrett, S. M. *Sociology of the American Indians.* Kansas City, 1946.

Barry, J. Neilson. "Astorians Who Became Permanent Settlers," *Pacific Northwest Quarterly,* XXIV, 3 and 4.

Beckwourth, James P. *The Life and Adventures of James P. Beckwourth,* ed. T. D. Bonner. New York, 1931.

Benedict, Ruth. *Patterns of Culture.* New York, 1949.

Berry, Don. *A Majority of Scoundrels.* New York, 1961.

Beverley, Robert. *The History and Present State of Virginia,* ed. with an introduction by Louis B. Wright. Chapel Hill, 1947.

Biddle, Nicholas (ed.). *The Journals of the Expedition under the Command of Capts. Lewis and Clark,* with an introduction by John Bakeless. 2 vols. New York, 1962.

Bigsby, John. *The Shoe and Canoe.* London, 1850.

Bolton, Herbert E. *Coronado on the Turquoise Trail.* Albuquerque, 1949.

———. *The Spanish Borderlands.* New Haven, 1921.

———. *Wider Horizons of American History.* New York, 1939.

Bourne, Edward Gaylord. *Spain in America, 1450–1580.* New York, 1904.

Brackenridge, Henry Marie. *Journal of a Voyage up the River Missouri in 1811.* (Thwaites, *Early Western Travels,* Vol. VI.) Cleveland, 1904.

Bradbury, John. *Bradbury's Travels in the Interior of America in the Years 1809, 1810, and 1811*. (Thwaites, *Early Western Travels*, Vol. V.) Cleveland, 1904.

Bradford, William. *Bradford's History of the Plymouth Plantation, Collections of the Massachusetts Historical Society*, Series 4, Vol. III. Boston, 1856.

Brooks, Noah. *First Across the Continent*. New York, 1902.

Bruner, E. M. "Mandan," *Perspectives in American Indian Culture Change*, ed. Edward H. Spicer. Chicago, 1961.

Bryce, George. *The Remarkable History of the Hudson's Bay Company*. London, 1902.

Burpee, Lawrence J. *The Search for the Western Sea*. 2 vols. Toronto, 1935.

Burrage, Henry S. (ed.). *Early English and French Voyages* . . . New York, 1906.

Cadotte, Jean-Baptiste. Manuscript account book, kept at Sault Ste. Marie, 1772–1794, trans. and ed. Evan A. Hart and Elizabeth Hart Bennett. Notre Dame University Archives.

Calderón de la Barca, Frances Erskine (Inglis). *Life in Mexico*, with an introduction by William H Prescott. New York. (Dolphin Book, no date.)

Campbell, Marjorie Wilkins. *The North West Company*. New York, 1957.
———. *William McGillivray, Lord of the Nor'Westers*. Toronto, 1962.

Canadian Biography, Dictionary of, George W. Brown, gen. ed. Vol. I (years 1000 to 1700). Toronto, 1966.

Carley, Kenneth. *The Sioux Uprising of 1862*. St. Paul, 1961.

Carrington, Margaret I. *Absaraka, Home of the Crows*. Chicago, 1950.

Carson, Christopher. *Kit Carson's Autobiography*, ed. Milo M. Quaife. Chicago, 1935.

Carver, Jonathan. *Three Years Travels Throughout the Interior Parts of North America*. Boston, 1797.

Catlin, George. *North American Indians, Being Letters and Notes on Their Manners, Customs, and Conditions* . . . 2 vols. Edinburgh, 1926.
———. *O-kee-pa, a Religious Ceremony, and Other Customs of the Mandans*, ed. John C. Ewers. New Haven, 1967.

Champlain, Samuel de. *The Voyages and Explorations of Samuel de Champlain (1604–1616) Narrated by Himself*, ed. A. N. and E. G. Bourne. 2 vols. New York, 1906.

Chardon, F. A. *Chardon's Journal at Fort Clark, 1834–1839*, ed. Annie H. Abel. Pierre, S. Dak., 1932.

Charlevoix, Pierre F. X. de. *Journal of a Voyage to North America* . . . , ed. with historical notes and introduction by Louise Phelps Kellogg. 2 vols. Chicago, 1923.

Chittenden, Hiram Martin. *The American Fur Trade of the Far West.* 2 vols. New York, 1935.

Cieza de Leon, Pedro de. *The Travels of Pedro de Cieza de Leon, A.D. 1532–1550,* ed. and trans. Clements R. Markham. London, 1864.

———. *The Incas,* ed. Victor W. von Hagen, trans. Harriet de Onis. Norman, 1959.

Clark, Alice. *Working Life of Women in the Seventeenth Century.* New York, 1919.

Cleland, Robert Glass. *This Reckless Breed of Men.* New York, 1950.

Clyman, James. *James Clyman, American Frontiersman, 1792–1881,* ed. Charles Camp. San Francisco, 1928.

Columbus, Christopher. *The Journal of Christopher Columbus,* trans. and ed. Cecil James. London, 1960.

Conard, Howard Louis. *"Uncle Dick" Wootton,* ed. Milo M. Quaife. Chicago, 1957.

Cook, James. *The Voyages of Captain Cook Round the World,* ed. Christopher Lloyd. New York, 1949.

Cook, Sherburne F. "The Conflict Between the California Indians and White Civilization," *Ibero-Americana: 21.* Berkeley, 1943.

Coues, Elliott. *See* Alexander Henry (the Younger).

Cox, Ross. *The Columbia River,* ed. Edgar I. Stewart and Jane E. Stewart. Norman, 1955.

Croghan, George. *A Selection of George Croghan's Letters and Journals . . .* (Thwaites, *Early Western Travels,* Vol. I.) Cleveland, 1904.

Dale, Harrison Clifford. *The Ashley-Smith Explorations and the Discovery of a Central Route to the Pacific, 1822–1829.* Cleveland, 1918.

Danielsson, Bengt. *Love in the South Seas.* London, 1958.

Davidson, Gordon C. *The North West Company.* Berkeley, 1918.

Davies, K. G. (ed.). *Letters from Hudson Bay, 1730–1740.* Hudson's Bay Record Society Publication 25. London, 1965.

Davis, W. W. H. *El Gringo.* New York, 1857.

Denig, Edwin Thompson. *Five Indian Tribes of the Upper Missouri,* ed. John C. Ewers. Norman, 1961.

Densmore, Frances. *Chippewa Customs.* Bureau of American Ethnology Bulletin 86. Washington, 1929.

De Smet, Pierre Jean. *De Smet's Letters and Sketches . . .* (Thwaites, *Early Western Travels,* Vol. XXVII.) Cleveland, 1906.

De Voto, Bernard. *Across the Wide Missouri.* Boston, 1947.

Dewey, John. *Human Nature and Conduct.* New York, 1922.

Díaz del Castillo, Bernal. *The Bernal Díaz Chronicles,* trans. and ed. Albert Idell. New York, 1956.

Doddridge, Joseph. *Notes on the Settlement and Indian Wars of the Western Parts of Virginia and Pennsylvania*, ed. A. Williams. Albany, 1876.

Dodge, Richard I. *Our Wild Indians*. Hartford, 1883.

Douglas, David. *Journal Kept by David Douglas during his Travels in North America, 1823–1827*. New York, 1959.

Drummond, William Henry. *The Voyageur and Other Poems*. New York, 1905.

Ewers, John C. "An Anthropologist Looks at Early Pictures of North American Indians," *The New-York Historical Society Quarterly*, October, 1949, pp. 223–35.

————. *Artists of the Old West*. New York, 1965.

————. "Mothers of the Mixed Bloods," *Probing the American West*, pp. 62–70. Santa Fe, 1962.

Farnham, Thomas Jefferson. *Travels in the Great Western Prairies*. Poughkeepsie, 1841.

Folwell, William Watts. *A History of Minnesota*. 4 vols. St. Paul, 1930.

Ford, Clellan S., and Frank A. Beach. *Patterns of Sexual Behavior*. New York, 1949.

Fowler, Jacob. *The Journal of Jacob Fowler*, ed. with notes by Elliott Coues. Minneapolis, 1965.

Franchère, Gabriel. *Franchère's Narrative of a Voyage to the Northwest Coast of America . . .*, trans. and ed. J. V. Huntington. (Thwaites, *Early Western Travels*, VI, 164–410.) Cleveland, 1904.

Franklin, Sir John. *Narrative of a Journey to the Shores of the Polar Sea in the Years 1819–20–21–22*. London, 1924.

Gann, Thomas W. F. *The Maya Indians of Southern Yucatan and Northern British Honduras*. Bureau of American Ethnology Bulletin 64. Washington, 1918.

Garcés, Francisco. *On the Trail of a Spanish Pioneer: the Diary and Itinerary of Francisco Garcés in his Travels through Sonora, Arizona, and California, 1775–1776*, ed. Elliott Coues. New York, 1900.

Garcilaso de la Vega. *The Florida of the Inca*, ed. and trans. John Grier Varner and Jeanette Johnson Varner. Austin, 1951.

————. *The Incas; the Royal Commentaries of the Inca . . .*, ed. Alain Gheerbrant, trans. Maria Jolas. New York, 1961.

Garrard, Lewis H. *Wah-to-yah and the Taos Trail*. San Francisco, 1936.

Garry, Nicholas. "Diary of Nicholas Garry . . .," *Proceedings and Transactions of the Royal Society of Canada*, Ser. 2, Vol. VI, pp. 73–204. Ottawa, 1900.

Gates, Charles M. (ed.). *Five Fur Traders of the Northwest, Being the Narrative of Peter Pond and the Diaries of John Macdonell, Archibald N. McLeod, Hugh Faries, and Thomas Connor*. St. Paul, 1933.

Gist, Christopher. *Christopher Gist's Journals . . .*, ed. William H. Darlington. Pittsburgh, 1893.

Gómara, Francisco López de. *Cortés: the Life of the Conqueror by His Secretary*, trans. and ed. Lesley Byrd Simpson. Berkeley, 1964.

Greenbie, Sidney. *Frontiers and the Fur Trade*. New York, 1929.

Gregg, Josiah. *Gregg's Commerce of the Prairies, 1831–1839*. (Thwaites, *Early Western Travels*, Vols. XIX and XX.) Cleveland, 1905.

Grinnell, George Bird. *Pawnee, Blackfoot, and Cheyenne*. New York, 1961.

Hackett, Charles Wilson (ed.). *Historical Documents Relating to New Mexico, Nueva Vizcaya, and Approaches Thereto, to 1773*. 3 vols. Washington, 1923–37.

Hafen, Ann W. *See* LeRoy R. Hafen (ed.), *The Mountain Men and the Fur Trade of the Far West*.

Hafen, LeRoy R. (ed.). *The Mountain Men and the Fur Trade of the Far West*. (Six or more volumes projected, five in print.) Glendale, 1965——. The following articles are cited in the Notes and References for *Daughters of the Country:* Ann W. Hafen, "Lancaster P. Lupton," II, 207–17; LeRoy R. Hafen, "A Brief History of the Fur Trade in the Far West," I, 17–176; LeRoy R. Hafen, "Philip F. Thompson," III, 339–49; Janet Lecompte, "John J. Burroughs," III, 61–68; Ray H. Mattison, "William Laidlaw," III, 167–72, and "James Kipp," II, 201–5; Ray M. Reeder, "John Work," II, 363–79; Harvey E. Tobie, "Caleb Wilkins," III, 387–88.

—— and W. J. Ghent. *Broken Hand: the Life Story of Thomas Fitzpatrick, Chief of the Mountain Men*. Denver, 1931.

Hargrave, Letitia. *The Letters of Letitia Hargrave*, ed. Margaret Arnett Macleod. Champlain Society Publication 28. Toronto, 1947.

Harmon, Daniel Williams. *A Journal of Voyages and Travels in the Interior of North America*, ed. Daniel Haskell. Andover, 1820.

Hart, Evan A. "The Fur Trade in Wisconsin," *Wisconsin Tales and Trails*, Vol. III, Nos. 3 and 4; Vol. IV, No. 1. Madison, 1962–63.

Hassrick, Royal B. *The Sioux: Life and Customs of a Warrior Society*. Norman, 1964.

Havighurst, Walter. *Three Flags at the Straits: the Forts of Mackinac*. Englewood Cliffs, N.J., 1966.

Hearne, Samuel. *A Journey from Prince of Wales's Fort in Hudson's Bay . . .*, ed. J. B. Tyrrell. Champlain Society Publication 6. Toronto, 1911.

Henry, Alexander. *Travels and Adventures in Canada and the Indian Territories between the Years 1760 and 1776*. Chicago, 1921.

Henry, Alexander (the Younger). *New Light on the Early History of the Greater Northwest. The Manuscript Journals of Alexander Henry and*

David Thompson . . . *1799–1814*, ed. Elliott Coues. 3 vols. New York, 1897.

Hodge, Frederick W. *Handbook of American Indians North of Mexico.* Bureau of American Ethnology Bulletin 30. 2 vols. Washington, 1907 and 1910.

Hrdlička, Aleš. "Beauty Among the American Indians," *Boas Anniversary Volume, Anthropological Papers,* August 9, 1906, pp. 38–42.

⸺. "Origin and Antiquity of the American Indian," *Smithsonian Institution Annual Report, 1923,* pp. 481–84. Washington, 1925.

Hunter, John D. *Manners and Customs of Several Indian Tribes Located West of the Mississippi* . . . Philadelphia, 1823.

Idaho State Historical Society Reference Series No. 86. Boise.

Innis, H. A. *Peter Pond, Fur Trader and Adventurer.* Toronto, 1930.

Irving, Washington. *The Adventures of Captain Bonneville, or Scenes Beyond the Rocky Mountains of the Far West.* 3 vols. London, 1837.

⸺. *Astoria.* 2 vols. Philadelphia, 1836.

Isham, James. *James Isham's Observations on Hudsons Bay, 1743,* ed. E. E. Rich, asst'd by A. M. Johnson. Champlain Society Publication, Hudson's Bay Company Series XII. Toronto, 1949.

James, Thomas. *Three Years Among the Indians and Mexicans,* ed. Milo M. Quaife. Chicago, 1953.

Jenness, Diamond. *The Indians of Canada.* National Museum of Canada, Anthropological Series No. 15, Bulletin No. 65. Ottawa, 1958.

Johnson, Robert C. *John McLoughlin, Patriarch of the Northwest.* Portland, 1935.

Johnston, Charles M. (ed.). *The Valley of the Six Nations.* Champlain Society Publication, Ontario Series, VII. Toronto, 1965.

Jones, Evan. *Trappers and Mountain Men, by the Editors of American Heritage.* New York, 1961.

Josephy, Alvin M., Jr. (ed.). *The American Heritage Book of Indians.* New York, 1961.

⸺. *The Patriot Chiefs.* New York, 1961.

⸺. *The Nez Perce Indians and the Opening of the Northwest.* New Haven, 1965.

Kane, Paul. *Wanderings of an Artist among the Indians of North America* . . . (*Master-Works of Canadian Authors,* ed. John W. Garvin, Vol. VII.) Toronto, 1925.

Kardiner, Abram (with collaboration of Ralph Linton, Cora du Bois, and James West). *The Psychological Frontiers of Society.* New York, 1945.

Keating, William H. *Narrative of an Expedition to the Source of St. Peter's River* . . . 2 vols. London, 1825.

Kellogg, Louise Phelps (ed.). *Early Narratives of the Northwest, 1634–1699*. New York, 1917.

Kinietz, W. Vernon. *Chippewa Village, the Story of Katikitegon*. Cranbrook Institute of Science Bulletin 25. Bloomfield Hills, Mich., 1947.

Kinzie, Juliette A. *Wau-Bun, the "Early Days" in the Northwest*, ed. Milo M. Quaife. Chicago, 1932.

Knight, John. *Indian Atrocities: Narratives of the Perils and Sufferings of Dr. Knight and John Slover among the Indians during the Revolutionary War*. Cincinnati, 1867.

Kohl, J. G. *Kitchi-Gami*. Minneapolis, 1956.

Kurz, Rudolph Friedrich. *Journal of . . .* , trans. Myrtis Jarrell and ed. J. N. B. Hewitt. Bureau of American Ethnology Bulletin 115. Washington, 1937.

La Farge, Oliver. *A Pictorial History of the American Indian*. New York, 1956.

Lahontan, Louis Armande de Lom d'Arce. *New Voyages to North America*, ed. Reuben Gold Thwaites. 2 vols. Chicago, 1905.

Landes, Ruth. *The Ojibwa Woman*. New York, 1938.

Langer, William. *An Encyclopedia of World History*. Boston, 1940.

Lapérouse, Jean François de Galup, comte de. *A Voyage round the World*. Boston, 1801.

Larpenteur, Charles. *Forty Years a Fur Trader on the Upper Missouri*, ed. Elliott Coues. 2 vols. New York, 1898.

Las Casas, Bartolomé de. *An Account of the First Voyages and Discoveries Made by the Spaniards in America*. London, 1699.

Lauber, Almon Wheeler. "Indian Slavery in Colonial Times within the Present Limits of the United States," *Studies in History, Economics, and Public Law*, ed. by the Faculty of Political Science of Columbia University. New York, 1913.

Laut, Agnes C. *The Conquest of the Great Northwest*. 2 vols. New York, 1918.

Lavender, David. *Bent's Fort*. New York, 1954.

————. *The Fist in the Wilderness*. New York, 1964.

La Vérendrye, Pierre Gaultier de Varennes de. *Journals and Letters of . . . la Vérendrye and his Sons*, ed. Lawrence J. Burpee. Champlain Society Publication 16. Toronto, 1927.

Lawson, John. *The History of North Carolina, Containing the Exact Description and Natural History of That Country*. Raleigh, 1860.

Lecompte, Janet. *See* LeRoy R. Hafen (ed.), *The Mountain Men and the Fur Trade of the Far West*.

Le Froy, Sir John Henry. *In Search of the Magnetic North; a Soldier-*

Surveyor's Letters from the North-west, 1843–1844, ed. George F. G. Stanley. Toronto, 1955.

Leonard, Zenas. *Leonard's Narrative; Adventures of Zenas Leonard, Fur Trader and Trapper, 1831–1836*, ed. W. F. Wagner. Cleveland, 1904.

Lewis, Oscar. *Effects of White Contact upon Blackfoot Culture, with Special Reference to the Role of the Fur Trade.* Monographs of the American Ethnological Society, VI. New York, 1942.

Lindquist, G. E. E. *The Red Man in the United States.* New York, 1923.

Linton, Ralph. "The Comanche" and "Analysis of Comanche Culture," *The Psychological Frontiers of Society,* ed. Abram Kardiner and others, pp. 47–100. New York, 1945.

Long, John. *Voyages and Travels of an Indian Interpreter and Trader* . . . (Thwaites, *Early Western Travels,* Vol. II.) Cleveland, 1904.

Luttig, John C. *Journal of a Fur Trading Expedition on the Upper Missouri, 1812–1813*, ed. Stella M. Drumm. St. Louis, 1920.

Mackenzie, Alexander. *Voyages from Montreal . . . through the Continent of North America . . . in the Years 1789 and 1793 . . .*, ed. John W. Garvin. (*Master-Works of Canadian Authors,* Vol. III.) Toronto, 1927.

"Mackinac Register of Baptisms, Marriages, and Interments, 1695–1821," *Wisconsin Historical Society Collections,* XIX, 1–162. Madison, 1910.

"Mackinac Register of Marriages, 1725–1821 . . ." *Wisconsin Historical Society Collections,* XVIII, 469–513. Madison, 1908.

MacLeod, William Christie. *The American Indian Frontier.* New York, 1928.

Magoffin, Susan Shelby. *Down the Santa Fe Trail and into Mexico . . . 1846–1847*, ed. Stella M. Drumm. New Haven, 1926.

Malhiot, François Victor. "A Wisconsin Fur Trader's Journal, 1804–05," *Wisconsin Historical Society Collections,* XIX, 163–233. Madison, 1910.

Marcy, Capt. R. B. "Report on Route from Ft. Smith to Santa Fe," Reports of the Secretary of War, U.S. Government Documents, 31st Congress, 1st Session, Senate Executive Document 64.

[Massachusetts] *Records of the Governor and Company of the Massachusetts Bay in New England,* ed. Nathaniel B. Shurtleff. Vol. IV, Part III. Boston, 1853–1854.

Masson, Louis R. *Les Bourgeois de la Compagnie du Nord-Ouest . . .* 2 vols. New York, 1960. (Contains long introduction by Masson and journals, letters, and reminiscences of the following North West Company traders: Roderic McKenzie, W. F. Wentzel, Simon Frazer, François Victoire Malhiot, John McDonnell, François Antoine Larocque, Charles MacKenzie, John McDonald of Garth, George

Keith, John Johnson, Samuel H. Wilcocke, Duncan Cameron, Peter Grant, and James McKenzie.)

"Masson Papers." Nos. 1 to 14, manuscript journals of North West Company traders; Nos. 32 to 39, manuscript correspondence of traders. Public Archives of Canada, Ottawa.

Masson Transcriptions. Miscellaneous accounts, letters, journals, post records of North West Company traders; Nos. 1, 2, 5, 6, 7. (Copies of manuscripts at McGill University.) Public Archives of Canada, Ottawa.

Mattison, Ray H. *See* LeRoy R. Hafen (ed.), *The Mountain Men and the Fur Trade of the Far West.*

Maximilian, Prince of Wied. *Travels in the Interior of North America.* (Thwaites, *Early Western Travels,* Vols. XXIII, XXIV, and XXV.) Cleveland, 1904.

McClintock, Walter. *Old Indian Trails.* Boston and New York, 1923.

McDonnell, Anne (ed.). "The Fort Benton Journal, 1854–1856" and "The Fort Sarpy Journal, 1855–1856," *Contributions to the Historical Society of Montana,* Vol. X. Helena, 1940.

McKay, Douglas. *The Honourable Company: A History of the Hudson's Bay Company.* Indianapolis, 1936.

McKenney, Thomas. *Sketches of a Tour to the Lakes* . . . Baltimore, 1827.

McKenney, Thomas, and James Hall. *The Indian Tribes of North America, with Biographical Sketches and Anecdotes of the Principal Chiefs.* 3 vols. Edinburgh, 1933.

McKenzie, Roderic. *See* Masson Papers.

McLoughlin, John. *Letters of Dr. John McLoughlin, Written at Fort Vancouver,* ed. Burt Brown Barker. Portland, 1948.

McNitt, Frank. *The Indian Traders.* Norman, 1962.

Mead, Margaret. *The Changing Culture of an Indian Tribe.* New York, 1932.

Means, Philip Ainsworth. *The Spanish Main, Focus of Envy, 1492–1700.* New York, 1935.

M'Gillivray, Duncan. *The Journal of Duncan M'Gillivray of the North West Company* . . . *1794–95,* ed. Arthur S. Morton. Toronto, 1929.

Miller, Alfred Jacob. *The West of Alfred Jacob Miller (1837); from the notes and watercolors in the Walters Art Gallery, with an account of the artist by Marvin C. Ross.* Norman, 1951.

Moberly, Henry John. *When Fur Was King.* London and Toronto, 1929.

Moore, Irene. *Valiant La Verendrye.* Quebec, 1927.

Moorehead, Alan. *The White Nile.* New York, 1960.

Morgan, Dale L. *Jedediah Smith and the Opening of the West.* Indianapolis, 1953.

Morley, Sylvanus Griswold. *The Ancient Maya.* Stanford, 1956.

Morison, Daniel. *The Doctor's Secret Journal,* ed. George S. May. Mackinac Island, 1960.

Morton, W. L. "The North West Company, Pedlars Extraordinary,". *Aspects of the Fur Trade, Selected Papers of the 1965 North American Fur Trade Conference,* pp. 9–17. St. Paul, 1967.

Nadeau, Remi. *Fort Laramie and the Sioux Indians.* Englewood Cliffs, N.J., 1967.

Neill, Edward D. "History of the Ojibways and Their Connection with Fur Traders . . . ," *Minnesota Historical Society Collections,* V, 395–570. St. Paul, 1885.

———. "A Sketch of Joseph Renville, a 'Bois Brule' and Early Trader of Minnesota," *Minnesota Historical Society Collections,* I, 196–206. St. Paul, 1872.

———. "Dakota Land and Dakota Life," *Minnesota Historical Society Collections,* I, 254–94. St. Paul, 1872.

Nute, Grace Lee. *The Voyageur.* New York, 1931.

———. *Lake Superior.* New York, 1944.

Ogden, Peter Skene. *Traits of American-Indian Life and Character.* London, 1853.

———. *Peter Skene Ogden's Snake Country Journals, 1824–25 and 1825–26,* ed. E. E. Rich. Hudson's Bay Record Society Publication 13. London, 1950.

———. *Peter Skene Ogden's Snake Country Journal, 1826–27,* ed. K. G. Davies. Hudson's Bay Record Society Publication 23. London, 1961.

Olson, Julius. "The Voyages of the Northmen," *The Northmen, Columbus, and Cabot, 985–1503,* pp. 1–74. New York, 1906.

O'Meara, Walter. "An Adventure in Local History," *Minnesota History,* Vol. 31, No. 1, pp. 1–10.

———. *The Savage Country.* Boston, 1960.

———. *The Last Portage.* Boston, 1962.

———. *Guns at the Forks.* Englewood Cliffs, N.J., 1965.

Parkman, Francis. *The Oregon Trail.* New York, 1931.

———. *The Old Regime in Canada.* Boston, 1929.

———. *A Half-Century of Conflict.* Boston, 1892.

Pattie, James O. *Pattie's Personal Narrative, 1824–1830,* ed. Timothy Flint. (Thwaites, *Early Western Travels,* Vol. XVIII.) Cleveland, 1905.

Peixotto, Ernest C. *Our Hispanic Southwest.* New York, 1916.

Perrault, Jean Baptiste. "Narrative of the Travels and Adventures,

1783–1820, by Jean Baptiste Perrault," ed. John Sharpless Fox, *Michigan Historical Collections*, XXXVII, 508–619.

Peterson, Harold L. *American Indian Tomahawks*. New York, 1965.

Phillips, Paul Chrisler. *The Fur Trade*. 2 vols. Norman, 1961.

[Plymouth Colony] *Records of the Colony of New Plymouth in New England*, ed. Nathaniel B. Shurtleff. 12 vols. Boston, 1855–61.

Point, Nicolas. *Wilderness Kingdom, Indian Life in the Rocky Mountains, 1840–1847*, trans. and intro. Joseph P. Donnelly, S.J., with an appreciation by John C. Ewers. New York, Chicago, San Francisco, 1967.

Porter, Clyde and Mae Reed, *Ruxton of the Rockies*, ed. LeRoy R. Hafen, Norman, 1950.

Pratte, Bernard J. "The Reminiscences of General Bernard Pratte, Jr." *Bulletin Missouri Historical Society*, October, 1949.

Prescott, William H. *History of the Conquest of Peru*. 2 vols. Philadelphia, 1874.

———. *History of the Conquest of Mexico*. 3 vols. Philadelphia, 1894.

Quimby, George Irving. *Indian Life in the Upper Great Lakes, 11,000 B.C. to A.D. 1800*. Chicago, 1960.

Randle, Martha Champion. "Iroquois Women Then and Now," Bureau of American Ethnology Bulletin 149, pp. 169–80.

Reeder, Ray M. *See* LeRoy R. Hafen (ed.), *The Mountain Men and the Fur Traders of the Far West*.

Reuter, E. B. (ed.). *Race Culture and Contacts*. American Sociological Society. London, 1934.

Rich, E. E. (ed.). *Moose Fort Journals, 1783–1785*. Hudson's Bay Record Society Publication 17. London, 1954.

———. (ed., assisted by A. M. Johnson). *Cumberland and Hudson House Journals and Inland Journal, 1775–82*. Hudson's Bay Record Society Publication 15. London, 1951–52.

Robinson, Henry Martyn. *The Great Fur Land; or Sketches of Life in the Hudson's Bay Territory*. New York, 1879.

Ross, Alexander. *The Fur Hunters of the Far West*, ed. Kenneth A. Spalding. Norman, 1956.

———. *The Red River Settlement: Its Rise, Progress, and Present State*. London, 1856.

Ross, Hamilton Nelson. *La Pointe, Village Outpost*. St. Paul, 1960.

Rowe, John Howland. "Inca Culture at the Time of the Spanish Conquest." Bureau of American Ethnology Bulletin 143. (*Handbook of South American Indians*, ed. Julian Haynes Steward, 7 vols.), II, 183–330.

Rowlandson, Mary. "Narrative of the Captivity of Mrs. Mary Rowlandson," *Narratives of the Indian Wars*, ed. Charles H. Lincoln, pp. 107–67. New York, 1913.

Russell, Osborne. *Journal of a Trapper, or Nine Years in the Rocky Mountains, 1834–1843*. Boise, Idaho, 1921.

Ruxton, George. *Life in the Far West*, ed. LeRoy R. Hafen. Norman, 1951.

Sandoz, Mary. *Love Song to the Plains*. New York, 1961.

Sargent, Winthrop. *The History of an Expedition Against Fort Duquesne in 1755* . . . (Includes "Seaman's Journal.") Philadelphia, 1885.

Schoolcraft, Henry R. *Summary Narrative of an Exploratory Expedition to the Sources of the Mississippi River in 1820* . . . Philadelphia, 1855.

Seaver, James Everett. *A Narrative of the Life of Mary Jemison, the White Woman of the Genesee*. New York, 1925.

Selkirk, Thomas Douglas. *Lord Selkirk's Diary, 1803–1804* . . . , ed. Patrick C. White. Champlain Society Publication 35. Toronto, 1958.

Sibley, H. H. "Reminiscences, Historical and Personal," *Minnesota Historical Society Collections*, I, 457–85. St. Paul, 1872.

Simpson, Sir George. *Journal of Occurrences in the Athabasca Department, 1820–1821*, ed. E. E. Rich. Champlain Society Publication, Hudson's Bay Company Series, Vol. I. Toronto, 1938.

Skinner, Constance Lindsay. *Beaver, Kings, and Cabins*. New York, 1933.

Smith, James. *An Account of the Remarkable Occurrences . . . during his Captivity with the Indians* . . . Lexington, 1799.

Spargo, John. *Two Bennington-born Explorers and Makers of Modern Canada*. Bradford, Vt., 1950.

Stevens, Wayne Edson. *The Northwest Fur Trade, 1763–1800*. Urbana, 1928.

Stratton, Royal B. *Life Among the Indians; or the Captivity of the Oatman Girls Among the Apache and Mohave Indians*. San Francisco, 1935.

Sullivan, Maurice S. *Jedediah Smith, Trader and Trail Breaker*. New York, 1936.

———— (ed.). *The Travels of Jedediah Smith, a Documentary Outline Including the Journal of the Great American Pathfinder*. Santa Ana, 1934.

Sumner, William Graham. *Folkways, a Study of the Sociological Importance of Usages, Manners, Customs, Mores, and Morals*. Boston, 1906.

Swanton, John R. *The Indian Tribes of North America*. Bureau of American Ethnology Bulletin 145. Washington, 1952.

Tabeau, Pierre-Antoine. *Tabeau's Narrative of Loisel's Expedition to the Upper Missouri*, ed. Annie H. Abel. Norman, 1939.

Tanner, John. *A Narrative of the Captivity and Adventures of John Tanner* . . . , ed. Edwin James. London, 1830.

Thomas, Alfred Barnaby. *The Plains Indians and New Mexico* . . .

(Coronado Cuarto Centennial Publications, 1540–1940, ed. G. P. Hammond, Vol. XI.) Albuquerque, 1940.

—— (trans. and ed.). *After Coronado: Spanish Exploration Northeast of New Mexico, 1696–1727* . . . Norman, 1935.

Thompson, David. *David Thompson's Narrative, 1784–1812*, ed. Richard Glover. Champlain Society Publication 40. Toronto, 1962.

Thorp, Raymond, and Robert Bunker. *Crow Killer*. Bloomington, Ind., 1958.

Thwaites, Reuben Gold (ed.). *Early Western Travels, 1748–1846*. 32 vols. Cleveland, 1904–1907.

—— (ed.). "The Fur Trade on the Upper Lakes, 1778–1815," *Wisconsin Historical Society Collections*, XIX, 234–372. Madison, 1910.

—— (ed.). "The French Regime in Wisconsin, II," *Wisconsin Historical Society Collections*, XVII, 1–518. Madison, 1906.

—— (ed.). "The French Regime in Wisconsin, III," *Wisconsin Historical Society Collections*, XVIII, 1–222. Madison, 1908.

Trudeau, Jean-Baptiste. "Journal of Jean-Baptiste Trudeau Among the Arikara Indians in 1795," *Missouri Historical Society Collections*, IV, No. 1.

Twitchell, Ralph Emerson (ed.). *Spanish Archives of New Mexico, Compiled and Chronologically Arranged . . . by the Authority of the State of New Mexico*. 2 vols. Cedar Rapids, Iowa, 1914.

——. *The Leading Facts of New Mexican History*. 2 vols. Cedar Rapids, Iowa, 1911–12.

Tyler, Lyon Gardiner (ed.). *Narratives of Early Virginia, 1606–1625*. New York, 1907.

Vaughan, Alden T. *New England Frontier; Puritans and Indians, 1620–1675*. Boston, 1965.

Vaughn, J. W. "The Fort Laramie Hog Ranches," *The Westerners Brand Book* (New York Posse), Vol. XIII, No. 2, pp. 39–41.

Vega, Garcilaso de la. *See* Garcilaso de la Vega.

Vespucci, Amerigo. *Amerigo Vespucci's Account of His Third Voyage*, ed. and trans. Clements R. Markham. Boston, 1898.

Vestal, Stanley. *Mountain Men*. Boston, 1937.

Victor, Frances Fuller. *The River of the West*. Hartford, Conn., 1870. (Joe Meek.)

Von Hagen, Victor W. *Realm of the Inca*. New York, 1957.

——. *World of the Maya*. New York, 1960.

——. *The Aztec: Man and Tribe*. New York, 1958.

Wallace, Anthony F. C. *The Modal Personality Structure of the Tuscarora Indians, as Revealed by the Rorschach Test*. Bureau of American Ethnology Bulletin 150. Washington, 1952.

Wallace, J. N. *The Wintering Partners on Peace River . . . with a Summary of the Dunvegan Journal, 1806.* Ottawa, 1929.

Wallace, W. Stewart (gen. ed.). *The Encyclopaedia of Canada.* 6 vols. Toronto, 1935–37.

—————— (ed.). *Documents Relating to the North West Company.* Champlain Society Publication 22. Toronto, 1934.

Warren, William W. "History of the Ojibways . . .," *Minnesota Historical Society Collections,* V, 21–394. St. Paul, 1885.

Washburn, Wilcomb E. (ed.). *The Indian and the White Man, Documents in American Civilization.* New York, 1964.

Webb, Walter Prescott. *The Great Plains.* Boston, 1931.

Weitenkampf, Frank. "How the Indians Were Pictured in Earlier Days," *The New-York Historical Society Quarterly,* October, 1949, pp. 213–21.

Weyer, Edward Moffat, Jr. *The Eskimos, Their Environment and Folkways.* New Haven, 1932.

——————. *Primitive Peoples Today.* New York, 1959.

Willson, Beckles. *The Life of Lord Strathcona and Mount Royal.* 2 vols. Boston and New York, 1915.

Wissler, Clark. *Indians of the United States: Four Centuries of Their History and Culture.* New York, 1940.

Witthoft, John. "Archeology As a Key to the Colonial Fur Trade," *Aspects of the Fur Trade, Selected Papers of the 1965 North American Fur Trade Conference,* pp. 55–61. St. Paul, 1967.

Woods, John. "Woods' Two Years' Residence in the Settlement on the English Prairie—June 25, 1820–July 3, 1821." (Thwaites, *Early Western Travels,* X, 171–357.) Cleveland, 1906.

Work, John. *Journal of John Work,* ed. W. S. Lewis and P. C. Philips. Cleveland, 1923.